Witchcraft narratives in Germany

STUDIES IN EARLY MODERN EUROPEAN HISTORY

This series aims to publish
challenging and innovative research in all areas
of early modern continental history.
The editors are committed to encouraging work that
engages with current historiographical
debates, adopts an interdisciplinary
approach, or makes an original contribution
to our understanding of the period.

SERIES EDITORS
William G. Naphy and Penny Roberts

EDITORIAL ADVISORY BOARD
Professor N. Z. Davis, Professor Brian Pullan,
Professor Joseph Bergin and
Professor Robert Scribner

Already published in the series

The rise of Richelieu   Joseph Bergin

Sodomy in early modern Europe
ed. Tom Betteridge

Fear in early modern society
eds William Naphy and Penny Roberts

Religion and superstitition in Reformation Europe
Helen Parish and William G. Naphy

*Religious choice in the Dutch Republic: the reformation of
Arnoldus Buchelus (1565–1641)*
Judith Pollman

A city in conflict: Troyes during the French wars of religion
Penny Roberts

Witchcraft narratives in Germany

Rothenburg, 1561–1652

ALISON ROWLANDS

Manchester University Press

Manchester and New York

distributed exclusively in the USA by Palgrave

Published by Manchester University Press
Oxford Road, Manchester M13 9NR, UK
and Room 400, 175 Fifth Avenue, New York, NY10010, USA
www.manchesteruniversitypress.co.uk

Distributed exclusively in the USA by
Palgrave, 175 Fifth Avenue, New York,
NY10010, USA

Distributed exclusively in Canada by
UBC Press, University of British Columbia, 2029 West Mall,
Vancouver, BC, Canada V6T 1Z2

British Library Cataloguing-in-Publication Data
A catalogue record is available from the British Library

Library of Congress Cataloging-in-Publication Data applied for

ISBN 0 7190 5259 9 *hardback*

First published 2003

11 10 09 08 07 06 05 04 03   10 9 8 7 6 5 4 3 2 1

Typeset in Monotype Perpetua with Albertus
by Northern Phototypesetting Co Ltd, Bolton
Printed in Great Britain
by Biddles Ltd, Guildford and King's Lynn

Contents

Acknowledgements

There are many individuals and institutions without whose support this book would never have been written. I am grateful to my PhD supervisor Bob Scribner for encouraging my love of early modern German history and hope that he would have been proud of my contributions to our better understanding of it. Since 1992 I have been hugely indebted to my colleagues in the History Department at the University of Essex, who have given me constant support and intellectual stimulation, and to the Essex University students with whom I have discussed witchcraft in the course of teaching. I am grateful to Lynn Botelho, Anthony Fletcher, Brian Ward and Jenny Wormald for reading early drafts of the manuscript, to Robin Briggs and Tom Robisheaux for always being ready to answer my witchcraft-related questions, and to Franz Josef-Knöchel, without whose technical expertise this book would have no map. I am also indebted to Nick Rowlands for helping me understand early modern Latin, to Marla Rowlands for helping me understand early modern German, and to Renate Barker for all the books. Thanks also to everyone of CLFC and CULFC (1992–2002) for distracting me and keeping me sane.

In Franconia my biggest thanks go to the archivists of the State Archive in Nuremberg but most especially to the staff of the Rothenburg City Archive who made the many hours that I have spent there so productive and enjoyable: to Frau Hildegard Krösche, Professor Karl Borchardt, and especially Herr Waldemar Parr and Dr Ludwig Schnurrer. For their unfailing hospitality in Rothenburg and beyond over more than a decade my immense thanks go to Christa Joist and Michael Kamp, but most especially to Bernhard, Hanne, Ulrike and Judith Mall, who have generously allowed me to make their apartment in Rothenburg my second home. For financial support which helped expedite the completion of this book I am grateful to the Research Endowment Fund at Essex University, a research grant awarded in 1999 by the Arts and Humanities Research Board, and the research fellowships awarded in 2000 and 2001 by the Sonderforschungsbereich 235 (Teilprojekt Zauberei- und Hexenprozesse) of the University of Trier. I am indebted to Professor Franz Irsigler for inviting me to participate in the Sonderforschungsbereich and to Dr Herbert Eiden, Dr Rita Voltmer and the other researchers in the Sonderforschungsbereich who made my time in Trier so intellectually stimulating and socially enjoyable. For their hospitality in Trier in 2000, thanks to Franz and Marita Eiden and Margret Krämer and Stefan Schörer.

My warmest thanks go to my parents, Nick and Marla Rowlands, without whose love and support this book would never have been started, and to my husband, Herbert Eiden, without whose love and support it would never have been finished. This book is for all three of them.

Alison Rowlands

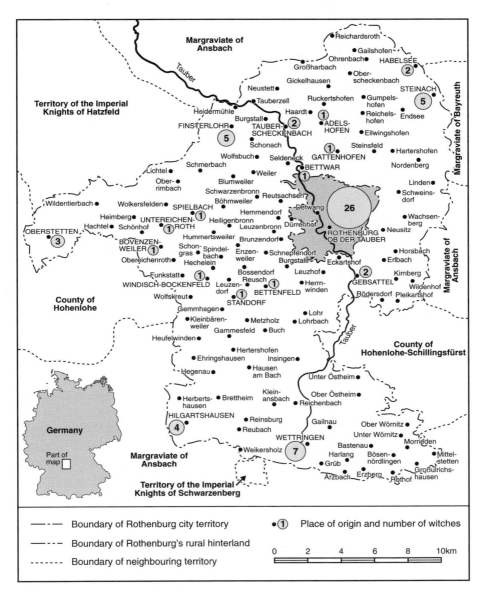

Place of origin of the sixty-five people involved as accused, self-confessed or reputed witches in witch-trials in Rothenburg ob der Tauber, 1549–1709

Design: Alison Rowlands; cartography: Franz-Josef Knöchel

Introduction

This book is a study of the trials involving allegations and confessions of mal-eficient or demonic witchcraft that took place in the German city of Rothenburg ob der Tauber between *c*. 1561 and *c*. 1652. It has two aims. First, it will explain why Rothenburg had a restrained pattern of witch-hunting during this period, with relatively few trials (even fewer of which ended in guilty verdicts against alleged witches); no mass-panics involving large numbers of accused witches; and the execution of only one alleged witch.[1] Second, it will offer detailed readings of the exceptionally rich records from the Rothenburg witch-trials to explore the social and psychic tensions that lay behind the making of witchcraft accusations and confessions, the popular and elite reactions to these accusations and confessions, and the ways in which participants in witch-trials pursued strategies, expressed emotions and negotiated conflicts through what they said about witchcraft.

These aims are important for various reasons. In 1996, Robin Briggs suggested that what was surprising about the early modern period was not how many people were prosecuted as witches, but – given the widespread belief in witchcraft and the existence of laws against it – how few were. Briggs argued that the witch-persecution of the early modern period 'was a relative failure, which only gained momentum in relatively few exceptional instances'. Persecution of witches was patchy both chronologically and geographically, Briggs concluded, with 'genuine witch-crazes' only touching 'the lives of a tiny fraction of Europeans'.[2] We still know little about where, when and why witch-hunts failed to gain momentum in early modern Europe, however, because so few historians have devoted attention to these questions since 1970. This is probably partly because it has been deemed less exciting and thus less marketable than accounts of large witch-hunts by publishers, partly because more radically feminist scholars have little interest in any work which apparently seeks to downplay the impact of witch-hunts on early modern women, and partly because cases of witchcraft that did not end in execution are harder to

identify and tease out from early modern legal records. The corpus of published work on the 'relative failure' of witch-hunts in Germany thus remains
small: Wolfgang Behringer and Bob Scribner published pioneering articles on
this theme in 1983 and 1990, respectively, while Hartmut H. Kunstmann's
account of witch-trials in Nuremberg (published in 1970) and Jürgen Michael
Schmidt's excellent analysis of witch-trials in the Palatinate (published in 2000)
are the only book-length studies of German territories that were characterised
by a restrained pattern of witch-trials throughout the early modern period.[3]
My study of Rothenburg will make a significant addition to this small but
important corpus, thereby adding weight to Briggs' idea that areas which did
not experience large-scale witch-hunts may well have been the early modern
norm rather than the exception. In the chapters that follow I will demonstrate
that complex and mutually reinforcing sets of beliefs and social, political and
religious priorities held not only by the ruling elites but also by the lower
orders of Rothenburg and its rural hinterland interacted to keep enthusiasm for
prosecuting witches at a low ebb at all social levels and to ensure that accusations and confessions of witchcraft did not herald an inevitable journey to the
stake for alleged witches.

Close reading of the records of the Rothenburg witch-trials is essential to
the analysis, as it is only at this level of detail, where the motives of the various
trial-participants can be re-created, where the complexity of their competing
narratives can be unpicked and evaluated, and where the twists and turning-
points of trial processes can be identified and interpreted, that explanations
about why things did or did not happen can be reached with any confidence.
Focusing on one area over a lengthy period of time also makes it possible to
show how ideas about witches and witchcraft developed over time, how the
experiences of early trials influenced the manner in which subsequent trials
were handled, and how individual trials were influenced by the specific circumstances in which they occurred. Last but by no means least, the personal
testimonies from the Rothenburg witch-trials give us uniquely detailed insights
into the otherwise often hidden social, cultural and imaginative worlds of early
modern peasants and townspeople. Through them we can explore communal
and domestic disharmony; perceptions of honour; experiences of motherhood,
childhood, marriage, illness and war; and beliefs about magic and religion, as
well as obtaining a vivid sense of the lives and personalities of individuals about
whom historical records are usually silent because of their gender, age and low
social status.

This book is organised around the following themes. Chapter 1 explores
popular speech about witchcraft, explains why the inhabitants of Rothenburg
and its hinterland were generally unwilling to accuse suspected witches at law,
and details the non-legal methods with which they more usually coped with

witches. Chapter 2 discusses elite beliefs about witchcraft and explains why the city councillors were unwilling to overstep the boundaries of due legal procedure in their prosecution of alleged witches. Chapter 3 analyses the first Rothenburg case involving a self-confessed child-witch from 1587 and explains why the councillors found such cases hard to deal with and what precedents this case set for the future. Chapter 4 analyses two trials from 1627 and 1629 to illustrate the ways in which they were shaped by the events of the Thirty Years' War and particularly by Catholic challenges to the city council's authority. Chapter 5 gives a new explanation for the gender-relatedness of witchcraft accusations through the prism of several seventeenth-century cases. Chapter 6 offers a detailed analysis of one accused witch's strategy of denying her guilt in council custody from 1652 and also shows how elite and popular attititudes towards witchcraft began to change in the course of the seventeenth century.

Rothenburg ob der Tauber

Rothenburg ob der Tauber is situated on a promontory overlooking the Tauber, the river from which it takes its name, about 66 kilometres due west from Nuremberg and 48 kilometres due south-east from Würzburg in south-central Germany. It was annexed by Bavaria in 1802 and forms part of that federal state today, its status reduced to that of a county town. From the fourteenth century, however, and until 1802, it was an imperial city, one of six such cities in Franconia, one of the Imperial Circles, or territorial sub-divisions of the early modern Holy Roman Empire. This meant that Rothenburg was autonomous, its city council subject to no higher authority other than that of the Holy Roman Emperor himself. As a result, the sixteen-member city council, constituted as the criminal court for Rothenburg and its rural hinterland, had the right to try all crimes committed by its subjects or on its territory, including cases of witchcraft. From the mid-sixteenth century the council appointed university-educated jurists to municipal posts and drew on their advice in particularly problematic legal cases, although the decision-making power in all cases always remained with the council.[4]

In the sixteenth century Rothenburg was one of the Empire's middle-sized urban settlements, with 5,000–7,000 inhabitants. Its population was dominated by craftsmen and their households, who produced goods for local and regional markets. These craftsmen belonged to guilds which regulated the standards of their particular craft, but they lacked political power within the city. Individual craftsmen might gain admission to the political elite if they made enough money and the right connections, but as a whole the craftsmen had no automatic right to representation on the city council. This was dominated by an urban patriciate which made its money chiefly from land-rents rather than trade and which became increasingly exclusive during the early modern period, particularly after 1650. The tension between the urban patriciate and craftsmen over the question of access to political power periodically reached breaking point in Rothenburg.[5] This occurred most spectacularly during the Peasants' War of 1525, when the craftsmen seized the chance offered by widespread rural rebellion to take over the government of the city, albeit for only a brief time.[6] The urban patriciate learnt the lesson of the events of 1525: for the rest of the early modern period its main aim was to defend its own power within the city – and the autonomy of Rothenburg externally – without antagonising either its urban or rural subjects to the point of unrest.

Starting in the fourteenth century, and spurred on by an awareness of the importance of possessing land and subjects beyond the city walls, successive generations of Rothenburg councillors gradually acquired a hinterland which became the fourth largest rural territory governed by a city in the early modern Empire. Covering about 400 square kilometres, it had 10,000–11,000 inhabitants living in 118 villages varying in size from tiny settlements like Hummertsweiler, with three households, to Gebsattel, the largest village, with eighty households. Most of these people were peasants, but the hinterland also contained rural craftsmen, blacksmiths, millers and parish clergymen. In 1430 the council had a barrier of hedges and ditches, punctuated by gates and towers, erected around the hinterland to protect the area against attack by rival neighbouring lords. However, the consolidation of power by the council within the hinterland was never as complete as this physical delineation of its territorial claims suggested. Rothenburg was situated in a part of the Empire where lordship rights over land and people were extremely fragmented and often the subject of competing claims. This meant that even by the sixteenth century, and despite the fact that the Rothenburg council had achieved its aim of becoming the dominant power within the hinterland, a thousand hinterland inhabitants were still the subjects of foreign lords, owing their land-rents and dues to them rather than to Rothenburg, while foreign lords still had the right to oversee four of the thirteen minor courts and to appoint pastors to several of the parish-livings in the hinterland.[7]

The period c. 1561–c. 1652 was one of extreme contrasts for Rothenburg. After the upheaval of the Peasants' War of 1525, the second half of the sixteenth century was a time of relative political and social calm. The council had increased its power as a result of its adoption of Lutheranism in 1544; the institutionalisation of its reformation was finally completed in 1559, by which time the council was no longer subject to the authority of the Bishop of Würzburg, within whose diocese Rothenburg had formerly lain, or to the Mergentheim chapter of the Order of Teutonic Knights, which had formerly held benefice-rights over the parish church in Rothenburg.[8] The council's confidence and the city's prosperity can be seen in the fact that the council undertook a variety of construction projects in the late sixteenth century, building a new town-hall, a grammar school, and several other municipal structures. There were, of course, short- and long-term problems in the late sixteenth century, suffered mainly by the lower orders: severe famine affected the area between 1570 and 1575, and population increase caused a subdivision of landholdings and social tension between wealthier peasants and poorer cottagers in some of the hinterland villages by the early seventeenth century. On the whole, however, the economic position of Rothenburg's peasant subjects before the Thirty Years' War was reasonably good: the council had not exploited rising land-prices by raising rents or special taxes and peasant indebtedness was not widespread.[9]

The Thirty Years' War of 1618–48 changed this picture completely. Rothenburg was at the crossroads of important north–south and east–west routes for troop movements during the war. This, and the vacillating political stance of the council, meant that from the 1620s the area suffered severely as troops marched through it or were quartered there for long periods, usually pillaging and demanding vast financial contributions from the peasants and citizenry as they went. The worst year was 1631, when the city was first taken over by Swedish troops, then besieged and captured by Catholic League troops under Tilly. By 1648 Rothenburg had been ruined financially, while its hinterland had been devastated. Scores of houses and many churches lay in ruins; most things of value, including livestock, had been stolen from those peasants who had been unable to flee to the city when the soldiers came; many of its parishes had been without pastors for long periods of time during the war; population loss, as a result of epidemic disease or flight, stood at an average of 58 per cent for the hinterland, and reached 75–100 per cent in certain villages; and agrarian production was virtually at a standstill.[10] This was arguably the worst experience ever suffered by the area and its inhabitants; I will suggest later that the events and aftermath of the Thirty Years' War also had subtle effects on popular and elite attitudes towards witchcraft that became apparent in the second half of the seventeenth century.

The Rothenburg witch-trials: historiography, sources, methodology

Little has hitherto been written about the Rothenburg witch-trials. The only substantial piece of research and writing that exists on the subject – although unfortunately without references – are the two articles published by

Rothenburg archivist Heinrich Schmidt in 1954 and 1959 as part of his broader project on seventeenth-century Rothenburg.[11] In them he identifies and sum- marises, in varying degrees of detail, twelve witchcraft cases from the period 1602–73, which provided a useful starting point for my own work on the seventeenth century. However, Schmidt did not analyse or contextualise these cases in depth, nor did he know of the witchcraft cases from the pre-1602 or post-1673 periods. Friedrich Merzbacher relies primarily on Schmidt's work in his brief discussion of Rothenburg in his 1957 monograph on witch-trials in early modern Franconia, as does Wolfgang Behringer for his discussion of Rothenburg in his 1987 book on witch-persecution in the territories covered by modern-day Bavaria – although in this excellent survey this was one of the few areas for which Behringer cited no manuscript sources.[12] Behringer was also correct in hypothesising in his book that the absence of evidence of execu- tions in Rothenburg indicated elite unwillingness to hunt witches,[13] although my research will prove and explain this unwillingness in detail and will also factor in the role the lower orders played in the restrained pattern of witch- trials in Rothenburg. For the late medieval period the punishment of sorcery is discussed briefly in Klaus-Peter Herzog's 1971 dissertation on criminal law in late medieval Rothenburg,[14] while Rothenburg archivist Ludwig Schnurrer was kind enough to share with me references from his own, unpublished research to cases of sorcery from the same period.

Unlike previous work on witch-trials in Rothenburg, this book is based on extensive and systematic research of a wide variety of manuscript sources from 1500 to 1800. I used the city Account Books, meticulously kept on an annual basis from 1530 until the twentieth century, to identify all the serious witchcraft cases tried by the council during the sixteenth, seventeenth and eighteenth centuries. 'Serious' cases were those that ended in execution or that involved a stay of more than a few days in gaol for the parties involved or the use of torture against them, as gaoling, torturing or executing suspects cost the council money which it accounted for carefully. Account Book entries usually specified the crime for which particular suspects had been gaoled or executed: where this was not made clear it was usually possible to find the relevant trial- records from the names and dates given in the Account Books in order to check whether or not it was a witch-trial. I am therefore confident that I have identi- fied all of the serious witch-trials that occurred in Rothenburg from 1500 to 1800. There are doubtless more witchcraft cases yet to be found in the city's criminal-court records, but it would have taken decades to examine the many hundreds of huge volumes of these records – which usually lack indices and are unpaginated – still held in the city archive. However, as cases which were not recorded in the Account Books would not have involved executions, torture or long spells in gaol for the suspects, future unearthing of hitherto-unknown cases from the criminal records will doubtless strengthen rather than weaken my arguments about the relatively restrained pattern of witch-hunting and treatment of suspected witches in Rothenburg.

These criminal-court records are the most important sources for the detailed analysis of the Rothenburg witch-trials. They fall into three categories. The *Urgichtenbücher* or Interrogation Books are the most important. Individuals arrested on suspicion of a crime were held in cells in the city gaol, where they were questioned by the two most junior members of the council (the *Turmherren*) about their alleged crimes, in an ordinary room if the interrogation occurred without torture, or in a subterranean dungeon if torture was to be inflicted by the municipal executioner. Records as close as possible to verbatim were made of these interrogations as they took place: these were then read and discussed by the rest of the council. When a trial was over these records were bound into the Interrogation Books, along with all other documents pertaining to the case: witnesses' statements, the opinions of legal, theological or medical experts and any letters written to or by the council about the case. The Rothenburg Interrogation Books therefore provide the historian with an exceptionally rich source, in some trials running to hundreds of pages, of personal testimonies from suspects, their accusers, witnesses and elite experts.

Once a verdict had been reached in a case, suspects might be released without punishment, at which point they had to swear a surety in which they promised not to revenge themselves on the council or its subjects for their treatment in custody: these were recorded and bound into *Urfehdenbücher*, or Surety Books. Suspects sentenced to corporal or capital punishment had their sentences recorded in the aptly named *Blutbücher*, or Blood Books. Records of sureties or sentences contained summaries of the respective criminals' crimes, which constitute a useful overview of the case and also the council's ultimate opinion about it. However, this neat division of source-types into Interrogation, Surety and Blood Books collapsed in Rothenburg in the early seventeenth century: thereafter the interrogations, sureties and/or sentences pertaining to particular cases were usually all bound into the Interrogation Books. Moreover, in the second half of the seventeenth century some witchcraft cases were bound into a special volume of the records of the Rothenburg Consistorium, or Church Council. This is why the Account Books rather than the Blood Books are the safest way to check on overall numbers of serious witchcraft cases, although all the Blood Books were also examined, as were most of the sixteenth-century Surety Books.

My analysis of the Rothenburg witch-trials is based on a careful reading of case-documents in order to capture nuances of meaning, the ways in which stories were shaped and told, and the personalities and perspectives of their tellers. In seeking to understand these texts and to offer explanations for why particular

individuals – as either alleged or self-confessed witches, their accusers, or witnesses – said what they did, in the way that they did, about witchcraft, I
privilege no single theoretical perspective. I have, for example, drawn on literary theory in my treatment of trial-records as created texts, on anthropological
and psychoanalytic theory in my analysis of the verbal and social exchanges and
personal crises that lay behind accusations and confessions of witchcraft, and on
gender theory in order to explain why the alleged Rothenburg witches were
most easily imagined as women.[15] I also seek to contextualise the witch-trials as
carefully as possible, using a range of other sources in order to establish the life-
histories of trial-participants, the immediate circumstances of particular trials,
and the broader social and cultural context of the beliefs and conflicts expressed
and negotiated within them. It is only in this most detailed of contexts that we
can best explain why inhabitants of early modern Rothenburg and its hinterland
said particular things about witches at particular times in their lives, whether
strategically – in order to pursue feuds, exact revenge or articulate defiance – or
in order to 'express and relieve their unconscious (and sometimes their
conscious) fears, conflicts and anxieties'.[16]

    I privilege trial-records in this book because they are the best sources
through which to fulfil its two main aims, outlined at the beginning of the Introduction. I say relatively little about demonology, other than where I can show
that a particular text had influence on a particular trial, as I am of Ian Bostridge's
opinion that the persecution of witches and discourses about witchcraft have
distinct, if overlapping, histories.[17] Feminists and literary scholars in particular
sometimes too readily assume simple causal relationships between what was
written by demonologists and how witches were treated by judicial elites, without teasing out the many complex influences at work in trial-processes.[18] Trial-
records are, of course, the product of an often lengthy legal process in which
alleged witches, their accusers and witnesses were constrained in the giving of
their testimony by various factors: alleged witches by the possible threat and
infliction of torture and the use of suggestive questioning techniques, witnesses
by the threat of sanctions governing slanderous speech, and all trial-participants
by the cultural resources available to them for the construction of credible narratives, either of witchcraft or of its denial. These constraints do not, however,
render trial-records valueless: to paraphrase Carlo Ginzburg, historical records
produced in the 'hostile' environment of the interrogation process can still 'fur-
nish precious testimony' about the motives, emotions and cultural worlds of
members of the lower orders.[19] The different ways – desperate, measured,
artful, enthusiastic, unwilling – in which accusers and witnesses shaped their
stories of witchcraft and participated in trial-processes to the advantage or disadvantage of the accused witch tell us a great deal about their reasons for so
doing and about their pre-trial relationship with the accused witch, as well as

about the narrative-telling strategies available to them and their awareness of the risks that they ran in speaking openly about witchcraft.[20]

Alleged witches were also not without agency in the interrogation process, primarily because of the fact that torture was used with considerable restraint – and often not at all – in the Rothenburg witch-trials. This meant that alleged witches were never simply forced through repeated torture into confessing guilt and on the contrary were likely to be able to maintain – sometimes sophisticated and usually impassioned – narratives of their innocence which often told a tale of bitter social conflict with their accusers but one lacking the sinister subtext of witchcraft. It was – ironically – usually individuals (children and weak-minded adults) who had suffered little or no physical or mental torment who admitted most freely to being witches, much to the bewilderment of the city councillors. The councillors were left with the problematic and unenviable task of trying to decide which of the competing testimonies they had heard was most likely to be true: their decisions in all cases were made in the context of broader legal, political and social concerns. The trial process was a complex one in which all participants operated under certain, albeit varying, constraints, yet at the same time had a certain, albeit varying, degree of agency. To imply, as some feminists do, that all parties to early modern witch-trials were simply the cowed or brutalised mouth-pieces of all-powerful patriarchal elites over-estimates levels of elite enthusiasm for witch-hunts, ignores the importance of the motives and personalities of alleged witches and their accusers to the trial-process, and misunderstands fundamentally how the law worked in early modern Germany.[21]

Chronology and the late medieval background

Between the late fourteenth and late fifteenth century no-one found guilty of using sorcery was executed in Rothenburg. The usual punishment was banishment, for a specified number of years or eternally. It was not, however, the automatic punishment. In 1435 two women who had used sorcery escaped any form of punishment, although records fail to explain why this happened.[22] Corporal punishments were inflicted only rarely in addition to banishment: I know of just one example from 1409 in which a woman was branded through both cheeks before being banished after she had promised, in return for payment, to teach many Rothenburg women how to find buried treasure and to work love-magic.[23] It is unclear, however, whether this punishment was inflicted for sorcery or for fraud: the boundaries between the two crimes remained blurred throughout the early modern period.

The same pattern – with its absence of executions, the possibility of escaping punishment for sorcery altogether if one's crimes were deemed insufficently grave, and the infliction of corporal punishments only in particularly heinous cases – persisted in Rothenburg in the early sixteenth century.[24] Between 1500 and 1544, however, the council inflicted branding more frequently on individuals found guilty of using sorcery in especially serious cases. Two women were branded through their cheeks and one man and two women were branded with the sign of the cross before being banished for crimes involving the use of black magic in 1519, 1525 and 1540, respectively.[25] This increased severity towards sorcery, however, appears to have reflected the council's growing concern with what it perceived to be growing irreligiosity on the part of its subjects in the early sixteenth century, and must be set against the backdrop of the social and spiritual unrest of the period which culminated in the Reformation and the Peasants' War.[26] As this book will show, Rothenburg's newly reformed Lutheran elites discontinued this severity from the mid-sixteenth century, largely discarding the use of branding in cases of sorcery and witchcraft and reverting to banishment as the normal, although by no means automatic, punishment. The policy of treating certain allegations of witchcraft as cases of slander was also well established in Rothenburg by the first half of the sixteenth century. Criminal and civil court records from this period show several cases in which allegations of witchcraft were handled as instances of slander to the advantage of the alleged witch, a trend which was to become arguably even more important in the second half of the sixteenth century.[27]

This book focuses on the period c. 1561–c. 1652 for several reasons. Apart from seven earlier volumes dealing with participants in the Peasants' War of 1525, Interrogation Books – the richest source for the study of witch-trials – are extant for the city only from 1550. The council adopted Lutheranism in 1544 and formalised its reformation between then and 1559. The focus on the post-1544 period thus allows us to see how a Lutheran city council treated witchcraft and how the reformation in Rothenburg affected its subjects' beliefs about magic and witchcraft. Moreover, although the restrained pattern of witch-trials in Rothenburg remained relatively constant throughout the entire early modern period, the ways in which witchcraft was imagined and treated changed subtly during the seventeenth century. The post-1652 period thus forms a distinct chapter in the history of Rothenburg witch-trials and one which I intend to discuss in depth elsewhere. Finally, the western European witch-hunts were generally at their worst in the second half of the sixteenth and first half of the seventeenth century. It therefore makes sense to look at Rothenburg for the same period to show how the inhabitants of this area lived through this period without experiencing large- or even small-scale episodes of witch-persecution. Details of all of the trials involving allegations or confessions of maleficient or demonic witchcraft that occurred in early modern Rothenburg are provided in an Appendix to this book, enabling the reader to set the cases from the mid-sixteenth to mid-seventeenth century in context.

Popular witchcraft belief

This book focuses primarily on the ways in which women, children and men of the lower orders in Rothenburg and its hinterland talked about witches. While they shaped their stories in idiosyncratic ways, they drew on common cultural resources of popular witchcraft belief which, by the mid-sixteenth century, coalesced around two main ways of imagining the witch. The first was as a worker of maleficient or harmful magic – someone who was believed capable of depleting and stealing, by magical means, the good health and material resources of other people, and causing them to fall ill, to become poorer, and even to die. These witches were often but by no means exclusively imagined as women. Witches were also popularly imagined as women who were capable of flying through the night sky and of entering buildings in order to plague people and livestock while they slept by means of 'pressing' or 'riding' them, also to the point of death. These ideas stemmed from pre-Christian beliefs in the wild ride which, as Charles Zika has shown, were still current in the sixteenth century and 'told of women who rode out on wild animals during certain nights of the year with Diana, Holda and other female goddesses, engaging in much feasting and often too in considerable destruction'.[28] These two ways of imagining witches could overlap in witch-trials in Rothenburg, but they could also remain conceptually distinct: allegedly maleficient witches were not necessarily also accused of night-flying, while women believed to have attended nocturnal gatherings of alleged witches did not necessarily also have reputations as workers of harmful magic.

During the second half of the sixteenth and early seventeenth centuries these beliefs were influenced by, and in their turn helped shape, elite beliefs about witches and their relationship with the devil. Elite belief in the witches' dance, or sabbat, as a gathering of witches overseen by the devil was easily incorporated into extant popular beliefs about night-flying women and was first formally encountered in Rothenburg in a story of witchcraft told by six-year-old Hans Gackstatt in 1587.[29] The idea that witchcraft was a form of heresy, involving the giving of one's soul to the devil, influenced popular belief more slowly and patchily, however, emerging in attenuated form for the first time in a story of witchcraft told by thirteen-year-old Margaretha Hörber in 1627.[30] Of more importance to many of the Rothenburg witchcraft narratives than the devil, however, was the figure of the adult female witch who was believed responsible for enticing or forcing other, younger people – especially children – into witchcraft. The way in which this particular witch-figure came to occupy such an important position in both elite and popular imaginings of the witch in early modern Rothenburg, and the consequences this had for women actually accused of witchcraft, is one of the key themes of this book.

Notes

1 Magdalena Dürr, who had also committed infanticide, was the only person executed for witchcraft before 1652: see Chapter 5. Two further executions for witchcraft took place in the late seventeenth century: that of self-confessed witch Anna Margaretha Rohn in 1673 and of Barbara Ehness, who had also attempted murder by means of poison in 1692: see Appendix for full list of all early modern trials.

2 Briggs, *Witches and Neighbours*, pp. 397–411, especially pp. 400, 402.

3 See Behringer, 'Scheiternde Hexenprozesse'; Scribner, 'Witchcraft and judgement'; Kunstmann, *Zauberwahn*; Schmidt, *Glaube und Skepsis*.

4 For narrative histories of Rothenburg's political development, see Bensen, *Historische Untersuchungen*, and von Bezold, *Die Verfassung und Verwaltung*. See Rowlands, 'Women, gender and power', pp. 10–29, for discussion of the council's accretion of legal power.

5 Schnurrer, *Rothenburg im Mittelalter*, pp. 272–286.

6 Vice, 'The German Peasants' War', pp. 30–193.

7 Woltering, *Die Reichsstadt Rothenburg*, especially vol. II.

8 Schattenmann, *Die Einführung der Reformation*, especially pp. 87–129.

9 Moritz, 'Die Folgen des Dreissigjährigen Krieges', pp. 44–52.

10 *Ibid.*, pp. 54–131; Rank, *Die Finanzwirtschaft*, pp. 125–129; Heller, *Rothenburg ob der Tauber*, pp. 36–190.

11 Schmidt, 'Vordringender Hexenwahn', and 'Aberglaube, Hexenwahn'.

12 Behringer, *Hexenverfolgung in Bayern*, pp. 43–47, 155–161, 228, 322–324, 338; Merzbacher, *Die Hexenprozesse in Franken*, pp. 46–47. Merzbacher also cites a witchcraft case involving Michael Würth from a reference to it by Weigel in his *Rothenburger Chronik*, p. 222, although Weigel wrongly dates it to 1649: it occurred in 1663.

13 Behringer, *Hexenverfolgung in Bayern*, pp. 46–47, 155, 228, 322.

14 Herzog, 'Das Strafensystem', pp. 12–14.

15 My approach to the reading of early modern witch-trials has been particularly influenced by the work of Diane Purkiss, Tom Robisheaux, Lyndal Roper, David Sabean and Bob Scribner.

16 Purkiss, *The Witch in History*, p. 93.

17 Bostridge, 'Witchcraft repealed', p. 310.

18 See for example Scholz Williams, *Defining Dominion*; Brauner, *Fearless Wives*; Barstow, *Witchcraze*. The works by Scholz Williams and Brauner are, however, helpful in suggesting ways in which elite thinking about witchcraft may have been influenced by particular demonological texts.

19 Ginzburg, *The Cheese and the Worms*, Preface, especially pp. xvii–xviii.

20 Natalie Zemon Davis points to similar constraints on the shaping of narratives in her analysis of pardon-tales in sixteenth-century France, see Davis, *Fiction in the Archives*, pp. 2–35.

21 Purkiss discusses the work of radical feminists in *The Witch in History*, pp. 7–29, and is critical of their emphasis on the witch as the helpless, silent victim of patriarchy.

22 Herzog, 'Das Strafensystem', pp. 12–14. The pattern was similar in other late medieval Franconian and Swabian imperial cities, although there were very rare instances of executions in, for example, Nuremberg and Lindau: Behringer, *Hexenverfolgung in Bayern*, pp. 44–46.

23 Herzog, 'Das Strafensystem', p. 84.

24 This conclusion is based on analysis of Rothenburg's Blood Books and Surety Books for the period 1501–50; see Stadtarchiv Rothenburg (hereafter abbreviated to RStA) Blood Book B329; Surety Books A842, A843, A844.

25 For the case from 1519, see RStA Blood Book B329 fol. 41verso (hereafter abbreviated to

v); from 1525, see Vice, 'The village clergy', pp.127–133; from 1540, see RStA Blood Book B329 fol. 91recto (hereafter abbreviated to r).

26 Quester, *Das Rad der Fortuna*, pp. 1–5, 122–137, 170–206.

27 For examples of allegations of witchcraft being treated as slander cases in this period, see RStA Peasants' Court Books B317 fols 20v, 76r, and B316 fol. 196r; Detwang Village Court Book B328 fol. 110v; Wörnitz Village Acts A769 fols 75r–76v; Surety Book A842 fols 94r–94v.

28 Zika, 'Fears of flying', p. 39.

29 See Chapter 3.

30 See Chapter 4.

1

'An honourable man should not talk about that which he cannot prove': slander and speech about witchcraft

On 29 January 1561, Paulus and Barbara Brosam, a married couple from Wettringen, one of the largest villages in Rothenburg's rural hinterland, brought a slander suit before the council in Rothenburg against two of their neighbours, brothers-in-law Hans Lautenbach and Leonhart Immell. The Brosams complained that Lautenbach and Immell had falsely claimed that Barbara was a witch and Paulus her accomplice, thereby threatening to rob the couple of their honour. Defendants Lautenbach and Immell refused to retract their claims, however, and because of this and the gravity of their allegations, the council gaoled both parties to the suit in order to examine the matter further. A few days later the case ended, in the Brosams' favour. Paulus and Barbara were allowed to return home after paying the costs of their brief imprisonment and promising to present themselves before the council if allegations of witchcraft were made against them in future, while Lautenbach and Immell were eternally banished from Rothenburg and its hinterland for malicious defamation, with Lautenbach first enduring the additional ignominy of a spell in the city's pillory.[1]

This was one of the earliest cases in which allegations of harmful or demonic witchcraft were brought to the attention of the post-reformation council in Rothenburg and one of eighteen such cases investigated by the council between c. 1561 and c. 1652. Of the forty-one individuals involved in these cases as alleged or self-confessed witches, nine were banished and only one was executed, in 1629.[2] Chapters 1 and 2 of this book will explain why Rothenburg and its hinterland had this restrained pattern of formal prosecution for witchcraft during the early modern period, exploring the web of legal, social and cultural factors at popular and elite levels which operated and interacted to deter the inhabitants of the area from accusing their neighbours of witchcraft at law, and to ensure that the allegations of witchcraft that reached the courts rarely led to convictions for the crime and never triggered mass trials. Using the Wettringen case from 1561 as a starting point, this chapter will focus on two legal factors central to this web of restraints: the unwillingness of the Rothenburg council to abandon due legal procedure in its treatment of witchcraft, and the role that the legal treatment of slander in Rothenburg played in dissuading people from accusing others formally of witchcraft, and even from voicing suspicions of witchcraft publicly at all. The Wettringen case proved to be the fore-runner of a case-type – in which allegations of witchcraft were treated as instances of slander and in which the slanderers rather than the alleged witches came off worst – which played an important part in shaping the council's judicial engagement with witchcraft in the late sixteenth and early seventeenth century and remained of some, albeit lesser, significance thereafter.

Brosam v. Lautenbach and Immell

Hans Lautenbach's story of alleged witchcraft, which precipitated the Brosams' slander suit and which he repeated to Wendel Ferg and Erhardt Schleeried, the councillors deputised to question him after his arrest, ran as follows. On 18 January 1561 he had been travelling home with several barrels of wine from Heidenfels, a village situated several miles to the southwest of Wettringen, when heavy snowfalls had forced him to abandon his cart at a tavern in another village called Wallhausen. By sunset he had managed to return home to Wettringen on horseback and, tired and cold, had lain down on a bench in front of the stove to warm himself. He had dozed off and been pressed by a witch while asleep.[3] On waking, Lautenbach had urinated into a glass container, stoppered it shut, and locked it in a chest. By this means Lautenbach hoped to identify the witch responsible for the pressing as – according to popular belief – she would thereafter be unable to pass water and would be forced to confront him in order to obtain and smash the container and thereby break its counter-magical power over her.[4]

A couple of days later Lautenbach's plan for identifying the witch had apparently worked. He had been drinking with companions in a Wettringen tavern belonging to Hans Kapp when one of the daughters of Paulus and Barbara Brosam arrived with a message from her father, in which Paulus offered to accompany Lautenbach on his journey to Wallhausen to retrieve his abandoned cart. Instead of going to meet Paulus, however, Lautenbach had dallied in the tavern. A short while later Lautenbach's own wife had turned up, to tell him that Paulus had just called at their house to repeat his offer personally. Again Lautenbach had stayed in the tavern, and it was at this point that he uttered the words that were to have such dire consequences for him. He told his companions of his recent pressing by the witch and of the method he had adopted to identify his tormenter, suggesting that Paulus Brosam's desire for his company 'was part of the same affair'.[5] This indirect reference was understood by those listening to

Lautenbach to imply that the witchcraft was the work of Barbara Brosam, on whose behalf Paulus was now acting to obtain the urine-filled container.

The account Lautenbach gave of his subsequent journey to Wallhausen to retrieve his cart underlined this conclusion. He had set off alone, but Paulus had followed the tracks of his horse in the snow to the tavern at Wallhausen. There he had insisted on speaking to Lautenbach and arranging that the two of them travel back to Wettringen together. On the return journey, Paulus had begged Lautenbach for the container, which was apparently causing great problems in the Brosam household. Lautenbach had initially made no promises, merely commenting that 'he had not thought that Paulus and his family were such people', meaning witches.[6] Paulus had asked for the container on two further occasions, once when Lautenbach's cart overturned in the snow – the idea being that he would help right the cart if Lautenbach promised to give him the container – and again when they reached Wettringen. At this point Lautenbach had relented to his increasingly desperate requests and given him the container, which he had smashed on the ground outside Lautenbach's house.[7] The allegation that Barbara Brosam was the witch who had pressed Lautenbach was subsequently repeated by his brother-in-law, Leonhart Immell, at another Wettringen tavern belonging to Georg Rigell.[8] It was in reaction to the ever-widening publicity that Lautenbach's story was gaining in Wettringen that the Brosams brought their slander suit.

In custody both Brosams refuted the allegations made by Lautenbach, although in different ways. Paulus told councillors Ferg and Schleeried a tale which accorded in many details with Lautenbach's, but which put a different gloss on the motives for his actions. He suggested that his offer to accompany Lautenbach on his journey had not been unusual or overly insistent, explaining that he had needed to travel in the same direction anyway in order to collect some money he was owed for a barrel of wine from a man who lived near Wallhausen. As he had been concerned about the threat posed by itinerant mercenaries to lone travellers, it had made sense to him to secure the company of Lautenbach for the journey. The arrangement had worked to Lautenbach's advantage as well, as he had been able to right his overturned cart on their return journey to Wettringen only with the assistance of Paulus. Paulus denied ever asking Lautenbach for the glass container. Instead, he gave his interrogators an everyday account of two men going about their business in the context of a neighbourly companionship which worked in both their interests, with no subtext of witchcraft to give sinister meaning to their exchanges.[9]

What Paulus implied – that Lautenbach's story was a malicious fabrication – Barbara made explicit in custody using three interlinked strategies: an assertion of her innocence, an attempt to discredit the defendants, and an emphasis on her piety. She insisted that she was not a witch, pointing out – by way of a negative proof of this fact, and as evidence of the popular under-standing of witchcraft as a mode of illicit material gain made by witches at the expense of their neighbours – that if she could work witchcraft she would not have suffered such poverty during her life. Her innocence was further shown by the fact that she and Paulus had come into Rothenburg voluntarily, leaving their six young children at home, to bring the case to the attention of the council in the first place. The implication was that these were not the actions of people who had anything to hide, but here Barbara was being disingenuous, glossing over the fact that the Brosams' decision to bring the suit had doubt-less been made after careful calculation of its risks and advantages. She accused Lautenbach and Immell of having plotted together to concoct lies about her out of envy and hatred and did all she could to undermine their credibility and the plausibility of their testimony. Immell had previously accused other women of being witches when drunk, she explained, while Lautenbach was a man tainted with vice, who lacked honour himself and therefore sought to deprive other people of their good names by defaming them. Barbara referred to a previous legal punishment that Lautenbach had received – for adultery in 1555, discussed below – and the fact that God had seen fit to inflict the serious illness of epilepsy upon him, as proof of his inherent sinfulness and dubious character. Barbara also called on God as a witness of her blamelessness and drew parallels between her own and Christ's suffering as a way of emphasis-ing her lack of guilt and of warning her interrogators against the unjust punishment of innocents by secular authorities.[10] From their fervour and fre-quency, Barbara's assertions of piety appear to have been heartfelt, but in voic-ing them she may also have been replicating narrative strategies she had already employed in response to the questions about her identity as a witch that had been put to her by the pastor of Wettringen, Johannes Zöllner, in the years before 1561.[11]

Leonhart Immell, Lautenbach's brother-in-law and a baker by trade, was questioned next. He had lost his nerve since being gaoled and now sought to escape the council's wrath by shifting the blame for the slander against the Brosams onto Lautenbach and by offering excuses for his own role in the affair. He admitted that he had mentioned Barbara's act of witchcraft to his drinking companions in Georg Rigell's tavern, but added that he had done so only after Lautenbach had first made the allegations against her public and that he other-wise knew nothing about her in connection with witchcraft. To excuse his rep-etition of the slander, Immell explained that he had been drunk at the time and provoked in his actions by the hostility which the Brosams had previously shown towards him. Barbara had once attacked him with a stick and Paulus with an axe and both Brosams had damaged his trade by criticising the quality of his bread. Immell expressed the wish that he lived far away from the couple, begged the councillors for merciful treatment, and implored them to ask his neighbours in Wettringen for testimony of his good character.[12]

The council did turn next to other Wettringen inhabitants for evidence, questioning pastor Zöllner and four men – Gilg Hoffman, Lorentz Herman, Steffan Haim and Gorg Kurtz – who were neighbours of the Brosams, on oath on 31 January. Such communal opinion was crucial to legal procedure in early modern Germany, as it could provide the circumstantial evidence on the basis of which a decision to question one or more of the protagonists under torture could be made by the judicial authorities. It was particularly important in cases such as those of alleged witchcraft or illicit sexual intercourse, where two parties maintained opposing versions of events which no-one else had witnessed and where the key issue for the authorities was that of which party was to be deemed most credible. The fact that the questioning of the Wettringen witnesses focused on the suspicions of witchcraft raised against Barbara Brosam showed that the council was still taking them seriously.

The statements given shed interesting light on other members of the Brosam family. Pastor Zöllner explained that, throughout the decade of his incumbency in Wettringen, rumours had circulated to the effect that the parents of Paulus, Veit and Elisabeth Brosam, were workers of sorcery who had taught their arts to Barbara. Zöllner stressed that he had done all he could to discover whether there was any truth in this talk, frequently exhorting Veit, Elisabeth and Barbara to admit their sin rather than take communion with it on their consciences. Here Zöllner had acted in accordance with the Rothenburg *Church Ordinance* of 1559, which decreed that village pastors were to summon and talk to any parishioners suspected of having heterodox beliefs or of working sorcery, in order to convince them of the errors of their ways.[13] The Brosams, however, had always maintained their innocence and continued to take communion. Zöllner had also watched their behaviour closely, but had seen nothing to confirm the rumours against them.[14] Hoffman, Herman, Haim and Kurtz stated that they personally had never seen or heard anything of Paulus and Barbara which would connect them with witchcraft and confirmed that the couple had behaved in a neighbourly fashion in Wettringen during the twelve years of their marriage. Since the time of the Peasants' War (1525), however, it had been rumoured in the village that Veit and Elisabeth Brosam, and Veit's brother Hans, were workers of sorcery.[15] Leonhart Immell had once publicly accused Hans Brosam of this, but had been fined after Hans had pursued a slander suit against him successfully at the village court in Wettringen.[16]

The Wettringen witnesses were thus unwilling to take sides, personally and unequivocally, with Lautenbach and Immell against Paulus and Barbara Brosam in the slander suit. However, their statements had at least the potential to swing the balance of the case against the couple in more subtle ways. This was because the *Carolina*, the code of criminal law procedure issued for the Holy Roman Empire in 1532, recognised as circumstantial evidence of possible guilt of alleged witchcraft two of the points implied in the testimony of the witnesses. These were first, that Paulus and Barbara were closely associated with other reputed workers of sorcery (Paulus' blood-relatives), and second, that Barbara, Veit, Elisabeth and Hans Brosam had long-standing reputations as workers of sorcery.[17] However, the councillors decided not to act on this evidence, on the basis of which they might have questioned the Brosams under torture, and instead brought Paulus and Lautenbach together in custody on 1 February to confront one another with their still-contradictory narratives.[18]

This decision was based on precepts – the tendency of the council to give the plaintiff rather than the defendant the benefit of the doubt in slanders involving witchcraft and its unwillingness to proceed too rapidly to the use of torture in the uncertain matter of witchcraft – which will be discussed later. It proved crucial for the ongoing case, however. On confronting Paulus, who still protested his innocence, Lautenbach broke down and confessed that he had never been pressed by a witch, but had been provoked into fabricating the story about Barbara Brosam by the hostility she had shown towards him.[19] It is unclear why Lautenbach executed this ultimately fateful about-turn in his narrative at this juncture, although some plausible explanations can be offered. He may have feared the possibility of being interrogated under torture or on oath as a test of his story, because he was in poor health at the time of the trial and thus doubtful of his ability to withstand physical pain, and because he knew that perjury was subject to potentially severe secular punishments as well as divine wrath. He may also have hoped that a retraction at this stage, combined with contrition and an explanation of the provocation by Barbara which he felt had justified his slander, would constitute sufficiently mitigating circumstances to earn him the council's mercy. He proved mistaken in his hopes, however, because his plea of provocation served merely to strengthen Barbara's claim that his words against her had been motivated by malice. His confession thus brought the case to an end and the council's judicial severity upon himself and his brother-in-law.

Honour, insult and feud

Why did Hans Lautenbach bear such ill-will towards Barbara Brosam that he slandered her as a witch? The explanation he gave to the councillors on 1 February rooted his enmity in various verbal exchanges he had had with her as he made his way home from Hans Kapp's tavern.[20] Barbara had been in the habit of accosting him and asking him in defiant tones, 'whether he had not already

been led around by the hangman's rope for long enough', adding that 'the hangman would lead him by the noose for a long time yet'.[21] It was 'because she had
hurt him so' with these words that Lautenbach had been goaded into spreading
the witchcraft allegations against her.[22]

Lautenbach reacted with such hostility to the insults offered by Barbara
because of the importance attached to honour and the need to defend it in early
modern German society. A person's honour was his or her good name, trust-
worthiness and integrity, and the main guarantor of an individual's standing and
reputation within a community. It was an invaluable asset: people with bad reputations not only risked being marginalised and disadvantaged within the nexus
of everyday exchanges between neighbours, but were also rendered more vulnerable to the deleterious effects of a legal system in which possession of ill-fame
was recognised at both elite and popular levels as an important indicator of possible guilt of a crime.[23] It was therefore with some justification that contemporaries likened honour to a precious jewel, worth more than gold or silver, or
expressed the wish that they would rather lose vast sums of money than suffer it
to be damaged.[24] In addition to being precious, however, an individual's honour
was precarious and in constant need of defence and affirmation. It could be jeopardised by an insult, by an allegation of discreditable behaviour, even by a rude
gesture, and anyone whose honour had been thus attacked had to retaliate
against the person or people responsible – with violence, a counter-insult, or a
legal suit – or risk a depreciation in the value of their good name.

The insult which Barbara Brosam offered Lautenbach as he walked home
from Hans Kapp's tavern had such power to hurt him for three reasons. First,
because it implied an association between Lautenbach and the hangman, or
municipal executioner, who was regarded in early modern German society as
dishonourable by virtue of his profession, which was that of torturing suspected criminals and carrying out the corporal and capital sentences on those
found guilty of their crimes.[25] Second, because hanging was the usual punishment for persistent theft in early modern Germany and was regarded as a more
dishonourable method of execution than, for example, beheading.[26] By suggesting that Lautenbach was led about by the hangman's rope, therefore, Barbara
implied that he was a thief, someone not to be trusted with other people's property and reputations, and damaged his honour still further. Finally, Lautenbach
had been publicly flogged by the Rothenburg hangman as punishment for an act
of adultery he had committed with his maidservant in 1555, a fact which probably rendered him more vulnerable to insults of this nature and put him under
greater pressure to react to them.[27]

Behind Lautenbach's personal grievance against Barbara Brosam, however, lay at least two other conflicts in which he was ranged against the Brosams
which help explain what he said and why Leonhart Immell repeated it. One of

these was a conflict which, he explained to the councillors, had arisen between Paulus and Barbara Brosam and Hans Kapp, who was his good friend and neighbour and at whose tavern he drank. As Barbara's insults towards Lautenbach had been offered as he made his way home from Kapp's, and as she had prefaced them with the accusation that he and Hans Kapp had been plotting together – presumably against the Brosams – Lautenbach's reaction to her words can thus be understood in the light of this Lautenbach–Kapp versus Brosam dispute.[28] The cause of it remains unclear, although it may have been related to a rivalry between Lautenbach and Paulus Brosam over the selling and supplying of wine, in which they both appear to have been engaged, and in which Kapp had taken sides with Lautenbach, or was perceived by the Brosams to have done so.

Lautenbach probably also felt loyalty towards his brother-in-law Immell, who was involved in his own disputes with Paulus, Barbara and Hans Brosam. Paulus and Barbara had threatened Immell's reputation and income as a baker by criticising the quality of his bread.[29] Immell may have been particularly sensitive to any threat to his financial position because of events which had occurred two decades earlier, before he moved to Wettringen. In 1541, while still living in Diebach, Immell had been ordered to pay a man named Hans Sorg the considerable sum of 95 gulden as compensation for injuries he had inflicted on Sorg in a fight. Pleading poverty, Immell had been granted permission to pay off the debt in eight instalments between 1541 and 1548. It actually took him until 1550 to complete the payments; he had moved to Wettringen in the meantime in 1544.[30] Further financial loss, caused by a decline in his trade, would have been unwelcome; it was small wonder that Immell lamented his close proximity to the Brosams.[31] His negative feelings against them would have been intensified by the fact that he had also been fined by the Wettringen court for having failed to prove his claim that Hans Brosam could work sorcery – another example of a Brosam victory at his expense.[32]

There is no reason to think that Lautenbach and Immell did not also genuinely believe that the Brosams could work witchcraft; after all, rumours to this effect had been circulating about Veit, Elisabeth and Hans for almost four decades and – according to the testimony of pastor Zöllner – about Barbara for at least a decade. For the inhabitants of Rothenburg and its hinterland, moreover, there was an emotional logic in imagining one's enemies to be witches, as both feuds and suspicions of witchcraft fed on common feelings of envy, hatred and fear of one's rivals. Despite these caveats, however, the story told by Lautenbach seems more like a move in an ongoing feud based on an unbearable sense of personal affront than a response to a deep-seated fear of witchcraft, particularly insofar as the efforts by Paulus Brosam to retrieve the urine-filled container from Lautenbach, rather than the initial pressing by

Barbara, dominated his account. The councillors understood this as an attempt by Lautenbach to implicate Paulus in Barbara's alleged witchcraft,[33] and it can also be seen as a way for Lautenbach to shift the focus of suspicion onto Paulus and to give added substance to the long-standing rumours connecting Paulus' parents and uncle with witchcraft. The creation of the story by Lautenbach and its repetition by Immell were thus expressions of their enmity towards the whole Brosam family, as well as an attempt to place its members at greater risk from a variety of sanctions, ranging from the communal to the judicial, as possible witches.

Slander in social and legal context

The decision by Paulus and Barbara Brosam to bring their slander suit before the council in Rothenburg can also be understood in the context of ideas about honour and would have been made after a careful evaluation by the couple of the risks and benefits of such a course of action. On the one hand, by bringing slanders against themselves to the attention of a court in an attempt to clear their names, plaintiffs subjected those slanders to legal scrutiny and possibly to further investigation by the judicial authorities. Plaintiffs thus ran the risk of suffering imprisonment, interrogation and even torture themselves if the investigation of the slander pointed towards the conclusion that they were guilty rather than innocent of the allegations it contained. This happened in Rothenburg in 1563, when Appolonia Kellner and her daughter Anna, inhabitants of the hinterland village of Finsterlohr, were gaoled and tortured – Anna with thumbscrews and Appolonia with thumbscrews and strappado – after an attempt to clear their names of allegations of witchcraft made against them by their relatives went awry. They were banished from Rothenburg and its hinterland as a result of the investigation of the allegations, despite the fact that they had refused to confess to being witches.[34]

On the other hand, to leave a slander unchallenged constituted tacit confirmation of the anti-social behaviour it implied. In the Finsterlohr case discussed above, for example, Leonhardt Knor – who was one of only two villagers willing to admit to the council in Rothenburg that he had ever publicly insulted Appolonia Kellner as a witch before 1563 – cited as evidence in support of his suspicions against her the fact that she had never taken action against his slanderous words.[35] Had Paulus and Barbara Brosam not reacted to the words of Lautenbach and Immell in 1561, therefore, this would have counted against them in the long term as proof of their possible guilt as witches. Moreover, given the widely held belief in witchcraft as an art passed on within households, Paulus and Barbara had to think not only of the need to clear their own names of the slander but also of the need to protect the reputations of other Brosam family members, including those of their six children.

The slander suit initiated by the Brosams can also be understood in the context of their feud against Lautenbach and Immell, although it is hard to judge whether it was an act of aggression against the brothers-in-law, pursued by the Brosams from a position of strength within Wettringen, or an act of desperation, pursued from one of weakness and social isolation. The unwillingness of their neighbours to testify unequivocally against them and the fact that Paulus Brosam's father, Veit, was a man of some standing in Wettringen, who had held important positions within the administrative structures of the village since the 1520s, supports the former interpretation.[36] However, the fact that four members of the Brosam family already had reputations as workers of sorcery within the village by 1561 and the fact that Paulus and Barbara felt it necessary to pursue their suit before the council, where the consequences of failure would have been far more damaging for them, rather than at the village court in Wettringen, suggests that they may have become increasingly vulnerable to slanders about witchcraft by 1561 and needed to show their neighbours that they would go to the highest available judicial authority to defend themselves against them. They may also have been encouraged in their decision to bring the suit by the fact that Immell had already failed to prove an allegation of witchcraft against Hans Brosam at the Wettringen village court and been fined for slander for his pains. Ultimately their gamble paid off – with perhaps even higher dividends than they had expected – with the banishment of their enemies and their own release from gaol, untortured and unpunished.[37]

The slander suit, or the threat of one, were thus important weapons which a reputed witch could wield, with some hope of success, against her detractors in early modern Germany: it was not the case, as Malcolm Gaskill assumes, that the threat of a prosecution for slander failed to deter people from making accusations of witchcraft in the context of continental inquisitorial procedure.[38] The significance of the deterrent effect of slander suits has hitherto been under-estimated and under-researched for early modern Germany, although some good work has been done for certain regions. For example, for the Principality of Bavaria Wolfgang Behringer points out that more people almost certainly appeared in the records of minor courts accused of having slandered others as witches than appeared as accused witches in witch-trials there, with most of the former cases ending with the punishment of the slanderer.[39] In her study of twenty-seven slander cases brought by alleged witches against their accusers before the court of Davensberg in the Prince-Bishopric of Münster in the early seventeenth century, Gudrun Gersmann shows that they also enjoyed a high success rate: only one of these alleged witches was subsequently prosecuted and executed for witchcraft by the authorities.[40] In

Rothenburg, the gamble of taking legal action against allegations of witchcraft was similarly successful for several alleged witches in the city and its hinterland after 1561.

In 1582, for example, it paid off for Gertraud Durmann, Anna Schneider and Anna Weh, who brought a slander suit before the council against Margaretha Seitz, one of their neighbours from the village of Oberstetten, after she had started rumours claiming that the trio were witches who had transported her against her will to their nocturnal gathering. As a result of their suit Seitz was imprisoned and interrogated and freed only after paying the costs of her stay in gaol, promising to present herself before the council if the plaintiffs brought further complaints against her, and providing two men to stand as sureties for her release. The plaintiffs were not imprisoned or questioned about her allegations.[41] A case from the village of Steinach from 1602, in which the blacksmith's apprentice, Leonhardt Brandt, claimed to have seen five village women at a nocturnal witches' gathering, followed a similar pattern. The women's husbands brought a slander suit against Brandt; he was imprisoned and interrogated, but none of the women were; and he had to pay his costs and promise to desist from his slanders and to present himself before the council if the matter went any further before being released from gaol.[42] Individuals deemed responsible for starting rumours of witchcraft against others could also be punished as slanderers by the council when their cases were investigated *ex officio* rather than as a result of a plaintiff's suit against them. In separate cases from 1629, for example, Barbara Rost of Rothenburg and Margaretha Harter of Bovenzenweiler were both banished, with Harter first suffering a flogging, for having spread such rumours. Unsurprisingly – given that they were the mayor's wife and one of the city councillors – the individuals slandered as witches by Rost were not involved at all in the legal investigation of her allegations, while the poor herdswoman who was accused of witchcraft by Harter was questioned but subsequently released from custody without punishment.[43]

Several factors explain why these cases ended with the punishment or reprimand of those who made accusations or who started and spread rumours of witchcraft, rather than the punishment of the alleged witches. Part of the explanation lies in the fact that the Rothenburg councillors took a dim view of all slanderers during the early modern period, as people who jeopardised the good names of others and who caused enmity between individuals and within communities with their damaging words. Indeed, the councillors were so firmly of the opinion that 'an honourable man should not talk about that which he cannot prove' – in other words, that no one should speak publicly against another person unless he or she was prepared to demonstrate the validity of his allegations in a court of law – that this dictum was displayed on a board which hung outside the council-chamber in the town-hall.[44] This meant that, particularly until about 1650, the councillors approached allegations of witch-craft with reasonably open minds, regarding most alleged witches as poten-tially innocent of the charges against them and their accusers as potentially guilty of slander. As it was difficult to prove charges of witchcraft at law in Rothenburg, for reasons which are discussed later, it was perhaps not sur-prising that several late sixteenth- and early seventeenth-century cases saw the alleged witches escaped unscathed.

Second, the councillors in Rothenburg appear to have realised from an early stage that the pursuit of allegations of witchcraft against individuals to the bitter end of verdicts of guilt, executions, and possibly even mass trials was inimical to one of their main political priorities: the maintenance of social stability and harmony in the city and its hinterland.[45] Their resolution of the Finsterlohr case in June 1563, for example, provides a good illustration of their awareness that discretion was the better part of valour as far as the handling of allegations of witchcraft was concerned. Alleged witches Appolonia and Anna Kellner were tortured during the investigation of the case, but the council was willing to accept their denials that they were witches without subjecting them to further physical torment, despite the fact that, in its final summary of their crimes, the council stated that it could have done this had it so chosen. The offi-cial summary of the case also concentrated as much on the fact that mother and daughter were part of a troublesome family, whose members quarrelled, cursed, blasphemed and slandered one another, as it did on their alleged witch-craft. Moreover, Appolonia's other daughter, Appolonia junior (about whom suspicions of witchcraft had also been raised), and the latter's husband, Leon-hardt Bretner, were also imprisoned, interrogated under threat of torture and banished along with Appolonia senior and Anna, for having frequently insulted their mother and sister as witches in the context of a bitter dispute over the family's material resources. By banishing all four of them the councillors rid Finsterlohr of a family which had caused great discord within the village and also impressed upon its subjects the idea that disruptive public speech, parti-cularly about witchcraft, was to be avoided at all costs.[46] This idea was also underlined by the council by the fact that Leonhardt Knor, the Finsterlohr vil-lager who had also once insulted Appolonia senior as a witch, was imprisoned and interrogated in the course of the case and released only after swearing a surety which pointed out that his allegations of witchcraft against her 'had not in the least been proven'.[47]

The council's resolution of this case may well have been influenced by its awareness of events that had taken place in Wiesensteig, a Protestant town in the southwest-German county of Helfenstein, in 1562. Between August and December of that year sixty-three witches had been executed under the aegis of Count Ulrich von Helfenstein, after fears had been raised that witchcraft was responsible for the severe hailstorms which had badly damaged vineyards in the area.[48] Although no mention was made of Wiesensteig in connection with the Finsterlohr case in 1563, it was mentioned by two jurists from Nuremberg, Christoph Hardessheim and Christoph Fabius Gugel, who were asked for advice on the Oberstetten case of 1582 by the Rothenburg council. They cited Wiesensteig as an example of the unpleasant consequences which could ensue if witchcraft cases were pursued on a dangerous, unstable basis by judicial authorities.[49] This suggests that the Wiesensteig trials, about which a sensational pamphlet had been published in 1563, had rapidly become a symbol of warning against the over-zealous pursuit of witches in certain southwest-German Protestant circles.

The resolution by the council in Rothenburg of the Oberstetten case from 1582 and the Steinach case from 1602 also underscored its lack of enthusiasm for hunting witches, as it chose to take the mildest course of action against the alleged witches from the differing opinions written on both cases by its legal advisers.[50] In 1582, for example, the three jurists called on by the council for advice on how best to handle the account given by Margaretha Seitz of the alleged witches' gathering in Oberstetten offered three different options for action against plaintiffs Gertraud Durmann, Anna Schneider and Anna Weh. Friedrich Renger advised the council that it could question the trio under oath about the allegations made by Seitz, but suggested that this be done in Oberstetten to spare them the ignominy of being called before the council in Rothenburg.[51] Johann Metzler, on the other hand, advised the council to concentrate its investigative efforts against Durmann, who could be called before the council or even imprisoned for further questioning. This was because other inhabitants of Oberstetten had testified that rumours, of at least seven years' standing, existed in Oberstetten to the effect that Durmann had fetched her since-deceased husband back to the village on a goat after he had left her on account of their bad marriage.[52] It was only the most recently appointed jurist, Cunradt Thalhaimer, who advised that none of the plaintiffs be imprisoned or questioned on oath, on the grounds that the evidence against them was of dubious quality, and who was supported in his conclusions by Gugel and Hardessheim, the two Nuremberg jurists also called on for advice in the case.[53]

The council followed Thalhaimer's recommendation and took no action against the trio of alleged Oberstetten witches.[54] Again, a concern for social stability and an awareness that witch-trials and thoughtlessly voiced accusations of witchcraft threatened to undermine good social order appear to have influenced the council's decisions. The legal opinions written by Thalhaimer and Gugel and Hardessheim played on these themes, with Thalhaimer pointing to the risk of an escalation of enmity between the women involved in the case if it were not resolved rapidly, and the Nuremberg jurists reminding the council of the fact that suspicions of witchcraft could provoke hostility and vengeful actions amongst people.[55] It is perhaps possible to set the concern of the councillors and their legal advisers with social order in 1582 against the backdrop of the severe dearth and inflation that Rothenburg – in common with much of Central Europe – had suffered as a result of a series of harvest failures caused by bad weather between 1570 and 1575.[56] Wolfgang Behringer has suggested that climatic catastrophes and the crop damage they caused could provide the trigger for episodes of witch-hunting in early modern Central Europe, because they encouraged desperate and fearful people to make demands for action against the witches believed responsible for magically causing the bad weather which judicial authorities found hard to resist.[57] In the aftermath of the famine of 1570–75, therefore, the Rothenburg authorities may have felt that the risk of such demands being made by their own subjects had increased, and resolved the Oberstetten case of 1582 in a manner which they hoped would diminish this risk.[58]

The council also took the most moderate line of action suggested by its jurists in its resolution of the Steinach case from 1602. Evidence offered by other villagers during the investigation of the claims made by Leonhardt Brandt had suggested that Appolonia Holenbuch, one of the five women allegedly seen by Brandt at the witches' gathering, had a reputation of at least six years' standing as a witch who could cause other people's cows to fall ill and whose own cow produced unusually large quantities of milk.[59] Working on the theory that there was no smoke without fire, jurist Michael Bezold told the council that it might subject Holenbuch's reputation to further investigation. Jurist Friedrich Prenninger, on the other hand, advised the council to take no action against her or any of the other alleged witches on the basis of Brandt's testimony, and it chose to follow his advice.[60] It was probably also significant in 1602 and 1582 that stronger suspicions of witchcraft existed against only one of a group of alleged witches, so that the council's enthusiasm for singling Durmann and Holenbuch out for more intense investigation may have been further diminished by the thought that this risked tarring their less suspect co-plaintiffs with the same brush of apparent guilt.

In another case, the decision by the councillors to treat allegations of witchcraft as slanderous stemmed as much from a desire to protect themselves from the slur of witchcraft as it did from a desire to maintain social harmony. Barbara Rost, a maidservant in the household of Georg Bezold, was banished in 1629 for having started and spread rumours to the effect that Bezold's wife, Anna Maria, was a witch who had caused the erysipelas from which another maidservant in the household was suffering. Rost had also helped spread rumours, which were being repeated by school-children, about a nocturnal dance which had allegedly taken place in a vineyard belonging to the wife of Johann Bezold and in which the most distinguished men and women of the

city, including Johann Georg Schnepf, had participated.[61] Georg and Johann
Bezold were two of the most powerful men in Rothenburg, council-members
since 1611 and 1612, respectively, and mayors from 1620 to 1632 and 1618 to
1634, respectively. Although younger than the Bezolds, Schnepf was of similar
social status and in 1629 was poised at the start of a political career which
would see him hold the office of mayor from 1633 to 1652.[62] Rost's words thus
threatened the honour of three of Rothenburg's pre-eminent men and their
families, as well as the peace of the city at a time when exceptionally fierce
witch-hunts were raging in the Franconian bishoprics of Würzburg, Bamberg,
Eichstätt and Mainz.[63] It was therefore unsurprising that Rost was banished for
slander and that the record of her sentence constituted one of the most viru-
lent condemnations of that sin drawn up by the council during the sixteenth and
seventeenth centuries.

Slander was punished in various ways in early modern Rothenburg. In
minor cases which came before the urban and rural civil courts there was a tendency for presiding judicial officials to nullify the alleged defamatory words in
order to restore the social peace between the parties involved. In addition, a
fine could be imposed on the defendant who failed to prove his or her slander
– as happened to Leonhart Immell at Wettringen's court – while short spells of
incarceration, and the shaming punishment of carrying a large stone around
Rothenburg were imposed more rarely, and for more serious slanders, on men
and women, respectively. In cases involving allegations so serious that they
risked exposing individuals to the rigours of criminal law procedure and which
were proven to be untrue and malicious, the council was willing to make an
example of the slanderers to the rest of its subjects with still more severe punishments. Banishment, with the option of time spent in the pillory and/or a
flogging, was the favoured option, and was inflicted not only on those who
falsely slandered others as witches, but also on men who falsely claimed to have
deflowered single women and on people who fabricated false allegations against
others for the purposes of extortion.[64] Hans Lautenbach and Leonhart Immell,
Leonhardt Bretner and his wife Appolonia, and Barbara Rost and Margaretha
Harter thus suffered the full force of the council's judicial wrath for their
unguarded words in 1561, 1563 and 1629, respectively. Their treatment was
in line with the law of talion, a medieval legal precept which continued to
influence proceedings in slander cases in early modern Rothenburg and which
decreed that individuals who brought but failed to prove charges at law risked
suffering the same punishments their adversaries would have suffered had the
charges been proven against them.[65] Their punishments were also in accord
with clause 68 of the *Carolina*, which threatened the bearers of false witness
with the same penalties they had tried to bring down on the heads of the innocent by means of their perfidious testimony.[66]

The councillors were more cautious in their treatment of Margaretha Seitz of Oberstetten and Leonhardt Brandt of Steinach, however. Jurist Thalhaimer had advised fining Seitz for her rumour-mongering and even suggested to the council that she could be threatened with banishment as a way of 'stopping her mouth' in 1582,[67] while in 1602 jurist Prenninger suggested that Brandt could be gaoled for eight days on bread and water or punished even more severely for his slander, according to the law of talion, as this might help put a stop to what Prenninger regarded as the bad habit of the lower orders in making false accusations.[68] The council opted to release both Seitz and Brandt without punishment, however, having perhaps decided that their incarceration and interrogation had already been punishment enough. It probably did this because the legal investigation of their cases had unearthed no evidence of any malice on their part towards the alleged witches which would have provided an explanation of their motives in starting the rumours about them. Moreover, the council had to be as mindful of social harmony in its handling of alleged slanderers as it was in its handling of alleged witches. Too severe a punishment of slander risked escalating, rather than assuaging, enmity between individuals. This can be seen in the aftermath of the Wettringen case from 1561. About five weeks after his banishment, Hans Lautenbach – enraged at the way in which the slander suit had ended and even more embittered against the Brosams – was arrested and gaoled in Rothenburg for a second time, after he had returned to Wettringen, repeated his accusations of witchcraft against Paulus and Barbara, and tried to stab another member of the Brosam family. That Lautenbach could still find four men willing to stand surety for his release after his second spell in gaol shows that he was by no means friendless at this stage; that the council merely banished him again, rather than punishing him more severely for having so violently broken his first surety, suggests that it was keen to show his friends that it was willing to exercise some mercy on his behalf.[69] In an attempt to restore communal harmony to the village of Steinsfeld in 1664 the council ensured even-handed treatment of both the slandered and their slanderers by ordering that anyone who repeated what it characterised as 'loose, careless children's gossip' about 'imagined witchcraft' was to be fined heavily.[70]

Witchcraft in legal context

The fact that the Rothenburg council was prepared to treat allegations of witchcraft as potential slanders and to punish with severity those allegations of witchcraft it deemed to be untrue, malicious, or particularly threatening to the social fabric, worked to the advantage of several of the alleged witches who appeared before it in the late sixteenth and early seventeenth century.

The other half of the legal equation which worked to their advantage was that allegations of witchcraft were generally difficult to prove at law, according to legal procedure as it was implemented by the councillors and interpreted by the jurists who advised them. This was primarily because torture was used either not at all, or with relative restraint, against alleged witches in the course of trials.

The manner in which early modern German courts were willing to use torture in witchcraft cases was crucial to their outcome, because the less frequently and severely torture was applied, the less likely it was that confessions of guilt would be elicited from suspects. In Rothenburg, torture was used against only nine of the forty-one people who were accused of witchcraft or who claimed to be witches between c. 1561 and c. 1652.[71] This restraint stemmed from a tendency on the part of councillors and jurists to subject the evidence that existed against alleged witches to careful scrutiny, in order to ascertain whether or not it constituted an indication of guilt sufficient to justify interrogating them under torture, rather than to assume their guilt as a foregone conclusion. In the Oberstetten case from 1582, for example, Thalhaimer – whose advice on the case proved most influential – argued that Seitz, as the only person who could testify to the alleged witches' gathering, did not constitute a good enough witness to justify even imprisoning, let alone torturing, the three plaintiffs. This was because, as the defendant in the defamation case, she had a vested interest in proving her story true, and because the generally inferior legal status of women meant that Seitz did not constitute a sufficient witness on her own in a criminal case.[72]

Thalhaimer was equally dismissive of Gertraud Durmann's alleged ill-fame as an additional proof of her guilt, pointing out that none of the Oberstetten villagers who had mentioned the rumours concerning her alleged transportation of her husband back to Oberstetten on a goat had specified from whom they had originated. He added, by way of devaluing the rumours, that it was the habit of the ignorant lower orders to call old women witches on the slightest whim.[73] This point was reiterated by Metzler, who told the council that the ill-fame in which Durmann stood would constitute a valid presumption of guilt against her only if the rumours which had created it could be shown to have been voiced first by honourable and credible people.[74] This was in line with clause 25 of the *Carolina* which, like clause 68, sought to minimise the influence of personal malice on legal procedure by stipulating that a suspect's ill-fame had to be proven to emanate from an impartial source, and not his or her enemies, before it could be counted against the suspect by a criminal court.[75] This proof was very hard for the council in Rothenburg to obtain, however, partly because some witches' reputations could be decades old before they came to its attention, and chiefly because the witnesses who testified in witchcraft cases were loathe to specify who had originally started rumours about alleged witches. Rumours against suspected witches in these cases therefore tended to remain general, in the sense that no-one was willing or could be made to take personal responsibility for them, and they were regarded as legally weak as presumptions of guilt of witchcraft as a result.

The councillors and jurists in Rothenburg were not always as scrupulous in their evaluation of the presumptions of guilt that existed against alleged witches as they were in 1582, however, and in some cases subjected suspected witches to interrogation under torture rapidly or on the basis of technically dubious testimony. This happened in 1587 and 1652, for example, in cases discussed in Chapters 3 and 6, respectively. It also happened in 1563, when Appolonia and Anna Kellner were subjected to torture during their first and only session of interrogation in custody and before the men of Finsterlohr had been questioned about the provenance of the rumours which were circulating against them in the village.[76] No legal opinions exist or appear to have been called for on this case. However, the final case summary suggests that it was the explicit and public accusations of witchcraft, frequently bandied about between the members of the Kellner family and repeated before the council during the attempt by Appolonia and Anna to clear their names of them, that had counted so heavily against mother and daughter and justified their rapid interrogation under torture.[77] This was probably because the council found it hard – at least initially – to believe that malice could be the cause of allegations of witchcraft made by such close relatives and therefore assumed that there might be some truth in them. It proceeded no further with its investigation, however, after Appolonia and Anna had denied the allegations under torture and the men of Finsterlohr had failed to substantiate the rumours of witchcraft that existed against them. This was because the council worked on the principle that, by withstanding the pain of torture and refusing to confess, an alleged witch purged herself of whatever presumptions of guilt had justified her interrogation under torture in the first place, and could not be tortured again unless new evidence against her came to light.[78]

When employed in witch-trials in Rothenburg, therefore, torture tended to be used in order to test the consistency of the statements made by suspects, rather than without restraint, to force them to confess their guilt. The highest number of bouts of torture inflicted on suspected witches in any one case was five, although between one and three bouts was more usual.[79] It was possible for adult women who possessed strong wills, sound minds, a conviction of their innocence, a fear of banishment or execution, a piety which sustained them during interrogation, and feelings of anger against both their accusers and judges, to resist even five bouts of torture and not only refuse to confess to being witches but, in some cases, to develop more sophisticated strategies of defiance

against their interrogators. No woman of this type who believed herself innocent at the start of a case was convinced otherwise in early modern Rothenburg.
It was rather children and weak-minded women, who had trouble differentiat-
ing between fantasy and reality or who had self-destructive tendencies, who
were willing to admit to being witches, often without suffering any torture
and to the perplexity of their interrogators. The absence of large numbers
of executions of witches in Rothenburg may have given individuals determined
to maintain their innocence the degree of confidence in the outcome of their
trials necessary to enable them to endure torture and the other privations of
a period of captivity in the city gaol without succumbing to the physical and
psychological pressures of the judicial process and conceding their guilt.

The relatively restrained use of torture against alleged witches in Rothenburg was in keeping with the general tenor of the *Carolina*, key aims of which
had been to eradicate local abuses of criminal law procedure, particularly in
relation to the infliction of torture, and to afford all alleged criminals a greater
degree of protection against arbitrary treatment by local courts, particularly by
stipulating that judges who tortured suspects improperly could be sued by
them for compensation.[80] This reluctance may also have been influenced by the
council's awareness that over-zealous use of torture was open to popular criticism. For example, in 1652 jurist Georg Christoph Walther suggested that
voices had been raised against the council's actions in two ongoing cases in
which alleged witches Catharina Leimbach of Wettringen and Margaretha
Horn of Bettenfeld had been subjected to the thumbscrews five times each.[81]
Popular disapproval of excessive or unjust use of torture stemmed from the fact
that torture risked injuring suspects and jeopardising their ability to earn a
living even if they were released from custody without punishment, as well as
rendering them dishonourable, because it was inflicted by the municipal executioner.[82] In areas where popular enthusiasm for prosecuting witches formally
remained at a low ebb, therefore, it was not something for judicial authorities
who cared about public opinion to resort to lightly.

More importantly, however, the reluctance of jurists and councillors to
advise and implement the use of torture with much enthusiasm against alleged
witches in Rothenburg – and, indeed, their reluctance to pursue allegations of
witchcraft with enthusiasm at law at all – stemmed from their belief that witchcraft, as an invisible and primarily spiritual crime, was extremely difficult to deal
with according to the fallible processes of human law. In 1582, for example,
Thalhaimer referred to cases of witchcraft as difficult and slippery matters,
while Metzler described the ongoing Oberstetten case as doubtful, difficult
and dangerous.[83] Jurists advising on later cases wrote in similar vein: Friedrich
Prenninger noted that witchcraft cases were difficult, doubtful and uncertain in
opinions he wrote in 1587 and 1602, Michael Bezold referred to the Steinach

case from 1602 as doubtful, and Georg Christoph Walther described witchcraft as the most unclear and puzzling form of magic in 1639.[84]

At certain times judicial authorities in certain other parts of Germany responded to the difficulty of proving witchcraft at law by treating it as an exceptional crime, one so heinous and threatening that all the inbuilt safeguards of due legal procedure, and particularly those pertaining to the use of torture, could be set aside in the pursuit of verdicts of guilt. It was in these circumstances, where torture was used without restraint, that confessions were most likely to be forced from suspected witches and large-scale episodes of persecution were most likely to occur.[85] In Rothenburg, however, the awareness that witchcraft was a difficult matter had the opposite effect, convincing jurists and councillors alike that discretion was the better part of valour in their handling of witchcraft cases, because the potential consequences of guilty verdicts – execution and the possibility of mass trials – were so dreadful for the alleged witch and the wider community alike.

This caution was evident in the ways in which the council handled and resolved cases of witchcraft: according to due legal procedure (as laid down in the *Carolina* and the legal precepts governing slander) and never as an exceptional crime. This caution was also clearly expressed in the words of the jurists who advised the council on witchcraft cases. In 1582, for example, Metzler advised the council to proceed in the Oberstetten case in a cautious and careful manner, while both Renger and Prenninger insisted that it was better to proceed too slowly rather than with too much haste in such cases.[86] In a variation on this theme, Prenninger noted in his opinion on the Steinach case from 1602 that, precisely because they were so serious, criminal cases should be pursued only on the basis of proofs that were 'clearer than the hot sun at midday'. These were clearly lacking in the Steinach case, because for Leonhardt Brandt to say that he had seen a witches' gathering by no means proved that it had really happened.[87] This counsel of caution was expressed most eloquently by Georg Christoph Walther in an opinion he wrote – and which the council followed – in 1652. He pointed out that if the secret and uncertain matter of witchcraft could not be proven according to due legal procedure, judges were not to exceed this, but were rather to release suspected witches unpunished. It was better for judges to free a hundred guilty individuals than to execute one innocent person unjustly; God would know if they were truly guilty and punish them accordingly himself. Here Walther underlined how hard it was for mere mortals to prove witchcraft unequivocally and suggested infallible divine judgement, rather than the treatment of witchcraft as an exceptional crime by earthly courts, as the best solution to the problem.[88]

Reluctance to accuse: witchcraft in popular perspective

The legal caution displayed by the council would have had much less effect on the frequency and severity of witchcraft prosecutions in Rothenburg, however, had the inhabitants of the city and its hinterland not evinced a marked lack of enthusiasm for accusing their neighbours of witchcraft formally at law during the early modern period. This is an important point, as historians of European witchcraft now agree that the initial impetus in most witchcraft trials came from the lower orders, in the form of accusations against specific suspects or general pleas from subjects to their lords demanding tougher action against witches.[89] This popular initiative was taken a stage further in parts of Germany where traditions of peasant autonomy remained strong, where concern about witchcraft became heightened, and where – either consciously or subconsciously – villagers realised the potential for pursuing social conflicts by means of witchcraft accusations most effectively. In much of the western part of Germany, for example, the witch-hunting initiative between the late sixteenth and mid-seventeenth century came from committees of village men, formed with the express purpose of starting and pursuing legal proceedings against suspected witches in their communities. Territorial lords were often powerless to ignore or abolish these committees, despite their desire to do so.[90]

In the villages of Rothenburg's hinterland, from where most witchcraft cases emanated until the later seventeenth century, no similar witch-hunting organisations were formed, however. This was despite the fact that traditions of peasant autonomy had also remained strong there: the widespread participation of Rothenburg's peasant subjects in the Peasants' War of 1525, for example, was organised in each village through the *Gemeinde*, the committee of propertied male householders responsible for regulating and overseeing the affairs of their community which continued to play an important role in hinterland village life until about 1630.[91] Petitions calling on the city council for action against witches were also conspicuous by their absence in early modern Rothenburg and accusations of witchcraft against specific individuals were brought before the council with relative infrequency. Given that belief in the ability of witches to work maleficient magic was as common in this area as it was in the rest of Europe, why was this the case?

Part of the answer to this question lies in the power which the laws pertaining to slander had not only to curb popular enthusiasm for the making of formal witchcraft accusations, but also to shape speech about witchcraft within communities more generally. Testimony from cases of witchcraft that did reach the council in Rothenburg suggests that knowledge of the risks run in speaking incautiously about witchcraft was widespread amongst the council's subjects, even if it was not always acted upon. For example, in 1602 Leonhardt Brandt

was so painfully conscious of his potentially parlous position as the creator of
the rumours against the five alleged witches of Steinach that he burst into tears
in custody, told his interrogators that he had been foolish in failing to consider
adequately the consequences of his talk about the women, and begged them
to forgive his mistake in having repeated his story of the witches' gathering to
other Steinach villagers.[92] In her statement to the council Brandt's fiancée,
Elisabetha Meck, claimed that she had warned Brandt against even peeping
in at the window of the house where the witches' gathering had supposedly
taken place, telling him that he could not be made answerable for something he
had not seen.[93]

Similar reactions were elicited from Barbara Rost, the woman held responsible for starting and publicising witchcraft rumours about mayor's wife
Anna Maria Bezold, and Susanna Negelein, a witness questioned about Rost's
rumour-mongering, in 1629. Like Brandt, Rost burst into tears in council custody, claimed that she had not really understood the implications of her words
about Anna Maria and expressed the wish that she could unsay them, while
Negelein told the councillors investigating the case that she had warned Rost
to keep quiet about Frau Bezold or risk being flogged out of the city as a slanderer.[94] It is impossible to tell whether the lamentations of Brandt and Rost in
custody were genuine, or tactical ploys to gain the council's sympathy, or
whether Meck and Negelein had really demonstrated such sagacity at the time
of the respective incidents, or were expressing it retrospectively, in order to
deflect any suspicion of complicity in the rumour-mongering away from themselves. What the four of them said and did during the investigation of the
respective witchcraft allegations, however, testified to their awareness of the
risks of prosecution and punishment run by people deemed personally repon-
sible for starting slanders against others.

The inhabitants of Rothenburg and its hinterland were so generally cautious in speaking of witchcraft that the depth of a person's conviction about
another's identity as a witch was equated with the manner in which they were
willing to talk about her. In a case from 1671, for example, witnesses Hans
Deeg and Michel Horn testified to the tenacity with which the deceased
Andreas Horn had believed that his former mistress, Appolonia Glaitter of
Windisch-Bockenfeld, had lamed him through witchcraft, by describing Horn
as having been without reserve in speaking about the suspicions he held against
Glaitter, and willing to repeat them publicly rather than secretly, to everybody,
and to her face.[95] It is, in fact, possible to discern four levels of publicity – or
openness, as a more literal translation of the German word *öffentlichkeit* – at
which speech about witchcraft circulated in Rothenburg and its hinterland villages. The first and most acceptable, because most secret, was when suspicions
of witchcraft were voiced within the confines of one's own house, or to just one

or two intimate acquaintances.[96] The second level was reached when rumours that someone was a witch began to circulate more widely within her community and in public spaces – such as streets, bath-houses and taverns – and the third when these rumours linked an individual with specific acts of witchcraft, like attending witches' gatherings and harming her neighbours, their families, livestock and livelihoods.[97] The fourth and most explicit speech about witchcraft was when individuals who believed that they or theirs had been bewitched accused the suspected witch personally, often after having identified her by means of consultations with cunning men. This direct accusation was known literally as 'saying it to someone's face' and often took the form of the standard plea for lifting a bewitchment: the witch was begged to do this for God's sake three times.[98]

Of course, as soon as a specific accusation was made against an alleged witch, or rumours about her were traced back to a specific individual, she had the option of a slander suit, or the threat of one, as a defensive weapon to silence her detractors. This also helps explain the unwillingness of individuals to take personal responsibility for accusations of witchcraft, a necessity circumvented in those parts of Germany where villagers formed witch-hunting committees who bore this responsibility and the financial risk it entailed collectively.[99] That the slander suit was acknowledged as at least one of the fairly standard and potentially effective ways of reacting to an accusation of witchcraft in the villages of Rothenburg's hinterland was shown by Martin Göller of Adelshofen in 1668, in a statement he made during an investigation into allegations of witchcraft made by seventeen-year-old Margaretha Fischer against her foster-mother, Susanna Lamer. Göller described Susanna and her husband Anthoni as quarrelsome and told the council that Anthoni was in the habit of calling his wife an old witch when he was drunk. As Anthoni had done this publicly at the village tavern as well as at home, Göller had told him to desist and explained to him that if other villagers called Susanna a witch he should go into Rothenburg to bring slander suits against them. As Anthoni and Susanna had moved to Adelshofen at the end of the Thirty Years' War from outside Rothenburg's hinterland, Göller's remarks were intended as instruction to them as newcomers of proper procedure in such matters, as well as a warning to them of the inadvisability of using so potentially damaging a word as 'witch' so openly and explicitly.[100]

Many of the statements made by witnesses called on to testify about allegations of witchcraft that became the subject of legal proceedings were also characterised by caution and indirectness. This suggests that popular awareness of the laws pertaining to slander and of the risks run in flouting them continued to influence speech about witchcraft even at this stage of proceedings, when it might, perhaps, have been expected that the council's willingness to investigate the allegations formally would have signalled to its subjects that more open speech was permissible. On the whole, however, witnesses might confirm that general rumours about an alleged witch – and/or her family or forebears – had been circulating for some time, but often added that they personally had never seen or heard anything to confirm the rumours, had no idea how they had originally started, and personally knew nothing bad about the suspect in question.

The statements given by Hoffman, Herman, Haim and Kurtz about Paulus and Barbara Brosam in the 1561 Wettringen case discussed earlier followed this pattern, as did those given by the eight men and four women of Oberstetten called on to testify about the alleged transportation of Margaretha Seitz to the nocturnal gathering of Gertraud Durmann, Anna Schneider and Anna Weh in 1582. All the Oberstetten witnesses claimed to know nothing of the matter beyond what Seitz herself had said about it. The eight men mentioned the old rumours to the effect that Durmann had allegedly transported her husband back to the village on a goat, but five of them were unwilling to say whether or not they believed them and the remaining three stated that they disbelieved them. The women witnesses claimed never to have heard the rumours at all. Five of the men offered additional evidence which might have been damaging for Durmann and Weh. They pointed out that Durmann had a brother living outside Rothenburg's hinterland who was a cunning man and that Weh's mother and grandmother, who also lived outside the hinterland, were rumoured to be witches. None of the other witnesses confimed these points, however, and the five men who had offered them lessened their significance, for Durmann at least, by adding that she had little to do with her brother. All the witnesses praised Durmann and Schneider as hardworking housewives and diligent churchgoers and were as positive about Weh, who had only recently moved into the village and kept herself to herself, as they could be.[101]

The witnesses called on to testify about the wives of Jörg Stahl, Frantz Kupfer, Daniel Kraft, Michel Lientschner and Leonhardt Holenbuch, the five women accused of being witches by Leonhardt Brandt in 1602, were similarly cagey in what they said about them to the council. Again, while they were willing to confirm that common talk existed connecting Appolonia Holenbuch with witchcraft, they added that they could not personally say anything bad about her and that they could specify no-one as personally responsible for the rumours which existed against her.[102] In 1629 the men of Bovenzenweiler, Obereichenroth and Untereichenroth were equally unwilling to say anything to the council to confirm the accusations of witchcraft that Margaretha Harter of Bovenzenweiler had made against Anna Dieterich, the old herdswoman of Untereichenroth.[103]

To an extent, of course, the inhabitants of Rothenburg and its hinterland were unwilling to accuse others of witchcraft or to testify explicitly against alleged witches because of the deterrent message that council policy with regard to witchcraft and slander conveyed to them: that speech of this sort was more likely to lead to their own punishment for slander than it was to a verdict of guilt against the alleged witch.[104] However, the aims behind the laws pertaining to defamation which influenced popular speech about witchcraft – to protect the honour of individuals and to prevent and defuse social conflict – were shared by, not simply imposed upon, the council's subjects, for whom at least the attempt to foster amity made more practical sense for the wellbeing of their communities than the fostering of enmity. These aims were also enshrined in various aspects of the customs of the hinterland villages, which had been established during the late medieval period in order to regulate communal life, and they motivated the application of law by the minor courts of the hinterland, which were staffed by jurors drawn from the male householders of the villages over which they held jurisdiction.[105]

Moreover, there is evidence to suggest that the council's subjects had no more patience for people who slandered others persistently and with potentially serious consequences than the councillors themselves had. This can be seen from the statements given by the nineteen men of Finsterlohr about the quarrelsome Kellner family in 1563. In what was to become a familiar pattern, they confirmed that Appolonia senior had been reputed a witch for at least thirty years, but added that they had no idea how the rumours against her had started and that no harm had been done to the villagers' cows – a favourite target of witches – while she had lived at Finsterlohr. However, they confirmed that Appolonia and her daughters had persistently and publicly accused one another of witchcraft and implied that they were held in disdain by their neighbours for behaving in this way. Some of them had even tried to persuade the women to stop slandering one another, for, if it was uncharitable for neighbour to call neighbour a witch, how much less charitable was it for members of the same family to do this to each other? The Finsterlohr men also conceded that something should have been done about this troublesome family a lot sooner, and the banishment of Appolonias senior and junior, Anna and Leonhardt Bretner was doubtless as much a relief to the Finsterlohr villagers as it was to the council.[106] In other cases the angry reaction of alleged witches and their families towards those they believed responsible for the public talk against them illustrates the depth of feeling such talk could arouse and the discord it could produce within communities. In the Hilgartshausen case from 1587 discussed in Chapter 3, for example, the story of witchcraft circulating in the village triggered inter-personal violence and even death-threats between accusers and accused, while in the Steinach case of 1602, one of the five women accused of witchcraft by Leonhardt Brandt accosted Brandt's fiancée, Elisabetha Meck, after the arrest of Brandt, called her a dissolute, stinking, thieving whore, and threw stones at her.[107] Thoughtless public talk about so potentially serious a matter as witchcraft always threatened an escalation of conflict within communities and was thus something not to be encouraged or undertaken lightly by their inhabitants.

The laws pertaining to slander and the ideal of curbing enmity which animated them thus formed an important part of the explanation for the reluctance to prosecute witchcraft evinced by the inhabitants of Rothenburg and its hinterland. The desire to preserve the stability of – and their own positions within – existing social hierarchies may also have motivated the men involved in certain cases to quash, rather than pursue, potential outbreaks of witchcraft accusations. In Steinach in 1602, for example, the husbands of the women who featured in Leonhardt Brandt's tale of the witches' gathering were quick to bring a slander suit against him on behalf of their wives. Brandt's words not only placed the reputations of their wives and households at risk, but also jeopardised the proper order of the village by suggesting that single, dependent youngsters could threaten established households by speaking out of turn about witchcraft. Before his arrest on the defamation charge Brandt seems to have been aware of the power that his briefly held position as the identifier of witches gave him over men who were his superiors in age, status and wealth. On being asked by Hans Bröschel, the village innkeeper and one of the richest men in Steinach, whether he had seen Bröschel's wife at the witches' gathering, Brandt replied magnanimously that he had not and that Bröschel need have no fear on that score.[108] Brandt's power was, however, shortlived, as was to be expected given that three of men whose wives he had slandered – Kraft, Stahl and Kupfer – were members of Steinach's *Gemeinde*, with Kraft as one of its leading figures.[109] The treatment of Barbara Rost by the Rothenburg councillors in 1629, discussed earlier, can be understood in similar terms, as the action of men keen to protect their own wives and positions within the community by quashing the thoughtless words of the socially and economically marginal.

It may also have been the case that the inhabitants of Rothenburg and its rural hinterland were less willing to prosecute witches formally, perhaps to the death, because they were not, on the whole, overwelmingly frightened of them.[110] The Rothenburg evidence offers glimpses of what is perhaps best described as a spectrum of popular concern about witchcraft, in which people felt varying degrees of envy, hatred and fear towards alleged witches and were thus differently disposed towards the question of how best to deal with them in specific contexts. At one end of this spectrum was the depth of feeling aroused in Benedict Wücherer of Schmerbach, who slit his wife Magdalena's throat with a knife in June 1627 because he thought she was a witch and because he wished to be rid of her so he could marry another woman; he was broken on the wheel for murder for his pains.[111] At the other end, however, lay an awareness of the possibility that talk of witchcraft could be the subject of humour, or could be used strategically by individuals in order to pursue feuds.[112] In the broad middle-ground of this spectrum it appears that people could adopt a pragmatic approach towards reputed witches and tolerate them within their communities for years, even decades, without taking any action against them which left its mark in written records. This approach is suggested in the communal testimony offered by the inhabitants of Wettringen, Finsterlohr, Oberstetten, Steinach, Bovenzenweiler, Untereichenroth and Obereichenroth, discussed above.

This spectrum of popular attitudes could be replicated and refined in specific cases, when it was usually the people who were involved in feuds or disputes with the alleged witch, or who were her nearest neighbours and thus felt themselves under greatest threat from their proximity to her allegedly malign influence, or who were weak-minded and particularly fearful of witchcraft as a result, who were most willing to testify against her, while people with less negative emotional investment in their relationships with her were correspondingly less driven to do so.[113] A person's fear of witchcraft could also vary according to the times at which they felt themselves to be most vulnerable to its threat. These might include life-cycle events such as childbirth or times of the year such as Walpurgis Eve (30 April) when witches were commonly believed to be especially active.[114] Popular concern about witchcraft was thus not uniform; it varied from individual to individual according to their psychological predisposition to anxiety, their personal relationships with alleged witches and the particular context of their own lives. Many of the inhabitants of early modern Rothenburg and its hinterland were therefore probably quite capable of believing in witchcraft without using the law against everyone ever suspected of it and without personally believing that a particular individual, accused by someone else, was necessarily a witch.

The rarity of executions in Rothenburg also helped keep popular concern about witchcraft at a low level. It seems reasonable to assume that the execution of people condemned as witches – and particularly of several or many at once, as was the case in larger-scale episodes of prosecution – carried out in front of large crowds and preceded by the promulgation of the crimes they had supposedly committed, could have increased the fear of witches felt by the inhabitants of an area. It may also have increased the vengeful desires of families who had already lost relatives to the executioner to demand the continued pursuit of other suspected witches by the authorities.[115] The idea that the legal mechanisms for dealing with witchcraft could whip up greater concern about the crime was recognised by contemporaries. For example, during the Navarre trials of the early seventeenth century, inquisitor Salazar suggested a connection between the public promulgation of sentences at executions and the perpetuation of trials, commenting that, 'there were neither witches nor bewitched until they were talked and written about'.[116] With relatively infrequent cases involving allegations, suspicions or confessions of witchcraft, no large-scale episodes of prosecution and just three executions for witchcraft in 300 years, the inhabitants and authorities of Rothenburg lacked the opportunity to stir each others' fears about witchcraft to the sort of frenzy which demanded sustained legal action to the point of mass trials and executions for its appeasement.

Their reluctance to prosecute alleged witches left the inhabitants of Rothenburg and its hinterland largely reliant on a set of non-legal options for coping with witchcraft. Given the paucity of guilty verdicts reached in witchcraft cases by the council, these were doubtless regarded as more effective than the law by the populace. The most important of these options was the vast panoply of strategies of white or beneficent magic with which most people believed that it was possible to counteract and contain the threat of witchcraft; these are discussed in more depth in Chapter 2. Other options also existed. The afflicted party might beg the witch for relief if other remedies against her bewitchments had been tried and found wanting.[117] To avoid bewitchment in the first place, neighbours might try to have little contact with a suspected witch, in their everyday exchanges with her and especially at times at which they regarded themselves and their households as particularly vulnerable to malevolent external influences.[118] Other people may have regarded placation as the best policy and tried to maintain at least the semblance of neighbourly exchange with suspected witches. It was only when the patience of an individual, household or village faction with a suspected witch became exhausted, or when their concern about her outweighed their ability or willingness to tolerate her presence, or when a particularly favourable set of cirumstances encouraged them to do so, that a formal charge against her might be brought or an attempt to drive her out of the community made.[119] None of these strategies was without risk or assured of success for the protagonists involved, however: to use cunning folk risked questioning or reprimand by the authorities,[120] while to accuse a suspected witch risked angering her and rendering oneself vulnerable to further bewitchment or a counter-accusation of slander.[121]

Suspected witches also had a set of options for trying to defend themselves against the suspicions of their neighbours which operated largely outside the law. For example, they might keep themselves to themselves as much as possible in order to minimise social exchanges with their neighbours, as such exchanges could always be interpreted or re-interpreted by people who believed them to be witches as a cause of bewitchment.[122] Or they might try to live as blameless a life as possible, seeking to convince their neighbours of their essential goodness by means of their good housekeeping and parenting, their

piety and peaceableness, and their willingness to help others.[123] Once suspected
of an act of bewitchment, they might challenge the maker of the accusation or
the starter of the rumours against them verbally (with insults or threats) or
physically (with violence),[124] or try to persuade them to retract their allegations
in an out-of-court settlement negotiated by other neighbours,[125] or accuse them
formally of slander at one of the hinterland courts or before the council itself.
The willingness of a reputed witch to bring a defamation suit against her detractors or to continue to live in a community despite the suspicions which existed
against her often depended on the amount of support she was able to call on
from her family and on the standing which her family enjoyed within the community. If the latter dwindled to a dangerous extent, the witch and her family
might decide to cut their losses and move elsewhere, or to appeal to the council as their overlord for protection aginst the hostility of their neighbours.[126] For
the alleged witch, the danger to survival lay in failing to take action against the
suspicions raised against her, as this risked her own exclusion from important
networks of social and economic exchange within her community and damage
to the reputations of the rest of her family.

The predominantly non-legal system of coping with suspected witches
was so strong and the incentives to abandon it in favour of more frequent use of
the law so weak, that it held firm in Rothenburg throughout the early modern
period. This was the case even during periods of dearth and inflation, times
which Wolfgang Behringer has identified as crisis points at which the lower
orders were most likely to press the authorities for action against the witches
believed to have caused harvest failures with their weather-magic.[127] This suggests either that the Rothenburg authorities had ways of coping with such crises
which obviated popular demand for witch-trials, or that the lower orders did
not perceive action against witches as the best solution to agrarian crises. As was
the case with the Rothenburg elites, however, the popular lack of enthusiasm
for prosecuting their neighbours as witches was not altruistic. It was rooted to
a great extent in the pragmatic self-interest of individuals and families and to
some extent in their awareness of what was best for their communities, and had
little or nothing to do with the well-being of the alleged witches themselves.
Moreover, as was suggested at the start of this chapter, the limited pattern of
formal prosecution for witchcraft in early modern Rothenburg was the result
of a complex and delicate equilibrium of mutually reinforcing factors which
operated at, and interacted between, both elite and popular levels. Just as elite
restraint in prosecuting witches was encouraged by popular unwillingness to
accuse them formally, so popular enthusiasm for accusation was discouraged by
the way in which cases were treated by the council when they came to court.
After all, witnesses offered many general clues that pointed towards the guilt of
certain individuals as witches in their testimony; what was significant was that

the councillors chose, on the whole, not to act upon them. Chapter 2 will explore further the other side of the balance: the beliefs and priorities which lay behind the unwillingness of the elites to use the law to hunt witches in early modern Rothenburg.

Notes

1 RStA Surety Book A846 fols 433v–441v.
2 See Appendix for details. I have included the 1549 case of Dorothea Klennckh and the 1663 case of Michael Würth (briefly discussed in Chapter 5) in these figures: the dates in the book's title refer to the first and last cases discussed in depth in Chapters 1 (1561) and 6 (1652), respectively. After 1652 there were only two other executions for witchcraft in Rothenburg, in 1673 and 1692.
3 Lautenbach did not say 'witch'; instead he said that 'something' ('etwas') had pressed him. This unwillingness to use the words 'witch' or 'witchcraft' when giving testimony was common in Rothenburg's witchcraft cases, supporting one of the main arguments of this chapter: that the area's inhabitants were reluctant to speak publicly and explicitly about witchcraft.
4 RStA Interrogation Book A858 fols 21v–22v.
5 *Ibid.*, fols 22v–23v, especially fol. 23r: 'Vnnd er besorget es dorffe wol derselbig Hanndell sein.'
6 *Ibid.*, fols 23v–24v, especially fol. 24v: 'er hete nit vermaindt das er vnd sein hauff sollche leuth were[n].'
7 *Ibid.*, fols 24v–25v.
8 *Ibid.*, fols 19r–20r.
9 *Ibid.*, fols 14r–16v.
10 *Ibid.*, fols 16v–19r.
11 See p. 18 for discussion of Zöllner's testimony.
12 RStA Interrogation Book A858 fols 19r–21v.
13 Sehling, *Die evangelischen Kirchenordnungen*, pp. 561–616, see pp. 612–614. If the pastor failed in this endeavour, such parishioners were to be sent to Rothenburg's Superintendent (the city's foremost ecclesiastical official) and then to the Consistorium (the city's Church Council) for further exhortation, and only in the last resort – and 'not hurriedly' – to the city council for possible punishment.
14 *Ibid.*, fols 28r–29r.
15 *Ibid.*, fols 29v–31v.
16 *Ibid.*, fol. 30r. This evidence was given by Hoffman, who had been in Hans Kapp's tavern when Lautenbach had first made public his allegation against the Brosams.
17 Radbruch, *Die Peinliche Gerichtsordnung*, clause 44, p. 52. The other indications of possible guilt of witchcraft, on the basis of which courts might use torture against suspected witches, were: if the suspect offered to teach others witchcraft; if he or she threatened to bewitch someone and the bewitchment subsequently occurred; and if he or she used suspicious objects, gestures, words or behaviour which suggested that they were working witchcraft.
18 The hope behind a confrontation was that one party would break down and admit that they had been lying: it put pressure on suspects without the need to torture them.
19 RStA Interrogation Book A858 fols 34r–36r.
20 *Ibid.*, fols 34v–36r.
21 *Ibid.*, fol. 35r: 'ob der Henngker Inne zuvor nit lanng genug an dem strick gefuert hete, so wurde er Inne lenng[er] fuern.'
22 *Ibid.*, fols 35v–36r: 'Allein das hab Ime so Whee thun.'
23 On the importance of honour in early modern German society, see Roper, 'Will and honour', especially pp. 64–66; Schwerhoff, *Köln im Kreuzverhör*, pp. 312–322; Müller–Wirthmann, 'Raufhändel'; Walz, 'Schimpfende Weiber'; Rowlands, 'Women, gender and power', pp. 40–89.

24 See RStA Blood Book B665 fol. 21v; Civil Court Book B304 fols 123r–123v.
25 Stuart, 'Des Scharfrichters heilende Hand', pp. 317–318. As Stuart points out in this article, however, the executioner's power to dishonour depended on context: no dishonour attached to people who had contact with the executioner in his capacity as a medical practitioner.
26 Burghartz, *Leib, Ehre und Gut*, p. 129.
27 RStA Blood Book B329 fols 156r–157v; Interrogation Book A854 fols 142r–143v.
28 RStA Interrogation Book A858 fols 34v–35r.
29 *Ibid.*, fols 20v–21r.
30 RStA Wettringen Village Acts A753 fols 89r–93v.
31 RStA Interrogation Book A858 fol. 21r.
32 *Ibid.*, fol. 30r.
33 RStA Surety Book A846 fols 433v–435v.
34 RStA Interrogation Book A861 fols 497r–517r; Surety Book A847 fols 353v–355v.
35 RStA Interrogation Book A861 fols 500v–501r.
36 For evidence of Veit's status, see Wettringen Village Acts A753 fols 47r, 93v.
37 There is no evidence that Paulus, Barbara or any other members of their family were officially accused of witchcraft after 1561, which suggests that the punishment of Lautenbach and Immell had a long-term deterrent effect.
38 Gaskill, 'The Devil in the shape of a man', p. 166.
39 Behringer, *Hexenverfolgung in Bayern*, pp. 63–64.
40 Gersmann, '"Gehe hin und verthedige dich!"', especially pp. 248–269.
41 RStA Interrogation Book A875 fols 186r–229v; Surety Book A853 fols 393r–394v; see also Rowlands, 'Eine Stadt ohne Hexenwahn'.
42 RStA Steinach Village Acts A739 fols 441r–480v; Surety Book A857 fols 499r–500v.
43 For the Rost case, see pp. 27–28, 35; for the Harter case, see pp. 124–130.
44 It was referred to by jurist Friedrich Prenninger in an opinion he wrote on the Steinach witchcraft case of 1602, see RStA Steinach Village Acts A739 fol. 472r.
45 See pp. 60–64 for more detail.
46 For the interrogations of Appolonia Kellner senior, see RStA Interrogation Book A861 fols 498v–499v; of Anna Kellner, fols 497v–498r; of Appolonia junior, fols 501r–502r; and of Leonhardt Bretner, fols 499v–500r. Georg Kellner, Appolonia senior's son, was also interrogated about his own and his family's activities as witches, after Bretner had called him a *Trutenkönig* (witches' king), fol. 497r.
47 *Ibid.*, fols 500v–501r; Surety Book A847 fols 379v–380r: 'welches sich dan hernacher mit dem wenigsten nicht befunden hat'.
48 Midelfort, *Witch Hunting*, pp. 88–90.
49 RStA Interrogation Book A875, fols 221r– 223v, especially fol. 223r.
50 See p. 24 for a summary of these cases.
51 RStA Interrogation Book A875 fols 209r–209v.
52 *Ibid.*, fols 217r–219r.
53 *Ibid.*, fols 211r–215r (Thalhaimer); fols 221r–223v (Gugel and Hardessheim).
54 They had, however, taken the existence of the rumour against Durmann seriously enough to have made some enquiries about it, see *ibid.*, fols 199r–200r.
55 *Ibid.*, fols 214r–214v (Thalhaimer); fols 221v–222r (Gugel and Hardessheim).
56 For discussion of the impact of this famine in Franconia, see Endres, 'Zur wirtschaftlichen und sozialen Lage', pp. 28–52.
57 Behringer, 'Weather, hunger, fear'.
58 Rumours to the effect that town midwife Anna Muller might have caused the unseasonably cold weather had circulated in 1569, during her trial for a bizarre fraud in which she had manufactured monstrous births out of puppies' corpses: see Rowlands, 'Monstrous deception', for more details. Recorded references to weather-magic were otherwise exceptionally rare in early modern Rothenburg.

59 RStA Steinach Village Acts A739 fols 449r, 458v–459r, 463r–465v.

60 *Ibid.*, fols 471r –472r (Prenninger); fols 473r–476r (Bezold).

61 RStA Interrogation Book A888 fols 1r– 32v; Blood Book B665 fols 21r–23v.

62 See RStA B186 (lists of councillors, 1230–1669) and B186a (council elections, 1300–1720).

63 Behringer, *Hexenverfolgung in Bayern*, pp. 238–241.

64 Rowlands, 'Women, gender and power', Chapter 1, especially pp. 46–49, 65–66; RStA Blood Book B331 fols 8r–11v.

65 The latest reference I have found to the law of talion dates from a case involving allegations of witchcraft from 1709 in which the couple responsible for having initiated the allegations were banished for slander; see RStA Interrogation Book A938 fols 297r–373v, especially fol. 373r and the Appendix.

66 Radbruch, *Die Peinliche Gerichtsordnung*, p. 61.

67 RStA Interrogation Book A875 fols 211r–215r, see fol. 215r ('das maul gestopfft').

68 RStA Steinach Village Acts A739 fols 471r–472r.

69 RStA Surety Book A846 fols 452r–455v.

70 B198 (Mayor Johann Georg Styrzel's Notebook), vol. II (1661–68), fols 407r–408r.

71 See Appendix for details.

72 RStA Interrogation Book A875 fols 211v–212v.

73 *Ibid.*, fols 212v–213r.

74 *Ibid.*, fols 217v–218r.

75 Radbruch, *Die Peinliche Gerichtsordnung*, pp. 42–43.

76 RStA Interrogation Book A861 fols 497v–499v.

77 RStA Surety Book A847 fols 353v–355v.

78 This principle was first mentioned in the 1587 Hilgartshausen witchcraft case discussed in Chapter 3, see RStA Interrogation Book A877 fol. 579v.

79 Catharina Leimbach and Margaretha Horn were both subjected to the thumbscrews five times in 1652. However, as all five bouts occurred in the same torture-session, the council may have considered them one bout overall: see pp. 150–160 and pp. 180–192 for discussion of their cases. The council's greatest severity was shown against two women tried in sixteenth-century fraud cases who were also asked whether they were witches in the course of their trials. In 1569, Anna Muller was subjected to three sessions of torture (two of strappado and one of strappado and thumbscrews) during interrogation, while in 1581 Anna Gebhart suffered the thumbscrews, strappado and then strappado with thumbscrews. Neither confessed to being a witch but both admitted their frauds, for which they were branded and banished. See above, n. 58 for details of the Muller case; pp. 49–50, 73–74 for the Gebhart case.

80 Radbruch, *Die Peinliche Gerichtsordnung*, pp. 19–20; Langbein, *Prosecuting Crime*, pp. 155–158, 179–186.

81 Staatsarchiv Nürnberg (hereafter StAN) Rothenburg Repertorium vol. 2087 fol. 96r.

82 For other examples of popular disapproval of torture, see Scribner, 'Witchcraft and judgement', p. 14; Gersmann, 'Injurienklagen', pp. 259–260.

83 RStA Interrogation Book A875 fols 215r, 217r.

84 RStA Interrogation Book A877 fol. 577r, Steinach Village Acts A739 fol. 471r (Prenninger); *ibid.*, fol. 473r (Bezold); Interrogation Book A895 fol. 171r (Walther).

85 For examples, see Midelfort, *Witch Hunting*, pp. 85–163; Behringer, *Hexenverfolgung in Bayern*, pp. 236–241.

86 RStA Interrogation Book A875 fols 217r, 209v; Interrogation Book A884 fol. 560r.

87 RStA Steinach Village Acts A739 fols 471r–472r: 'heller . . . dann die liebe Sonne vmb den heissen Mittag leuchtet.' Prenninger also argued for caution in the legal opinion that he wrote on the case of Hans Georg Hofmann in 1605 (discussed pp. 162–164), RStA Interrogation Book A884 fols 556r–560r.

88 StAN Ro. Rep. vol. 2087 fols 97r–97v.

89 See for example Briggs, *Witches and Neighbours*, pp. 7–10.

 90 Labouvie, *Zauberei und Hexenwerk*, pp. 135–154; Rummel, *Bauern, Herren und Hexen*, pp. 26–67; Dillinger, 'Hexenverfolgungen in Städten', pp. 151–152, 160.
 91 Vice, 'The German Peasants' War', pp. 30–74.
 92 RStA Steinach Village Acts A739 fols 443v–44r.
 93 *Ibid.*, fol. 450r.
 94 RStA Interrogation Book A888 fols 22v–23v.
 95 RStA Interrogation Book A908 (unpaginated); testimony of Deeg (25 July), and of Horn (31 July).
 96 RStA Interrogation Book A875 fol. 203v; Steinach Village Acts A739 fol. 471v.
 97 RStA Interrogation Book A858 fols 19v, 23r; A888 fols 13r, 15r.
 98 See Deeg's testimony ('ins gesicht sagen'), n. 95; RStA Interrogation Book A896 fol. 263v.
 99 Imperial law stipulated that the accuser was to pay the costs of a trial that ended without a guilty verdict himself. However, such was the power of these witch-hunting committees in parts of western Germany that they managed to overturn this stipulation and make released witch-suspects pay their own costs, see Rummel, *Bauern, Herren und Hexen*, pp. 32–35.
100 RStA Interrogation Book A906 (unpaginated), 25 August 1668.
101 RStA Interrogation Book A875 fols 192r–98v.
102 RStA Steinach Village Acts A739 fols 449r–450r, 463r–463v, 464r–465v.
103 See p. 128.
104 Ruling elites elsewhere also sent out this deterrent message to their subjects. In Munich in 1608, for example, the authorities issued an ordinance threatening those who denounced others as witches with punishment (Behringer, 'Scheiternde Hexenprozesse', p. 77), while in 1590 Nuremberg's city council executed a man whose main crime had been to identify women of the city as witches (Kunstmann, *Zauberwahn*, pp. 74–78).
105 Ziegler, *Die Dorfordnungen*, pp. 70–91; Village Acts A719, A753–A754, A515, A539; Detwang Village Court Books B327–B328, B659.
106 RStA Interrogation Book A861 fols 505r–513r.
107 RStA Steinach Village Acts A739 fol. 451r.
108 *Ibid.*, fols 468r–468v.
109 *Ibid.*, fols 288r, 308r–309r, 367r–367v, 602r–603v.
110 As Eva Labouvie points out, witchcraft was just one of many threats to their existence that peasants faced; others were war, famine, epidemic disease, fire and bad weather, see Labouvie, 'Hexenspuk', pp. 74–75.
111 RStA Interrogation Book A886 fols 308r–343v.
112 RStA Interrogation Book A888 fol. 603v; A858 fol. 17v.
113 See the cases involving Margaretha Horn (pp. 180–192) and Catharina Leimbach (pp. 150–160).
114 This idea of the importance of ritual time is taken from Robisheaux, 'Witchcraft and forensic medicine', p. 206. Leonhardt Brandt thought that he had seen the Steinach witches' gathering on Walpurgis Eve, RStA Steinach Village Acts A739 fol. 441r. In 1652 Leonhardt Gackstatt linked his neighbour Margaretha Horn's alleged witchcraft with Shrove Tuesday, while in the same year Eva Schurz became worried about her neighbour Catharina Leimbach's witchcraft as the birth of her child approached (see pp. 153, 181).
115 Schormann, *Der Krieg*, pp. 62–63.
116 Henningsen, 'The greatest witch-trial', p. 39.
117 RStA Interrogation Book A896 fol. 263v.
118 See for example StAN Ro. Rep. 2087 fol. 24r; see also n. 114.
119 See the cases involving Margaretha Horn and Catharina Leimbach, discussed on pp. 180–192, 150–160.
120 See pp. 68–72.
121 Cf. Briggs, 'Verteidigungsstrategien', p. 121. Another defensive strategy Briggs shows suspected witches in Lorraine using was that of the threat that they would denounce their accusers as witches if formal proceedings were brought against them, *ibid.*, pp. 123–126.

122 Anna Weh, whose mother and grandmother had been reputed witches, was known to keep herself to herself in Oberstetten in 1582, see RStA Interrogation Book A875 fol. 194r.

123 *Ibid.*, fols 192v–193v. In 1652, Margaretha Horn offered the fact that she was a good wife and housekeeper and had been godmother to twenty-six children as evidence of the lack of veracity of the witchcraft accusation against her, RStA Interrogation Book A898 fol. 489v.

124 See for example the reactions of Hilgartshausen villagers to Hans Gackstatt's story of witchcraft (discussed in Chapter 3); RStA Interrogation Book A875 fol. 187v; StAN Ro. Rep. 2087 fol. 679r.

125 *Ibid.*, fol. 11r; RStA Interrogation Book A898 fol. 517v.

126 This happened in the aftermath of the cases involving Margaretha Horn and Catharina Leimbach, discussed on pp. 180–192, 150–160.

127 See p. 27 for details.

2

The devil's power to delude: elite beliefs about witchcraft and magic

The Rothenburg elites have left us few personal testimonies of their beliefs about witchcraft and magic during the sixteenth and seventeenth centuries. No record of council meetings was kept in Rothenburg until 1664, when popular pressure for greater openness forced the councillors to lift the shroud of secrecy from their gatherings. However, even after 1664 the meeting minutes recorded only the decisions made by the council and not the deliberations by which they were reached. The often detailed testimonies elicited from the women, children and men of the lower orders who became involved in witch-craft cases, which frequently give us a real sense of their personalities, emotions and discursive strategies, thus stand in ironic contrast to the silence of the councillors who judged their cases, whose personal opinions about witchcraft and influence on individual witchcraft cases were never recorded and whose reasons for resolving cases in particular ways were never stated explicitly.

We can, however, draw conclusions about elite belief with reasonable confidence from other sources. The opinions written by jurists and, occasion-ally, clerics for the councillors on particularly problematic witchcraft cases are most important in this regard, as they set case-specific advice in the context of wider demonological and jurisprudential thinking about the crime of witch-craft and usually cited the legal or theological texts on which their conclusions were based. Jurist Georg Christoph Walther also wrote a twenty-nine-page treatise to better inform the councillors about witches and their activities in September 1652.[1] These jurists and clerics were council appointees whose religious affiliation and educational and social background had to be acceptable to the councillors for them to acquire their positions in the first place, and their advice was frequently followed by the councillors in specific witchcraft cases. It thus seems reasonable to assume that the beliefs about witchcraft they expressed in their opinions reflected a similar spectrum of beliefs held by the councillors themselves. We can also establish the broader framework of elite beliefs about beneficient witchcraft and popular use of magic from council ordinances issued against these practices and from the records of the Consistorium, the post-reformation church council staffed by three councillors and three clerics which was largely responsible for trying to implement these ordinances. Fortunately the minutes of Consistorium meetings, detailing personal statements by its members, survive from 1605.[2]

Harmful magic

Elite beliefs about maleficient or demonic witchcraft were expressed around three themes in early modern Rothenburg: maleficium, or the causing of harm by magical means; the making of pacts with the devil; and the flight to and attendance at witches' dances, or sabbats. Broadly speaking, Rothenburg's councillors and their advisers thought that witches really could cause harm by magical means and make pacts with the devil, although they were far less sure about whether sabbats existed in reality or were imaginary delusions. Of most importance to their handling and resolution of witchcraft cases, however, were their doubts about how effectively specific individuals could be proven guilty of any of these activities at law: it was chiefly this doubt which explained their relatively mild treatment and punishment of alleged witches during the early modern period.

Like their subjects, the Rothenburg elites believed that witches could interfere in all manner of damaging ways with the lives and bodies of people and animals. In 1587, for example, the questions put to alleged witch Magdalena Gackstatt of Hilgartshausen asked her whether she had caused bad weather, created discord between married couples, attacked pregnant women, or otherwise caused harm to people and livestock – the standard acts of maleficia according to traditional demonology.[3] The range of destructive activities that maleficient witches were thought able to engage in remained much the same in Rothenburg throughout the seventeenth century. In his treatise of 1652, for example, jurist Walther condemned witches for killing, blinding and crippling other people, harming and killing animals, and destroying crops with bad weather in order to cause dearth, inflation and hunger,[4] while alleged witches continued to be tried for harmful magic – on the admittedly rare occasions when their activities were brought to the attention of the council by its subjects – in cases which occurred in 1663, 1671 and 1689.[5]

Unlike their subjects, however, who imagined that the ability of the witch to work magic depended on the supernatural powers and skills that she had acquired for herself, the Rothenburg elites believed that her maleficient powers depended in important ways on her relationship with the devil. Although doubtless current among the elites from an earlier date, the first written record of this idea dates from the interrogation of itinerant cunning woman Anna Gebhart in 1581. Gebhart arrived in Rothenburg in September of that year, claiming that – for a price – she could heal disease, make bad marriages good, restore potency to men and fertility to women and, most importantly, find buried treasure for people with the help of a spirit she could conjure for this purpose. She and her husband were arrested after getting into a fight with an innkeeper and she was closely questioned about her activities, by means of which she had defrauded several inhabitants of Rothenburg out of significant sums of money. During interrogation she was asked whether her treasure-seeking ability was the result of a pact with the devil rather than of the skill she boasted of as her own – an allegation she denied vigorously.[6] In subsequent cases the ability to work harmful magic was assumed by Rothenburg's elites to follow from a pact with the devil: in 1587, for example, Magdalena Gackstatt was asked whether she had given herself to the devil before being asked about her acts of maleficium, as if the latter were a logical consequence of the former.[7] Rothenburg's foremost cleric, Georg Zyrlein, and jurist Walther likewise considered maleficium in the context of the witch's pre-existing pact with the devil. In 1627 Zyrlein categorised maleficent witches as those who had willingly given themselves to the devil and who caused harm to people and livestock,[8] while in 1652 Walther observed that the pact was the basis for all subsequent acts of maleficium on the part of witches.[9]

The exact roles of the devil and witch in working maleficium were not, however, explored in detail by Zyrlein and Walther. Both noted that the devil might give the witch poisons and poisonous salves by means of which she could work harm,[10] and the fact that the councillors had Magdalena Gackstatt's house searched for suspicious tins of ointment and boxes of herbs in 1587 suggests that they shared this belief.[11] Neither Zyrlein nor Walther went into much detail about the power dynamics of the witch–devil relationship, although what they did write hints at the image of a witch who was not the powerless plaything of a demonic puppet-master. In 1627, for example, Zyrlein wrote that maleficent witches caused harm 'in accordance with the devil's will',[12] but the manner in which he described them working their magic – 'with harmful spoken charms, with poison prepared by the devil, or other improper arts, *with the devil's help*' – suggested more of a partnership, albeit an unequal one.[13] Similarly in 1652 Walther allowed for some agency on the part of the witch in causing maleficium when he wrote that, while the devil was capable of plaguing humankind without assistance, he also used the witches who had bound themselves willingly to him in order to cause harm 'when *they desired and called upon him*' to do so.[14]

These, then, were not the entirely powerless witches written of by sceptical German demonologists such as Johannes Brenz and Johann Weyer, who were capable of effecting nothing by supernatural means themselves but were deluded by Satan into thinking that they could cause harm,[15] but rather individuals imagined as contributing in some way and of their own volition towards the doing of maleficium. The councillors and their advisers may have reinforced the idea of the agency of the witch unintentionally in certain seventeenth-century cases when they investigated with great thoroughness allegations of maleficium made against alleged witches who refused to confess to dealings of any description with the devil: technically, the absence of a pact should have led the councillors to conclude that the witches in question were incapable of executing the acts of maleficium of which they stood accused.[16] That the councillors did not press suspects for confessions about their pacts as the essential starting point in every case of alleged maleficium suggests that the traditional popular idea of the powerful maleficient witch who could harm others without diabolic assistance still exerted an influence on elite imaginings of witchcraft, occasionally proving difficult to reconcile with accepted demonological logic.

As for the fate of maleficient witches, and following the biblical dictum 'thou shalt not suffer a witch to live', Georg Zyrlein thought that witches who willingly made pacts with the devil and caused harm deserved death.[17] This was in accordance with clause 109 of the *Carolina*, which decreed that the practice of harmful magic was to be punished with death by fire, while non-harmful magic was to be subject to discretionary, non-capital punishments.[18] In practice, however, Rothenburg's councillors adopted a more cautious approach towards the punishment of maleficium. In the second half of the sixteenth century, for example, only two women were punished for the crime, and with banishment rather than death, after they had been arrested and interrogated under torture about their activities. Unfortunately the records of their interrogations have not survived, so we cannot assess how their testimony was shaped by the interrogation process. However, the case-summaries contained in their sureties suggest that the first, Dorothea Klennckh, really had used a magical ritual to try to inflict the pox on someone in 1549, without specifiying what – if any – effect her attempt had had on her intended victim.[19] The second, Magdalena Weinmaÿr, was a lying-in maid and children's nurse with a long-standing reputation as a witch who, in 1571, was accused of having tried to kill one of the infants in her charge by putting mercury into its broth. Again it appears that she really had done this, although she insisted that she had administered the mercury in order to cure the child of the dysentery from which it had been suffering. Luckily for her the child fell ill but did not die as a result of her actions.[20]

Weinmaÿr was lucky to escape with her life, as even attempted poisoning carried the death penalty according to the *Carolina*, because it implied a premeditated intention to murder.[21] Although there is no evidence to this effect, Weinmaÿr may have been banished rather than executed in 1571 because her case was tried during the dearth of 1570–75 when the council may have been particularly keen not to foster popular enthusiasm for witch-hunts.[22] Dorothea Klennckh may have escaped harsher punishment in 1549 because she had influential relatives who begged the council for mercy on her behalf.[23] In other late sixteenth-century cases Rothenburg's councillors showed little enthusiasm for pursuing allegations of maleficium at law once the accused women involved had denied them, and usually simply dismissed the suspected witch – and sometimes her accuser as well – with a warning to keep the peace.[24] For many years succeeding generations of Rothenburg's councillors appear to have believed that only a witch who had killed another person deserved the death penalty. Before 1673 the only person executed for witchcraft in Rothenburg was Magdalena Dürr of Standorf, who had killed her own baby and then claimed that she was a witch who had done the deed at the devil's bidding. As infanticide carried the death penalty according to the *Carolina* anyway, Dürr's admission of witchcraft made little difference to her ultimate fate, other than to ensure that her body was burned after she had been beheaded in 1629.[25]

Demonic pacts

The Rothenburg jurists and clerics spent more time discussing the making of pacts with the devil by witches than their perpetration of maleficium, partly because so few explicit allegations of maleficium were brought to their attention by their subjects, but also because they regarded the making of such pacts as the most serious of witches' sins. In 1652 jurist Walther criticised those people who thought that witches ought to be punished for their acts of maleficium, arguing that these were of secondary importance to her apostasy, which was the most heinous sin against God because it contravened the first commandment: maleficium was a matter of external circumstances, Walther noted, whereas making a pact with the devil reflected the internal evil of the witch's heart.[26] The elites believed that witches confirmed their pacts with the devil in various ways: by shaking hands or having sex with him or, as Zyrlein noted in 1627, by means of swearing oaths to him or signing pledges to him in their own blood.[27] That their subjects shared – and could parody – these beliefs was seen in 1614, when a group of men which included the city's executioner were banished from Rothenburg for having tried to defraud Hans Unger of Gebsattel out of 400 gulden. One of the group had disguised himself as Satan using soot and horsehair, while the others had persuaded Unger to sign his soul over to 'Satan' using his own blood for ink. The idea was that, in return for 400 gulden, 'Satan' would grant Unger's wishes for ten years. Unger fell for the trick even though 'Satan' rejoiced in the unlikely name of *Wischauf* ('Wipe-Up'). The fraud was discovered only because a city gatekeeper found Unger in possession of this large sum of money — which he had stolen from his father Jobst — on his return to Rothenburg.[28]

In 1627 Georg Zyrlein drew a distinction between two types of witches who made pacts in different ways and consequently deserved different treatment in the opinion he wrote on the case of self-confessed child-witch, Margaretha Hörber. His ideas and their derivation are worth explaining in detail, as they not only proved influential in the handling of Hörber's case but probably also shaped the way in which the councillors treated self-confessed child-witches for the rest of the seventeenth century. As we have already seen, in the first category Zyrlein classed witches who gave themselves willingly and intentionally to the devil and worked harm with his assistance: they made explicit spoken or written promises to the devil and deserved the death penalty.[29] In the second, however, were witches who had neither caused harm nor promised themselves explicitly or willingly to the devil but who had been deceived or forced through violence or fear by the devil to believe as true events and sights which were not and could not be true in reality, such as flights to witches' dances. These passive witches with their implicit pacts did not deserve the death penalty, Zyrlein noted, because their only crime was that of apostasy — a spiritual failing which only God, not the courts of this world, could judge. Such individuals deserved pity and better religious instruction rather than punishment.[30]

Zyrlein relied heavily on Theodor Thumm's 1621 work, *Tractatus Theologicus de Sagarum Impietate*, for this moderate stance on non-maleficient witchcraft specifically and for much of what he wrote generally about the devil's power to delude people in his opinion of 1627.[31] Thumm was a theologian at Tübingen University in the neighbouring Duchy of Württemberg who, following the view of Johann Weyer that death was too extreme a punishment for a spiritual crime, divided witches into three categories in his treatise: those who suffered from melancholy fantasies and were entirely deluded by the devil; those who made pacts with the devil but caused no harm; and those who had express pacts with the devil and caused harm with his help. According to Thumm, the first needed medical help and the second, admonition and better religious instruction: only truly harmful witchcraft deserved death.[32] Zyrlein clearly followed Thumm's schema in his opinion of 1627, although he also more briefly cited Rostock jurist Johann Georg Gödelmann, whose 1591 work *Tractatus de Magis, Veneficis et Lamiis* had categorised witches and the treatment they deserved along very similar lines, again following Weyer.[33] The third text on which Zyrlein based his advice was an extract from Luther's *Table Talk*, which dealt with an event which had occurred in 1538 when a Wittenberg student called Valerius

Glockner had told Luther that he had given himself to the devil. Instead of handing Glockner over to the secular courts for trial and punishment, Luther and his colleagues had convinced him of the error of his ways and persuaded him to take an oath admitting his sin, expressing his contrition, and forswearing the devil.[34] The idea that the penitent apostate should be forgiven rather than punished also figured significantly in the Rothenburg *Church Ordinance* of 1559, which gave people who had fallen into various types of heterodoxy (including witchcraft) at least four chances to repent of their sins before excommunication or a worse fate awaited them.[35]

In practice, however, the Rothenburg councillors and their advisers regarded self-confessed child-witches as most worthy of pity and as most redeemable from the sin into which they had fallen. It was for this reason that thirteen-year-old Margaretha Hörber, eight-year-old Brigitta Hörner and eight-year-old Barbara Schürz were all sent to the city hospital for religious instruction at the end of their respective trials in 1627, 1639 and 1652. Case-specific circumstances played their part in explaining the moderate stance of the council in all three cases. However, generally speaking the council was willing to show these girls mercy for two reasons. First, because they had freely admitted that they were witches: this was important because confession of one's sins was regarded as the first essential step on the road to contrition and forgiveness. And second, because they had allegedly been beguiled or forced into giving themselves to the devil when very young. Roman law held that a child could not be held culpable for crimes of intentional malice because, as its reason and will were not yet fully formed, it could not be deemed responsible for its actions; this point of view influenced the trials of all three girls.[36]

The views of jurist Walther on pacts and the punishments they deserved, expressed in his witchcraft treatise of 1652, were – theoretically at least – much harsher than those of Zyrlein. In a return to what had been the commonly held view at the University of Tübingen before Theodor Thumm's espousal of a more liberal position, Walther asserted that witches deserved the death penalty even if they had only made a pact with the devil and not committed any acts of maleficium, because their apostasy was so heinous a sin. However, Walther allowed himself a rhetorical loophole in his treatise by writing only of witches who had willingly and voluntarily made such pacts.[37] This implied that there might be another type of pact in which the witch's will and consent was lacking, and in practice Walther regarded self-confessed child-witches in this context. In his opinion on the Brigitta Hörner case of 1639, for example, he categorised Brigitta as a poor little girl who had been seduced into witchcraft when she was too young to have known better, and it was on his advice that she was sent to the city hospital for religious instruction. Indeed, youth was so important a mitigating factor for Walther that he raised doubts about whether Brigitta, who claimed to have killed a foal belonging to her cousin, could be held responsible and punished even for an act of maleficium because of her age and lack of reason.[38]

Elite thinking on pacts, then, was relatively moderate as far as self-confessed child-witches were concerned. However, as subsequent chapters will show, the stories of witchcraft told by these youngsters invariably included an older female witch who had allegedly first seduced them into witchcraft by acting as an intermediary between themselves and the devil. The Rothenburg elites regarded and treated these women in a far less merciful manner and they usually escaped legal punishment as witches only because of their own courage during interrogation and the unwillingness of the council to abandon all legal restraint in the handling of their cases. However, the fact that the elites tried these women at all seems illogical. Why should the devil have needed these women to act as go-betweens for him, when he was capable of corrupting children of his own volition? And why, given that the jurists and councillors doubted other aspects of these children's stories – such as their claims to have attended sabbats – because of their youthful unreliability as witnesses, did they tend to believe the children's narratives of seduction by these women? The answers to these questions are partly to be sought in the influence on the minds of the Rothenburg elites of traditional demonological accounts of seduction into witchcraft: part two of the famous late fifteenth-century demonological treatise, the *Malleus Maleficarum*, for example, talks of older women initiating others – including their own children – into witchcraft and was cited by Rothenburg jurist Johann Schäfer in his comments on the trial of Margaretha Hörber in 1627.[39] However, I will argue later that this image endured and was strengthened for the post-reformation elites in Rothenburg because it fitted in important ways with their ideas about, and fears of, the power of mothers for good and evil over their children.[40] It was so central to elite concerns that questions about such alleged seductions into witchcraft of children by older women, rather than questions about the latter's pacts with Satan, usually constituted the focal point of their interrogations.

Sabbats, demonic delusion, and legal caution

Most elite scepticism was expressed in the records of witchcraft cases from Rothenburg about witches' sabbats and the flights to them. The jurists and clerics who commented on these issues tended to believe that sabbats did not take place in reality, but that self-confessed witches and other people who claimed to have seen witches' gatherings had been deluded by the devil into imagining that they had done so. This view was first recorded by jurist Cunradt

Thalhaimer in 1582, when he suggested that Margaretha Seitz might have been deluded by the devil into imagining her transportation to the nocturnal gathering of her three Oberstetten neighbours.[41] Gugel and Hardessheim, the two Nuremberg jurists who also wrote an opinion on the Oberstetten case, agreed with Thalhaimer's interpretation of events, citing the *Canon Episcopi* in support of their views.[42] This was the famous ninth-century canon which, as part of the attempt by the Church to eradicate pagan and superstitious beliefs among the lower orders, had been issued in order to condemn the widely held popular belief 'that certain women rode out at night on the backs of animals in the company of the goddess Diana' by explaining that these women were merely deluded by the devil into thinking that they did such things.[43] The *Canon Episcopi* strongly influenced a strain of sceptical thought about the powers of witches to fly to sabbats which emerged at the University of Tübingen in the sixteenth century and which was also important in Rothenburg.[44] Jurist Friedrich Prenninger, for example, cited the *Canon Episcopi* explicitly in support of his belief that witches' sabbats did not really take place in the advice he gave the council on the Hilgartshausen witchcraft case of 1587, while in 1602 he suggested that Leonhardt Brandt had been deluded by the devil into seeing five of his neighbours at the witches' gathering Brandt claimed to have observed in Steinach.[45] The same ideas were still current later in the seventeenth century. In his opinion on the Brigitta Hörner case of 1639, jurist Walther noted his belief that flights to sabbats did not take place in reality,[46] while both Zyrlein and jurist Johann Schäfer believed that Margaretha Hörber had been deluded by the devil into imagining her attendance at sabbats in 1627.[47] Schäfer, however, allowed for the possibility that the devil might really transport people physically to different places in other cases.

As might have been expected, given this emphasis on sabbats as diabolic delusions, the Rothenburg elites showed little zeal for starting or pursuing legal proceedings against alleged sabbat-attenders during the early modern period. This is an important point, as it was usually only in areas where the judicial authorities were willing to take action against alleged witches purely on the grounds that they had been 'seen' by other witches at sabbats, and where torture was used without restraint to obtain confessions and denunciations of further sabbat-attenders from alleged witches, that a chain-reaction effect occurred to escalate witch-hunts in terms of size and speed. This could, potentially, have happened in Rothenburg: in 1627, for example, Margaretha Hörber named twenty-two people she claimed to have seen at witches' dances.[48] However, in practice in Rothenburg no legal action was taken against any of the alleged witches 'seen' at their gatherings by Margaretha Seitz in 1582, Leonhardt Brandt in 1602 or Brigitta Hörner in 1639.[49] In the cases involving Margaretha Hörber and Barbara Schürz from 1627 and 1652, respectively, a total of only three people were questioned after the girls had allegedly seen them at sabbats. However, in both cases other evidence, primarily their close association with the women who had allegedly seduced the girls into witchcraft in the first place, also counted against them.[50] The only individual to be arrested and interrogated purely on the grounds of having been 'seen' at a sabbat in late sixteenth- and early seventeenth-century Rothenburg was Babelein Kuch, during the Hilgartshausen witchcraft case discussed in Chapter 3. None of these four people were found guilty of or punished officially for witchcraft as a result of their involvement in these cases, however.

I do not want to suggest that there was a simple causal connection between elite scepticism about the reality of sabbats and elite unwillingness to pursue alleged sabbat-attenders at law in Rothenburg. Compelling legal reasons almost always also existed in specific cases to discourage the councillors and their advisers from taking action against alleged sabbat-attenders. In 1582, 1602 and 1628, for example, the fact that the allegations about witches' gatherings made by Margaretha Seitz, Leonhardt Brandt and Barbara Rost were handled according to the precepts governing slander helped ensure that the legal scales were tipped in favour of the alleged sabbat-attenders rather than their accusers.[51] In cases in which self-confessed child-witches claimed to have attended sabbats, jurists were more likely to cast doubt on the child's testimony by questioning the child's status as a witness than they were to spend pages debating the reality or otherwise of witches' sabbats. As far as they were concerned, a child who claimed to be a witch was, on grounds of both age and character, hardly a reliable enough witness on which to base the arrest and legal pursuit to the death of other people as witches.[52] Case-specific and more general religious and political reasons, which often had little to do with witchcraft itself, also help explain why it made little sense for the council to take or pursue legal action against alleged sabbat-attenders in particular witchcraft cases.[53]

Scepticism about the reality of witches' dances did, however, help to sow sufficient doubt in the minds of the councillors and their advisers to encourage them to treat allegations of sabbats in particular and witchcraft in general with caution when trying them at law. This was because the scepticism about sabbats stemmed from a broader set of beliefs about the devil's power to delude human beings: to make them believe as true sights and events which might not be true in reality, as Superintendent Zyrlein had put it in 1627. And, because the Rothenburg elites believed that, as a secret crime, witchcraft was difficult enough to prove unequivocally anyway, add the devil's trickery, malice and power to delude to the equation and proving witchcraft at law became even more problematic.[54] As jurists noted in 1582, 1602 and 1639, the devil might well have deluded Margaretha Seitz, Leonhardt Brandt and Brigitta Hörner into thinking that they had seen other people at sabbats because he hoped

thereby to endanger the lives of innocent people.[55] The council would therefore be doing the devil's work if it pursued the allegations against these potentially blameless people too vigorously. The idea that the councillors themselves
were not immune to the devil's trickery by virtue of their wisdom and status
was suggested by Zyrlein in 1627, when he commented that the devil's cunning
was so great that, while he regarded weak, melancholy women as easier targets
for his deceptions, no-one, not even the most steadfast and intelligent of men,
was safe from them. Zyrlein painted such a vivid picture of the power and
speed of the devil in playing tricks on the human mind and senses, which were
coarse and slow by comparison, that one wonders whether the Rothenburg
councillors had any confidence in their ability to use the law to reach conclusions about what was real and what imaginary, what true and what false, in
witchcraft cases.[56]

These doubts were expressed most clearly by jurist Walther in the witchcraft treatise he wrote on 14 September 1652. Walther organised his treatise
around four questions: (1) What should we believe about witches and their
activities? (2) Which of the witch's sins most deserve punishment? (3) How
should suspected witches be tried? and (4) How should witches be punished by
courts? Walther's responses to questions (1) and (2) reflected a fairly harsh
view of witches. He began by stating that, despite the fact that melancholy
imaginations and the devil's delusions played some role in the matter of witchcraft, witches really did exist and always had done: God would not have said so
much about them in the Bible if they were merely creatures of fantasy.[57]
Walther then listed the witches' various sins – their apostasy and acts of maleficium – explaining that their apostasy was the most heinous and deserving of
death.[58] However, in response to question (3), Walther's tone changed from
one of condemnation to one of caution. He noted that witchcraft was a weighty
and dangerous matter and advised judges to take care not to anger God and
assist the devil by subjecting suspected witches to rapid and unlawful trials.
They should rather make diligent enquiries, not only about suspected witches
but also about their accusers, to ensure that the latter were honourable and not
motivated in their actions by envy, enmity or a desire for vengeance. Judges
were also to investigate thoroughly the veracity of deeds confessed by alleged
witches under torture before reaching verdicts against them. Caution and thoroughness were needed because witchcraft was a secret crime and the devil was
the arch-deceiver.[59]

Walther gave his solution to the problems posed by witchcraft to judges
in the opinion that he wrote on the ongoing trials of alleged witches Margaretha
Horn and Catharina Leimbach on 23 September 1652. Stick to due legal procedure, he advised the council and, if Horn and Leimbach cannot be proven
guilty according to it, they should be released without punishment and their

eternal fate left to the all-seeing wisdom of God. The risk of executing the innocent along with the genuinely guilty was otherwise too great.[60] For Walther, then – and perhaps also for the councillors, who followed Walther's advice in these cases – it was possible to hold and express harsh opinions against witches in theory while remaining cautious in the handling of specific witch-craft cases in practice. Walther's tract may well have been modelled, con-sciously or otherwise, on the famous legal treatise, *Practicae novae imperialis Saxonicae rerum criminalium*, published by the Saxon jurist Benedict Carpzov in 1635. As Tom Robisheaux has shown, Carpzov also condemned witchcraft harshly as one of the most heinous crimes possible in Part One of his treatise, then advocated scrupulous adherence to due legal procedure as laid down in the *Carolina* in trying witches in Part Three.[61] This gap between the 'bark' of their demonological rhetoric and the 'bite' of their jurisprudential advice on the part of both Carpzov and Walther should thus perhaps warn us against the danger of taking demonological rhetoric at face value, without exploring how – and if – its ideas actually influenced trial procedure.

Doubts about their ability to prove witches unequivocally guilty accord-ing to due legal procedure, fears that they would invoke God's wrath against themselves and their subjects if they overstepped its bounds, and a certain humility in thinking that witchcraft was a matter best left up to God, all played a part in encouraging the Rothenburg councillors and their advisers to handle witchcraft cases with caution. It was therefore a marked degree of jurispru-dential scepticism, and not a well-defined and dogmatically maintained scepti-cism about the reality of witchcraft, which was the defining feature of the city's early modern witchcraft cases. Thus, while a particular set of beliefs about the devil's powers of delusion influenced and strengthened this legal caution, it was the refusal by the council to treat witchcraft as an exceptional crime, subject to no legal restraints or safeguards, which was most important in explaining the relatively restrained treatment of witchcraft suspects, the paucity of guilty ver-dicts in witchcraft cases, and the absence of larger-scale episodes of persecu-tion in the city during the early modern period.

This attitude towards witchcraft had much in common with the stance adopted in the treatises published between 1617 and 1635 by the four most important early seventeenth-century opponents of witch-hunting in Germany: Adam Tanner, Paul Laymann, Friedrich von Spee and Johann Matthäus Mey-fart. Stuart Clark has argued that the four:

> assumed (in print at least) that there was such a crime as witchcraft, involving real contact with demons, and that men and women were capable of and could properly be found guilty of it . . . Delusion appeared occasionally in these . . . texts but only as a reason for regarding revelations about the sabbat with cau-tion, not as a threat to the entire reality of witchcraft.[62]

However, Tanner, Laymann, Spee and Meyfart did not become embroiled in the minutiae of ongoing demonological debates in their works. Instead they attacked the practice of witch-hunting, criticising the mistreatment of witches at law, arguing for the introduction of various procedural safeguards and the more careful regulation of the use of torture in witchcraft trials, and demanding that trials be conducted 'according to the standards of natural reason and equity'.[63]

The similarities between their ideas and those of successive Rothenburg councillors, in terms of their belief in the possibility of witches causing maleficium and making pacts, their doubts about the reality of sabbats, and their overriding emphasis on the circumspect legal treatment of suspected witches, are striking. Still more striking was the fact that the Rothenburg councillors adopted what Clark has called this 'radically sceptical position concerning these legal issues' at so early a date: from the 1560s rather than the 1620s and 1630s.[64] Moreover, the councillors had not learned the lesson of legal caution through bitter experience: no large-scale episode of witchcraft prosecution, based on excessive infliction of torture and other legal abuses, had occurred in Rothenburg to teach them that discretion was the better part of valour when it came to trying witches. This suggests that older legal ideas connected with the law of talion and the treatment of slander, the procedural safeguards stipulated by the *Carolina*, and the conviction that witchcraft was a spiritual crime best left to God's ultimate judgement were sufficient, in Rothenburg at least, to ensure and maintain legal caution in the treatment of witchcraft without the need for any radical re-appraisal of the legal issues pertaining to the crime.[65] It also suggests that the councillors and their advisers had a wider set of concerns, which had little to do with witchcraft itself, but which influenced their handling of witchcraft cases and helped explain why they were unwilling to throw legal caution to the winds in the process.

Wider social and political priorities

If hunting witches without regard for due legal procedure risked doing the devil's work by executing the innocent along with the guilty, it also made little sense to the Rothenburg councillors for more practical reasons. Take the importance of the rural hinterland, from where most witchcraft cases emanated until the later seventeenth century, to the city and its elites as an example. The hinterland had always been vital to Rothenburg's survival as an autonomous political unit and to the continuing political dominance within the city of the urban patriciate, whose wealth came primarily from the land that they owned rather than from craft-based trade and commerce. Ever since Heinrich Toppler, the best-known late-medieval mayor of Rothenburg, had begun to increase the city's landholdings outside the city walls from the late fourteenth century, the fates of the city, its hinterland and their own power were regarded by the urban elites as inextricably connected. Rothenburg's hinterland subjects provided essential foodstuffs and raw materials to the inhabitants of the city, money in the form of rents and dues to the city coffers and individual patrician families, a market for the goods of the urban craftsmen, and a peasant militia as the first line of defence against attack from external enemies.[66] The importance of the hinterland and its inhabitants to the city was emphasised in many ways during the early modern period. After the Peasants' War of 1525, for example, the council acknowledged the military importance of the men of the hinterland when it quickly re-armed the peasants who had just raised their weapons in rebellion against its authority so that they could help defend the city in a feud with a neighbouring lord.[67] The economic importance of its peasant subjects to the city can be seen from council ordinances which ordered the hinterland inhabitants to sell their produce only at markets in Rothenburg and not to flee the hinterland with their possessions during the Thirty Years' War.[68] After the Thirty Years' War had wrought terrible destruction on the hinterland villages, the council adopted policies which would ensure that they were rebuilt and repopulated as quickly as possible, offering financial assistance to its peasant subjects to achieve this aim.[69] Council concern for the well-being of the peasants was at work here, but so too was concern for the economic well-being of the city and its inhabitants.

The importance of the hinterland to the city and its survival, then, helps explain why the councillors showed little enthusiasm for pursuing the allegations of witchcraft raised by villagers in the late sixteenth and early seventeenth century beyond the limits of due legal procedure and why they often emphasised the restoration of social harmony in their resolution of witchcraft cases. Partly as a result of their traditional policies regarding slander and partly as a result of observing the effects of large-scale witch-trials in other areas, the councillors seem to have realised from an early date that thoughtless talk about witchcraft on the part of their subjects risked triggering witch-trials and plunging communities into a spiral of accusation, counter-accusation and enmity, and that the zealous pursuit of witch-trials on a dubious legal basis risked the persecution and perhaps execution of large numbers of their subjects.[70] Neither scenario was conducive to the traditional aim of the councillors: that of maintaining order and harmony in well-populated hinterland villages in the economic, political and military interests of the city. It is also interesting to note that the five villages which became the focus of investigations into allegations of witchcraft between 1561 and 1602 — Wettringen, Finsterlohr, Oberstetten, Hilgartshausen and Steinach — were all situated close to the territorial boundaries of the hinterland, with Oberstetten lying beyond the line of hedges and ditches the city had erected to protect its rural possessions.[71] The council may have been particularly keen to maintain order and authority at its outer territorial reaches by deciding not to allow allegations of witchcraft among its inhabitants there to escalate out of control.

In Chapter 1 I argued that we can clearly see council concern for order and harmony in its handling of the allegations of witchcraft from Finsterlohr in 1563, Oberstetten in 1582 and Steinach in 1602.[72] However, this concern also shaped the way in which the council resolved urban witchcraft cases. In 1605, for example, the councillors followed the advice of jurist Friedrich Prenninger to banish joiner Hans Georg Hofmann rather than investigate the suspicions of witchcraft against him any further in order to quell the rising tide of talk about witchcraft among the common people of Rothenburg, while elite concern for social stability in the city, mingled with self-interest on the part of the councillors, lay behind their treatment of Barbara Rost's allegations of witchcraft as slander in 1629.[73] This same concern helps explain why eight-year-old Brigitta Hörner of Spielbach was sent to the city hospital with no further investigation of her witchcraft confessions in July 1639. Hörner was one of the many children orphaned during the Thirty Years' War and she wandered Rothenburg largely unchecked, telling people that she had been seduced into witchcraft, had promised herself to the devil, had flown to sabbats which various women from Spielbach and Rothenburg had also attended, and had committed acts of maleficium.[74] The sources note that Hörner had stirred up great trouble among the common people and especially the children on the streets of Rothenburg with her witchcraft stories.[75] The type of trouble she had caused was not specified, although it was probably similar to that caused by six-year-old Hans Gackstatt's witchcraft stories in the village of Hilgartshausen in 1587, discussed in Chapter 3: furthering suspicions about already-reputed witches, increasing the likelihood of public accusations of witchcraft, and raising the level of enmity within the community. Moreover, the records of the Consistorium suggest that some city-dwellers had asked Hörner whether she had seen individuals they personally suspected of witchcraft at the sabbats she claimed to have attended.[76] Had the council taken her confessions too seriously, it might have elevated her authority as an identifier of witches in the minds of some of its subjects, who might then have brought formal witchcraft charges against other reputed witches. By taking Hörner off the streets and placing her in the hospital, the council doubtless hoped to calm feelings and speech about witchcraft in Rothenburg.

Case-specific political circumstances also influenced the legal treatment of allegations of witchcraft by the council, often in a manner which encouraged caution. This can be seen in the case involving Margaretha Hörber of Gebsattel from 1627 discussed in Chapter 4 and the cases from Bettenfeld and Wettringen from 1652 discussed in Chapters 5 and 6. In all three cases factors which had little to do with witchcraft itself – rivalries with neighbouring lords, the immediate political and religious context of the Thirty Years' War, ongoing disputes with their subjects, and the desire to maintain their own judicial authority and autonomy – helped shape the handling of the allegations of witchcraft by the council. More general political issues also help explain why the council showed little desire for prosecuting witches beyond the limits of what they perceived as due legal procedure. Territorial rulers who presided over particularly large episodes of witch-hunting based on abuses of the law and the excessive use of torture could render themselves vulnerable to external interference in early modern Germany. For example, Gerhard Schormann has shown that the action of the *Reichshofrat*, one of Germany's two central imperial courts, helped end the terrible witch-hunts in the Franconian Prince-Bishopric of Bamberg in 1630. This happened after refugees from the hunts in Bamberg fled to Nuremberg and made formal complaints against Prince-Bishop Johann II Fuchs von Dornheim from there to the *Reichshofrat*, thereby persuading the Emperor to issue mandates ordering von Dornheim to hand over the records of the Bamberg hunts to the imperial court.[77] The same pattern of an assertion of imperial authority on grounds of legal abuses also helped end the terrible witch-hunts which took place in the Electorate of Cologne and the Prince-Bishopric of Würzburg between 1626 and 1631.[78]

Of course, the Rothenburg councillors could not have known in advance how the Bamberg, Würzburg and Cologne witch-trials were going to end in 1630 and 1631. They were, however, the governors of a medium-sized Lutheran imperial city which owed its status as an autonomous political unit within the Holy Roman Empire to the rights and privileges given to it and protected by Catholic Emperors. This meant that after their adoption of Lutheranism in 1544, successive generations of councillors tried consistently to pursue both internal and external policy in a way that would draw as little imperial attention to themselves as possible and give the Emperor as few excuses for interfering in their affairs – and perhaps curbing their powers and judicial autonomy – as possible. This policy of quiet caution in order to remain on good terms with the Emperor can be seen, for example, in the slow and legalistic nature of the city's reformation between 1544 and 1559, and in the circumspect political stance taken by the city during the Schmalkaldic War in the mid-sixteenth century and the early years of the Thirty Years' War in the seventeenth century.[79] It was therefore possible for successive generations of councillors and their advisers to have made the links between abuse of the law, excessive witch-hunting, and imperial displeasure at an early stage of their judicial engagement with witchcraft allegations, and shaped their legal treatment of these allegations accordingly. In 1605, for example, one of the reasons given by jurist Friedrich Prenninger in support of his advice to the council to pursue allegations of witchcraft against a citizen and joiner, Hans Georg Hofmann, no further, was that Hofmann might complain to the Emperor about his treatment if he were tortured during his trial, and thereby embroil the council itself in lengthy legal proceedings.[80]

External influences on elite thinking?

The Rothenburg councillors were content to keep witchcraft cases an almost exclusively in-house affair during much of the early modern period. They asked 'foreign' jurists for advice in only three instances: Johann Höfel of Schweinfurt in 1663 and 1673 and Nuremberg jurists Gugel and Hardessheim in 1582.[81] However, although Gugel and Hardessheim were employed by and lived in the city of Nuremberg, they were also paid an annual retainer for their services by the council in Rothenburg.[82] This meant that the councillors could ask them for advice directly, without having to submit a request to this effect to their counterparts in Nuremberg. Moreover, the advice proffered by Gugel and Hardessheim in 1582 was very similar to that given to the councillors by their own jurist Thalhaimer, which it in many ways confirmed.[83] Apart from these three instances, the Rothenburg councillors relied on their own appointees for legal, theological and medical opinions on witchcraft cases until 1671 when, for the first time, they sought advice from a law faculty at a university (Tübingen) on a witchcraft case.[84] As the *Carolina* had ordered judges to seek advice in this way in difficult criminal cases nearly a hundred and forty years earlier in 1532, we can perhaps see in the council's determination to consult only its own experts on witchcraft before 1671 a deliberate assertion of its judicial and political autonomy as well as an expression of confidence in its ability to handle witchcraft cases without external assistance.[85]

This is not to say that elite ideas about witchcraft and how it was best handled at law were immune to external influence in Rothenburg – just that any signs of such influence were almost entirely absent from specific cases. It seems likely, for example, that connections with Nuremberg, the most powerful imperial city in Franconia, helped shape the attitudes of the Rothenburg elites towards witchcraft. Both cities became Lutheran, and both had similarly restrained patterns of witchcraft prosecution, based on similar beliefs about witchcraft, about the need to try witches according to due legal procedure, and the need to maintain social order for practical reasons.[86] And, while the Gugel–Hardessheim opinion is the only example of a direct link between the two cities in a specific witchcraft case, there were other contexts in which ideas about witchcraft could have been exchanged.[87] For example, the Rothenburg council looked to Nuremberg for help and advice in the implementation of its own Lutheran reformation between 1544 and 1559, drawing heavily on the services of Nuremberg jurist Christoph Gugel, to whom it paid an annual retainer between 1530 and 1577.[88] It also 'borrowed' Nuremberg cleric Thomas Venatorius, who had helped advise the council in Nuremberg on a witchcraft case in that city in 1536, to be Rothenburg's first evangelical preacher in 1544.[89] After 1559 the municipal account books show that mayors and jurists made numerous advice-seeking visits to Nuremberg throughout the early modern period, when ongoing witchcraft cases from either city could have been discussed, while most of the jurists active in Rothenburg in the seventeenth century and an increasing proportion of its councillors studied at the newly established Nuremberg university at Altdorf.[90]

The Rothenburg council also continued to pay annual retainers to certain Nuremberg jurists for their services. By the late 1580s the two jurists retained in this way were Andreas Stöckel and Johann Heroldt.[91] They wrote no opinions about witchcraft cases in Rothenburg but we know of their views on the subject from opinions they wrote for the council of another Franconian city, Weissenburg, in 1590. Like several of the Rothenburg jurists, Stöckel and Heroldt regarded witchcraft as a real crime deserving of severe punishment but recommended caution in its legal treatment, especially as the devil could delude alleged witches into accusing other people, who were in fact innocent, of the crime.[92] Stöckel and Heroldt may have discussed their ideas privately with their Rothenburg acquaintances in the late sixteenth century, but no reference was made to their formal written opinions in Rothenburg until 1652, when jurist Walther mentioned them fleetingly in his witchcraft treatise.[93]

The Rothenburg elites were probably also influenced in their attitudes towards witchcraft by the links they forged with the nearby Lutheran Duchy of Württemberg. Erik Midelfort has shown that, from the early sixteenth century, theologians from Württemberg's Tübingen University combined the emphasis from the *Canon Episcopi* on the devil's power to delude with a providential belief that God was ultimately responsible for all things – good and bad – that happened on earth to produce a particularly sceptical view of the power of witches. The most famous proponent of this Württemberg view of witchcraft was the Lutheran reformer Johannes Brenz. After his congregation blamed a particularly severe hailstorm on witchcraft in 1539, Brenz drew on the story of Job in order to tell them that bad weather came from God to test and punish them and to encourage them to repent, and not from witches, who were merely deluded by the devil into thinking that they could cause storms.[94] Jacob Heerbrand, a theologian from Tübingen University, preached in the same vein in the 1570s.[95] The Tübingen jurists wrote little about witchcraft during the sixteenth century, but 'their occasional opinions show definite restraint in regard to procedures used against witches'.[96]

The councillors in Rothenburg also looked to Württemberg for advice and assistance during the implementation of their reformation. Württemberg theologian Jakob Andreä drafted the Rothenburg *Church Ordinance* of 1559, relying heavily on Württemberg precedents in the process, while the first Superintendent, or foremost cleric and ecclesiastical official, in Rothenburg was Johannes Hoffmann, another Württemberger.[97] Johannes Brenz himself was an important influence on proceedings and enjoyed a personal friendship and correspondence with Johannes Hornburg, the Rothenburg councillor responsible for instigating the adoption of Lutheranism in the city.[98] The library in Rothenburg also contained copies of the complete works of Brenz, including his *Sermon on Hailstorms*, and of Heerbrand.[99] The links between Rothenburg and Württemberg, and especially Tübingen University, continued throughout the sixteenth century. In 1578 the council sought the advice of the Tübingen theologians in a dispute about usury which had arisen among its own pastors.[100] The number of students from Rothenburg matriculating at Tübingen rose significantly after Rothenburg became Lutheran, while six of the eight jurists who advised the council on witchcraft cases between 1582 and 1652 had also studied at Tübingen: Renger, Metzler, Thalhaimer, Prenninger, Bezold and Seuter.[101] They all advocated caution and adherence to due legal procedure in handling allegations of witchcraft and two of them – Thalhaimer in 1582 and Prenninger in 1587 and 1602 – expressed beliefs in line with the *Canon Episcopi* in their opinions on witchcraft cases.[102]

I do not want to suggest that the Rothenburg councillors and their advisers slavishly followed a Tübingen or Nuremberg 'line' in their treatment of witchcraft. For example, despite the influence of Brenz on Rothenburg's reformation, he was not cited in relation to witchcraft in the city until jurist Walther mentioned him briefly in his witchcraft treatise of 1652.[103] Nor were Brenz's ideas about the powerlessness of witches entirely followed by jurists and councillors in Rothenburg: as we have seen above, case-specific evidence suggests that they continued to think that witches were able to cause storms as well as other sorts of maleficium, while emphasising the devil's powers of delusion mainly in relation to witches' sabbats. By the early seventeenth century views on witchcraft had anyway become sharply divided in Tübingen itself. Whereas Brenz and his followers argued that witches deserved execution just for apostasy, Theodor Thumm and other moderates argued against the death penalty for a spiritual crime.[104] The important point from a Rothenburg point of view was that the councillors chose to opt for the moderate Thummian position in 1627, on the advice of Wittenberg-educated Georg Zyrlein and because this made good sense to them for other reasons.[105] The similarities in the treatment of witchcraft between Rothenburg and Nuremberg may have stemmed as much from their political similarities as they did from any explicit exchange of ideas on the subject: they were both imperial cities with rural hinterlands, ruled by patrician councils which introduced Lutheranism. The most that can be concluded at present is that there were channels of communication between Rothenburg and its two staunchest local Lutheran allies through which ideas about witchcraft and its legal treatment could have been exchanged, from Rothenburg to Tübingen and Nuremberg as well as vice versa.[106] Any more detailed conclusions about the networks of mutual influence that existed between the elites in Rothenburg and their counterparts elsewhere must await much-needed research on the lives, careers and correspondence of the leading men of Rothenburg throughout the early modern period.

A final factor influencing the cautious legal treatment of witchcraft in Rothenburg was probably the fact that alleged witches, like all other suspected criminals, were tried by the sixteen-man city council, constituted as the city's criminal court. Johannes Dillinger has argued that the trial of witches by councils or council subcommittees in early modern German cities probably militated against witch-trials spreading rapidly and with scant regard for the law. This was because it involved a relatively lengthy process of discussion and consideration of the issues which no individual was able to control and in which a variety of opinions had to be aired and discussed so that a final consensus could be reached.[107] The same processes were at work in Rothenburg. The progress of criminal cases was controlled by the full council, which considered them and planned the next course of action during its meetings. Suspects were interrogated in the city gaol by the two most junior councillors who, because of their lowly status, were least likely to pursue a case at variance with council dictates. Any sudden change in the progress of a case was reported back to the council for further consideration. Rothenburg also had its own municipal hangman, who was paid by the council and had no personal influence on witchcraft cases. This is a noteworthy point, as travelling hangmen who offered their services in identifying, torturing and executing witches to judicial authorities at times of witch-panics could help exacerbate and spread these panics, as they had a vested interest in so doing.[108] In Rothenburg control was always kept by the council, although its five most powerful members, the five mayors, almost certainly exerted a disproportionate influence over proceedings. By encouraging and even prolonging discussion about cases, therefore, the trial process in Rothenburg probably helped ensure that doubts about their ability to prove witches guilty at law remained uppermost in the minds of successive generations of councillors, whatever they believed about witchcraft as individuals. A consensus about legal caution may, in fact, have hidden a greater variety of opinions about witchcraft among the councillors than the decisions they reached en masse in particular cases suggests.

White magic

The Rothenburg elites had to deal with what they perceived to be the problem of popular use of beneficient or white magic as well as maleficient or demonic witchcraft during the early modern period. Like the lower orders throughout the rest of Europe, their subjects drew on deep resources of white magic in order to try to ensure success in their daily undertakings; to find lost or stolen objects or missing people; to protect themselves and their livestock against witchcraft, disease and other misfortunes; and to limit the damage caused by these threats to their health and livelihoods once they had taken effect.[109] People sewed herbs and seeds blessed in special ways into cloth pouches and wore them about their bodies or placed them in their bed-straw to protect themselves against witches, or put them into door-lintels to protect the live-stock that passed under them against witchcraft.[110] Amulets containing written blessings were worn for the same purpose, while women swept their homes and left their brooms outside in a ritual manner on Shrove Tuesday to ensure that their houses were protected against dirt, disease and witchcraft for the coming year.[111] Of particular importance to the web of white magic rites were blessings: prescribed formulae invoking God, Jesus, Mary or the saints which were spoken aloud – often to the accompaniment of other rituals – and which were believed to invest particular objects with magical power or to protect or cure by virtue of their own power. Blessings were spoken to protect soldiers against being wounded in battle, to cure wounds, open sores and failing eye-sight, and to protect sheep against wolves.[112] In Rothenburg these blessings cir-culated in written as well as spoken form. The earliest reference to a hinterland inhabitant possessing a book of blessings dates from 1582,[113] although such ref-erences became more common during the seventeenth century.[114] This may have reflected rising levels of literacy among the peasantry, or more probably the fact that more blessings and blessing-books had entered circulation as a result of troop and population movements through the area during the Thirty Years' War.

Most inhabitants of Rothenburg and its hinterland would have had their own repertoire of white magic blessings and rituals to draw on in their daily battle against misfortune. However, they often also used the services of cun-ning folk – men and women renowned for their skills as purveyors of white magic. It is usually unclear how cunning folk first acquired their reputations. However, for the blacksmiths and herdsmen and -women among them, this probably occurred because they were already regarded as experts in identify-ing and curing diseases in livestock. Other cunning folk built up their reputa-tions deliberately – and played down the skills of their competitors for custom – by means of judicious self-advertisement. In the early seventeenth century cunning man Jorg Fronhöfer of Ober Breitenau solicited customers by spreading the news that he travelled long distances to find the herbs he used in his magic, and that he could do things that no physician or barber-surgeon could achieve.[115] Some cunning folk may have chosen or continued in the job because it was a good way of earning money: in 1582 Georg Kissling, cunning man and blacksmith of Ergersheim, claimed that he had earned 10 gulden for protecting a peasant's livestock against witches and six gulden for healing a woman's diseased thigh.[116] These were considerable sums of money and would have constituted a welcome addition to the income of any household.

The records of the Consistorium, or church council of Rothenburg, identify many cunning folk who operated in the hinterland during the early modern period, although many more who never surfaced in official records doubtless also existed. In 1577 Thomas Zipfel of Detwang was chastised for having used the services of Els the Herdswoman, who had tried to cure Zipfel's wife's diseased leg with a ritual involving molten lead, a pair of scissors and a blessing.[117] In a list of cunning folk and their users made in 1612, the herdsman of Gammesfeld and his wife were identified as purveyors of blessings, while various hinterland inhabitants were criticised for having consulted the Sorcerer of Feuchtwangen and the executioners of Ellwangen and Rothenburg about witches.[118] Feuchtwangen and Ellwangen were towns situated well beyond the boundaries of Rothenburg's hinterland, showing how far people were willing to travel to consult particularly renowned wizards. The two most notorious early seventeenth-century cunning men in Rothenburg also came from outside the hinterland. One was Jörg Grönn, a carpenter from the town of Aub, who made regular forays into hinterland villages, visiting taverns in order to obtain news of local people who might be interested in his services. In 1612 alone he had been used by villagers from Tauberscheckenbach, Hardt, Schweinsdorf, Finsterlohr, Detwang and Gattenhofen to protect themselves and their livestock against witches and to cure disease. He may have pushed his luck too far that year, however, as in 1613 he was arrested by the council and banished from Rothenburg and its hinterland for his use of magic.[119] The other, Peter Fischer, who was known as the Little Miller from Buch am Wald, was also arrested and interrogated by the council in 1624 but was released without punishment and continued to ply his trade until the 1640s, when he surfaced in the trial for witchcraft against Margaretha Rost of Finsterlohr, discussed in Chapter 5.[120] While women could be cunning folk, the sources suggest that at least twice as many more were men, as were all the most renowned cunning folk of the area, Fronhöfer, Grönn and Fischer included. Just as maleficient witchcraft was gender-related to women, beneficient witchcraft was gender-related to men.[121]

Inhabitants of Rothenburg and its hinterland regarded white magic in a pragmatic light, as one method of trying to combat misfortune and cure

disease which was worthwhile using along with other, non-magical methods in
the hope that one of them would have the desired effect. Cunning folk were
thus often just one of a range of experts called on in times of need. For
example, in 1612 Kirch Hans of Gattenhofen called Jörg Grönn into his house
to treat his sick wife while he was waiting for a barber-surgeon to come to the
village from Rothenburg to let his wife's blood. The pastor of Gattenhofen,
Michael Beringer, was in Kirch Hans's house at the same time, offering spiritual
solace to his wife, and was subsequently criticised by the Consistorium for
having failed to accost and chastise Grönn while he had the chance.[122] In 1613
Michael Bendig of Detwang was reprimanded by the Consistorium for having
used the services of Grönn and the executioner of Feuchtwangen against his
own wife, whom he suspected of having bewitched him, causing his thigh to
become diseased. Bendig had also consulted one of the Rothenburg physicians,
Jeremias Seng, about his condition. The striking aspect of this consultation was
that Bendig had tried to use university-educated Seng as he would have used
Grönn or any other cunning man – in order to gain confirmation of the identify of the witch he already suspected of having bewitched him. Seng was forced
to make a statement to the Consistorium to clear himself of any suspicion in his
dealings with Bendig, stressing that Bendig was mistaken in thinking that he,
Seng, had blamed Bendig's disease on Bendig's wife.[123]

In contrast to their subjects, and like elites elsewhere in Protestant
Europe, the Lutheran councillors and clerics of Rothenburg viewed the use of
white magic as a sin.[124] This was because they believed that God sent misfortunes to punish people for their sins and to test their faith; the only theologically appropriate response to misfortune was therefore prayer and repentance,
although acceptable medical methods – natural remedies or the services of
physicians and barber-surgeons – could be used to combat disease. The use of
white magic, however, 'questioned God's providential control over affairs' and
attributed powers to objects, rituals and words which were neither natural nor
sanctioned by Scripture.[125] If white magic worked, and it was neither natural
nor godly, then 'the devil must be held to have co-operated'.[126] To the Rothenburg elites, white magic was thus theoretically as sinful and as worthy of
punishment as maleficent magic, as both implied co-operation with the devil
and denial of God on the part of the perpetrator. As the first ordinance issued
in Rothenburg specifically against white magic noted in condemnatory tones in
1612, people who used white magic and consulted cunning folk committed
'abominable apostasy' for the most minor of material gains and were ordered
to desist on pain of corporal punishment, while cunning folk were described as
idolatrous, blasphemous and deserving of death for their activities.[127]

Despite their loathing of beneficent magic, however, the councillors
failed to eradicate its use by their subjects during the early modern period.

Council ordinances and Consistorium minutes repeated the same laments about the problem throughout the seventeenth century, while court records show that inhabitants of Rothenburg and its hinterland were still consulting cunning folk in the late eighteenth century.[128] Moreover, research undertaken in Franconia in 1970 showed that beliefs about both maleficient and beneficient magic had persisted, albeit doubtless in attenuated form, among the rural populace into the twentieth century.[129] How can we account for this failure on the part of the Rothenburg elites, contrasting as it does with the apparent severity of the 1612 ordinance?

The secular and clerical elites in Rothenburg elites used three tactics to try to persuade their subjects that the use of white magic was a sin: teaching them in Catechism classes and sermons that this was the case, admonishing individuals identified as users of white magic, and punishing the worst recidivists with excommunication or secular punishments. The first tactic – teaching – may not have been particularly effective, for two reasons. Consistorium records from the sixteenth and seventeenth century suggest that many Rothenburg subjects lost interest in formal church teaching once they had learned enough to take their first communion.[130] To compound the problem, the structures and processes of institutionalised religion all but collapsed in Rothenburg's hinterland during the Thirty Years' War, at the same time as access to and reliance on the forms and formulae of white magic on the part of its inhabitants increased.[131] Even if the conditions and resources for teaching their subjects had been more favourable, however, it is unlikely that the councillors would have convinced their subjects that white magic was sinful. This idea made so little practical sense to them, and the consequences of embracing it were so uncongenial, that most of them probably chose prudently to ignore it.

Individuals known or rumoured to have used white magic could be called to answer for their actions before the Consistorium, which met in Rothenburg, or before the councillors who periodically visited the hinterland's villages to check on standards of piety among their inhabitants. These individuals often sought to minimise their culpability in the eyes of their elite questioners by offering various mitigating explanations for their behaviour. The magic they had used had not really worked, they claimed; they had used it with good intentions, because other people had advised them to do so, or because they or their family members had been so ill and all other remedies had failed; anyway, they had not known that to use white magic was a sin, because their parents had used it before them and because blessings invoking God could surely not be sinful.[132] These excuses point to the conceptual gulf that existed between the elites and lower orders on the question of white magic, at least in the early years of Rothenburg's reformation, although as the years passed and awareness of elite opinion on the issue spread, peasants probably offered these excuses disingenuously, in the hope that they would thereby escape official sanctions.[133]

Official sanctions were not exceptionally severe anyway. A verbal warning was usually all that the sinners who appeared before the Consistorium suffered. In 1612, for example, Michael Bendig was simply told to stop using cunning folk, after much ink had been expended explaining in the minutes of the Consistorium why he deserved to be harshly punished for consulting Jörg Grönn about his allegedly bewitched leg.[134] In 1615 the Consistorium resorted to the even tamer method of asking Hans Müller of Gailnau's wife to admonish her husband on its behalf when she returned home. Müller was rumoured to have used cunning folk but was unable to appear personally before the Consistorium because he was infirm.[135] In the sixteenth century the council occasionally gaoled recidivists, who were usually released after a short spell in custody, while in the seventeenth century it imposed fines more regularly on offenders – if they confessed their sins.[136] However, the general tactic of admonition of offenders, combined with exhortations to them to live better lives, appears to have remained relatively consistent throughout the early modern period.

This approach made theological sense according to the Rothenburg *Church Ordinance* of 1559, which had emphasised that sinners were to be given every chance, by means of persuasion, to repent and return to the Lutheran fold of their own volition.[137] However, it would have been practically impossible for the councillors to have punished with any great severity – with corporal punishments, as the 1612 ordinance suggested – all users of white magic within the city and its hinterland, as this would have meant gaoling, flogging or otherwise punishing a significant number of their subjects. Moreover, pastors in some hinterland villages had reported hostile and incredulous reactions on the part of their parishioners to the public promulgation of the first post-reformation ordinances against various sins, with villagers accusing the council of wanting to erect a new priestly tyranny over them.[138] For the sake of social and political order, then, the council may have feared antagonising its subjects by disciplining the users of white magic too zealously and accordingly adopted more cautious policies.

The council's greatest ire was reserved for the purveyors rather than users of white magic. This was because it believed that cunning folk encouraged popular use of white magic in opposition to church teaching on the subject, deprived the physicians and barber-surgeons of Rothenburg of custom, defrauded the council's subjects out of money for remedies and services which did not work, and exacerbated social discord by confirming their customers' suspicions against alleged witches.[139] The anger of the Consistorium against cunning folk occasionally reached boiling point: the 1612 ordinance issued by the council against them can be traced directly to the increasing impatience of the Consistorium with the activities of Jörg Grönn in Rothenburg's hinter-land,[140] while in 1643 the impatience of the Consistorium with Peter Fischer of Buch am Wald prompted the council to issue another ordinance against white magic in which Fischer was mentioned by name.[141] The council's rhetorical venom was only periodically translated into judicial action against cunning folk, however, and their usual fate was not execution but banishment beyond the boundaries of Rothenburg's hinterland: in 1571, for example, itinerant cunning woman Ursula Hespel was banished for practicing divination and other forbidden arts using herbs, roots and blessings.[142] More severe punish-ments were rarely inflicted and then only on itinerant quacks or local cunning folk who had committed other crimes in addition to the sale of their magical skills. In 1551, for example, a woman from Trier and three mercenaries were set in the pillory and then banished – after the men had also been flogged – for having sold plants which they falsely claimed to be mandragora to unsuspect-ing peasants,[143] while in 1581 itinerant quack Anna Gebhart had a cross burnt into her forehead and holes burnt through both cheeks before being banished after she had defrauded several inhabitants of Schwäbisch Hall, Nördlingen and Rothenburg by claiming, among other things, that she could find buried treasure with the help of a spirit.[144] In 1582 blacksmith Georg Kissling of Erg-ersheim was flogged and banished after being found guilty of acts of extortion and slander which he had perpetrated in the course of his activities as a cunning man against an inhabitant of Rothenburg's hinterland village of Wettringen, while in 1616 blacksmith Leonhardt Geuder from Gattenhofen enjoyed the dubious honour of being the only cunning man ever to be executed in Rothen-burg. He was beheaded mainly because he had committed adultery and bigamy, however, although the final summary of his crimes did mention his activities as a purveyor of forbidden remedies and blessings.[145]

These punishments must be set in context, however. To begin with, the individuals listed above undoubtedly represented only a fraction of all the cun-ning folk active in Rothenburg and its environs; as was almost certainly the case with the majority of reputed witches, most cunning folk probably lived out their lives without ever coming or being brought to the attention of the secu-lar or ecclesiastical authorities. Second, while arrest and banishment may have made cunning folk more cautious about plying their trade in Rothenburg's ter-ritory, they may not have experienced it as a terrible, life-destroying punish-ment because many of them – like Hespel and Grönn – lived outside Rothenburg's hinterland anyway. Finally, the Rothenburg council tended not to conflate white and black magic in trials of cunning folk, despite the fact that – according to Lutheran thinking on the matter of magic – they might have been tempted to do so. For example, they never showed great enthusiasm for trying to force cunning folk into admitting that they were in league with the devil in the course of their trials. They tried hardest to do this with Anna Gebhart, who stoically resisted torture to deny that she had made a pact with the devil; the fact that she was branded with a cross reflected the council's lingering suspicion that she was a witch as well as its desire to make an example of her because of the audacity of her crimes.[146] Generally, however, and in line with its relatively restrained treatment of witchcraft as a whole, the councillors were satisfied to accept the denials of cunning folk on this issue; by the seventeenth century the question of a cunning person's pact with the devil had become a largely formulaic part of the trial process.[147] There was no need to force such individuals into confessing that they were in league with the devil or guilty of maleficient magic when their illicit and fraudulent use of magic was almost invariably grounds enough to justify their banishment anyway.

Why do the Rothenburg court records contain a relatively meagre haul of cunning folk punished for their activities? Part of the answer lies in the fact that the council was largely reliant on the customers of cunning folk to turn them over to the authorities. In the ordinance against white magic issued in 1612 the council ordered its rural subjects to capture any cunning folk caught sneaking in and out of the hinterland and to hand them over to the council for punishment.[148] The council seems to have missed the point that, for as long as they believed that white magic worked, peasants had a vested interest in keeping cunning folk out of the clutches of the authorities. It was only when relationships between cunning folk and their customers soured significantly – if cures went wrong, for example – that cunning folk were at risk of being accused of fraud or maleficium.[149] This does not appear to have happened very often in Rothenburg. A second problem for the council was that its judicial authority stopped at the boundaries of its hinterland. This meant that foreign cunning folk could travel in and out of the hinterland and Rothenburg subjects could visit cunning folk in neighbouring territories with relative impunity. Disputes over political and judicial rights appear to have made it difficult for the council and the lords of neighbouring territories to co-operate and take concerted action against renowned cunning folk in their respective territories, who thus fell between the gaps of the various judical systems.[150]

Finally, the councillors had to take immediate circumstances – and particularly the maintenance of social harmony – into account when taking action against cunning folk, just as they did when trying allegedly maleficient or demonic witchcraft. This point was illustrated in 1613, when Rothenburg chaplain Michael Hornung brought the activities of a 'so-called' doctor, Lazarus Schmid, to the attention of the Consistorium. Hornung had called on the services of Schmid – a newcomer to Rothenburg – when his wife fell ill, but had been shocked when Schmid had given her an amulet, containing a paper on which strange characters were written, and some herbs, over which he had spoken strange words, to cure her. The concern that Schmid was in fact a wizard, who used blessings and other forbidden arts, was raised again by clerical members of the Consistorium in 1616, when they demanded that the council expel Schmid from the city with the pointed reminder that magicians deserved to be burned to death. Johann Bezold, Michael Reichshöfer and Johann Offner, the three councillors who sat on the Consistorium, responded almost wistfully that, while they wished they could do something about Schmid, they saw no possibility of proceeding against him, because no-one apart from the clerics had complained about him and because he had a large following of apparently satisfied customers among the citizenry. The gap between theological theory and its practical application in the case of Schmid was uncomfortably plain for all members of the Consistorium, and presumably many of the townsfolk, to see.[151]

I do not want to suggest that the attempt by the council to police the use of white magic was entirely without effect. Its best-educated and most pious subjects may have come to share its view that the use of white magic was a sin, while those who continued to use white magic probably did so more furtively, knowing that the risk of some sort of official sanction had increased. Cunning folk in particular were forced to become more circumspect in what they said and did and faced an increased risk of formal prosecution and banishment as a result of their activities.[152] However, on the whole the system of beneficient magic and the beliefs that underpinned it survived relatively intact in early modern Rothenburg and its hinterland to remain the most crucial weapon in the armoury of strategies for coping with witchcraft that the inhabitants of the area possessed. And as long as this system retained its resilience, there was less reason for the inhabitants of city and hinterland to look to the law as the most important or effective means of dealing with suspected witches.

Notes

1 StAN Ro. Rep. 2087 fols 99r–113r. The only books published by a Rothenburger on the subject of magic were *Neue Teuffels-Stücklein* (Frankfurt, 1678) and *Greuel des Segensprechens* (Nuremberg, 1680), written by Superintendent Johann Ludwig Hartmann against the sin of white magic.

2 Although the first volume of Consistorium minutes (1559–1605) is missing, extracts from it were recorded in the eighteenth century by Johann Ludwig Schäfer in *Auszug aus den Consistorialacten des ehemal. Rothenburg. Consistorium* (held in the archive of Rothenburg's parish church of St Jakob). The Consistorium was dominated by its secular members, as two of the three councillors who staffed it were city-mayors. The clerics were the Superintendent (Rothenburg's foremost cleric), the preacher of St Jakob's and one of its deacons, who kept the minutes.

3 RStA Interrogation Book A877 fols 557v–558v. These were similar to the acts of maleficium listed by Pope Innocent VIII in his Bull *Summis Desiderantes* of 1484, which forms the Preface to the *Malleus Maleficarum*; see Kramer, *Malleus Maleficarum*, pp. 101–107.

4 StAN Ro. Rep. 2087 fols 103v–104r.

5 RStA Interrogation Book A902 (unpaginated), 22 December 1662–31 July 1663 (case

involving Michael Würth); RStA Interrogation Book A908 (unpaginated) 11 July–11 October 1671 (case involving Appolonia Glaitter); StAN Ro. Rep. 2087 fols 621r–739r (1689).

6 RStA Interrogation Book A873 fol. 389r.
7 RStA Interrogation Book A877 fols 555r–558v.
8 RStA Interrogation Book A886 fol. 283r.
9 StAN Ro. Rep. 2087 fol. 105v.
10 Ibid., fol. 104v; RStA Interrogation Book A886 fol. 283r.
11 RStA Interrogation Book A877 fol. 567v.
12 RStA Interrogation Book A886 fol. 283r: 'dem teufflischen willen nach'.
13 Ibid., 'mit schedlichen Zaubersegen, mit gifft vom Teuffel zubereittet, oder andern ungebürlichen künsten, durch hülffe dess Teuffels' (emphasis mine).
14 StAN Ro. Rep. 2087 fols 102r–102v: 'auff ihr sonder gebett vnd anruffen' (emphasis mine).
15 For the work of Brenz, see Midelfort, Witch Hunting, pp. 36–33; for Weyer, see Midelfort, A History of Madness, pp. 196–213.
16 See for example the cases involving Margaretha Horn (pp. 180–192) and Catharina Leimbach (pp. 150–160).
17 RStA Interrogation Book A886 fol. 283v: 'die Zauberer soltu nicht leben lassen' (Exodus 22: 18).
18 Radbruch, Die Peinliche Gerichtsordnung, p. 78.
19 RStA Surety Book A844 fols 199v–200r.
20 RStA Surety Book A849 fols 296r–298r.
21 Radbruch, Die Peinliche Gerichtsordnung, p. 87.
22 See pp. 26–27.
23 See above, n. 19.
24 See for example a case involving Kunigundt, who accused her sister Anna of having lamed her husband through witchcraft in 1572, RStA Surety Book A851 fols 509v–510r, and Appendix. In 1576 a woman called Barbara Muller was banished with her family: during interrogation she was asked about her alleged ability to lame people through witchcraft. However, her punishment was for quarrelsomeness, slander and generally verbally disruptive behaviour, with which she had upset her neighbours for many years, see RStA Interrogation Book A870 fols 137r–138r; Surety Book A851 fols 367r–368v.
25 See pp. 136–143 for discussion of Dürr's case. In 1673 Anna Margaretha Rohn was executed after she had claimed to have been possessed by the devil for seven years and after confessing to several acts of infanticide, which she had almost certainly not committed. In 1692 Barbara Ehness was executed after poisoning her lodgers – although none of them died – and then confessing that she had done this at the devil's bidding. See Appendix for both cases.
26 StAN Ro. Rep. 2087 fols 105r–105v.
27 RStA Interrogation Book A886 fol. 283r.
28 RStA Blood Book B331 fols 202v–208r. This was probably the same Jobst Unger who was the guardian of self-confessed witch Margaretha Hörber, whose case is discussed pp. 105–124.
29 RStA Interrogation Book A886 fols 283r–283v.
30 Ibid., fols 283v, 285v–286v.
31 Ibid., fols 285v–286r.
32 On Thumm, see Midelfort, Witch Hunting, p. 50; Clark, Thinking With Demons, p. 166, 210. On Weyer, see Midelfort, A History of Madness, pp. 204–205.
33 RStA Interrogation Book A886 fol. 286r. On Gödelmann, see Clark, Thinking With Demons, pp. 203–204, 209–210, 519.
34 RStA Interrogation Book A886 fol. 286v; see also Haustein, 'Martin Luther', p. 40.
35 See Chapter 1, n. 13. The idea that the apostate should be taught the error of her ways rather than punished was also central to thinking about witchcraft in the Palatinate and helps explain why the elites there showed no enthusiasm for prosecuting witches: see Schmidt, Glaube und Skepsis, pp. 131–137, 215, 479.

36 See Midelfort, *A History of Madness*, p. 194, although Midelfort points out that the *Carolina* decreed that a child could be punished as an adolescent or adult if it was felt that his/her malice made up for his/her age. For Hörber's trial see pp. 105–124; for that involving Schürz, see pp. 150–160 (especially 150–151); for Hörner's trial, see p. 62 and Rowlands, 'The "Little witch girl"'. Self-confessed boy-witches could also be treated in this way: see the case of Hans Adam Knöspel, 1689, in the Appendix.
37 StAN Ro. Rep. 2087 fols 104v–106r. For discussion of this view at Tübingen see Midelfort, *Witch Hunting*, pp. 34–46.
38 RStA Interrogation Book A895 fols 172r–173r.
39 Kramer, *Der Hexenhammer*, pp. 360, 366–368, 372, 373–374, 381, 479, 480–481; RStA Interrogation Book A886 fol. 274r. This was the first citation of the *Malleus* in a Rothenburg witchcraft case.
40 See Chapters 3 and 5.
41 RStA Interrogation Book A875 fol. 211v.
42 *Ibid.*, fols 221r–222r.
43 Midelfort, *Witch Hunting*, pp. 15–16. These were the popular beliefs in the wild ride discussed in the Introduction.
44 For the *Episcopi* tradition at Tübingen, see Midelfort, *Witch Hunting*, pp. 34–46.
45 RStA Interrogation Book A877 fols 577r–577v (1587); RStA Steinach Village Acts A739 fol. 471v (1602).
46 RStA Interrogation Book A895 fols 171r–171v.
47 RStA Interrogation Book A886 fols 284v, 274r–274v.
48 *Ibid.*, fols 269(a)r–269(a)v.
49 See p. 24 for the Seitz and Brandt cases; p. 62 for the case of Hörner.
50 See pp. 105–124 for the trial of Hörber and pp. 150–160 for that involving Schürz.
51 See pp. 23–24, 27–28.
52 See for example the advice given by the jurists in Margaretha Hörber's case in 1627, RStA Interrogation Book A886 fols 275v–276r, 277v–278r; and in Brigitta Hörner's case in 1639, RStA Interrogation Book A895 fol. 172v. However, this caution was a result of the elites' problematic encounter with Rothenburg's first child-witch in 1587, in a case in which their treatment of the child and his mother was severe by their standards: see Chapter 3 for details.
53 See for example Margaretha Hörber's trial, pp. 105–124.
54 See Chapter 1, pp. 32–33, for the elites' belief in the difficulty of proving witchcraft at law.
55 See n. 41 (1582); n. 45 (1602); n. 52 (1639).
56 RStA Interrogation Book A886 fols 283r–283v.
57 StAN Ro. Rep. 2087 fols 101r, 102r–102v.
58 *Ibid.*, fols 103r–105v.
59 *Ibid.*, fols 107v–110v.
60 *Ibid.*, fols 95r–97v.
61 Robisheaux, 'Zur Rezeption Benedict Carpzovs'.
62 Cark, *Thinking With Demons*, p. 205.
63 *Ibid.*; see pp. 204–208 for general discussion of their works.
64 *Ibid.*, p. 205.
65 See pp. 24–33 for discussion of these ideas.
66 Woltering, *Die Reichsstadt Rothenburg*, vols. I and II; Moritz, *Die Folgen des Dreissigjährigen Krieges*, pp. 21–53.
67 Woltering, *Die Reichsstadt Rothenburg*, vol. II, p. 99.
68 Schnurrer, 'Die Rechtssatzungen', nos. 801, 803, 805, 807, 842, 869, 901, 942, 957.
69 Moritz, *Die Folgen des Dreissigjährigen Krieges*, pp. 132–176.
70 See Chapter 1, pp. 24–29.
71 See map of Rothenburg and its hinterland.
72 See pp. 24–25.

73 For Prenninger's advice, see RStA Interrogation Book A884 fols 559v–560r; for the Rost case, see pp. 24, 27–28.
74 RStA Interrogation Book A895 fols 165r–174v, 408r–420v. See also Rowlands, 'The "Little witch girl"'.
75 RStA Municipal Account Book R528 fol. 591v.
76 StAN Ro. Rep. 2092 fols 53r–54r.
77 Schormann, *Der Krieg*, pp. 160–163.
78 *Ibid.*, pp. 67, 168–169; Merzbacher, 'Geschichte des Hexenprozesses', p. 175.
79 Schattenmann, *Die Einführung der Reformation*, pp. 86–118; Moritz, *Die Folgen des Dreissigjährigen Krieges*, pp. 54–62.
80 RStA Interrogation Book A884 fol. 559r.
81 RStA Interrogation Book A902 (unpaginated) 2 February 1663 (Michael Würth case), and RStA Interrogation Book A909 (unpaginated) 22 June 1673 (Anna Margaretha Rohn case), for Höfel; RStA Interrogation Book A875 fols 221r–223v for Gugel and Hardessheim.
82 They were retained by the council between 1577 and 1586 (Gugel) and 1577 and 1585 (Hardessheim); see RStA Account Books R525a, R526 (General Expenditure sections).
83 RStA Interrogation Book A875 fols 211r–215r.
84 RStA Interrogation Book A908 (unpaginated) 19 August 1671 (Appolonia Glaitter case). The council had asked for advice from the law faculty at the University of Altdorf in a case of treasure-seeking in 1659, see StAN Ro. Rep. 2087 fols 296r–307r. It also looked to Altdorf for advice in the case of self-confessed witch Anna Margaretha Rohn in 1673, see RStA Interrogation Book A909 (unpaginated) 6 June 1673.
85 Radbruch, *Die Peinliche Gerichtsordnung*, pp. 130–131.
86 See Kunstmann, *Zauberwahn*, for details.
87 There is, for example, no evidence of correspondence between Rothenburg and Nuremberg about Rothenburg's witchcraft cases in the Nuremberg sources: *Ratsverlässe* (Council Minutes, StAN Rep. 60a); *Briefbücher* (Council Correspondence, StAN Rep. 61a); *Ratschlagbücher* (Books of Legal Opinions, StAN Rep. 51 and 51a). Nor is there evidence of any links in further volumes of Rothenburg's Books of Legal Opinions and Legal Correspondence: RStA B230, B231, A372–A382, A390, A394.
88 RStA Account Books R524, R525, R525a (General Expenditure sections); Schattenmann, *Die Einführung der Reformation*, pp. 105–118.
89 *Ibid.*, pp. 93–96; Kunstmann, *Zauberwahn*, pp. 63–65.
90 RStA Account Books R525–R529 (External Travel Expenditure sections); RStA B186 (lists of councillors, 1230–1669) and B186a (council elections, 1300–1720); RStA B511 (lists of council appointees), preface: list of jurists; Steinmeyer, *Die Matrikel der Universität Altdorf*.
91 RStA Account Book R526 (General Expenditure sections from 1586).
92 Kunstmann, *Zauberwahn*, pp. 188–191.
93 StAN Ro. Rep. 2087 fol. 109v.
94 Midelfort, *Witch Hunting*, pp. 36–38. The Brenz sermon on hailstorms has been discussed most recently by Sönke Lorenz, 'Brenz' Predigt vom Hagel'.
95 Midelfort, *Witch Hunting*, pp. 40–41.
96 *Ibid.*, pp. 51–52.
97 Schattenmann, *Die Einführung der Reformation*, pp. 118–129.
98 *Ibid.*, pp. 121–122.
99 RStA Council Library, Theology Section nos. 463, 284–286; Miscellaneous Section no. 68.
100 RStA Account Book R525a fol. 292r; Schattenmann, *Die Einführung der Reformation*, pp. 142–146.
101 Schattenmann, 'Rothenburger Studenten', pp. 31–33; Hermelink, *Die Matrikeln der Universität Tübingen*; RStA Account Books R524–R526 (General Expenditure sections); RStA B511 (council appointees), preface: list of jurists.
102 RStA Interrogation Book A875 fols 209r–219r (Renger, Thalhaimer, Metzler); RStA Interrogation Book A877 fols 577r–579v (Prenninger); RStA Steinach Village Acts A739 fols

471r–476r (Prenninger and Bezold); RStA Interrogation Book A886 fols 277r–278v, 298r–300r (Seuter).

103 StAN Ro. Rep. 2087 fol. 106v.

104 Midelfort, *Witch Hunting*, pp. 36–56.

105 RStA Interrogation Book A886 fols 283r–286v; Dannheimer, *Verzeichnis*, p. 144. See also pp. 53–54, 114–115, 123, for further discussion of Zyrlein's advice.

106 Behringer argues that Nuremberg and Augsburg were leaders of opinion and exerted a restraining influence on smaller cities in southern Germany, *Hexenverfolgung in Bayern*, p. 156. However, the myriad channels of communication between the south-German cities on the subject of witchcraft remain largely unexplored.

107 Dillinger, 'Hexenverfolgungen in Städten'.

108 This point is made by Behringer, *Hexenverfolgung in Bayern*, pp. 196–198.

109 Rowlands, 'Witchcraft and popular magic', pp. 114–115.

110 See for example RStA Interrogation Book A874 fol. 29v; RStA Interrogation Book A981 fols 470r–484r.

111 See for example StAN Ro. Rep. 2090 fol. 125r; RStA Interrogation Book A898 fols 486r–488r.

112 RStA Interrogation Book A911 (unpaginated) 13 May 1676 (case of Hans Horn and son); RStA Interrogation Book A920 fols 143r–150v; StAN Ro. Rep. 2090 fol. 163r.

113 RStA Interrogation Book A874 fol. 39r.

114 See for example StAN Ro. Rep. 2091 fol. 137r (1623); RStA Interrogation Book A902 (unpaginated), Michael Würth case, 22 December 1662–31 July 1663.

115 StAN Ro. Rep. 2089 fol. 108r.

116 RStA Interrogation Book A874 fols 35v–36r, 40v–41r.

117 StAN Ro. Rep. 2089 fol. 80v.

118 *Ibid.*, fols 101r–101v.

119 See *ibid.*, fols 101r–101v, and StAN Ro. Rep. 2090 fol. 114r for Grönn's activities; RStA Account Book R527 fol. 325r for his banishment. No interrogation or surety has survived for his case.

120 For Fischer's arrest on the complaint of a dissatisfied customer, see RStA Account Book R528 fol. 116v; no other records of his case survive. For his activities in 1641, see discussion of the Margaretha Rost case, pp. 144–150.

121 See Chapter 5 for discussion of the gendering of witchcraft in Rothenburg.

122 StAN Ro. Rep. 2090 fol. 114r.

123 *Ibid.*, fols 120v–121r.

124 StAN Ro. Rep. 2091 fols 139r, 232r; 2089 fols 38v, 80v; 2090 fols 112r, 123r, 177r; Rücker, *Mundus personatus*, pp. 66–71; Hartmann, *Greuel des Segensprechens* and *Neue Teuffels-Stücklein*.

125 Clark, 'Protestant demonology', p. 60.

126 *Ibid.*, p. 66.

127 RStA Ordinances A363 fols 49v–50r.

128 RStA Interrogation Book A981 fols 470r–484r (case from 1760); on the continuity of popular use of magic into the eighteenth century in Lutheran Germany, see Rublack, 'Success and failure', especially pp. 159–161. For ordinances, see RStA Ordinances A1269 fols 42r–42v (1643), A365 fols 282r–285v (1666), A366a fols 185r–198v (1685).

129 Wagner, 'Hexenglaube in Franken heute'.

130 See for example StAN Ro. Rep. 2089 fol. 43v; 2091 fols 38r, 141r.

131 There were no visitations between 1621 and 1642, many churches fell into disrepair and many parishes were without pastors: StAN Ro. Rep. 2096 fols 33r–65r; Moritz, *Die Folgen des Dreissigjährigen Krieges*, pp. 17–32.

132 See Rowlands, 'Witchcraft and popular religion', p. 116; StAN Ro. Rep. 2089 fol. 80v; RStA Interrogation Book A921 fols 147r, 149r.

133 This was part of what C. Scott Dixon has usefully labelled the 'process of dissimulation'

parishioners had to engage in when talking to the authorities about magic after the Reformation in Lutheran areas; see Dixon, *The Reformation and Rural Society*, pp. 162–202.

134 StAN Ro. Rep. 2090 fols 120v–121r.

135 *Ibid.*, fols 163r–163v.

136 See for example the case of Dorothea Lang, RStA Surety Book A851 fols 210r–210v, StAN Ro. Rep. 2089 fols 72r–72v (1574); RStA Council Minutes B45 fol. 128r (fine of Michel Klenck for consulting a cunning man, 1671).

137 See Chapter 1, p. 18 and n. 13.

138 StAN Ro. Rep. 2089 fols 32r, 33r–35r, 83v.

139 StAN Ro. Rep. 2090 fols 176r–176v. The *Carolina* stated explicitly that nobody should be arrested or questioned under torture on the basis of the testimony of a cunning man or woman, but rather that the latter should be punished for their activities; see Radbruch, *Die Peinliche Gerichtsordnung*, clause 21, pp. 40–41.

140 StAN Ro. Rep. 2089 fols 101r–101v; 2090 fols 112r, 114r–114v, 120v–121r.

141 StAN Ro. Rep. 2092 fols 48v, 50r; RStA Ordinances A1269 fols 42r–42v. Fischer had already been mentioned by name in an ordinance issued by the council in 1639, see RStA Ordinances A363 fols 279r–282r.

142 RStA Surety Book A849 fols 258r–259r.

143 RStA Blood Book B329 fols 138r–139r. Worn in an amulet, mandragora was highly valued as a means of protecting the wearer against illness and misfortune; see Labouvie, *Verbotene Künste*, p. 99.

144 RStA Blood Book B331 fols 3r–6v; Interrogation Book A873 fols 296r–399v.

145 See RStA Blood Book B331 fols 8r–11v, Interrogation Book A874 fols 24r–54v for Kissling's case; Blood Book B331 fols 220r–222r for Geuder's sentence.

146 See above, n. 144 for Gebhart's case documents.

147 See for example the case of Christoph Vogel of Bettwar from 1687, RStA Interrogation Book A920 fols 143r–150v.

148 RStA Ordinances A363 fols 48r–50r.

149 See for example the case of Peter Fischer, n. 120.

150 This appears to have happened with Peter Fischer, whose home in Buch am Wald lay in territory belonging to the Margrave of Brandenburg-Ansbach; see the case involving Margaretha Rost, pp. 144–150.

151 StAN Ro. Rep. 2090 fols 125r–125v, 176r–177v.

152 Peter Fischer was cautious about identifying anyone specifically as responsible for Michael Rost's bewitchment in 1641, for example, and also gave Rost remedies for his bewitched leg which involved no use of quasi-religious blessings, perhaps in order to avoid undue arousal of the authorities' anger: see pp. 144–150 for discussion of this case.

3

'One cannot ... hope to obtain the slightest certainty from him': the first child-witch in Rothenburg, 1587

It is, of course, only with the benefit of hindsight that we can draw conclusions about the relative restraint with which the council in Rothenburg treated witch-craft during the early modern period; this restraint was never a foregone con-clusion in any particular witch-trial. The intricate web of factors which accounted for it could be tested to the limits in certain cases when an individual's story of witchcraft and the manner in which the council chose to investigate it threatened – albeit usually only fleetingly – to produce verdicts of guilt against alleged witches, and even to foster larger-scale episodes of witch-hunting. This happened for the first time in Rothenburg in 1587, when a six-year-old boy called Hans Gackstatt from the hinterland village of Hilgartshausen, told a tale of nocturnal flight to a witches' dance which started an investigation of dubious legality and physical severity against his mother and himself from which other inhabitants of Hilgartshausen were not initially entirely safe. The Hilgartshausen case was, in fact, the precursor of an increasing number of particularly prob-lematic trials involving self-confessed child-witches dealt with by the councillors and their advisers in the seventeenth century. Their engagement with these cases had the long-term effect of deepening their concern about witchcraft and of intensifying their hostility towards what they increasingly came to regard as the archetypal witch-figure: the bad mother.

Hans Gackstatt began telling a story of night-flying with his mother and a black, horned man in the late summer of 1587. He claimed to have eaten a supper of bread rolls and milk before the three of them had flown out of a hole in the Gackstatt's cow-stall on a fire-iron which had first been smeared with a magical salve; the black man had signalled the start of their journey by firing a shot into the air. Hans had been seated in the middle of the fire-iron, with his mother behind him and the black man in front. First they had flown into vari-ous houses in Hilgartshausen to look for money and eggs, some of which they had stolen. Then they had flown into the cellar of the village tavern belonging to Lorentz Dolmann and had drunk the wine stored there. Here the black man had given Hans' mother a leather sack full of wine which she had taken home with her, and from which Hans and his mother had drunk their fill, giving his father, Martin Gackstatt, none of it. Then they had flown to the common meadow of the village, where the black man had played the pipes and they had danced near a tree called the Witches' Tree. Other Hilgartshausen women, including Anna, the wife of Jörg Brodt, had accompanied them on the ride, and Hans claimed to have partnered Babelein, the thirteen-year-old daughter of Hans Kuch junior, at the dance.[1]

Hans initially told his tale to other Hilgartshausen boys, but it soon spread among the adults, and by early September the village was full of it. Like stones thrown into a pond, Hans' words spread enmity and discord in ever-widening ripples within the community. Beginning in his own family, it provoked an extremely angry reaction from his mother, Magdalena. Lienhardt Herman, the village official who brought the story of witchcraft to the attention of the council on 8 September, claimed to have seen Magdalena twice chase Hans out of their house at night, hitting him and threatening to stab him with a knife; once she had also carried a rope and had threatened to hang herself as well.[2] Later, in custody, Magdalena denied that she had threatened to commit suicide, but admitted that she had once said, in anger, that it would be no surprise if she did kill her son, when he falsely accused her of such a thing – meaning witchcraft.[3] That this degree of hostility was regarded as a justifiable response on the part of a mother who had been made the subject of a potentially life-threatening accusation of witchcraft by her own son is evident from the statement given by another inhabitant of Hilgartshausen, Georg Rigel's wife Ursula, who was later asked to testify in the case. She stated that she herself had once told Hans that he was a villain who was making his parents' life a misery with his talk of witchcraft, and that he deserved to have been drowned in his first bath, or to be hung up by his toes now, as a punishment for it.[4]

Hans' talk also caused enmity between his mother and one of her neighbours: Anna, the wife of Jörg Brodt, who Hans claimed had accompanied them on the night-ride. In his report to the council on 8 September, Lienhardt Herman described how the two women had exchanged insults and threats as a result of the story told by Hans. Anna had learned what Hans was saying about her during the six-week lying-in period following the birth of her youngest child and had acted on the news the minute her lying-in had ended. She had accosted Magdalena Gackstatt, called her an old baggage, and accused her of bringing Hans up badly – in other words, to spread rumours of witchcraft – and of teaching him to call her (Anna) a witch. Anna had said that while Magdalena herself might be a witch, she (Anna) was not, and had promised Magdalena that she would not leave the allegations made by Hans unchallenged, even if she had to take the matter before the council in the form of a slander suit. Magdalena had denied the suggestion that she was to blame for Hans' talk, the anger between the two women had increased, and they had threatened to stab one another.[5] The altercation between the women hinted at two themes which were to be taken up later in the case by the councillors. The first of these was that Magdalena, rather than Hans' father Martin Gackstatt, was held responsible for the boy's behaviour. The second was that this responsibility put Magdalena in a double bind. If Hans' story were deemed true, it threatened to confirm her guilt as a witch. If this did not happen, however, it still threatened to give her a reputation as a bad mother, who had brought her son up to talk loosely and to slander other people with unfounded allegations.

Finally, Hans' story spread discord among the men of Hilgartshausen. On 6 September, Jorg Dolman had been discussing it in the village tavern with his cousin, Hans Stoll, and several other men. During their discussion Dolman had ventured to suggest to Stoll that Stoll's wife had been implicated in Hans' story as one of the night-flying witches. Dolman had, however, been careful to preface his comments with a plea for forgiveness, so that Stoll would not misconstrue them as a public accusation of his wife which needed avenging by Stoll or proving by Dolman, and they had taken leave of one another that night amicably. Matters went differently the next night, however, as the Hilgartshausen *Gemeinde* – all the male household heads, constituting the formal political community of the village – were gathered in the tavern for a communal drinking session. At the end of the evening Dolman had woken Stoll and told him that he should be helping to organise the settling of the bill. Stoll had reacted angrily, and possibly drunkenly, to this implied dereliction of duty, and accused Dolman of having called his wife a witch the night before. Dolman had denied this, insisting that his remarks about her had been made in jest and had not been meant seriously. Stoll had called Dolman a liar, Dolman had thrown a pitcher of wine in Stoll's face, and the two of them had begun brawling. Lienhardt Herman, who was the village official with special responsibility to help maintain order in Hilgartshausen on behalf of the council in Rothenburg, had intervened to try to stop the fight, but without success.[6]

Herman went into Rothenburg to tell the council about the damaging effects Hans Gackstatt's story was having on life in Hilgartshausen on 8 September because, as he put it, he feared that 'no good, but perhaps rather a murder will result from the affair'.[7] Herman's concerns on this score were probably genuine, but the fact that he reported to the council the day after the brawl in the tavern and devoted most of his report to it suggests that he had also taken umbrage at the fact that his own authority had been slighted. Dolman and Stoll had not only refused to heed his order to keep the peace in the tavern, but Dolman had sworn at him and denied his authority to fine him for starting the brawl, claiming instead that only the *Gemeinde* could legitimately do this. In addition, a bystander called Adam Siler had entered the fray in support of Dolman and sworn at Herman, who Siler had thought was trying to interfere in the settling of the drinking bill of the *Gemeinde*.[8] This was a very touchy subject, as the men of the *Gemeinde* had been bitterly divided among themselves since October 1586 by a legal dispute over the village accounts which centred on disagreements about money spent at communal drinking sessions and in which Siler and Herman took different sides.[9] In this context, and with this dispute still on-going, Herman evidently thought it best to pass the peace-keeping buck to the council.

The council responded by arresting Jorg Dolman, Adam Siler and Hans Stoll and by calling Hans Gackstatt, his mother and Anna Brodt into Rothenburg to give an account of themselves on 15 September. The three men were soon released from custody after swearing sureties, with Dolman and Siler also being fined 10 gulden each for brawling and insulting the authority of Lienhardt Herman.[10] With order restored among the men, the council turned its attention to the cause of all the trouble: the story told by Hans Gackstatt. In keeping with the usually cautious manner in which the inhabitants of Rothenburg and its hinterland spoke about witchcraft to the authorities, Herman had repeated it in only a very cursory fashion at the end of his report to the council on 8 September and had been careful to add that he could not say whether or not it was true.[11] The statement that Hans himself made in Rothenburg on 15 September did not, however, get the councillors any nearer the truth of the matter. First Hans said that another youngster from Hilgartshausen, thirteen-year-old Peter Streng, a goose-boy whose widowed mother lodged with householder Bartl Kurtz, had taught him the whole night-flying story and had instructed him to spread it about the village. Then Hans repeated the story as if it had really happened, but concluded his statement with the remark that he had learned the whole thing, including the names of the people he claimed to have seen at the dance, from Peter.[12] Magdalena Gackstatt confirmed the suspicions against Peter, informing the council that Hans had told her that Peter had taught him the story and had promised him some marbles as a reward if he would tell it to others.[13] In the face of the contradictory testimony given by Hans and in line with its usual policy of consulting communal opinion, the council called various other inhabitants of Hilgartshausen into the city over the next few days to ask them what they knew about the rumours of witchcraft that were circulating in their village.

Peter Streng was the first to testify. Perhaps unfortunately for the councillors, who probably hoped to end the case rapidly by pinning the blame for the witchcraft story on the older boy, Peter denied having taught Hans anything and asserted that Hans had first told him the story one day in late July, as he had been sheltering from the rain in a stable belonging to Bartl Kurtz.[14] Kurtz's ten-

year-old son, another Hans, and his twenty-year-old farm-hand, Michl
Kupper, had also been there, and they subsequently gave accounts of the occasion which agreed closely with that given by Peter.[15] Peter also reported having
heard that Hans had threatened to stir up a wind which would blow away the
recently harvested corn in Hilgartshausen, while Michl Kupper said that Hans
had been heard to boast that he had ridden tavern-keeper Lorentz Dolman's
horse to exhaustion on a nocturnal visit to the tavern.[16] Goose-herd Endres
Sturmer and Georg Rigel's wife, Ursula, added further details about threats
made by Hans in their statements to the council: they both reported that they
had heard Hans threaten to press to death two other village boys because they
would not give him a marble and a ribbon that he coveted.[17]

The testimony offered by other villagers regarding Magdalena Gackstatt
was, at best, ambivalent. Ursula Rigel said that she had not heard any suspicions of witchcraft raised against Magdalena other than those that her son was
now voicing, but added that she herself had not lived in Hilgartshausen for very
long.[18] Anna Brodt said the same, although as the alleged night-flying companion of Magdalena she had an obvious interest in testifying as positively about
her as possible.[19] Two of the oldest villagers, Wendel Ackerman and Hans Kuch
senior, also said that they had never heard any suspicions of witchcraft or complaints of maleficium raised against Magdalena or any other women of Hilgartshausen. Again, however, they may have had their own reasons for saying
this. The girl named Babelein whom Hans claimd to have partnered at the
witches' dance was Hans Kuch senior's grand-daughter and Hans later testified
in custody that the wives of Hans Kuchs senior and junior and of Wendel Ackerman had also been at the dance. If, as seems likely, rumours to this effect had
been circulating in Hilgartshausen before the case was brought to the attention
of the council, then the testimony given by Ackerman and Hans Kuch senior
was probably shaped by a desire to protect their own families from possible
entanglement in the legal investigation.[20]

Other villagers were less positive about Magdalena. A man named Hans
Herman stated that about ten or twelve years earlier rumours had circulated
about her in Hilgartshausen on account of this 'evil business', adding crypti-
cally that suspicions had also existed about the other women Hans Gackstatt
had named as witches.[21] However, the testimony given by tavern-keeper
Lorentz Dolman was the most detailed and potentially damaging to Magdalena. It was also a masterpiece of subtle insinuation, in which Dolman
managed to offer as much negative evidence as he could against her without
ever accusing her of anything specifically and personally. Dolman confirmed
that general rumours of witchcraft had existed against Magdalena some years
ago, but then pointed out that, just because something was said about a person
did not necessarily mean that it was true.[22] This caveat was, of course, entirely

in keeping with the council's thinking on the gulf that existed between an individual saying something and being able to prove it at law, discussed in Chapter 1, but its effect in Magdalena's favour was undercut by the fact that Dolman immediately proceeded to offer the council evidence that seemed to support the idea that witches' gatherings might have taken place in Hilgartshausen. He told the council that, about six years earlier, an old man called Peter Naiffer had often talked in his tavern about certain 'strange goings-on' he had seen taking place under the Witches' Tree in a meadow outside Hilgartshausen when walking home at night to Hilgartshausen from the neighbouring village of Brettheim.[23] Naiffer had died since – allegedly – saying this, so Dolman was able to offer the old man's testimony knowing that neither of them would have to take personal responsibility for it. Dolman stressed that he, personally, was not a rumour-monger by explaining to the council that he had instructed his servants to ignore, rather than become involved in, any conversations about Hans' night-flying story that they happened to overhear in Hilgartshausen.[24]

As Dolman's tavern figured significantly in Hans' story, Dolman was asked specifically by the council whether he had recently lost any wine or livestock in suspicious circumstances. In response to these questions Dolman again managed to insinuate much without committing himself to anything, while demonstrating an apparent ignorance of commonly held beliefs about the activities of witches which was surely feigned for the benefit of the council. For example, he said that for the past two years he had been puzzled at the rate at which the wine had seemed to disappear from his cellar, with no money to show for it. He added that it had not occurred to him to think that the wine could have been stolen by witches and had satisfied himself with the explanation his servants had given him for this state of affairs: that he served too much wine on credit![25] With regard to his livestock, Dolman explained losses he had suffered a decade or more ago in terms which made no reference to possible witchcraft. This was not the case with more recent incidents, however. For two years his cattle had fallen ill every so often, losing weight, shaking and sweating. One of Dolman's maidservants had apparently hinted at the idea that they were being plagued by witches, but Dolman claimed that he had not thought that this was possible until a recent visit to the Duchy of Württemberg, where he had heard that some women had been burned as witches there for this crime. He added that his two horses had behaved strangely over the past six weeks and that one of them was found to be dripping with sweat in its stall first thing in the morning. Dolman had thought something was wrong – the implication being that the horse was being ridden at night by witches – but was careful to emphasise that he had voiced his suspicions to no-one but his wife and could not accuse anyone of anything specific.[26]

The testimony of Dolman and Herman thus did little to help Magdalena Gackstatt. However, neither had mentioned from whom the allegedly long-standing rumours against her had originated; the repetition by Dolman of what Peter Naiffer claimed to have seen under the Witches' Tree was hearsay; and Dolman had studiously refrained from accusing her of any acts of maleficium directly. The case of witchcraft against her was thus still largely based on the testimony of Hans as the source of the night-flying story. And Hans was only six years old. Judicial opinion tended to regard children below the age of seven as legally incompetent,[27] and the idea that Hans was so young as to be almost worthless as a witness had already been suggested at the end of the contradic-tory statement made by Hans to the council on 15 September, when his inter-rogators had noted that nothing could be achieved with him on account of his youth.[28] Given the apparent weakness of the case against Magdalena, therefore, we might have expected the council to bring the matter to a close at this point, perhaps with an admonition to Hans for having spread the night-flying story so heedlessly and to his parents for having failed to discipline their son's unguarded speech adequately.

Exactly the opposite happened, however. On 23 September Magdalena was interrogated in the city gaol by councillors Georg Guckenberger and Bern-hard Mader, who began by asking her to say the creed and Our Father. Any stumbling over the words would have counted against her as additional evidence that she might be a witch who had given herself to the devil, but Magdalena acquitted herself well, falling to her knees and reciting the words with under-standing.[29] She was then asked thirty-five questions which had been drawn up in advance by the council in consultation with its jurists.[30] The questions not only reflected an apparent assumption of Magdalena's identity as a witch, but also aimed to lead her into confessing her guilt, an interrogatory tactic technically prohibited by the *Carolina*.[31] For example, Guckenberger and Mader asked her: had she given herself to Satan? What had Satan promised her in return, and had she had sex with him? Could she work magic to disrupt marriages, to interfere with men's potency and women's fertility, to cause bad weather and to harm livestock? All the livestock problems that tavern-keeper Lorentz Dolman had recounted in his earlier statement were put to Magdalena at this point, despite the fact that he had neither attributed them all to witchcraft nor accused Mag-dalena of them specifically.[32] Had she gone night-flying, or did she think that it was all merely a diabolic delusion? Where had she flown to, how often, and by what means? Here Mader and Guckenberger told her that Hans had described the magical salve that her fire-iron had supposedly been smeared with as having been made from sandstone and ashes.[33] Who were her companions? Were there other witches in Hilgartshausen? Had she taken her son night-flying with her, or otherwise taught him her arts? Did her husband have any knowledge of this, and did she keep any of the paraphernalia of her arts, such as tins of salve, in their house? Magdalena insisted vigorously on her innocence of any witchcraft throughout the interrogation, told her interrogators that they were welcome to search her house, and said that her husband was as shocked as she was that their son was causing her such misery.[34]

Hans was brought into the cell to confront his mother at this point and exhorted by Mader and Guckenberger to tell the truth on pain of a flogging. He immediately reverted to the claim that Peter Streng had taught him the whole story, leaving the authorities no nearer the truth of the matter than they had been on 15 September.[35] After some deliberation, the council decided to confront Hans with Peter Streng, who still denied having taught the younger boy anything, and with his mother, who still maintained her innocence of any witchcraft. He was also confronted with Babelein, the daughter of Hans Kuch junior, who had also been taken into custody as a result of the claims made by Hans that he had danced with her at the witches' gathering. She denied that this had ever happened. Hans reacted with inconsistency to these three encounters, repeating that Peter had taught him the story when face to face with Peter and Magdalena, then asserting that he had danced with Babelein in her presence as if the witches' dance had really happened. The session ended with Mader and Guckenberger noting that Hans said nothing consistent or credible.[36] Surely at this point, with the childish unreliability of Hans highlighted for a second time, proceedings would be halted?

Again, this did not happen. Instead, the council seems to have pinned its hopes on obtaining some physical evidence of Magdalena's guilt to buttress the shaky circumstantial evidence on which the case against her had hitherto been built. On 25 September it ordered the pastor of Hilgartshausen to search the Gackstatt residence for the leather sack Magdalena had allegedly been given by the black man of Hans' story and for her alleged night-flying equipment.[37] On 27 September, Magdalena was again interrogated on the basis of a prepared list of questions by Mader, Guckenberger and jurist Friedrich Renger.[38] The municipal executioner was also present and Magdalena was bound by him at the start of the interrogation.[39] This increased the pressure on her to confess, as it indicated to her that she was probably about to be tortured. Magdalena still maintained her innocence, however, explaining that the objects which the pastor had fetched from her house and which were solemnly shown to her by her interrogators were all put to innocent use – the fire-iron for raking ashes, and a tin of salve and a box of herbs for home remedies such as any other housewife would employ.[40] Mader, Guckenberger and Renger then took the allegedly suspicious objects to show Hans, and he obligingly identified his mother's fire-iron as the one on which he had gone night-flying. The boy added that it had been given to his mother by a black man called Hans or Lucifer, and that she had smeared it with a magical salve made out of white sand, vinegar, salt and pear-wine. These were not the same ingredients that Hans had described earlier, and at this point his interrogaters seem to have lost patience with him. They had thumbscrews put onto him – without them actually being tightened – and confronted him with his mother in an attempt to 'persuade' him to adhere to one fixed versions of events.[41]

Perhaps unsurprisingly, the threat of torture did nothing to encourage Hans to greater consistency. He still oscillated between the two contradictory statements that he had been flying with his mother, and that Peter had taught him to tell the story. Magdalena was therefore subjected once to strappado, a form of torture where the victim's arms were tied behind her back and she was hoisted up by them by means of a rope and pulley. Additional weights could be attached to the victim's feet to add to the agony; in this instance Magdalena was tortured without them, but she was hoisted up as high as possible by the executioner to increase her suffering. Peter and Babelein were both shown the instruments of torture and threatened with them, and Babelein also had her finger put into the thumbscrew without it being tightened. However, all three of them still denied everything of which Hans accused them.[42]

Later that same day, after further deliberation by the council, another, arguably even more desperate, effort was made to force Hans tell the truth, in the legal sense of a statement which was credible and, crucially, consistent in all its details no matter how often it was repeated. Hans was threatened with the thumbscrews and a flogging, but in response he only added more details to his two, still-contradictory stories. He claimed that his mother, Babelein and the black men called Hans and Lucifer had appeared at his bedside at night with cudgels and beaten him to force him into going flying with them; then, that not only Peter, but some other village boys had taught him what to say. At this point Hans was flogged by the executioner, but he continued in the same, confused vein, now telling of the milk and butter his mother had stolen on their nocturnal flight, and describing the way in which she was able to milk other people's cows magically by means of a thread wound around a bodkin. Hans was flogged again for his inconsistency – hard enough for a person of adult years, as the sources grimly note – and also subjected to the thumbscrews, but concluded by maintaining that he really had been night-flying with his mother, and that Peter the goose-boy had taught him the whole story. Peter was brought in to confront Hans again and threatened with a flogging himself, but he refused to admit having taught Hans the night-flying story.[43]

In the face of these still-contradictory versions of events, the council turned for advice about the case to another of its jurists, Friedrich Prenninger, who had been in post in the city since 1583.[44] Prenninger's legal opinion is interesting for two reasons. First, because there was no published material specifically on child-witches on which he could draw for precedents in his discussion of the Hilgartshausen case. The first German text to consider this subject explicitly was *Tractus de confessionibus maleficiorum sagarum*, published by Peter Binsfeld in 1589 and based on his personal experience of the major outbreak of witchcraft persecution that had occurred in the Electorate of Trier between 1585 and 1589 and in which self-confessed child-witches had emerged as a new problem for demonologists and judicial experts alike.[45] The advice given by Prenninger was also noteworthy because he seemed as concerned to justify what the council had already done in the case and to put a quasi-legal gloss on some of the more dubious actions the council had already authorised, as he was to advise on how to proceed in the case. This suggests that at least some of the councillors had become uneasy with the way in which the case had progressed and wished to have some vindication of the handling of the case by the council on record for posterity.

Citing the *Canon Episcopi*, Prenninger began by pointing out that he was of the opinion that witches did not really fly through the air, nor eat, drink and dance at witches' gatherings, but were deluded by Satan into merely thinking that they had done such things. However, Prenninger added that they still deserved severe treatment at the hands of the authorities because, by believing these thoughts, they denied God and bound themselves to the devil. The council had therefore been fully justified in arresting the people involved in the Hilgartshausen case.[46] Prenninger then considered the specifics of the case, and particularly the question of whether Hans' story constituted a sufficient presumption of guilt against his mother for her to have been tortured, or for her to be tortured again.[47] Prenninger approached this question from two angles, first considering the validity of the testimony given by Hans on the basis that he had already confessed to the crime of witchcraft himself, and then in view of the fact that he was a minor.

Prenninger suggested that much disagreement existed among doctors of law on both issues. On the first point, he stated that many of them argued that a self-confessed criminal who accused someone else of the same deed should not be believed, nor should his or her accusation count as a presumption of guilt against the person so accused. Other jurists, however, argued that it could be counted as a presumption of guilt sufficient to justify interrogation of the second suspect, although torture could not be used against him or her in the absence of other evidence. There was no absolute answer on this question, Prenninger concluded; procedure was left to the discretion of the presiding judge.[48] Prenninger also suggested that opinion was divided on the second issue, with many jurists arguing that the testimony of a minor constituted no, or only a 'very poor or trifling' presumption of guilt against a suspect. Others, however, suggested that the testimony of a minor might be regarded as sufficient justification for proceeding to interrogate a suspect under torture in cases where the truth could be arrived at in no other way – in other words, where no other witnesses to the alleged crime existed.[49]

Prenninger seems to have been rather uncomfortable with this second position – and possibly aware that the council was as well – as he went on to list the presumptions of guilt that had existed against Magdalena other than her son's testimony upon which the council had acted: the general rumours that had circulated against her in Hilgartshausen, the denunciation by Lienhardt Herman, and the altercation between Magdalena and Anna Brodt.[50] Here Prenninger glossed over, or appeared to have forgotten, the fact that the rumours against Magdalena had never been traced back to their original source and that the altercation between the two women and the denunciation of Magdalena by Herman had both been caused by Hans' testimony anyway. Of most importance, however, was the fact that Prenninger came to the conclusion that this evidence against Magdalena had been cancelled out by the torture she had already suffered without conceding her guilt, and that no further action against her or any of the other people Hans had implicated in his story was justified on the basis of the existing evidence against them.[51]

As far as Hans was concerned, Prenninger was keen to stress that the council had not contravened the law in having had Hans flogged for his contradictory testimony,[52] a point of view which pre-empted the argument of Binsfeld in *Tractus de confessionibus* that beatings could be inflicted on child-witches below the age of fourteen if they proved recalcitrant during interrogation.[53] Behringer warns us against seeing the beating of children in a legal context during the early modern period as exceptionally severe, as they were also beaten in other contexts.[54] The records of the Rothenburg Consistorium, for example, contain instances of children being physically punished – sometimes quite severely – by pastors in Catechism classes, by teachers in schools, and on the orders of Consistorium members, who believed that domestic discipline should be upheld by parents by means of beatings as well as words.[55] What was unusual about the treatment of Hans was that he had been subjected to the 'adult' form of torture of the thumbscrews. This severity on the part of the council can perhaps be explained by its increasing frustration with him and by the fact that this was their first encounter with the perplexing phenomenon of the self-confessed child-witch, and was not repeated in later cases.[56] Significantly, however, the council did not continue to torture either Hans or his mother in the hope that this would eventually elicit the 'truth' from them. Prenninger ended his advice to the council by concluding that Hans' statements had remained so inconsistent that there was no point in torturing him any further, because 'one cannot obtain or hope to obtain the slightest certainty from him'.[57] Prenninger therefore advised the council to drop a case in which 'one can neither discover the truth nor come to any certain conclusions', which it duly did with the release of the suspects by early October.[58]

But why had the council pursued the case for so long, given that the unreliability of Hans as a witness had been apparent from the beginning? Why had the council arrested, interrogated and tortured a six-year-old child and his mother, and arrested, interrogated and threatened to torture two other children, on the basis of such dubious testimony, when in 1582 the story told by Margaretha Seitz of a witches' gathering in Oberstetten had been dismissed without any of the alleged witches being taken into custody?[59] Council policy in 1587 cannot be accounted for in terms of a sudden change in council personnel, with new men adopting a tougher stance in witchcraft cases. Of the sixteen men who had been councillors in 1582, fourteen, including all five mayors, were still there in 1587.[60] Of the two jurists involved in the Hilgartshausen case, Prenninger had been newly appointed since 1582, but his advice in 1587 and subsequent witchcraft cases showed him to be anything but an advocate of the zealous pursuit of suspected witches.[61] It was rather the case in 1587 that the council became convinced enough of the possibility that a witches' gathering might *really* have occurred in Hilgartshausen, concerned enough about the spiritual good of the boy who had apparently been taken to it, and – ultimately – frustrated enough by his inconsistent testimony about the affair, to abandon momentarily its usually cautious legal approach in its efforts to investigate the case.

In Chapter 2 I argued that elite opinion in Rothenburg on the question of whether or not witches' dances and the flights to them took place in the imagination or in reality tended to veer towards scepticism. However, this scepticism about the reality of witches' dances was by no means absolute. Jurists in Rothenburg were well aware of the body of demonology that existed arguing that flights and sabbats occurred in reality; in 1627 jurist Schäfer hedged his bets on the issue by concluding that, whereas he believed that Margaretha Hörber had not really flown to a witches' dance, in other cases the devil might physically transport people from place to place.[62] Each allegation of witchcraft that jurists and councillors were faced with challenged and tested their scepticism afresh, and their reactions were by no means a forgeone conclusion. What tested it to the limit in 1587 was the fact that the teller of the tale of witchcraft with which they were confronted was so young and his tale so detailed. Where could a six-year-old boy possibly have obtained such a detailed knowledge of such evil matters from? And what possible motivation could he – unlike an adult, who might have made a witchcraft accusation in pursuit of a feud – have had for telling a story with such potentially damaging consequences for his own mother, not to mention himself? As far as the council was concerned there were only two possible answers to these questions:

either Peter Streng had taught him the tale, or the events Hans described had really happened. Because Peter denied any part in the affair, and because his denials were supported by the testimony of the other boys who claimed to have first heard Hans recount his story, the councillors were faced with the thought that the night-flight and witches' gathering might really have happened. While their failure to entertain the possibility that Hans could have invented the tale by himself says little for their ability to acknowledge the fertility of young children's imaginations, it does suggest that they found it hard to regard such children as so wilfully sinful that they could create and disseminate damaging rumours deliberately and maliciously.

Wolfgang Behringer and Rainer Walz have also argued that self-confessed child-witches were usually taken seriously elsewhere in early modern Germany, because the belief in the inherent innocence of children, combined with the fact that they accused themselves and others of witchcraft voluntarily and apparently without motive, made it very difficult for adults who believed in the possibility of witchcraft to dismiss their statements as lies or childish fantasies.[63] Walz in fact argues that the testimony of self-confessed child-witches was regarded as 'a proof of the existence of witches that was virtually impossible to refute',[64] and one which tended to reinforce whatever particular suspicions of witchcraft were currently under discussion within their communities.[65] Behringer also suggests that voluntary confessions and accusations of witchcraft made by children were particularly shocking and difficult to deal with because they shattered the code of relative silence that most adults maintained on the subject of witchcraft most of the time.[66] This was almost certainly the case in Rothenburg. In the eyes of the councillors the wealth of detail of Hans' story and his willingness to repeat it must have contrasted vividly with the usually brief, vague comments that many of the adults who testified in other witchcraft cases – either as plaintiffs, defendants or witnesses – were willing to offer. Hans' story had doubtless also caused such disruption in Hilgartshausen before it came to the attention of the council because he had uttered it in blissful ignorance of the customary codes and formulae by which most adults regulated their speech about witchcraft among themselves. This rendered it almost impossible to handle in the village without the intervention of the authorities, and also inclined the villagers to think that there might be some truth in the matter because, as Hans Stoll put it, Hans Gackstatt talked so much of it.[67]

At the start of the case, then, Hans seems to have been perceived by the councillors and jurists as a child whose innocence had been corrupted and whose spiritual well-being had been placed in jeopardy by the pernicious influence of older individuals upon his impressionable mind and conscience: either by Peter Streng, who had taught him to spread the night-flying story, or by his mother, who had initiated him into the evil arts of witchcraft. Had Hans managed to stick to just one of his two contradictory statements after his arrest, the case would have taken a different course. Either Peter or Magdalena would have faced a great deal more pressure to confess their alleged guilt and possible punishment as a slanderer or witch, respectively, while Hans might have been able to preserve his persona as corrupted innocent in the eyes of the council, with perhaps no worse a consequence to himself than a spell of re-education in the city hospital to wean him off his witchcraft beliefs. However, as the case progressed, the inconsistency of Hans – or his inability to tell the truth, as the councillors saw it – gradually lost him whatever sympathy he had once enjoyed in their eyes, and ultimately convinced Prenninger that he was a 'young villain', rather than the innocent party of the affair.[68]

The council appeared to have had little sympathy for Magdalena Gackstatt throughout the case. At worst, she was a woman who had not only given up her own soul to witchcraft, but also introduced her own son to the same black arts, thereby transgressing the most natural of human emotions – a mother's love for her child – and the most sacred of parental duties – the raising of God-fearing children in the Lutheran faith. At best, she was a negligent mother, who had failed to bring up her son to know that it was wrong to tell stories of witchcraft about other people to all and sundry with no heed of the consequences. The council's low opinion of the mothering abilities of Magdalena was implied at the beginning of the case on 15 September, when it was noted that, despite the fact that he was six years old, Hans was not yet able to say the Lord's Prayer, and made explicit on 23 September, when Magdalena was asked why she had neither taught Hans to pray properly nor raised him to be more God-fearing.[69]

Lutherans placed huge emphasis on the inculcation of the tenets of their faith through rote learning of the Ten Commandments, the Creed, the Lord's Prayer and the sacraments of baptism and communion, which all children had to learn and recite verbatim – preferably with understanding – before they could take their first communion.[70] Knowledge of these articles of faith, displayed through accurate recitation of them, was believed to provide individuals with the spiritual armour necessary to protect them from any temptations to stray away from God and Lutheran orthodoxy.[71] This can be seen from the records of the Consistorium from 1616, for example, when its members noted with surprise and disappointment that a citizen called Görg Hahn had discussed his doubts about the physical resurrection with a foreign artist called Hans Görg Jung; such epicurean opinions were to be expected of foreign, frivolous types like artists, they implied, but not of a 'child of the city', who had been brought up in the articles of faith since his youth.[72] Ideally, these articles of faith were to be taught to children as early as possible in life, before their innate, human sinfulness was allowed to blossom forth and make them intractable, so that they would have this spiritual protection from a young age.

Luther and his followers had originally hoped that the teaching of the young in the articles of Lutheran orthodoxy would be a joint endeavour, undertaken by parents in the home, teachers in schools, and pastors in sermons and catechism classes. These initial hopes for significant parental participation in the education of the young had faded by the 1530s, however: thereafter the main aim of Lutheran authorities was to exhort parents to discharge their pedagogical responsibilities by sending their children regularly to catechism classes and, where available, schools.[73] This tactic was also used in Rothenburg: ordinances were issued exhorting parents to send their children and household servants to church, while the failure of parents to do this or to support the teaching efforts of pastors and school-teachers with sufficient diligence was a common complaint in the records of the Consistorium.[74] However, evidence from the Hilgartshausen and later witchcraft cases suggests that, despite their emphasis on teaching outside the home as the most important method for inculcating the tenets of Lutheranism, the authorities in Rothenburg still regarded the role of parents in beginning the teaching process with their own children, with the teaching of the Lord's Prayer and other prayers at home, as an important stage of the pedagogical process. And, in the same way that Anna Brodt had held Magdalena Gackstatt responsible for Hans' upbringing, the comments about Magdalena noted during the investigation of the Hilgartshausen case suggest that the councillors also thought that the initial responsibility for teaching a child these prayers was thought to lie with mothers, with whom children spent most time before the age of about seven, rather than with fathers.[75] This idea accorded with the elevation by Lutherans of the status of motherhood – as both the bearing and raising of children – to the only natural and God-ordained role for women, but it somewhat ironically undercut the marginalisation within Lutheranism of women within the realm of the sacred and the Lutheran emphasis on the theory of patriarchal authority as the ideal in all things.[76] Precisely because it emphasised the power of mothers, for good or evil, over their children, this idea may also have put pressure on mothers whose attempts at instruction of their children fell short of the ideal. This would have been particularly likely among women of the lower orders, who probably often lacked the necessary time and knowledge to devote themselves to the task. Magdalena Gackstatt explained that she had tried to teach Hans the Lord's Prayer, but had been thwarted by the fact that he had only started to speak properly at the age of about four, but her protestations seem to have fallen on unsympathetic ears.[77] She had had the initial responsibility for guiding her son away from sin and, in the councillors' eyes at least, she had failed.

In 1587, then, we can first observe a convergence of two beliefs that would occur repeatedly in seventeenth-century witchcraft cases from Rothenburg in which children or adolescents claimed to have been seduced

into witchcraft by their mothers or other women who had quasi-maternal relationships with them. The first belief, commonly held at both popular and elite
levels and discussed in more depth in Chapter 5, was that witches were individuals – and often women – who passed on their knowledge of witchcraft to
those with whom they had contact and over whom they exercised influence in
the context of the household: usually their children, but also servants and other
family members. The second belief was the elite concern that proper maternal
responsibility could be abdicated either by women who deliberately corrupted
children by seducing them into witchcraft, or by women who unwittingly left
their children open to the threat of corruption from others by failing to provide
them with the foundations of a solid Lutheran upbringing. It was the convergence of these two beliefs, combined with genuine sympathy on the part of the
urban elites for such apparently corrupted youngsters, which encouraged
the Rothenburg council to take the claims of children allegedly seduced into
witchcraft by older women so seriously and increasingly to view their alleged
seducers with a mixture of fear, contempt and anger.

Magdalena Gackstatt was doubtless no better or worse a mother than
most other women of Rothenburg's hinterland; what was different about her
was that she had the misfortune to become the subject of her own son's story
of witchcraft. She emerges in the trial records as a strong-minded woman,
whose ability to resist the pressures of interrogation and the pain of torture
without deviating from her claims of innocence was crucial to the decision
reached by the council to pursue the case no further. While in custody she also
managed to curb the anger she had shown towards Hans before their arrests,
but not the sense of bewilderment about his behaviour. The rest of this chapter
will try to answer the questions Magdalena must often have asked herself as she
awaited her fate anxiously in gaol in September 1587: where had Hans' story
come from, and why had he told it?

The trials records suggest that Hans' story came from his own fertile
imagination with the help of promptings from Peter Streng and Michl Kupper.
The statements given by Streng and Kupper about how Hans had told the tale
in Bartl Kurtz's barn agreed that the initiative had come from Hans, who had
entered the barn claiming that he had a secret to impart and boasting about how
wonderful it was to go night-flying. Much of the remainder of their statements
recounted Hans' tale as if it had flowed from him without any intervention
from them. However, they testified to sufficient promptings of Hans to suggest
that these had strongly encouraged him in the shaping of his tale, and to hint at
the likelihood that similar questions – perhaps asked of Hans on previous occasions by other village children – had contributed significantly to the fashioning
of his story. For example, Peter had asked Hans how he flew, and with whom.
He had also shown Hans a pitchfork and asked him if that was what he flew on,

and when Hans had replied that it was not the right kind of fork, Kupper had fetched a fire-iron from the kitchen and asked Hans what his mother did with it to make it fly. Peter and Kupper had also asked Hans with whom he had danced at the witches' gathering. Unfortunately for Peter, he had also promised Hans some marbles if he would go and fetch his magical salve so that they could all see him fly.[78] Peter's questions and this promise of marbles in return for a demonstration of Hans' powers seem to have suggested to Hans that Peter had taught him the night-flying tale and bribed him to spread it. This idea may have become particularly appealing to Hans as a way of shifting the blame away from himself and onto Peter in the face of his mother's wrath over the night-flying story; the more angry she became with him, the more he may have clung to this explanation of the genesis of the story. Certainly by the time of his arrest Hans appears to have convinced himself that both versions of events – that he had really gone night-flying, and that Peter had taught him what to say – were equally credible. During interrogation he tended to shift from one version to the other depending on whether or not his mother was present and on what he thought his interrogators wanted him to say, until he became completely confused and simply oscillated wildly between the two.

The presence in Hans' tale of a black man in charge of proceedings, who was named by Hans during interrogation as Hans or Lucifer, shows that the devil was beginning to be integrated into beliefs about witchcraft in Rothenburg's rural hinterland. However, the black man of Hans' tale was not a terrifying demonic presence, but rather an admired leader of revels and a thoughtful provider of all the things that were needed to make the night-flight and dance a success. Hans also saw the presence of both the black man and his mother as protective and comforting, rather than threatening or frightening; his description of being seated between the two of them on the fire-iron suggests that they would have prevented him from falling off no matter how high they flew.[79] Hans began to suggest that they had shown violence towards him during his last interrogation in custody on 27 September, when he claimed that he had been beaten with cudgels by his mother, Babelein and the black man to make him go flying. However, Hans only said this after he had seen his mother tortured and had been threatened with torture and floggings himself, which suggests that he was adapting his story in accordance with an increasingly threatening line of official questioning.[80]

Hans' original story of the sabbat was primarily a festive tale, which drew its inspiration not from elite demonology, but from the popular beliefs about the flight and gatherings of witches Hans must have learned from his elders; from Hans' own experience of the festivals and dances enjoyed throughout the year by the villagers; from old Peter Naiffer's story of the strange goings-on under the Witches' Tree that Hans had doubtless heard discussed in the village; and from memories of moments of particular companionship that Hans had enjoyed with his mother.[81] The elements of Hans' tale were probably the stuff of which little boys' greatest imaginary adventures were made in the sixteenth century: flying through the night sky on a magical fire-iron as high as the heavens, sneaking into other people's houses without them being aware of it, visiting the tavern, dancing with an older village girl, and having good things to eat and drink. As far as Hans was concerned, night-flying and witches' dances were wonderful fun, and he fully expected other boys to envy him his imagined experiences.[82]

Given the existence of his mother's reputation for working witchcraft, Hans may already have been called a witch himself by the time he was six. However, his main motive for telling his tale in 1587 was a desire to impress other, older village boys and youths. This can be seen from the boastful, eager-to-impress tone of the recitation of his tale to Peter Streng, Michl Kupper and Hans Kurtz. It was also evident in the response by Hans to Peter's demand that he provide a flying demonstration, which showed that he was keen to protect his boasts from possible derision: he refused to go and fetch the magical salve on the basis that it was a disgrace to fly during the day.[83] At six years old, Hans was younger than the other boys whose ages were specified in the sources. The reference by Magdalena Gackstatt to the fact that Hans had started to speak at quite a late stage of his infancy, and a reference made by Lorentz Dolman to the effect that Hans had the habit of secretly creeping into the tavern to hide under the tables, hint at the idea that he may have been something of a loner.[84] He may therefore have told his story with a view to gaining membership of the peer-group of these older, more influential boys, who doubtless arbitrated questions of reputation and standing within their own social milieu in much the same way as the adult men did within the *Gemeinde*, and whose acceptance of Hans would have considerably enhanced his status. The attempt by Hans to increase his own social credit backfired, however, as he managed to raise suspicions about his possible identity as a witch without providing the proof of his magical powers that the practical Peter Streng demanded. When Hans subsequently demanded trinkets from other village boys with threats of violence and boasted about his other maleficent powers it was as though he had grown further into his self-fashioned role as a witch, recognising and utilising the power of his words to provoke fear or anger in other people, and especially his mother, at the same time as he unwittingly alienated their sympathy from him.[85] He became the centre of attention, but only at the cost of increasing social isolation.

Hans' story also offers us insights into his relationships with his parents. The absence of his father, Martin Gackstatt, from his story is particularly striking. Hans went night-flying and dancing close to the protective presence of his mother and they were given a magical leather sack of wine from which they,

but specifically *not* his father could drink their fill, and which Magdalena subsequently hid near her trunk in the bedchamber.[86] On one level, Hans' story
may have mirrored an everyday life in which he had a close relationship with
his mother, consisting of companionship and small treats enjoyed together in
the absence of his father. Hans' attempts to shift the blame for the story onto
Peter Streng, and his inability or unwillingness to adhere consistently to the
claim that his mother really had taken him night-flying once he was in council
custody may therefore hint at an underlying emotional bond with his mother
that the boy was ultimately unwilling to sever, as much as they attest to his
increasing confusion as the official questioning progressed. On another level,
however, the way in which Hans imagined and told the story may have enabled
him to create a surrogate father in the figure of the black man who accompanied the boy and his mother on the flight to the dance. The description Hans
gave of flying on the fire-iron with his mother behind him and the black man
in front provides a telling image of a family group in which the black man
replaced Hans' father as the leader of the revels. Martin Gackstatt was aged in
his mid-to-late sixties in 1587, which would have made him a good deal older
than Magdalena, who was probably at least his second wife, and probably a distant and ancient figure to six-year-old Hans.[87] Perhaps Hans simply could not
imagine his real father indulging in the enjoyable antics of the night-flight as he
imagined them, and so had to create a more convivial substitute; or perhaps the
black man was what he wished his own father to be – a more entertaining and
mischievous playfellow and companion.

    The focus by Hans on Lorentz Dolman's tavern and his emphasis on the
gift of the leather sack of wine from the black man to his mother may also have
had a significance beyond the obvious interpretation that a tavern and the con-
tents of its wine-cellar might be expected to figure in tales of secret nocturnal
revelries. Since June 1586 the men of Hilgartshausen had been bitterly divided
by a legal dispute over the accuracy of the village account books. The dispute
centred on the money spent at communal drinking sessions – which, ironically,
were supposed to foster communal harmony – during the year 1585–86. The
men of the *Gemeinde* had accused the two outgoing officials of that year of
having drunk to excess at the expense of the *Gemeinde* after the drinking sessions involving all the men of the village had ended; of having hatched a plot to
falsify the figures recorded in the account books in order to keep the council in
Rothenburg in the dark about how much money was spent in the village on
alcohol; and of managing the finances of the *Gemeinde* so badly that the poorest
men of Hilgartshausen were in dire financial straits trying to make good their
contributions to the communal drinking kitty. The two officials denied the allegations and blamed any irregularity in the account books on old drinking debts
from 1584–85 which they had been forced to make good. The case dragged on

until February 1588, when the council reached a verdict in favour of the officials, but not before many men of the *Gemeinde*, including Martin Gackstatt, had testified against them. Lorentz Dolman and his tavern figured significantly in this case: Dolman was a crucial witness in defence of the outgoing officials and many of the allegedly excessive private drinking sessions, and the meeting which had discovered the alleged discrepancies in the account books, had taken place in his tavern. The whole affair was doubtless discussed at great length in Hilgartshausen between 1586 and 1588, particularly by the men of the *Gemeinde*. Perhaps Hans was tired of hearing his father and other village men talking about wine and the discord it had caused, and instead created in his story a vision of a convivial drinking session among the night-flyers at Dolman's tavern, unfettered by concerns over payments or account books, and of an enjoyment of wine between himself and his mother from which his father, as a representative of the litigious *Gemeinde*, was excluded.[88]

Finally, some clue as to why Hans told his story in 1587 may be found in his age at the time, of six years. The age of around seven had long been regarded as a significant milestone in the mental and physical development of children, and it may have been a milestone of particular significance for boys. Anthony Fletcher has argued that, because of an early modern belief in conception as a concoction in which the woman's seed mattered almost as much as the man's, boys and men found it impossible 'to think of themselves as wholly gendered male beings until they had struggled free of maternal making and maternal influence'.[89] In infancy, boys' upbringing was dominated by women, particularly their mothers, and boys and girls were dressed alike. Boys were put into adult male dress for the first time at around six or seven years, and this was also the age at which it was thought appropriate for boys to start to move away from the tutelage of their mothers.[90] Hans told his story, then, at an age which was recognised to be an important milestone in the long progression from infancy, with its uncertain gender boundaries, towards full, adult masculine identity. It is therefore perhaps not too fanciful to suggest that the inclusion by Hans of the black man as a surrogate father in a story otherwise dominated by his mother and other women, and his use of the night-flying story to try to impress older village boys, were both means which enabled Hans to begin to negotiate a shift away from a close relationship and identification with his mother, to a wider set of relationships with other village boys and a greater sense of identification with his father.

In the end, Hans' inability either to distinguish reality from his imagined experiences or to comprehend the possibly serious consequences of his story for himself and his mother brought them both nothing but trouble. They both suffered the pressures and terrors of incarceration and interrogation, and the ignominy and agony of physical torture. By telling his story, and then showing himself unable to maintain consistently whether it had really happened or just been taught to him, Hans also managed to alienate the sympathies of everyone else involved in the case: the other villagers, his own mother, and, ultimately, even the Rothenburg councillors. There is no evidence to tell us what happened to Hans and Magdalena once they had been released from custody, although a reference to a daughter of Martin Gackstatt in village records from 1590 suggests that at least some of the family still lived in Hilgartshausen by that date.[91] Some villagers, like Ursula Rigel, may well have had sympathy for Magdalena and the fact that her own son had brought such disgrace upon her head, and she might have been able to continue living in Hilgartshausen, although she was probably more isolated and vulnerable to allegations of witchcraft than before. Hans, however, may well have lost the sympathy of his own parents as well as that of the wider community, and they may well have packed him off to fend for himself as soon as they could reasonably do so.[92]

The reliance on Hans as the chief witness, the torture used against himself and his mother, the leading questions put to Magdalena which implied a belief in the reality of the Hilgartshausen witches' dance, and the fact that Babelein, as another alleged participant in the dance, was also arrested and interrogated, all hinted at the possibility that the council in Rothenburg was veering towards the treatment of witchcraft as an exceptional crime in 1587, in a case which had the potential to drag many other people into the legal investigation and perhaps to initiate prosecution on a wider scale. However, the councillors stopped short of abandoning all restraint in the use of torture in its interrogation of the suspects and instead decided to drop the case when they became convinced that no amount of effort on their part would uncover the truth of the matter. The inconsistency of the testimony given by Hans, compared with the consistency of the statements given by his mother and Babelein Kuch, did much to persuade Friedrich Prenninger and the councillors that this was the best course of action to take. Unease over the fact that they had already overstepped the mark of what was legally proper in their handling of the case seems also to have played a part in persuading them to this resolution, as did a sense of humility, which encouraged them to conclude that God was the only power capable of seeing and judging the hidden truth of Hans Gackstatt's story.

Notes

1 For all case documents, see RStA Interrogation Book A877 fols 532r–579v; Surety Book A855 fols 446v–447v. Hans' story is reconstructed from A877 fols 535v, 537r, 538r, 545r–546r, 551v–552v.
2 *Ibid.*, fol. 535r.
3 *Ibid.*, fol. 538r.
4 *Ibid.*, fol. 551r.
5 *Ibid.*, fols 535r, 538r–538v.

6 *Ibid.*, fols 533r–534v, 539r–540r, 543r–544r. It was legally recognised in Germany that an alleged slanderer (Dolman, in this case) might try to defend his behaviour by claiming that his/her potentially slanderous words had been uttered in jest or in the context of convivial drinking, or had been prefaced with some sort of verbal or physical greeting between him/herself and the allegedly slandered party; see Maclean, 'The law of defamation', p. 156.

7 RStA Interrogation Book A877 fols 535r–535v: 'und also kein guter handel sonder noch ein mordt aus disen sachen erfolgen mocht'.

8 *Ibid.*, fols 533v–534v, 540r.

9 This dispute is discussed later in this chapter: see n. 88 for details.

10 *Ibid.*, fols 536v, 539r–540r; RStA Surety Book A855 fol. 446v.

11 RStA Interrogation Book A877 fol. 535v.

12 *Ibid.*, fol. 537r.

13 *Ibid.*, fols 537v–538r.

14 *Ibid.*, fols 545r–546r.

15 *Ibid.*, fols 551r–553r.

16 *Ibid.*, fols 546r, 553r.

17 *Ibid.*, fols 550r–550v.

18 *Ibid.*, fol. 550r.

19 *Ibid.*, fol. 538v.

20 *Ibid.*, fols 547r, 564r.

21 *Ibid.*, fol. 547r: 'böser hendel'.

22 *Ibid.*, fol. 549r.

23 *Ibid.*, fols 549r–549v: 'wer er zu einem seltzamen handel kommen'.

24 *Ibd.*, fol. 549v.

25 *Ibid.*, fols 547v–548r.

26 *Ibid.*, fols 548r–549r.

27 Erler and Kaufmann, *Handwörterbuch zur deutschen Rechtsgeschichte*, vol. I, p. 136, vol. II, p. 721.

28 RStA Interrogation Book A877 fol. 537r.

29 *Ibid.*, fols 560r–560v.

30 *Ibid.*, fols 560v–563v. For the list of thirty-five questions – reduced from an original total of 52 – see fols 555r–558v.

31 Radbruch, *Die Peinliche Gerichtsordnung*, p. 57.

32 RStA Interrogation Book A877 fols 562v–563r.

33 *Ibid.*, fol. 562r.

34 *Ibid.*, fol. 563v.

35 *Ibid.*, fol. 564r.

36 *Ibid.*, fols 565v–566v.

37 *Ibid.*, fol. 567v.

38 *Ibid.*, fols 568r–569r (list of questions); 570r–574r (Magdalena's replies to them).

39 *Ibid.*, fol. 568r.

40 *Ibid.*, fol. 570v.

41 *Ibid.*, fols 571r–571v.

42 *Ibid.*, fols 571v–572r.

43 *Ibid.* fols 572v–574r.

44 On Prenninger and his background, see Wulz, *Die Prenninger von Erding*, pp. 31–34. Born in Remlingen in 1556, Friedrich had studied at Rothenburg's grammar-school and then Tübingen University.

45 Behringer, 'Kinderhexenprozesse, pp. 34–36.

46 RStA Interrogation Book A877 fols 577r–577v. For discussion of the *Canon Episcopi*, see pp. 55–56.

47 *Ibid.*, fols 577v–578r.

48 *Ibid.*, fols 578r–578v.

49 *Ibid.*, fols 578v–579r: 'ein gar schlechtes vnd geringes . . . Indicium'.

50 *Ibid.*, fol. 579r.
51 *Ibid.*, fol. 579v.
52 *Ibid.*, fol. 579r.
53 Behringer, 'Kinderhexenprozesse', p. 35.
54 *Ibid.*
55 See for example StAN Ro. Rep. 2091 fols 38r, 57r–58r; 2090 fol. 189v; 2096 fol. 283r.
    Parents often thought that the authorities had treated their children too severely in beating
    them: the third case cited concerned a woman who was reprimanded by the Consistorium
    in 1616 for insulting one of Rothenburg's school-teachers after he had beaten her daughter
    'blue and bloody' ('blau und blutig', fol. 189v).
56 Another self-confessed child-witch, Hans Adam Knöspel, was, however, beaten and threat-
    ened with beatings during questioning in 1692, see StAN Ro. Rep. 2087 fols 787v, 848v.
57 RStA Interrogation Book A877 fol. 579v: 'dz man die geringste gewissheit nit von Ime haben
    od[er] mutmassen kan.'
58 *Ibid.*: 'dieweil man Ja vf kein gewissen grund kommen, vnd die Warheit nit erfaren könne'.
    Anna Brodt was released on 25 September (RStA Surety Book A855 fol. 447r), and Peter
    Streng and Babelein were released four days later (*ibid.*, fols 447r–447v). I have been unable
    to find sureties for Hans Gackstatt and his mother, but as there is no evidence in the Blood
    or Municipal Account Books or in any later cases of any punishment having been meted out
    to them, it can be assumed that they were released on sureties which have since got lost.
59 See pp. 24, 26–27, 30–31.
60 See relevant years in RStA B186 (lists of councillors, 1230-1669); B186a (council elections,
    1300–1720).
61 See RStA Steinach Village Acts A739 fols 471r–472r (case from Steinach, 1602); RStA
    Interrogation Book A884 fols 556r–560r (case from Rothenburg, 1605).
62 See pp. 56, 113.
63 Behringer, 'Kinderhexenprozesse', especially pp. 43–44, 46; Walz, 'Kinder in Hexen-
    prozessen', especially pp. 220–221.
64 *Ibid.*, p. 220: 'ein kaum zu widerlegender Beweis für die Existenz von Hexen.'
65 *Ibid.*, p. 230.
66 Behringer, 'Kinderhexenprozesse', pp. 44–45.
67 RStA Interrogation Book A877 fol. 539v.
68 *Ibid.*, fol. 579v: 'der jung bösswicht'.
69 *Ibid.*, fols 537r, 563v, 567v.
70 Sehling, *Die evangelischen Kirchenordnungen*, pp. 581–582; Leder, *Kirche und Jugend in Nürn-
    berg*, especially pp. 28–29, 36, 47–49, 53–60; Strauss, *Luther's House of Learning*; Strauss,
    'Success and failure', pp. 33–34.
71 Gawthrop and Strauss, 'Protestantism and literacy', pp. 37–39; Sabean, *Power in the Blood*,
    pp. 110–112.
72 StAN Ro. Rep. 2090 fols 191r–192v.
73 Leder, *Kinder und Jugend in Nürnberg*, pp. 38, 54–56, 60, 117–119; Strauss, 'Success and fail-
    ure', pp. 31–41.
74 See for example StAN Ro. Rep. 2091 fols 29r, 38r, 141r, 213r, 413r; RStA Ordinances
    A362 fols 79r–79v; A363 fols 22r, 48r–50r, 69r, 224r–232v; AA122a fols 387r– 98v.
75 On the idea that children spent most time with their mothers rather than their fathers before
    the age of seven, see Cunningham, *Children and Childhood*, p. 34; Ulbricht, 'Der Einstel-
    lungswandel zur Kindheit', pp. 167–168; Fletcher, *Gender, Sex and Subordination*, pp. 86–87.
    The idea that women were responsible for the care and guidance of children of both genders
    during infancy is also suggested by the early modern writers on the household economy
    analysed by Marion W. Gray in *Productive Men, Reproductive Women*, p. 65.
76 For a discussion of these ideas, see Karant-Nunn, 'Kinder, Küche, Kirche'; Lorenz, 'Vom
    Kloster zur Küche', especially p. 23; Wiesner, 'Luther and women'; Plummer, 'Reforming
    the Family', especially pp. 208–209; Ahme, 'Wertung und Bedeutung', especially p. 65.

77 RStA Interrogation Book A877 fol. 563v.
78 See *Ibid.*, fols 545r–546r for Peter's statement; fols 551v–553r for Michl Kupper's.
79 *Ibid.*, fol. 545v.
80 *Ibid.*, fol. 572v.
81 Stories of sabbats told in subsequent Rothenburg witchcraft cases were also firmly anchored in notions drawn from the realities of popular festival culture, into which the devil and his activities were incorporated. On this point, see also Labouvie, 'Hexenspuk', pp. 91–92; Biesel, 'Die Pfeifer', pp. 300–301.
82 A similar glee in his imagined activities as a witch emerges from the confession of a nine-year-old boy in Bamberg in 1629, see Sebald, *Der Hexenjunge*, especially pp. 28–33.
83 RStA Interrogation Book A877 fols 546r, 552r.
84 *Ibid.*, fols 549v, 563v.
85 *Ibid.*, fol. 550r.
86 *Ibid.*, fol. 546r.
87 When called on to testify in the ongoing dispute over the village accounts on 26 February 1587, Martin Gackstatt had said that he could remember the Peasants' War (of 1525) when asked how old he was, see RStA Hilgartshausen Village Acts A597 fol. 224r.
88 See *ibid.*, fols 183r–332v for the case documents of this lengthy legal dispute.
89 Fletcher, *Gender, Sex and Subordination*, p. 59, and chapters 3, 5 and 15.
90 See *ibid.*, pp. 87–88, 297 on breeching. Most of the evidence on breeching exists for the middle and upper social orders in the early modern period. However, the idea that it was more generally practised can be seen in the testimony offered by child-witch Hans Adam Knöspel in Rothenburg in 1692. When asked how young he had been when he had first given himself to the devil, Knöspel told his interrogators that he had been as young as the gaoler's little son, who was still running around in skirts, StAN Ro. Rep. 2087 fol. 797v.
91 RStA Hilgartshausen Village Acts A599 fols 317r–318r.
92 There is evidence to suggest that this happened to another self-confessed child-witch, Barbara Schürz of Wettringen (see pp. 150–160, especially p. 157). The pastor of Wettringen noted some years after her trial that her father had felt ashamed of the effect his daughter's confessions of witchcraft had had and had sent her away from home as a result, see StAN Ro. Rep. 2087 fol. 163r.

4

'When will the burning start here?': the Catholic challenge during the Thirty Years' War

The authorities in Rothenburg were spared another problematic encounter with a self-confessed child-witch until 1627, when thirteen-year-old Margaretha Hörber from the hinterland village of Gebsattel began claiming that she had been seduced into witchcraft and taken to witches' dances by older women. As befitted a teenager, her story was more detailed than that told by six-year-old Hans Gackstatt in 1587, particularly in terms of her descriptions of the witches' dance and her encounters with the devil. However, the questions of whether the experiences of a self-confessed child-witch had been real or illusory and of whether his or her testimony against others was to be trusted, which had perplexed the councillors and their advisers in 1587, also helped shape their dealings with Margaretha in 1627. What was different about the case in 1627 was the political context within which it took place. The Thirty Years' War had started in 1618, and the late 1620s were years of ascendancy for the Catholic Habsburg Emperor, Ferdinand, and the Catholic League, the coalition of Catholic allies under the leadership of Duke Maximilian of Bavaria. This ascendancy culminated in the promulgation by Ferdinand of the Edict of Restitution in March 1629 which, among other provisions, ordered the return to the Catholic church of all ecclesiastical properties seized by Protestants since 1552 and constituted 'a staggering blow to German Protestantism, before which all earlier setbacks paled in comparison'.[1] Margaretha Hörber's narrative of witchcraft and the manner in which the Rothenburg council handled it proved to be firmly embedded in, and expressive of, this wider context of religious conflict, in which a beleaguered Lutheranism appeared to be fighting for its survival against the resurgent forces of counter-reformation Catholicism.

Unable to pray:
Margaretha Hörber's tale of witchcraft, 1627

In the early years of the Thirty Years' War, between 1622 and 1631, Rothen-burg's subjects were forced to endure the almost continual mustering and quar-tering of imperial and Catholic League troops in the city's hinterland.[2] In line with a long tradition of trying to remain on good terms with the Emperors to whom the city owed its privileges, the city councillors doubtless hoped that this toleration of the Catholic military effort would prevent an irrevocable break with Ferdinand. However, after the collapse in 1621 of the Evangelical Union – the alliance of Protestant princes and cities formed in 1608 against the growing threat of Catholic militancy – the council had no real choice in the matter. The presence of these troops weighed heavily upon the inhabitants of the hinterland villages and it is likely that Margaretha Hörber's parents, who died in early 1626, fell victim to an outbreak of plague spread by soldiers to her home village of Gebsattel.[3] Margaretha was left an orphan under the guardianship of her stepbrother, Michael Hörber, and her brother-in-law, Jobst Unger, who also both lived in Gebsattel.[4] Apparently unwilling to take Margaretha into their own homes, Hörber and Unger sent her to live for a year with Hans Herman and his family in the Siechen Mill, which was situated on the outskirts of Geb-sattel, in late October 1626. In return for 8 gulden, Herman and his wife were to feed and care for Margaretha and to make sure that she learnt her prayers and catechism so that she would soon be able to take her first communion at the nearby Lutheran church of St Leonhard's.[5]

Margaretha did not make the progress in religious instruction her guardians hoped for. On the contrary, she seemed incapable of fulfilling her pious obligations adequately. The pastor of St Leonhard's lamented that she wanted to learn nothing in church and she evinced a similar lack of enthusiasm for the instruction offered by the schoolmaster in Gebsattel. Matters were even worse at the Siechen Mill, where no amount of exhortation could persuade Margaretha to say her prayers willingly. When the time came for the recitation of morning and evening prayers by all members of the household, Margaretha either sought excuses which would enable her to absent herself from them or said the prayers in a confused manner when she was made to participate. Anna, the seventeen-year-old daughter of the miller with whom Margaretha shared a bed, had to force the younger girl to say her prayers before they went to sleep at night. Anna also hit Margaretha for refusing to wash her hands before meals, which was another habit of disobedience she had acquired.[6]

Margaretha's recalcitrance came to a head in the spring of 1627, when she ran away from the mill to her stepbrother in Gebsattel. She claimed that she was treated badly in the Herman household, but Michael Hörber showed little sympathy for her complaints and sent her back to the mill. There she was questioned about the reasons for her flight and for her continued refusal to pray willingly by Anna, who threatened to beat her with a stick if she refused to answer, and then by the miller and his wife. In response, Margaretha claimed that she could not pray because Satan prevented her from so doing. He beat her whenever she wanted to say her prayers and had appeared to her in the mill in the guise of an ox, a piebald goat and a snail in order to reiterate his prohibition. Margaretha added that Ursula, the old midwife of Gebsattel, and her own mother, had also beaten her to stop her praying and had tried to teach her witchcraft before their recent deaths and that she had been taken to a witches' dance on a golden fire-iron by Ursula's daughter, Eva, who was still alive and living in Gattenhofen.[7]

These claims shocked and frightened the miller and his wife and they summoned Michael Hörber to the mill for advice on what to do next. Hörber also questioned Margaretha about her inability to pray and was particularly concerned about a chair which the old midwife Ursula had given to his stepsister as a sign of her affection before her death. According to Margaretha, Ursula had instructed her to let no-one else sit in the chair and, when she sat in it herself, to say aloud that 'as this chair was given to me by my dear mother, so I am her dear daughter'. Margaretha had taken the chair with her to the Siechen Mill, where the miller had ordered it to be put away in the attic. The miller and Hörber feared the chair, regarding it as bewitched or as capable of bewitching and either way as a symbol of the hold that the midwife still had over Margaretha. Hörber fetched the chair from the attic and burned it in order to destroy the midwife's power and the onlookers' worst fears of the chair's supposedly magical properties were confirmed by the fact that even its ashes behaved strangely, jumping about like grains of gunpowder that only Margaretha could extinguish. This was too much for the miller and his wife. They refused to have anything more to do with Margaretha and she was taken back to Gebsattel by her stepbrother.[8]

Margaretha's strange behaviour was first brought to the attention of the council on 15 May, when the miller and his wife reported it to the city chancellery.[9] It is unclear whether they had been asked to do this by the councillors, who may have heard rumours about Margaretha's story and the burning of the chair at the mill and wanted an official report on the matter, or whether – as Rothenburg subjects – the Hermans had gone into the city of their own volition in order to apprise the council of an affair which threatened deleterious consequences for its authority in Gebsattel.[10] Given the long history of conflict over the exercise of lordship in Gebsattel, the latter explanation is the more likely. The arrest of Margaretha by the council on 18 May can certainly only be understood in the context of a long-standing and extremely acrimonious battle to defend its judicial and political power in Gebsattel, a battle which had acquired an additional religious edge in the spring of 1627.

As discussed in the Introduction, Rothenburg was situated in a part of early modern Germany where rights over land and people were particularly fragmented and subject to competing claims from rival lords.[11] The village of Gebsattel was one of the biggest thorns in the flesh of the city councillors in the context of their attempts to defend and extend Rothenburg's lordship rights over its rural territory in the late medieval and early modern periods. With eighty-nine households, Gebsattel was the largest hinterland village. However, only thirteen of these households belonged and owed their seigneurial dues to the city. The remaining seventy-six belonged to Komburg, a large Catholic monastery situated near the city of Schwäbisch Hall.[12] Komburg appointed an official to exercise authority on its behalf in Gebsattel; he lived in a small castle-cum-manor-house in the village which was scathingly called the 'so-called castle' by the Rothenburgers.[13] Disputes between Rothenburg and Komburg over the rights that each possessed in Gebsattel began in the late fourteenth century and continued to be so numerous and acrimonious that the documentation they generated between 1575 and 1798 fills 161 volumes still held in the Rothenburg city archive.[14] In many disputes legal argument was abandoned in favour of force of arms and several disagreements could be settled only by the highest court of appeal and arbitration in the Holy Roman Empire, the *Reichskammergericht*. The perpetually tense situation was not helped by the fact that Gebsattel, with its large concentration of 'foreign' inhabitants, was situated barely 2 kilometres to the south of Rothenburg.

A major source of conflict between Rothenburg and Komburg, and of particular relevance for Margaretha Hörber, was the fact that Komburg constantly sought to challenge what the Rothenburg council regarded as the most important expression of its territorial overlordship: its claim to exercise authority as the dispenser of high criminal justice over all inhabitants of the city and its hinterland.[15] Two examples can serve as an illustration of the level of animosity which existed between the two rival lords in Gebsattel on this issue before 1627. In 1561 a Komburg subject called Leonhardt Lullich committed suicide in his house in Gebsattel and the city council, who claimed the right to dispose of suicides' bodies as part of its high criminal justice authority, had the body ceremonially burned by the city's muncipal executioner. However, because this was done in one of Lullich's fields, on wood which had belonged to him and which had been carried to the field by horses led by male householders chosen by lot from all the Komburg and Rothenburg villagers, Komburg felt that its own authority in Gebsattel had been compromised. A dispute over the disposal of suicides' corpses ensued between Komburg and Rothenburg which was settled only in 1567 after reaching the *Reichskammergericht*.[16] In

1590 it was the turn of the council to take umbrage after the Komburg offical in Gebsattel placed a mill-hand who had slandered another villager in the castle stocks. The council felt that the matter came under its jurisdiction as dispenser of high criminal justice and demanded that the mill-hand be sent to Rothenburg for punishment. The Komburg official refused to comply, so a force of 500 armed Rothenburg peasants and citizens was dispatched to Gebsattel to break into the castle to fetch him into the city, seriously – and probably deliberately – damaging the castle as they went.[17]

The potential for conflict in Gebsattel was further increased by the intro-duction of Lutheranism to Rothenburg and its hinterland in 1544. Komburg held the patronage rights to the parish church of St Laurence in Gebsattel, but the council in Rothenburg had managed to persuade the monastery to reach an agreement in 1567 by which it promised to appoint only suitable individuals, who gave no grounds for complaint, to the living.[18] As far as the council was concerned, this meant Lutherans, and the first pastor to be appointed to the living after 1567 was the Lutheran Johann Fuchs, who held it until 1584.[19] After 1584, however, Komburg played on the vague wording of the 1567 agreement in order to justify a succession of short-lived appointments of osten-sibly Catholic priests, despite the fact that Rothenburg tried unsuccessfully to block their appointments through the *Reichskammergericht*.[20] Unfortunately for Komburg the spiritual damage had already been done in the village during the long incumbency of Johann Fuchs. By the turn of the sixteenth century about two-thirds of Komburg's subjects in Gebsattel had become Lutheran and looked to St Leonhard's, the chapel attached to the leprosarium which lay between Gebsattel and Rothenburg, rather than to Gebsattel's parish church, as the focus of their religious life.[21] The religious divisions within Gebsattel as a whole were reflected in the religious divisions within the Hörber family, who were all Komburg subjects: Margaretha Hörber had been baptised a Catholic,[22] while her stepbrother Michael Hörber and brother-in-law Jobst Unger had either been raised as Lutherans or had converted to Lutheranism by 1626.[23]

The balance of religious power swung dramatically in Komburg's favour in the late 1620s, however. With Alexander Schreckenfuchs, a particularly zealous and belligerent Komburg official in post in Gebsattel, and a Catholic military presence in Rothenburg's hinterland as a result of the Thirty Years' War, Komburg and its powerful Catholic protector, Prince-Bishop Philipp Adolf von Ehrenberg of Würzburg, seized the opportunity to win back the lost souls of Gebsattel for Catholicism.[24] They enforced the principle of the Peace of Augsburg – that each ruler had the right to determine the official religion of his own territory – by ensuring that all of Komburg's subjects in the village returned to the Catholic fold, despite the appeals made by the Rothenburg council on behalf of the Komburg Lutherans that they be allowed to remain

Lutheran.[25] In March and April of 1627 officials representing the Bishop of Würzburg attempted to persuade the Komburg Lutherans to convert to Catholicism. This had little effect, so Philipp Adolf gave them a stark choice: they had to convert to Catholicism or sell their landholdings to Catholic buyers and leave Gebsattel by 13 May. This deadline was subsequently extended, but some of the most committed Komburg Lutherans made the decision to sell up and settle elsewhere by December 1627 and twelve families eventually left Gebsattel. They included Michael Hörber, who moved to the hinterland village of Steinach. The rest, faced with the unenviable task of trying to find Catholic buyers for their land in the midst of a war-zone, were 'persuaded' to become Catholic in a series of religious examinations held by Komburg and Würzburg officials in the village between December 1627 and August 1628.[26]

This was the complex and conflict-ridden background against which the arrest and trial of Margaretha Hörber was set. But one element is still missing from the picture: the terrible series of mass executions for witchcraft which occurred at the same time in the Prince-Bishopric of Würzburg, just to the north-west of Rothenburg. An initial wave of trials had seen possibly as many as 300 executions for witchcraft there during the episcopate of Julius Echter von Mespelbrunn in 1616 and 1617, but worse was to come under the aegis of Bishop von Ehrenberg. Isolated executions in 1625 gave way to a swell-tide of denunciations in 1626, to produce a witch-hunt which lasted until 1631, peaked in its ferocity between 1628 and 1629, and sent possibly as many as 900 people, including at least thirty-nine priests and numerous children, to the stake.[27] It proved to be the largest witch-hunt ever seen in Franconia, although the Prince-Bishopric of Bamberg, with about 300 executions between 1625 and 1631, ran it a close second.[28] There were also mass trials and executions in the Bishopric of Eichstätt and the Upper Archbishopric of Mainz in the same years.[29] The hunts experienced by these Catholic ecclesiastical teritories in early seventeenth-century Franconia were exceptionally savage, realising what Wolfgang Behringer has described as 'the sombre dream of unconditional persecution, of persecution without regard for political, social or humanitarian obstacles, but only for the logic of the persecutions themselves'.[30]

The arrest of Margaretha Hörber on 18 May 1627 was thus prompted primarily by the Rothenburg council's fear that its judicial authority over her would otherwise be usurped by Komburg and the Prince-Bishop of Würzburg. On 15 May the Siechen miller Hans Herman had told the council that Margaretha had been questioned on suspicion of witchcraft on her return to Gebsattel by Komburg official Schreckenfuchs, who was now keeping her in custody while he decided what course of action to take next.[31] Then on 16 May the council received an anonymous letter from Gebsattel which reported that Schreckenfuchs intended to send Margaretha to be dealt with by the Jesuits in Würzburg and advised the council to act quickly if it wanted to assert its authority in the matter. The situation was particularly urgent, the letter suggested, because Margaretha's relatives were keen to be rid of her, so would presumably not leap to her protection if Schreckenfuchs put his plan into action.[32] As a self-confessed witch, Margaretha would hardly have been popular with her relatives at this time. Moreover, although we do not know whether or not she had inherited any money or property from her parents, it may have been the case that her relatives had financial motives for failing to leap to her defence; perhaps they hoped thereby to rid themselves of the need to support her, or to gain access to any inheritance she may have been entitled to if she were executed as a witch.[33]

As dispenser of high criminal justice over Gebsattel, the council in Rothenburg had the right to arrest and try any inhabitant of the village who was suspected of heresy, sorcery or witchcraft, a right which had been confirmed explicitly in treaties agreed between the city and Komburg in 1614 and 1618.[34] It therefore seems that Schreckenfuchs was trying to capitalise on the Catholic ascendancy in Gebsattel in the spring of 1627 by challenging this right and spiriting Margaretha away to Würzburg before the council had time to act. Given the context in which these events occurred, the challenge by Schreckenfuchs and the reaction of the council to it had significant religious and political implications. Had Schreckenfuchs succeeded in sending Margaretha to Würzburg, he would have struck a blow for Catholicism against the Lutheran imperial city. Moreover, given that Rothenburg had been subject to the ecclesiastical authority of the Bishop of Würzburg before the city had adopted Lutheranism, the sending of Margaretha to Würzburg would have suggested that 'proper' Catholic episcopal authority was in the process of being restored over the 'heretical' Lutheran city. By arresting her first, the Rothenburg council reasserted its judicial authority against a rival lord, its autonomus status as an imperial city against an autocratic prince-bishop, and its Lutheranism against the threat of counter-reformation Catholicism. At the same time, and perhaps aware of what Margaretha's likely fate would have been as a suspected witch in Würzburg, the council may also have been striking a deliberate blow for Lutheran moderation against what it had come to regard as a Catholic ferocity in witch-hunting which was inextricably bound up with a resurgence of Catholic political and military power.[35]

Margaretha in custody, May 1627–February 1628

Margaretha was questioned for the first time in the city gaol on 18 May. Perhaps unsurprisingly, given that she had already been browbeaten into telling her story of witchcraft before her arrest by Hans Herman and his wife and daughter, by

Michael Hörber and by Schreckenfuchs, she repeated it in custody with little prompting from her interrogators. Her story fell into two parts, one recounting her attendance at witches' dances, in which her central relationship was with Ursula, the old midwife of Gebsattel, and the other explaining her inability to pray in the context of her encounters with Satan. Magaretha told her interrogators that, while her parents were still alive, Ursula had offered to teach her witchcraft, with her mother's knowledge. At first Margaretha had declined the offer, but Ursula had persisted in her entreaties and had finally succeeded in taking Margaretha to a witches' dance on a golden fire-iron. Many other people had been there, dancing to the music of two bagpipers. Margaretha named twenty-two of them, most of whom came from Gebsattel: nineteen women, including her own dead mother and godmother, and three men. Three old women and the old herdsman of Gebsattel had illuminated proceedings by standing on their heads at the corners of the dance with torches stuck in their backsides. There had been a feast of meat and wine, but no bread or salt, and people had blessed each other in the devil's name as they shared out the food. Satan, in the guise of a handsome young man, dressed in black, with a black feather in his hat, a green badge on his coat and a gilded dagger at his side, had taken charge of the dance. It had lasted three or four hours and then Ursula had taken her home. Ursula had taken Margaretha to four more dances; after her death her daughter Eva had taken Margaretha to another four and a woman from the village of Bockenfeld had taken her to a futher three. Margaretha was keen to stress to the councillors that she could not fly to dances on her own; that she had not learned how to do this or any other witchcraft; and that she had refused to be persuaded by the old midwife to promise herself to Satan. Margaretha's description of the dance was also suffused with this sense of her unwillingness to participate rather than of her enjoyment of the revels. She had been taken there by the midwife against her will; she had refused to obey the devil's suggestion that she stand on her head to act as a 'light' for the others; and she had blessed others at the feast in the devil's name only at the midwife's behest.[36]

The devil had also appeared to Margaretha in her parents' house and in the Siechen Mill, usually as a black, horned man who offered to teach her witchcraft in return for a promise that she would be his. Margaretha went into particular detail about his visits to the Siechen Mill. The first time he had appeared to her there he had told her that, because she had been christened a Catholic, she must now let herself be re-baptised by him. Margaretha had been stopped from complying with his suggestion only by the intervention of a white figure, like that of a young man, which she had assumed was an angel and which had suddenly appeared at her side to assist her. Later, and on successive Sundays when Margaretha had been alone in the mill while the others were at church, the devil had appeared to her as a piebald goat which could open and close doors with its hooves and as an ox which distracted her so much from her work that the fire had gone out, disrupting her cooking. He had also appeared to her in order to stop her praying and washing her hands from behind the vinegar jar and from under the stove in the shape of a snail which only she could see. She even thought that he sat next to her when she went to church and urged her not to pay attention to the services.[37]

After hearing this disturbing narrative from Margaretha, and perhaps having learned its lesson from 1587, when legal advice had been called for only at a late stage of the Hans Gackstatt case,[38] the council turned immediately to jurists Christoff Conrad Seuter and Johann Schäfer for counsel on how best to proceed. Schäfer began his opinion on the case by considering whether or not Margaretha's claims that she had been seduced into witchcraft and had flown to witches' dances were to be believed. The problem as far as her alleged seduction was concerned was that the old midwife and Margaretha's mother were now dead and could not be questioned on the matter. Schäfer pointed out that the devil could have deluded Margaretha into 'seeing' the two dead women as her seductresses. However, he offered another explanation of their central roles in Margaretha's story which evinced a potentially low opinion of her, suggesting that she might be seeking deliberately to shift the blame for her seduction into witchcraft onto them precisely because they were dead and unable to deny her allegations for themselves.[39] On the question of witches' dances, Schäfer discussed whether they and the flights to them took place in reality or were diabolic delusions and concluded by subscribing to a middle way of thinking on the issue. He believed that the devil exploited people of weak faith, sometimes by transporting them corporeally to other places and sometimes by deluding them into dreaming that they had been so transported. Schäfer thought that the alleged attendance at the witches' dance by Margaretha belonged in the latter category, but found it hard to believe that she had not paid homage to Satan, given the number of encounters she admitted to having had with him. He advised the council to question her more vigorously on this point.[40] Had she been of age (fourteen) Schäfer thought it would have been acceptable to have tortured her 'moderately', but as she was still a minor, all he could advise was that she might be flogged at the council's discretion if she proved obstinate under interrogation.[41]

Seuter was more kindly disposed towards Margaretha. He argued that she should not be punished as a witch as she had not confessed to learning or practising any witchcraft. He suggested instead that the council try to establish the exact nature of her relationship with the devil; like Schäfer, Seuter thought it likely that Margaretha had promised herself to the devil as she admitted that he had enough power over her to stop her praying. However, Seuter thought that the question of how Margaretha was to be freed from the devil's clutches was

better answered by theologians than jurists. He advised the council to seek theological advice on the matter and to ensure that Margaretha was given daily
religious instruction in custody so that her trust in God was restored.[42] Neither
Seuter or Schäfer thought that the testimony given by Margaretha against the
other alleged participants in the witches' dance was enough, without other evidence, to justify any legal action against them, although they both pointed out
that the council could make further enquiries against those named as participants by Margaretha if it so wished.[43]

     The council followed the milder of the two courses of action suggested by
its jurists and turned to its foremost cleric and ecclesiastical official, Superintendent Georg Zyrlein, for advice. This was the first theological opinion asked
for in a witchcraft case in Rothenburg and it presaged an increasing involvement of clerics in such cases, particularly in the later seventeenth century. Zyrlein questioned Margaretha three times in early July 1627, then delivered a
lengthy opinion on her case to the council on 15 July. From this opinion it is
clear that Margaretha had repeated to Zyrlein much of what she had said in custody in May, emphasising her reluctance to attend or participate in the witches'
dances and the fact that she could work no witchcraft herself. However, she had
added more details in response to Zyrlein's questions. She dated her seduction
into witchcraft by the old midwife to six years ago. She also confessed that she
had, in fact, given herself to Satan and had sex with him, but only because he
had tempted her with promises of sugar (which she had not received), and
because the old midwife had told her she must do this. Margaretha had actually
been afraid of him and expressed the wish to be free of his snares, with God's
help.[44] From this, Zyrlein concluded that Margaretha belonged in the category
of witches who had not actively and willingly made pacts with the devil, but
who had been terrified, forced or deceived into making such pacts; who had
not given the devil their signature as a pledge of their servitude to him; and who
had worked no harmful magic against other people. Such witches, whose consent was entirely lacking from their dealings with the devil, ought not to suffer
legal punishments as they had already suffered enough at the devil's hands. Margaretha was especially to be pitied because she had been seduced by the forces
of evil at so young an age, before she had acquired the constancy of will or
maturity of intellect necessary to enable her to resist them.[45]

     Zyrlein was convinced that diabolic delusion was the cause of all of the
events allegedly experienced by Margaretha; indeed, it was the only explanation for the glaring incongruities in her testimony. How could she have had sex
with the devil when the devil was an incorporeal being? How could Margaretha's mother have appeared to her after her death, as Margaretha now
claimed? How could Margaretha have flown to the witches' dance, yet remained
in bed at the same time? How could she have eaten and drunk at the dance, yet

suffered hunger and thirst on her return?[46] Zyrlein cited extracts from the works of St Augustine, Luther, Melanchthon, Conrad Dietrich, Johann Geiler von Kaisersberg and Niels Hemmingsen in support of his belief that Margaretha had only dreamed or imagined her flight to and participation in the dances. He concluded by advising the council that Margaretha be helped to make good the lack of faith in God which had laid her mind open to the influence of the devil's delusions in the first place. Drawing on the ideas of Württemberg theologian Theodor Thumm, who believed that no-one should suffer the death penalty simply for apostasy, Zyrlien advised that Margaretha be given religious instruction to teach her how greatly she had sinned and to comfort her with the prospect of God's mercy and be kept stringently to a programme of praying and hearing God's word so that she would always know how to resist the devil's wiles. In this way, she would be brought back onto the right path spiritually and snatched from the clutches of Satan by proper Lutheran teaching.[47]

Jurist Seuter readily agreed with Zyrlein's interpretation of Margaretha as a girl who had been led astray by the old midwife and deluded by Satan when she was too young to have known any better and who deserved to be taught the errors of her ways rather than to be physically punished for them in the next opinion he wrote on the case on 9 September.[48] He even suggested ways of proving that Margaretha's experiences had been diabolic delusions, although it is unclear whether this was for her benefit or that of the council. He advised the council to ask Anna, the miller's daughter with whom Margaretha had shared a bed at the Siechen Mill, whether Margaretha had ever gone missing during the night.[49] Anna was asked to testify on this matter on 9 October and she stated that, although Margaretha had often made strange noises in her sleep and had been hard to wake up, she had never actually left their bed, nor had Anna ever seen anyone come to fetch her from it.[50] Seuter also advised the council to have Margaretha examined by the city midwives, if she persisted in claiming that she had had sex with the devil.[51] This was done on 11 October, after Margaretha had repeated her assertion that the devil had deflowered her under interrogation on 10 October: the three midwives called on to perform the examination confirmed that Margaretha was still a virgin.[52] In late October, both Seuter and Schäfer advised that Margaretha be released from gaol without punishment and committed to the guidance of theologians and the care of pious people.[53]

In the meantime the council had made some effort to discover more about some of the other people Margaretha had implicated in her story. The old midwife's daughter Eva, who Margaretha claimed had taken her to four dances after the midwife's death and the main, living suspect in the case, had been called into Rothenburg to testify on 22 May. She denied the allegations vehemently and pointed out that she neither knew the girl well nor had had much to do with Margaretha's mother when she was alive. She also denied that her own mother had ever worked any witchcraft. On the contrary, the midwife had taught Eva and her sisters how to pray; she had, in short, been a good mother to them. Eva did, however, state that the old herdsman of Gebsattel, who had allegedly provided one of the undignified lights at the witches' dance, had a reputation for working witchcraft among the inhabitants of Gebsattel.[54] This suspicion against the herdsman was strengthened in a report written in early September by Georg Phoss, the Gebsattel official answerable to the Rothen-burg council, who had been asked by the council to investigate it further. Phoss' report implied that the villagers suspected the herdsman of being able to harm livestock, although they appear to have intimated this to him in the indirect manner usually adopted by other villagers when expressing suspicions of witchcraft against their neighbours to the council or its representatives. What they had actually said was that the herdsman had been in the habit of blocking the way when the village livestock was driven back into Gebsattel at night, until he had been ordered to stay in his house until all the beasts were safely returned to their stalls.[55]

This was as far as the investigations against the other alleged sabbat-atten-ders progressed, however. As jurist Seuter pointed out in early September, as it had not been proven that Margaretha had really attended these dances her-self, there was little firm basis on which to justify further legal action against other people who may or may not have been there as well. Seuter was also scathing about the evidence Phoss had gathered against the herdsman. He argued that it did not amount to a legally recognisable presumption of guilt against him and instead criticised the Gebsattel inhabitants for believing that Satan and his minions were to blame for the misfortunes visited upon them by God as punishments for their sins. Instead of encouraging the villagers in their suspicions against the herdsman, Seuter advised, the pastor of St Leonhard's should preach with zeal against these superstitions.[56] Once the questioning of Anna and the examination of Margaretha had added weight to the idea that her experiences had been illusory rather than real, there was even less justification for action against any of the twenty-two individuals she claimed to have seen at the dance.

Margaretha was finally released from custody without punishment on 8 December 1627. She was then sent to the city hospital, where her religious instruction continued, until 13 February 1628, when she was finally set at liberty after promising to live a good Christian life and after her guardians had, reluctantly, paid the considerable costs incurred by her incarceration.[57] It might be argued that the nine-month stay in custody endured by Margaretha constituted physical and psychological punishment enough for her confessions. However, the council kept her imprisoned for so long for what it deemed to be good reasons. Once they had accepted Zyrlein's categorisation and the jurists' confirmation of Margaretha's crime as apostasy, for example, they would have taken seriously the idea that she needed religious instruction to teach her the error of her ways. This was something which could hardly be achieved overnight, particularly as Seuter noted that it would also be necessary to observe Margaretha's behaviour for a time in order to establish that her repentance was genuine and not a sham.[58] The council also prolonged Margaretha's stay in custody for the same reason it had arrested her in the first place: to keep her out of the clutches of Schreckenfuchs in Gebsattel. On 9 September Seuter suggested further interrogation and physical examination of Margaretha as a deliberate tactic to delay her release, because he had heard that Schreckenfuchs still intended to send her to Würzburg as soon as she was free.[59] On 28 October Schäfer suggested a ploy by means of which the council might free Margaretha but continue to protect its judicial authority in Gebsattel against attack from Schreckenfuchs. Margaretha was to be released, but Schreckenfuchs was to be told that the case against her was still open and subject to the jurisdiction of the council and that the council was still conducting enquiries in relation to it.[60] The council may have thought that this strategy was too risky, however, and opted to keep Margaretha in custody instead. Margaretha may even have seen this as the lesser of two evils herself: while begging for her release from gaol on 10 October she had asked not to be sent back to Gebsattel, because she was afraid of Schreckenfuchs.[61]

Spiritual crisis: Margaretha's narrative in personal and political context

Margaretha's witchcraft narrative became more elaborate as she repeated it in response to questioning in custody, but its central elements – the reason for her inability to pray, her frequent encounters with the devil, the role of the old midwife in seducing her into witchcraft, and her attendance at the sabbats – remained constant throughout. On one level, her narrative can be read in the context of her life story, as a response to, and attempt at coping with, the emotionally difficult situation in which she found herself in 1627. She had lost both her parents in 1626 and then experienced rejection at the hands of her guardians, Unger and Hörber. They had sent her away to the Siechen Mill and then Hörber had made her return there even after she complained that the Herman family treated her badly. The old midwife Ursula had been a good friend of Margaretha's mother and Margaretha recalled in custody how Ursula and two other women, Georg Windtsheimer's wife and Leonhard Unger's wife, who was also Margaretha's godmother, had been in the habit of visiting her mother to eat and drink together while her father was absent from their house.[62] Margaretha named Windtsheimer's wife and her mother and god-mother in the list of sabbat-attenders she gave to her interrogators on 18 May, which suggests that the sabbat Margaretha imagined being taken to by Ursula was an embellished version of her memories of the actual, convivial gatherings of women-friends which had taken place in her home before her mother's death.[63] That she claimed to be able to see her mother and godmother at these sabbats even though they were both dead suggests a sense of loneliness and abandonment felt by Margaretha after their deaths, as did her later claim that her mother had visited her after her death, appearing to her while she was in bed and calling 'little Margaret, little Margaret'.[64]

Margaretha's loneliness may also help explain her fantasies of the visits by the devil to the Siechen Mill. There she was particularly isolated and the focus of psychological and physical pressure to conform to the daily routine of Lutheran prayers: she was subjected to constant exhortation to pray, was beaten by Anna, the miller's daughter, to make her pray, and was left alone in the mill to perform domestic chores in the absence of the Herman family.[65] In this context, imagining even the devil as a visitor was probably a welcome distraction, insofar as he offered her companionship and, in the case of the devil-as-ox who made the fire go out, a scapegoat for her unfinished housework.[66] Margaretha's description of the devil as the snail which only she could see and which hid behind the vinegar jar or under the stove in the mill, suggests a poignant desire for company on the part of the friendless girl which was increasingly being fulfilled by the powers of her own imagination.

It is unclear why Margaretha fixed on the old midwife, who apparently did not have a reputation as a witch in Gebsattel, as the person who had tried to teach her witchcraft and taken her to sabbats, rather than on her own mother, as Hans Gackstatt had done in 1587.[67] Perhaps Ursula had told tales of witchcraft at the women's gatherings in the Hörber household before the deaths of Margaretha's parents and thus planted an association between herself and witchcraft in Margaretha's mind. Perhaps Margaretha wanted to protect her dead mother from the worst stigma of witchcraft by claiming that Ursula had been chiefly responsible for her seduction into it, with her mother simply allowing this to happen. However, there is evidence to suggest that Margaretha may have enjoyed a close, quasi-filial relationship with Ursula. Margaretha claimed to have been made a present of the allegedly bewitched/bewitching chair by her 'dear mother' Ursula, upon which only she, as Ursula's 'dear daughter', could sit.[68] This suggests that a degree of special affection had existed between the two of them, or had been wished for by Margaretha, of which their imagined flights to witches' dances were an extension. It also suggests that early modern girls could identify women other than their blood-mothers, perhaps with whom they spent time or who paid them particular attention, as mother-figures in relation to themselves.

Margaretha's narrative was also an expression and dramatisation of the attempt which was being made in the Siechen Mill at the behest of her guardians to convert her, a baptised Catholic, to Lutheranism, and of her struggles to resist this conversion. In this sense, her narrative reflected in reverse the struggles of conscience which the Lutheran inhabitants of Gebsattel were being made to undergo by the re-Catholicisation programme started by the Bishop of Würzburg in the spring of 1627 and which continued throughout Margaretha's time in custody.[69]

By claiming that she could not pray because Ursula, her mother, and especially the devil in all his guises prevented her from doing so, Margaretha was able to blame her disobedience to her guardians' wishes and to the daily exhortations of the miller's family on others. This was probably not a deliberate strategy on Margaretha's part. It was rather an expression of her youth and powerlessness and of the fact that she was entirely dependent, materially and emotionally, on the very people who were trying to make her give up the Catholic faith into which she had been baptised. In this position she could hardly meet the attempts to teach her to pray properly with open defiance. Moreover, before she was even gaoled Margaretha had wept bitterly and lamented the fact that the devil kept her from praying and expressed her desire to be able to pray properly and to live a pious life, if only she could be helped thereto.[70] This suggests that her habit of imagining her struggles of religious conscience in terms of a personal relationship with the devil had become so entrenched that she genuinely believed she was in thrall to him and powerless to escape without external assistance.

A couple of the imagined exchanges with the devil which Margaretha described for her interrogators suggest that she was suffering a genuine spiritual crisis, wanting to remain loyal to the Catholic faith of her birth but knowing that her life would be easier if she converted. For example, for the most part Margaretha imagined the devil as the cause of her inability to become Lutheran: he stopped her saying her prayers and told her they were in vain. However, she also imagined the devil telling her that her Catholic baptism was invalid, that she would not go to heaven because of it, and that she must allow him to rebaptise her properly as a Lutheran.[71] Here, then, Margaretha imagined the devil as the personification of the Lutheran effort to convert her, rather than her desire to remain Catholic, and as expressing arguments which Margaretha's guardians and the miller's family had probably often used to try to persuade her of the errors of her Catholic ways. She was only prevented from submitting to the devil's offer to rebaptise her by a white being like a guardian angel which appeared, as a personification of Catholicism and her only ally in her isolated situation, to save her from this temptation.

Why did the council accept Margaretha's presentation of herself as a hapless individual ensnared by Satan and the forces of evil against her own will and

therefore treat her leniently? It need not have done so. Early in the case jurist
Schäfer mentioned the possibility that she might have been guilty of wilful
deceit in the telling of her stories and that the council was within its rights to
have her flogged to loosen her tongue. Moreover, at some point after her arrest
in 1627 Margaretha turned fourteen, the age at which, according to Schäfer, it
would have been legally acceptable to have had her tortured.[72] Why then did
the council choose to regard her as a corrupted innocent and to question and
release her without torturing or formally punishing her, when it had treated the
younger Hans Gackstatt more severely in 1587?

Part of the answer to this question lay in the political and religious situation of 1627–28. The council had always regarded witch-hunts as a threat to
social stability and harmony, but in 1627 the spectre of unconditional persecution, which had been raised in Würzburg, must have reiterated – and warned
them against – this threat particularly powerfully. As Zyrlein noted in July, in a
reminder to the council that one execution for witchcraft had the potential to
start a large-scale panic, 'the more witches one executes or burns, the more
numerous they seem to become'.[73] It was probably also for this reason that no
action was taken against the alleged sabbat-attenders named by Margaretha. By
treating Margaretha leniently and keeping her out of the clutches of the
Catholic authorities in Gebsattel and Würzburg, the council may also have been
asserting a point about Lutheran restraint in witchcraft prosecution, in comparison to Catholic severity, as well as about its judicial authority. Its actions can
be seen in the same light as the succour offered by the council of Nuremberg,
another Franconian Lutheran imperial city with a record of restrained treatment of witches, to refugees fleeing from the terrible witch-persecutions in the
nearby Prince-Bishopric of Bamberg in the late 1620s: as an affirmation of
religious identity and alleged theological superiority.[74] Set in this context of
religious one-upmanship, it was not surprising that Margaretha's story of a
young soul torn between the forces of evil (witchcraft/Catholicism) and good
(Lutheranism) appealed to the councillors and their advisers. It mirrored the
wider conflict of the Thirty Years' War while enabling the council to achieve a
small victory over Catholicism by winning Margaretha's soul for Lutheranism.

Crucial to the struggle for Margaretha's soul was whether or not she could
say her prayers. As I suggested in Chapter 3, Lutherans placed huge emphasis
on the rote learning and recitation of prayers and other central tenets of their
faith by their subjects because, as David Sabean argues, in the still predominantly oral culture of early modern Germany, 'there was and could be no word-
less salvation' for Lutherans.[75] In the Siechen Mill Margaretha had been unable
to adhere to this standard of Lutheran orthodoxy: she had either recited her
prayers improperly or had not said them at all. She did, in fact, know several
prayers and the main points of the Catechism and was able to recite them to the

satisfaction of her interrogators on her first day in gaol.[76] However, before then her will to say them properly had been lacking, distracted by the siren calls of the devil, midwife Ursula and her own mother. By taking Margaretha into custody, the council had lessened the hold that the forces of evil had over her, cancelling them out with its own judicial and religious power. All that was then needed was intensive religious instruction to give Margaretha the trust and faith in God's mercy which would enable her to say her prayers properly and confidently in future, thereby proclaiming her adherence to Lutheranism.

The treatment by the councillors of Margaretha was thus shaped by their desire to prove a point in wider religious, political and judicial battles. However, what Margaretha said and the manner in which she said it, played into their hands, making it easier for them to pity rather than blame her. Unlike Hans Gackstatt in 1587, she was consistent in custody and did not alienate the councillors' sympathies by offering different explanations for the genesis of her story. Moreover, neither she nor anyone else claimed that she had worked any harmful magic, a point which was cited throughout the case by both jurists and in the final case-summary as one of the key factors justifying her lenient treatment.[77] Any confession of maleficium by Margaretha would have put her into Superintedent Zyrlein's category of active, willing witches who were potentially worthy of the death penalty and thereby increased her risk of being questioned under torture and punished in some way.[78]

Equally importantly, Margaretha expressed remorse for what she had done and the wish to be freed from the devil's clutches with increasing fervour as the case progressed. She probably realised how important it was for her to express the penitence which the councillors and their advisers valued so greatly as a sinner's first step back on the road to piety as a result of her interrogation sessions with Zyrlein in early July. By late October jurist Schäfer had come to the conclusion that the question of whether Margaretha's tale of the sabbats was true or not was less important than the fact that she had repented of her sins and shown contrition; it was this latter fact which absolved her of any corporal or capital punishment.[79] The final summary of her case also cited her penitence and her humble pleas for forgiveness as another key factor justifying her lenient treatment.[80] It seems likely that Margaretha's appeal for assistance to be freed from the devil's influence pandered to the egos of the councillors and their advisers, enabling them to imagine themselves as the stern but merciful rescuers of this apparently helpless girl from diabolic clutches, at the same time as it fitted their theological interpretation of her as a penitent sinner.

Finally, the fact that Margaretha was pronounced a virgin by the city midwives helped the council justify its merciful treatment of her. Had her examination shown that she had been deflowered the council might have found it harder to regard her sins as purely spiritual and would have had a piece of physical evidence about her alleged relationship with the devil that would have been harder to dismiss as illusory. Ironically, the sexual element of her confession, which had been absent from the narrative she had told before her arrest and during her first interrogation on 18 May, was a product of specific questions put to her in custody, probably for the first time by Zyrlein in early July.[81] That Margaretha confessed to having had sex with the devil at this point suggests either that she thought this was what Zyrlein wanted her to say or that she was becoming more deeply convinced of her own sinfulness and identity as a witch as the case progressed.

Margaretha and the men who questioned her thus reinforced their perceptions of one another in what they all came to regard as the unfolding drama of the battle for her soul. This was a drama in which, of course, the councillors and their advisers held all the power as arbiters not only of Margaretha's ultimate fate but also of her alleged experiences, with the power to redefine events she claimed had really happened as delusions. Margaretha's only hope for escaping punishment was to play the part of the seduced but still-redeemable innocent, led astray by the forces of evil against her will and when she was too young to have known any better; luckily she proved able to do this with conviction and the necessary remorse and humility. She was helped enormously in this endeavour by the fact that midwife Ursula and her own mother, who Margaretha named as responsible for her seduction into witchcraft, were both dead by 1627 and therefore unable to complicate the council's handling of the case with protestations of their innocence. This was a vital point. Had they been alive to defend their good names at law the case might have ended very differently, with an admonition or punishment of Margaretha for defamation in keeping with the more usual outcome of other Rothenburg witch-trials. At the very least, their consistent denials of any involvement in witchcraft in the absence of any other incriminating evidence against them would have rendered Margaretha's story less credible and the authorities less confident in dealing with it, as they had been in 1587 in the face of Magdalena Gackstatt's dogged refusal to admit that she had taken her son Hans to a witches' dance.[82] In their absence Ursula and Margaretha's mother constituted convenient scapegoats for both Margaretha and the council; they were the bad mothers who were ultimately to blame for the diabolic seduction of Margaretha.

Margaretha's claims that she had been tempted into witchcraft by midwife Ursula, as her 'surrogate' mother, with the consent of her blood-mother drew on the widespread belief that the arts of witchcraft were passed on by mothers to daughters. However, they also struck chords with the council's fear of bad mothers as women who failed in their duty of teaching their offspring the basic tenets of Lutheranism.[83] Margaretha told the council that her mother had been unable to teach her how to pray because she was unable to pray herself, a claim that may well have been 'true', in the sense that her mother (as a Catholic) had not raised her to be a good Lutheran as defined by the council.[84] The councillors doubtless imagined that this lack of early religious instruction had first rendered Margaretha vulnerable to the devil's snares, with Margaretha's mother then compounding this failing by allowing Margaretha to be tempted into witchcraft by Ursula and by joining Ursula in discouraging Margaretha from saying her prayers in the Siechen Mill. Ursula had behaved even more wickedly, making every effort to teach Margaretha the evil arts of witchcraft. The low esteem in which the authorities held the two dead women can be seen in the reference by Seuter to Ursula as the old witch of Gebsattel, as if her status were an unequivocally proven fact,[85] and in the suggestion in the final summary of the case that Margaretha's mother and Ursula had, like procuresses, been responsible for persuading Margaretha to have sex with the devil.[86] The inclusion of this suggestion in the summary was unnecessary, given that it then went on to point out that Margaretha had never actually had sex, and shows that the council was having some difficulty reconciling its emphasis on the culpability of the two women in the case with its tendency to believe that Margaretha's alleged experiences had been illusory rather than real.

Finally, Zyrlein's report on the case probably helped confirm for the jurists and councillors a perception of Margaretha as worthy of pity rather than condemnation, dispelling earlier suspicions about her possible blameworthiness and providing compelling theological justification for treating her with clemency. Zyrlein (conveniently?) established that Margaretha had only been eight when Ursula had first taken her to a witches' dance and thus too young to have known right from wrong. His argument that her flights to the dances were probably diabolic delusions gave theological backing to the jurists' earlier advice not to arrest the other sabbat-attenders and consitituted the most cogent and best-documented statement about the tricks the quicksilver cunning of the devil could work on the human mind and senses that a Rothenburg witchcraft case had ever seen. Finally, his categorisation of Margaretha as a harmless witch, guilty only of apostasy and therefore undeserving of punishment, gave the council a way out of the case which was legally and theologically acceptable and in line with the some of the most liberal Lutheran thinking about witchcraft.

After her release from custody on 13 February 1628 Margaretha was probably sent to live with her stepbrother Michael Hörber in Steinach. Hörber had not been eager to take her into his household after her parents' deaths in 1626, nor had he shown much kindness towards her when she had complained to him of her harsh treatment at the Siechen Mill in 1627. However, he was her legal guardian and would have found it hard either to hand Margaretha over to the Würzburg authorities or to refuse to take her in himself once he had declared himself for Lutheranism, left Gebsattel, and become a Rothen-burg subject by buying a landholding which owed its dues to the city in Steinach.[87] Still, it seems unlikely that Hörber would have wanted to be closely associated with a self-confessed witch, who had doubtless gained huge notori-ety locally as a result of her trial, for very long. He probably sent her away into service somewhere far beyond the boundaries of Rothenburg's hinterland at the earliest opportunity.

The second Catholic challenge: the Schöneburg cavalrymen, 1629

An even more blatant Catholic challenge to the council's judicial authority over witchcraft occurred in August 1629, when Catholic League cavalrymen from the Bavarian regiment of Otto Friedrich von Schöneburg tried to start a witch-hunt in Rothenburg's hinterland, where they were permanently quartered between 1628 and 1631 after several earlier, briefer visits to the area. They rapidly acquired a reputation as particularly callous and brutal soldiers among the hinterland's rural population, and Surety Books of the time contain several instances of murders and attacks carried out by them on villagers which the Rothenburg council was virtually powerless to punish with adequate severity.[88] In addition to the immediate threat posed to life and limb, social order, and the council's judicial authority by the presence of von Schöneburg's cavalrymen and other imperial troops in the hinterland, by August 1629 the Lutheran posi-tion in the Thirty Years' War generally and Rothenburg's position *vis-à-vis* its local Catholic rivals was even more parlous than it had been in 1627. In Janu-ary 1629 the council had begun legal correspondence in defence of its secular-isation of the religious houses of the city in anticipation of the promulgation of the Edict of Restitution by Emperor Ferdinand in March.[89] Emboldened by the edict, our old friend Alexander Schreckenfuchs from Gebsattel went into Rothenburg on 5 August with some Jesuits from Munich and told the rector of the grammar school there that all the schools and churches in Rothenburg would soon be back in Catholic hands, a gloating prophecy which must have underlined for the councillors the reality and proximity of the Catholic threat to their Lutheran reformation and political power.[90]

The attempt by the cavalrymen to start a witch-hunt occurred around the same time in the three neighbouring villages of Obereichenroth, Bovenzen-weiler and Untereichenroth, which had eight, five and six households, respec-tively. In early August a fifteen-year-old girl called Margaretha Harter from Bovenzenweiler was fetching water from the well in Obereichenroth when she accidentally spilled some on a baker's apprentice who was standing nearby. He

swore at her in anger and called her a witch. Some of the Schöneburg cavalrymen who were quartered in Obereichenroth heard this, took Harter captive,
and presented her to their captain, Johann Caspar von Eltz, whose horse had
recently died in mysterious circumstances. Witchcraft was suspected, and
Caspar and his cronies seized the opportunity offered by the animal's death and
the public slandering of Harter as a witch to start their own investigation into
the matter. Von Eltz claimed that it was possible to tell whether someone was
a witch by looking into their eyes to see whether or not they had pupils; his
wife subjected Harter to this identification ritual and, unsurprisingly, concluded that she had no pupils and was therefore a witch. Von Eltz and his companions then asked Harter whether other local women were also witches and,
by means of leading questions and threats of violence, terrorised her into fabricating a story of witchcraft which would justify their instigation of a more
widespread witch-hunt.[91]

Harter was forced to admit that she had been seduced into witchcraft by
Anna Dieterich, the sixty-one-year-old widowed herdswoman of Untereichenroth and one of the first women suggested by the cavalrymen to Harter as
a probable witch.[92] Harter claimed that she and Dieterich had once met the
devil on their way home after they had been out begging for bread and alms
together. He had offered his hand to Harter but she had refused to shake it and
had hurried home alone while Dieterich talked to him. About a week after this
incident Dieterich had taken her night-flying against her will to a stable in
Oberstetten where the horse belonging to von Eltz was kept. There Dieterich
had ridden the horse to the point of exhaustion, which explained why it had
died three days later. Dieterich had then taken Harter to a nearby cellar where
they had feasted and to a witches' gathering where they had danced in the
devil's presence with other women from Obereichenroth and Bovenzenweiler,
whose names were also suggested to Harter by the cavalrymen. Harter also
claimed that at the dance the devil had instructed her to spit out rather than
swallow the bread and wine she received at communion, but that she had not
promised to obey him.[93]

Once the cavalrymen had 'persuaded' Harter to incriminate other
women in her witchcraft narrative they led her by a rope tied around her neck
through Bovenzenweiler and Obereichenroth and called the men of the two
villages together to hear her allegations. They asked Adam Strauss and Hans
Simon of Bovenzenweiler and Hans Stinzenberger, old Dümler, Georg Strauss
and the herdsman of Obereichenroth, whose wives' names had been forced out
of Harter as participants in the sabbat she had attended, whether they knew
that their wives were witches? Von Eltz then suggested to Georg Strauss that
his wife had been responsible for the deaths of Georg's horses. Georg replied
that if his wife were a witch who had killed his horses he would kill her

himself, but that no suspicions of witchcraft had been attached to the horses'
deaths at the time of their demise. Georg added that Harter and her allegations
of witchcraft should be taken before the proper judicial authorities for investigation and this cry was taken up by the other men present. The cavalrymen
were not keen on this idea. They knew of the council's restraint in trying
witches, commenting to Harter that if they allowed her to be taken into custody in Rothenburg the matter would end there, with the peasants and their
wives escaping arrest. They took Harter instead to Dunzendorf, a village outside Rothenburg's hinterland, in a short-lived attempt to remove her from the
council's jurisdiction. However, after a couple of days they let her go, after
either losing interest in their plan or realising that the villagers of Rothenburg's
hinterland were not to be stirred easily into an enthusiasm for witch-hunting.
Harter was taken into Rothenburg on 13 August for investigation of her allegations, which had already been brought to the attention of the council, probably by the men of Bovenzenweiler and Obereichenroth.[94]

Poor Harter. Thinking that she was now safe in council custody, she told
the councillors assigned to interrogate her how the cavalrymen had captured
her, told her they could do what they liked with her, and threatened to crush
her thumbs with their pistols if she did not answer their questions. She had tried
to insist on her innocence but had finally told them that she was a witch and
accused other women of witchcraft because she had been so afraid of their
threats and because she had hoped that they would release her if she told them
what they wanted to hear.[95] Her interrogators did not appear satisfied with this
account of events, however, and asked her instead to repeat the story she had
told the cavalrymen, showing particular interest in her meeting with the devil
and the death of von Eltz's horse. After much exhortation by her interrogators
and much reluctance on the part of Harter, she repeated her witchcraft narrative as though it had actually happened, and the council duly began an investigation of her alleged seduction into witchcraft by Anna Dieterich![96] Eight men
from Bovenzenweiler, Obereichenroth and Untereichenroth were questioned
about Dieterich's alleged reputation as a witch, while Harter was interrogated
for a second time on 17 August and forced to confront Dieterich in custody
on 18 August.

Why was Harter pressed to repeat her witchcraft narrative after she had
offered what appears to have been an eminently plausible explanation of why
she had invented it in the first place? Her interrogators might have done this
simply to test the consistency of her testimony, as they did with suspects in all
criminal cases. However, the willingness of the councillors to contemplate
beginning an investigation against Dieterich once Harter had repeated her allegations suggests that they must have thought that there was more than a grain of
truth in them. After all, they mirrored closely the witchcraft narrative they had

just heard in 1627, when they had been inclined to believe the worst of the women who had allegedly seduced Margaretha Hörber into witchcraft.[97] More-over, both the Hörber case and the Hans Gackstatt case discussed in Chapter 3 showed that the councillors and their advisers found it very difficult to believe that youngsters could simply fabricate witchcraft narratives, either subconsciously or strategically, from their own imaginative resources and for their own reasons. Finally, the fact that Rothenburg's councillors had sentenced Magdalena Dürr, a woman who had confessed to both infanticide and witchcraft, to death on 12 January 1629, in what was to be the first execution for witchcraft in Rothenburg, may have meant that they were disposed to take allegations of witchcraft particularly seriously just a few months later in August 1629.[98]

Harter doubtless repeated her narrative to the councillors as if it had really happened because she had just endured one terrifying experience of captivity and interrogation at the hands of the cavalrymen and feared that she would endure a similar experience if she did not tell her new set of interrogators what they apparently wanted to hear. During her second interrogation on 17 August she even gave the councillors additional evidence against Dieterich in a desperate attempt to win their sympathy and to shift the focus of the case onto the herdswoman. Harter told the councillors that she had heard that the Untereichenroth villagers wanted to get rid of Dieterich because they feared she would harm their livestock; that Dieterich had used blessings to cure headaches in Untereichenroth; that strange noises and fiery lights, indicative of mysterious nocturnal gatherings, had been heard and seen to emanate from the room where Dieterich lodged in the village; and that once, after Dieterich had had a bruised face for five weeks, it had been rumoured that she had been beaten by the devil.[99]

Rumours connecting Dieterich with witchcraft do seem to have circulated in Untereichenroth, Bovenzenweiler and Obereichenroth before August 1629; this was doubtless why she had been one of the first women suggested by the cavalrymen to Harter as a probable witch. It is unclear how generally and seriously Dieterich was reputed a witch in Untereichenroth and its environs, however. Harter traced virtually all the rumours she had heard linking Dieterich with witchcraft back to a single source: Dieterich's own son and daughter-in-law, with whom Dieterich had taken lodgings in the village after the death of her husband in 1627 and who appear to have hated and wanted to be rid of her with an alarming degree of enthusiasm. The cause of their animosity is unclear, although Dieterich and her daughter-in-law were reported to have quarrelled over the alleged bad housekeeping of the latter, a situation which cannot have been improved by the fact that soldiers had plundered their household, leaving them largely reliant on begging to survive.[100]

The eight men of Bovenzenweiler, Untereichenroth and Obereichenroth called on to testify about Dieterich by the council, however, all claimed that they personally knew nothing about her in connection with witchcraft, other than what Harter and the cavalrymen had recently said.[101] If anyone had ever called Dieterich a witch, Michael Dehner of Obereichenroth commented, this was simply because it was the general habit of people to call old women witches.[102] The men of Untereichenroth praised Dieterich's diligence as a herdswoman during the thirty-four years she had lived in their village and professed to know nothing about any of the additional evidence Harter had cited against Dieterich during her second interrogation.[103] Hans Strauss confirmed that the men of Untereichenroth had commented that it would be better for the rest of the village if Dieterich lived elsewhere, but explained that this was because they feared that she might involve the rest of them in a witch-hunt, not because they feared that she would harm their livestock.[104] This fear of finding themselves and their families dragged in a witch-hunt, and particularly one started by the hated Schöneburg cavalrymen, was also uppermost in the minds of men from other villages and helps explain their unwillingness to testify against Dieterich. As Adam Strauss and Hans Kaufman of Bovenzenweiler put it in a statement which highlighted the gulf that existed between the villagers and the cavalrymen on the question of how best to deal with witches, even if Dieterich had been called a witch in the past, this had only been done to tease and vex her. It had not been meant as a serious matter, which was what the cavalrymen were now trying to make of it, as they rode through Bovenzenweiler shouting 'when will the burning start here?' to its inhabitants.[105] Popular concern about the risks of formal prosecutions for witchcraft were probably heightened at this point because of the ongoing mass witch-trials in Würzburg and also because of the execution of Magdalena Dürr for infanticide and witchcraft in Rothenburg in January 1629.[106]

Anna Dieterich was thus helped significantly by the absence of negative communal testimony against her. Unfortunately for Harter, the herdswoman was also only too willing to appear in person in Rothenburg to protest her innocence vehemently to the councillors and to Harter when the two of them were brought face to face in gaol on 18 August. At first Harter attempted to stick to her allegations against Dieterich, despite Dieterich's lamentation that Harter was trying unjustly to deprive her of her good name in her old age and her reminder to Harter that she would have to answer for her false accusations at the Day of Judgement. However, after Dieterich was removed from the room and Harter was exhorted to tell the truth by the councillors, Harter retracted the accusation against Dieterich that she had never wanted to make in the first place, admitted that none of her witchcraft narrative had ever really happened, and repeated that she had only spoken of it because the cavalrymen had terrorised her into so doing.[107]

Harter's admission that she had falsely accused Dieterichin of witchcraft brought the case to an end and earned the fifteen-year-old a flogging in the city gaol followed by banishment from Rothenburg and its hinterland for slander on 22 August.[108] This doubtless satisfied the men of Bovenzenweiler and Obereichenroth whose wives had also been accused as witches by Harter; Georg Strauss of Obereichenroth had already planned to bring a slander case on behalf of his wife against Harter had the necessity arisen.[109] Harter's punishment was relatively harsh, however. The much older Barbara Rost had only been banished in January 1629, despite the fact that her slanders had touched some of the most eminent families in Rothenburg,[110] and the fact that the cavalrymen had initially forced Harter into inventing her slander was played down by the council as a mitigating circumstance in her case. Moreover, if the council had been concerned chiefly with the consistent punishment of slander in August 1629, then it should also have arrested the baker's apprentice who had called Harter a witch in Obereichenroth in the first place. Harter had complained to the councillors of his unfounded accusation of her during her first interrogation on 13 August, but there is no evidence to suggest that he was ever made to answer for it at law.[111]

Harter's inconsistency in custody – and her final admission that she had, indeed, falsely accused Dieterich of witchcraft – doubtless did little to endear her to the councillors. They appear also to have decided to categorise her as a malicious slanderer because she had repeated her allegations against Dieterich in custody as if they were true without suffering torture: she was asked at the end of her second interrogation why she had said such things about Dieterich when she had not been forced to do so.[112] This inability or unwillingness on the part of the councillors to comprehend that Harter had probably been so traumatised by her experience at the hands of the cavalrymen that she would probably have said whatever anyone interrogating her subsequently appeared to want to hear suggests a marked lack of sympathy for her on their part. This unsympathetic stance was probably also motivated by practical and political reasons. Given the ease with which the Schöneburg cavalrymen had escaped the council's justice for other crimes they had committed, the councillors doubtless realised that it would have been very hard even to try to punish them for attempting to start a witch-hunt. It was much easier for the councillors to gloss over the fact that the cavalrymen had tried to start a rival and unofficial witch-hunt in the city's own hinterland and to assert their judicial authority in the matter by making an example of the defenceless Harter as an evil slanderer. They therefore used Harter, as they had used Hörber in 1627, to make a point about their judicial authority over witchcraft cases which had political and religious resonances beyond the immediate context of the cases themselves.

From the point of view of the Schöneburg cavalrymen, their attempted witch-hunt was another way of terrorising the villagers in whose midst they were quartered and also a way of showing them how witches ought to be tried and hunted, in contrast to what they regarded as the mealy-mouthed treatment of suspected witches by the council in Rothenburg. They were careful to give a semblance of legitimacy to their actions by aping recognised legal procedures in their treatment of Harter: they 'arrested' and 'interrogated' her, threatened to 'torture' her using their pistols as a makeshift version of thumbscrews, and subjected her to an identification ritual that was used by municipal executioners in other parts of southern Germany.[113] However, in stark contrast to the usually cautious legal handling of witchcraft allegations by the council, the cavalrymen's only aim in their 'trial' of Harter was to force her to confess to being a witch and to accuse other people of witchcraft as quickly as possible, in order to start a witch-panic which they hoped would result in many executions. Here they seem to have been drawing on knowledge of the mass witch-trials currently ongoing in the Catholic ecclesiastical territories of Franconia, which relied for their impetus on excessive use of torture and forced denunciations by suspected witches of their accomplices, in order to 'teach' the inhabitants of Untereichenroth, Obereichenorth and Bovenzenweiler the mechanisms by which such trials might be replicated in Rothenburg and its hinterland.[114] Fortunately for all concerned, the villagers in question proved to be intractable pupils and neither participated in the cavalrymen's 'trial' of Harter nor demanded harsher action against witches generally from the council. This, combined with the continued caution of the council in its handling of witchcraft allegations, ensured that Rothenburg was spared the swell-tide of executions which engulfed the Catholic territories of Franconia between 1627 and 1629.

Notes

1 Gagliardo, *Germany Under the Old Regime*, p. 54.
2 The same was the case in the rest of Franconia; Nuremberg, for example, also became a mustering and provisioning centre for the Catholic armies, see Endres, 'Der Dreissigjährige Krieg', pp. 487–488.
3 Moritz, *Die Folgen des Dreissigjährigen Krieges*, pp. 54–60, 70–76; Müller, *Gebsattel. Chronik eines fränkischen Dorfes*, pp. 62–63.
4 This was probably the same Jobst Unger whose son Hans had almost been tricked out of 400 gulden belonging to his father in 1614, see pp. 52–53. This, and the fact that Michael Hörber could afford to move out of Gebsattel rather than convert to Catholicism, suggests that neither of Margaretha's guardians was financially incapable of caring for her themselves.
5 RStA Interrogation Book A886 fols 264r, 265r.
6 *Ibid.*, fols 264r–264v, 291r–291v.
7 *Ibid.*, fols 264r–266r.
8 *Ibid.*, fols 266v–267r, 291v.
9 *Ibid.*, fols 264r– 267r.
10 All sixteen of the mills situated along the Tauber River in Rothenburg's hinterland belonged to the city; their millers had to swear annual oaths of loyalty to the council, promising to uphold Rothenburg's mill ordinances, see Bedal, *Mühlen und Müller in Franken*, pp. 141–144, 178.

11 See p. 4.
12 Müller, *Gebsattel. Chronik eines fränkischen Dorfes*, p. 74.
13 *Ibid.*, p. 146: 'das sogenannte Schloss.'
14 See RStA Gebsattel Village Acts, disputes with Komburg, vols A105–A166.
15 On the importance of the exercise of high criminal justice to the consolidation and assertion of the Rothenburg council's territorial overlordship, see Rowlands, 'Women, gender and power', pp. 7–8, 10–11.
16 RStA Blood Book B333 fols 86v–98v, 107v–109r; Müller, *Gebsattel. Chronik eines fränkischen Dorfes*, pp. 44–45.
17 *Ibid.*, p. 49. Müller's book contains an excellent account of the medieval origins of the rivalry between Rothenburg and Komburg over their respective rights in Gebsattel (pp. 35–44), as well as several other examples of disputes between them which occurred during the sixteenth century (pp. 44–51).
18 *Ibid.*, p. 160; Dannheimer, *Verzeichnis*, p. 33.
19 Müller, *Gebsattel. Chronik eines fränkischen Dorfes*, pp. 172–173.
20 *Ibid.*, pp. 173–176. One of the most popular incumbents of late-sixteenth-century Gebsattel was Jakob Artmeier, who provided both Catholic and Lutheran services, *ibid.*, pp. 160, 174.
21 *Ibid.*, pp. 63, 76, 160, 197, 199.
22 RStA Interrogation Book A886 fols 270v, 294r.
23 Hörber and Unger were listed as Lutherans by the Bishop of Würzburg in 1627, see Bauer, *Gebsattel im 17. Jahrhundert*, p. 204.
24 Schreckenfuchs held this post from 1618 until 1632, then again from 1636 until 1650, see Müller, *Gebsattel. Chronik eines fränkischen Dorfes*, pp. 150–151. This action of von Ehrenberg's was a continuation of his predecessor Julius Echter von Mespelbrunn's counter-reforming efforts as Bishop of Würzburg, which had started in the 1580s, see Schubert, *Gegenreformation in Franken*.
25 Bauer, *Gebsattel im 17. Jahrhundert*, pp. 202, 263.
26 *Ibid.*, pp. 202–207, 263–267, 278–279; Müller, *Gebsattel. Chronik eines fränkischen Dorfes*, pp. 63–66; RStA Steinach Village Acts A739 fols 654r–654v. Hörber had become Rothenburg's village official in Steinach by 1635, see *ibid.*, fols 645r–645v.
27 Kunstmann, *Zauberwahn*, p. 17; Merzbacher, 'Geschichte des Hexenprozesses im Hochstifte Würzburg'; Schwillus, '"Der bischoff lässt nit nach"'. Robert Walinski-Kiehl suggests that the estimate of 900 witches executed in Würzburg (which comes from a pamphlet printed c. 1629) is almost certainly too high, but that accurate figures for the Würzburg persecutions are hard to obtain because many trial-records from the period are missing, see Walinski-Kiehl, '"Godly states"', p. 13. Wolfgang Behringer, however, suggests that the high figures are probably reasonably accurate, especially for the witch-hunts that occurred in the late 1620s, *Hexenverfolgung in Bayern*, pp. 237–238.
28 Walinski-Kiehl, '"Godly states"', p. 13.
29 Behringer, *Hexenverfolgung in Bayern*, pp. 236–241.
30 *Ibid.*, p. 239: 'Die fränkischen Verfolgungen verwirklichten den düsteren Traum der unbedingten Hexenverfolgung, in welcher ohne Rücksicht auf politische, gesellschaftliche oder humanitäre Hindernisse allein der Logik der Verfolgungen gefolgt wurde'.
31 RStA Interrogation Book A886 fol. 266r.
32 *Ibid.*, fols 268r–268v.
33 The Prince-Bishop of Würzburg issued a mandate ordering the confiscation of the property of witches executed in his territory only on 10 June 1627, see Merzbacher, 'Geschichte des Hexenprozesses im Hochstifte Würzburg', p. 173.
34 Müller, *Gebsattel. Chronik eines fränkischen Dorfes*, pp. 52–53, 59.
35 Robert Walinksi-Kiehl, for example, argues that the witch-hunts in the Prince-Bishoprics of Bamberg and Würzburg in the late 1620s 'should be viewed as a product of the new vigour of emerging Catholic absolutist-style states', see '"Godly states"', p. 21. Jürgen Schmidt

argues that the authorities in the Calvinist Palatinate, who deliberately refused to foster witch-trials there from 1561, also regarded the mass-trials in the Catholic ecclesiastical territories disparagingly as evidence of typically Catholic confusion, see *Glaube und Skepsis*, p. 480.

36　RStA Interrogation Book A886 fols 269r–270v.

37　*Ibid.*, fols 270v–271v.

38　See Chapter 3, especially pp. 89–92.

39　RStA Interrogation Book A886 fols 273r–273v.

40　*Ibid.*, fols 274r–275r.

41　*Ibid.*, fols 275r–275v. Although not mentioned specfically, the treatment of Hans Gackstatt in 1587 may have influenced Schäfer's opinion on this point: see Chapter 3.

42　*Ibid.*, fols 277r–278v.

43　*Ibid.*, fols 275v–276r, 277v–278r.

44　*Ibid.*, fols 283v–284r.

45　*Ibid.*, fols 283r–283v, 284v. See also pp. 53–54 for further discussion of Zyrlein's division of witches into 'active' and 'passive' categories.

46　*Ibid.*, fol. 284v.

47　*Ibid.*, fols 285v–286v. See also pp. 53–54 for the influence of Thumm, Gödelmann and Luther on Zyrlein's ideas.

48　*Ibid.*, fols 298r–300r.

49　*Ibid.*, fol. 298v.

50　*Ibid.*, fols 291r–292r.

51　*Ibid.*, fols 298v–299r. The expertise of midwives in ascertaining whether or not women were still virgins had been legally acknowledged in Rothenburg in two sixteenth-century slander cases, see RStA Interrogation Book A852 fols 264r–265r (1554); RStA Marriage Acts A1477 fols 138r–145v (1565).

52　RStA Interrogation Book A886 fol. 301r; although performed by the midwives, the examination was carried out in the presence of one of the city's physicians.

53　*Ibid.*, fols 302r–304r.

54　*Ibid.*, fols 280r–281v. Eva had recently married: see Appendix for details.

55　*Ibid.*, fol. 287r. This report also implicated the herdsman's wife and maidservant in these suspicious activities.

56　*Ibid.*, fols 299r–300r.

57　*Ibid.*, fols 279r, 282r, 305r–305v, 306r–307r.

58　*Ibid.*, fol. 300r.

59　*Ibid.*, fol. 299r.

60　*Ibid.*, fols 303v–304r.

61　*Ibid.*, fol. 297r.

62　*Ibid.*, fol. 269r.

63　*Ibid.*, fol. 269 (a)r.

64　*Ibid.*, fol. 284r: 'Meigelein! Meigelein!'. Brigitta Hörner, another girl who claimed to be a witch in the seventeenth century, was also an orphan and unwanted by her relatives: see p. 62 and Rowlands, 'The "Little witch girl"'. Perhaps Margaretha and Brigitta coped with their emotional trauma by means of their witchcraft narratives.

65　*Ibid.*, fols 264r–267r, 291r–292r, 270v–271v.

66　*Ibid.*, fol. 265r.

67　See Chapter 3 for discussion of Hans Gackstatt's case.

68　*Ibid.*, fols 266v, 271v.

69　The process of questioning that the Komburg Lutherans were forced to undergo in Gebsattel at the hands of Schreckenfuchs, Gebsattel's Catholic priest Georg Holzapfel, and the Bishop of Würzburg's representatives, in order to convert them to Catholicism, is transcribed by Bauer in *Gebsattel im 17. Jahrhundert*.

70　RStA Interrogation Book A886 fols 266r–266v.

71　Margaretha expressed this idea during her first interrogation on 18 May, see *ibid.*, fol. 270v.

She repeated it when questioned by Superintendent Zyrlein in early July (fol. 284r), and again under interrogation on 10 October (fol. 294r).

72 See Schäfer's first opinion on the case dated 20 May, *ibid.*, fols 273r–276r.

73 *Ibid.*, fol. 286r: 'ie mehr man hexen vmbbringet oder verbrennet, ie mehr derselben werden.'

74 Schormann, *Der Krieg*, p. 162–163. On the probable exchange of ideas about witchcraft between Rothenburg and Nuremberg during the early modern period, see pp. 64–67.

75 See pp. 94–96; Sabean, *Power in the Blood*, p. 111.

76 RStA Interrogation Book A886 fol. 272v.

77 *Ibid.*, fol. 307r.

78 However, leniency would probably have been shown towards Margaretha because of her youth even if she had confessed to maleficium, as happened in the case of Brigitta Hörner in 1639, see Rowlands, 'The "Little witch girl"'.

79 RStA Interrogation Book A886 fols 303r–303v. On this point, see also Zyrlein's use of the example of the penitent sinner taken from Luther, pp. 53–54.

80 *Ibid.*, fol. 307r.

81 *Ibid.*, fols 283v–284r.

82 See Chapter 3.

83 See pp. 94–96.

84 RStA Interrogation Book A886 fol. 271v.

85 *Ibid.*, fol. 298r.

86 *Ibid.*, fol. 306v. This way of imagining procuresses had some basis in reality; Lyndal Roper's work on procuresses in early modern Augsburg suggests that they tended to be older, married women, while the prostitutes they controlled tended to be younger and unmarried. See Roper, 'Mothers of debauchery', pp. 6–7.

87 RStA Steinach Village Acts A739 fols 645r–45v, 654r–654v. The records say nothing about Margaretha's fate after her release from custody. However, the fact that a formal investigation into self-confessed child-witch Brigitta Hörner's death occurred in 1640, after she had been released from council custody but rejected by the relatives who were supposed to have taken responsibility for her, suggests that Rothenburg's council did not turn a blind eye to the fate of child-witches after their release from custody, see Rowlands, 'The "Little witch girl"'. Hörber would therefore probably not have found it easy to turn Margaretha out of his house after her trial.

88 Schmidt, 'Das Kriegsjahr 1628', pp. 59–68. Endres also notes that these cavalrymen were notorious, see 'Der Dreissigjährige Krieg', pp. 488–489.

89 StAN Ro. Rep. 2086 fols 11r–14r (this entire volume is devoted to correspondence about the Edict of Restitution).

90 Heller, *Rothenburg ob der Tauber im Jahrhundert des grossen Krieges*, pp. 40–41.

91 This account is taken from Harter's first statement in council custody on 13 August, RStA Interrogation Book A888 fols 595r–600r, especially 595r–598r. The Rothenburg sources refer to the cavalrymen's ringleader as Hans Caspar, but records from Nuremberg suggest that this was Captain Johann (Hans) Caspar von Eltz, StAN Council Correspondence Books Rep. 61a, vol. 245, fol. 30v.

92 RStA Interrogation Book A888 fols 596r, 614r.

93 *Ibid.*, fols 598v–600r. This was the story that Harter repeated to Rothenburg's councillors during interrogation on 13 August. We know that this was the story she had been forced to fabricate by the cavalrymen before her arrest, as the councillors interrogating her already knew all about its key elements (her alleged meeting with the devil, the sabbat, the death of the horse) from reports it had received from unspecified sources before her arrest.

94 *Ibid.*, fols 596v–97v, 619v.

95 *Ibid.*, fols 595r–598r.

96 *Ibid.*, fols 598v–600r.

97 See above, pp. 122–123.

98 See RStA Interrogation Book A887 fols 592r–594v for Dürr's sentence; pp. 136–143 for discussion of her case.
99 RStA Interrogation Book A888 fols 606r–608r.
100 *Ibid.*, fols 596r, 607r, 609v, 614r.
101 *Ibid.*, fols 601r–603v, 609r–612r.
102 *Ibid.*, fol. 601r.
103 *Ibid.*, fols 603r, 609r–612r.
104 *Ibid.*, fols 611r–612r.
105 *Ibid.*, fol. 603v.
106 See above, n. 98.
107 RStA Interrogation Book A888 fols 614r–616v.
108 *Ibid.*, fols 618r–619v.
109 *Ibid., fol.* 619v.
110 See pp. 24, 27–28.
111 RStA Interrogation Book A888 fol. 598r.
112 *Ibid.*, fol. 616r.
113 In 1590, for example, Friedrich Stigler identified several Nuremberg women as witches because of their alleged lack of pupils, after he had learnt this identification method from his master, the executioner of Eichstätt; Kunstmann, *Zauberwahn*, p. 76. Stigler was ultimately executed for bigamy, sorcery and falsely accusing these women of witchcraft, *ibid.*, pp. 76–78.
114 Although Heinrich Schmidt suggests that the Schöneburg cavalrymen probably served as the guard that accompanied condemned witches to the stake in Würzburg in 1627 (Schmidt, 'Vordringender Hexenwahn', p. 77), I have been unable to find any evidence of this. It is, however, virtually certain that the cavalrymen would have travelled through or been quartered in or near those areas of Franconia where large-scale witch-hunts took place between 1627 and 1629, and that the differences in Catholic and Lutheran patterns of witch-prosecution during those years must have plain for them and others to see.

5

Seduction, poison and magical theft: gender and contemporary fantasies of witchcraft

As was the case in many other places in early modern Europe, most of those who were accused of or who confessed to witchcraft or who were formally questioned as suspected witches in Rothenburg were female.[1] They ranged in age from eight to eighty-eight years but most were aged twenty-one and above,[2] with those aged from around thirty to sixty – and perhaps particularly those in their fifties – most at risk of becoming the subject of a legal investigation into an allegation of witchcraft.[3] Most were married at the time of involvement in a trial: the remainder were predominantly widows.[4] Why were adult women most likely to become caught up in witch-trials in early modern Rothenburg? Was it because they were most readily imagined as witches by their neighbours and accused accordingly? Or was the gender-bias more marked at the elite level, ensuring that any men who were accused as witches were less likely to face formal prosecution? This chapter explores answers to these questions through analysis of a series of seventeenth-century cases and in the light of ideas about how witches were conceptualised which are gaining increasing currency within the historiography of early modern witchcraft. These ideas suggest that women were more likely to be accused of and confess to being witches because witches were predominantly imagined by contemporaries as the evil inverse of the good housewife and mother; as women who poisoned and harmed others rather than nurturing and caring for them.

Diane Purkiss, for example, has argued for early modern England that 'For women, a witch was a figure who could be read against and within her own social identity as housewife and mother'; the witch was a 'usurper of the authority of other women over the domestic realm' who polluted food supplies, disrupted household order and harmed children and childbearing women.[5] Lyndal Roper has suggested that motherhood was a central theme of the witch-trials of seventeenth-century Augsburg. Most accused witches there were old, widowed lying-in maids who were imagined as 'evil mothers' who harmed rather than nurtured the parturient mothers or newborn babies in their charge. This was partly because their post-menopausal bodies were imagined negatively as dried up and poisonous, the inverse of the fertile female body which flowed with menstrual blood and breastmilk, and partly because the childbearing women who were their accusers projected their own feelings of anxiety or hostility towards their babies or their own mothers onto these lying-in maids.[6] In her work on the German town of Horn, Ingrid Ahrendt-Schulte has postulated that the skills of harmful magic were imagined as the inverse of the positive skills of housewifery: both were rooted in women's powerful yet ambiguous abilities to transform substances within their bodies (in terms of childbearing), and in their daily work (in terms of cooking, brewing and dairying).[7] Similar ideas have been used to interpret women's voluntary confessions of witchcraft. Louise Jackson, for example, has suggested that women in seventeenth-century Suffolk also judged themselves against the ideal of the good housewife. Should they find themselves wanting they might articulate their 'insecurities as wives and mothers as well as traumas about experiences or events . . . through the framework of the witchcraft confession', adopting 'the language of demonology' to explain their feelings.[8]

A 'murdering' mother? Magdalena Dürr, 1628–29

Can these ideas help us understand the gender-bias of the Rothenburg witch-trials? Let us begin to answer this question by examining the case of Magdalena Dürr, a twenty-eight-year-old woman from the village of Standorf who was arrested on 23 December 1628 on suspicion of having killed her eleven-week-old daughter four days earlier. Magdalena claimed that she had found the baby lying dead next to its cradle with a bruise on its head on returning to her house after fetching some milk from a neighbour with which to feed the child; she was incapable of feeding it herself because she had no nipples, probably meaning inverted nipples or nipples which had been damaged through infection. Her cries of alarm had brought her husband, Hans Dürr, and the couple's two servants rushing into the house to see what was wrong.[9] Rumours that Magdalena might have harmed the child herself arose rapidly in Standorf for various reasons. To begin with, she gave muddled answers to her husband when he questioned her about the baby's death in the presence of their servants and a neighbour, Hans Unger, saying first that the baby must have suffocated, then that it must have fallen out of its cradle while she was out.[10] Magdalena then ran off, spent three nights sleeping rough, and missed her baby's funeral in the process. She later claimed that she had only done this to escape her husband's violence: he had beaten her on 19 December for her inconsistent replies to his questions and had treated her so violently during their married life that she was deaf and hardly knew what she was doing at times as a result.[11] One of their servants, two of their neighbours, and Dürr himself confirmed that he beat Magdalena frequently, but this was doubtless insufficient to stop damaging inferences from being drawn from Magdalena's absence from her child's funeral: that she cared little for it and had therefore perhaps been responsible for its death.[12]

Magdalena's vulnerability to the negative rumours which occasioned her arrest probably also sprang from her social isolation: had she been a popular individual with a supportive husband and network of friends, it is possible that her baby's death would never have reached the attention of the council. Her unpopularity seems to have stemmed from three things: the fact that she was incontinent, her disorderly speech and behaviour, and her bad marriage. Her incontinence may well have resulted from complications following the birth of twins by Hans Dürr in the late summer of 1627; the babies had died shortly after birth but Magdalena's condition encouraged her neighbours to regard her with distaste.[13] For example, Eva Klenck, who had prepared all three of the Dürrs' babies for burial, told the council that she had made Magdalena touch her daughter's corpse in December because she had heard that if a murderer touched her victim's body it would bleed as a sign of her guilt. Eva explained that she suspected Magdalena of having harmed the child because she was a filthy woman whom people held in horror.[14] Klenck, Magdalena, and Hans Dürr all suggested that the couple's bad marriage was due largely to Magdalena's incontinence: Dürr described Magdalena as 'worthy of no man, coarse, dirty'.[15]

Magdalena's words and behaviour were also regarded as disorderly by her neighbours. Hans Unger described her as inconstant of speech while another villager, Georg Gackstatt, reported that she behaved at times as if out of her senses and had run around out of doors instead of staying at home during her pregnancy with the now-dead baby.[16] Such behaviour would not have endeared her to her neighbours: verbal unreliability and the damage it could do to others was scorned in an age which valued reputation so highly,[17] while her behaviour when pregnant would have been seen as a disturbing abdication of the proper responsibilities of an expectant mother.[18] The Dürrs' bad marriage was probably a source of concern for their neighbours. Early modern communities valued harmonious marriages as these were least likely to disrupt the communal peace or to necessitate the intervention of outside authorities in the settling of disputes. And, while neighbours were capable of blaming violent husbands for bad marriages, it seems likely that what communal sympathy existed for the Dürrs in Standorf probably lay with Hans; his violence was probably seen as a justified response to, rather than an unjust cause of, his wife's disorderly behaviour.

During her first interrogation in custody on 23 December Magdalena continued to maintain that she had found her child lying dead next to its cradle without knowing how it had died. This was despite the fact that her interrogators tried to undermine her story and also implied that all her babies had a sinister habit of dying young. How could the child have died from a fall from its cradle, they asked, surely she had maltreated it in some way? Why had her child by her first husband died so rapidly?[19] Magdalena's only hope of escaping from custody with her life lay in maintaining this denial of knowledge of, or culpability for, her baby's death. However, four days later her second interrogation took a different course. In the interim Magdalena had confessed to her gaolers that she had indeed killed her baby. Her interrogators, who would have been informed of this confession, thus opened proceedings on 27 December by accusing Magdalena of having lied to them in making her first statement. Magdalena responded by admitting that she had killed her baby, explaining that she had been moved to do so by anger. The baby had been crying because it was hungry and, thinking of the beating she would receive from her husband for failing to quieten it, she had thrown it across the room against its cradle in a rage. It had hit its head and fallen to the floor, sustaining fatal injuries in the process. She had not intended to kill it and was heartily sorry for what she had done.[20]

This confession did not satisfy her interrogators, however; they urged Magdalena to account more specifically for the bruise on the baby's head. After hesitating Magdalena added that she had crushed the baby's temples with her thumbs because Satan had been standing behind her encouraging her to do this. Her interrogators asked for more details about her relationship with Satan; after more hesitation and pressure, she said that she had first met him while working in the fields as a child and that he had wanted to teach her how to murder people. As it was believed that the arts of witchcraft could be taught by mothers to daughters, her interrogators then demanded whether her mother had taught her anything? Magdalena hesitated again, but then said that her mother (who had died three months earlier) had told her that she must murder her children and that she had also killed the twins she had had in 1627 by crushing their temples. Her mother had also taken her to witches' dances on a fire-iron but infrequently, as Magdalena had been unenthusiastic about attending. She was again asked about the death of her baby by her first husband but insisted that it had died of convulsions. When asked how she could have killed her other children, she explained that she had had to do it on her mother's orders and because Satan had been standing behind her with a stick threatening to beat her.[21]

During her third interrogation on 30 December Magdalena vacillated between natural and supernatural explanations for her babies' deaths. She continued to maintain that she had killed her baby daughter, although she first said that Satan had forced her into doing this, then that she had acted out of anger and fear of her husband's violence. Regarding her twins she at first described their deaths as if they had occurred naturally. It was only after further pressure from her interrogators that she claimed to have crushed their temples with her thumbs, first saying that she had done this to stop them crying, then because she had desired to murder them. She added that her mother had taught her to do this and had also threatened her with a beating to ensure that she killed the babies. After further questioning about what other witchcraft she had learned she said first that she had been taken to witches' dances by her mother, then that another woman who had been at the dance, Stern Katharin from Insingen, had tried to teach her witchcraft. Magdalena refused to admit that she had learned how to work harmful magic from Katharin, however, despite the fact that her interrogators recorded their suspicion that Magdalena had been responsible for the deaths of her first husband and her child by him.[22] It was only under threat of torture during her fourth interrogation on 5 January 1629 that Magdalena finally admitted that she had forsworn God and given herself to Satan at the witches' dance. Satan had given her a witches' mark and some money and they had had sex. On being asked what other acts of maleficium she had committed she claimed to have stabbed to death two cows belonging to Georg Gackstatt.[23] Gackstatt subsequently reported that one of his cows had died as a result of witchcraft but that he could not accuse anyone specifically as responsible for its demise.[24]

The council's patience with Magdalena's inconsistency ran out on 7 January when she was taken to the torture-chamber at the start of her fifth interrogation and exhorted to tell the truth about all the murders she had committed. Magdalena now claimed that, in addition to killing her children, she had strangled Stern Katharin and her two maidservants with her mother's help, that she had strangled a man called Peter Lenck from Buch on her own, and that she had strangled one – rather than stabbed two – of Georg Gackstatt's cows. In light of these new confessions and inconsistency, Magdalena was tortured twice with thumbscrews, although this elicited no additional admissions; Magdalena remained adamant that she had killed neither her first husband nor her child by him, insisting that both had died of natural causes.[25]

On 10 January the councillors made a final attempt to force Magdalena into making a consistent statement. They had discovered that Stern Katharin had died of the plague and that Peter Lenck was still alive.[26] This information was put to Magdalena but she still maintained that she and her mother had killed them both. She also repeated that she had flown to witches' dances with her mother and promised herself to Satan. She had reconsidered her explanations of her children's deaths, however. She said that the twins had been weak at birth because of Dürr's violent treatment of her during her pregnancy with them. She repeated her original admission about the events of 19 December – that she had thrown the baby into its cradle out of anger because she had feared her husband's reaction to its cries – adding that Satan had put the idea into her head. She finished by asking for mercy, saying that she did not think she deserved to be executed for the killing of just one child.[27] The councillors thought otherwise, however. On 12 January she was beheaded – the usual punishment for infanticide – and then her corpse burned to suggest that she might have been a witch.[28]

How can we explain Magdalena's muddled and, as her interrogators described it, 'very . . . marvellous and strange' narrative?[29] It seems likely that the accounts of the deaths of her babies by Dürr to which she returned in her final interrogation were nearest any 'truth' of what had happened to the children. It was entirely plausible that her twins had died of natural causes; no-one else had raised suspicions about their deaths in 1627, Magdalena herself had maintained that they were premature, while the most that Eva Klenck was willing to say on the matter was that Magdalena had worked too hard during her pregnancy and was hard-hearted towards the twins once born.[30] Magdalena's account of her unintentional killing of her third baby was also plausible, if tragic. It is unlikely that a baby so weak from poor feeding could have fallen from its cradle of its own volition. It was possible that Dürr rather than Magdalena could have killed it, but certain factors – the fact that he had been working outside with his servants at the time of its death and the fact that he so rapidly made the death public knowledge – suggest that this was improbable. He had fled Standorf by 10 January but Magdalena offered the most likely explanation for his action: because he feared being arrested and questioned about his ill-treatment of her.[31] Why then did Magdalena turn her accounts of her babies' deaths into tales of murder prompted by Satan and admit to being a witch under interrogation?

As Louise Jackson has suggested for seventeenth-century Suffolk women, Magdalena may have used the process of confession subconsciously in order to articulate her sense of failure to live up to the ideal of the good housewife and to express her feelings about her babies' deaths.[32] Married women in early modern Rothenburg gained good reputations by having harmonious marriages, bearing and raising children successfully, managing the economy of their households efficiently, and being good neighbours. Magdalena probably saw herself and was seen by others as a failure on all these counts. Her marriage was characterised by enmity rather than harmony, yet Dürr's detestation of her was caused by the physical problem of her incontinence which she could not rectify. Her mothering was characterised by failure rather than success; her babies had all died young and Magdalena's inability to breastfeed, which she could likewise not rectify, must have ensured their failure to thrive. When her daughter started crying on 19 December Magdalena may have been reminded of the babies she had failed to mother successfully before and of the threat of another beating at the hands of the husband whose wish to quieten the child she could not obey. Her outburst of rage in throwing the child stemmed probably from a desire to stop the noise which symbolised her shortcomings as a wife and mother and from the anger towards her husband which she could demonstrate in no other way. That she then claimed during interrogation that she had been doing Satan's bidding and that she had killed her twins as well may testify to feelings of guilt for her failings as a mother which she could articulate only by imagining herself as a baby-killing witch, particularly as it was Magdalena rather than her interrogators who first introduced Satan and the murders of her twins into the interrogation process. Her refusal to admit that she had done her first husband or her child by him any harm was also striking. This suggests that her first marriage had been happy in comparison to the misery she endured at the hands of Dürr and that she therefore had no desire to imagine it in diabolic terms.

We can, however, only push this interpretation of Magdalena's confession so far; other explanations for it are equally plausible. In claiming that Satan and her mother had prompted her to kill her children Magdalena may – naively – have been trying to escape the full rigours of the law for her actions. During her third interrogation she was accused of trying to blame her mother for the twins' deaths by claiming that her mother had told her to kill them: Magdalena responded by saying that 'it was the person who told one to do such a deed who was guilty of it'.[33] She also tried hard, at least until the threat and then the reality of torture were introduced into the proceedings, to suggest that she had been forced by threats of violence into the 'murders' and that she had been reluctant to go to witches' dances or to learn witchcraft. Moreover, while Magdalena occasionally took the narrative initiative in the interrogation process, the insistent questioning by her interrogators provided its overall driving force. Such relentless questioning was normal in criminal cases where the aim of the authorities was to establish the 'truth', meaning an account of events which was consistent in all its details no matter how often it was repeated. Furthermore, her interrogators' questions did not dictate Magdalena's replies: in response to the question of what her mother had taught her, for example, she could have said 'nothing', or 'to pray', rather than that she had tried to teach her witchcraft. However, Magdalena was probably particularly incapable of resisting the psychological pressure of interrogation for two reasons.

Before her arrest Magdalena had had a reputation for disorderly speech and behaviour, characteristics which, in combination with her own claim that she sometimes did not know what she was doing, suggest that she may have been weak-minded and thus not well-suited to bearing the rigours of the interrogation process. Second, because Magdalena regularly endured violence at her husband's hands she was probably in the habit of responding to questions by those who wielded power over her by telling them what they wanted to hear, with little thought for the consistency or long-term consequences of what she said.[34] Once violence or its threat was introduced into the equation

she became even more desperately loquacious: at the appearance of the tor-
turer she confessed to having forsworn God while under torture she admitted
four more murders. Her interrogators were puzzled by her inconsistency and
constant introduction of new information and during her final interrogation
asked her why she had confessed initially to her twins' murders without being
forced to do so when she now retracted that confession. Magdalena replied
that, while force had not been used against her initially, she had been terrified
by the questions put to her.[35] In the light of her inconsistent statements about
the twins and after establishing that she could not have killed either Stern
Katharin or Peter Lenck the final summary of her crimes was couched in suit-
ably cautious terms, explicitly mentioning only the murders of her daughter
and Georg Gackstatt's cow.[36]

If the fantasy of Magdalena as a baby-killing witch shaped the dynamic of
her interrogation process at all then it perhaps assumed most importance in the
minds of her interrogators and the other councillors and jurists who discussed
and handled her trial. They could have stopped proceedings as soon as she
admitted having killed her daughter as this admission was enough to have
earned her the death penalty for infanticide. The fact that this was not done and
that the process of questioning continued relentlessly, eager to uncover every
detail of Magdalena's actions and their motivations, suggests that the councillors were horrified yet also fascinated by her unmotherly behaviour. This fasci-
nation can be seen in the way in which they questioned her about how she had
killed her daughter, pressing for an explanation of the bruise on the baby's
head, asking her whether she had pressed its temple hard or softly, and how she
had known that it was dangerous to crush a baby's skull in that particular
place.[37] They also asked how she, as a mother, could have treated her own child
in this way,[38] a question suggesting a feeling of revulsion echoed by jurist
Christoff Conrad Seuter, who wrote a legal opinion on the case and described
Magdalena's murder of her baby as 'piteous', a 'terrible deed' which went
'against nature' and 'maternal feeling'.[39] Seuter was so horrified by Magdalena's crimes that he recommended that her flesh be torn with red-hot
pincers before her execution, once for every child she had murdered.[40] This
was not done, probably because the councillors deemed the burning of her
corpse deterrent enough for the onlookers.

The councillors also believed that a woman who confessed to having
killed her own child was capable of any foul deed imaginable; hence the
assumption that Magdalena must also have been responsible for the deaths of
her first husband and her child by him. They appear to have been unable or
unwilling to accept Magdalena's initial explanation of the unintentional murder
of her baby in a fit of anger. This was partly because condonable manslaughter
was almost exclusively understood by such men as the killing of one man by

another in a fight over honour,[41] and partly because it was more problematic for women than men in early modern Europe to use a rhetoric of rage in order to justify acts of violence.[42] Moreover, Lutheran idealisation of domestic roles held motherhood to be so sacred a duty and maternal love so natural an emotion that the idea of a woman who would harm her own baby to save herself from a beating would have been profoundly disturbing to the councillors, who therefore pressed for another explanation for Magdalena's behaviour.[43] The notion that Satan and Magdalena's own unmotherly mother had motivated Magdalena's actions was thus probably comforting as well as plausible to these men as it obviated the need for any deeper understanding of Magdalena's anger or the miserable reality of her married life from which it sprang.

The idea of the witch as a woman who directed her malevolence with particular vehemence against infants, childbearing women and children was not, in fact, of overwhelming importance in the Rothenburg witch-trials. The only other case in which infanticide figured significantly was that of another self-confessed witch, Anna Margaretha Rohn in 1673, although the many admissions of child-murder she made were almost certainly without foundation.[44] An earlier case for which interrogation records have not survived was similar to those discussed for early modern Augsburg by Lyndal Roper. It involved a widow called Magdalena Weinmayr who worked as a lying-in maid and children's nurse and who was accused of having tried to poison a baby in her care. She admitted that she had put mercury into the child's pap – a fact confirmed by the physician who examined its vomit – but only in order to cure it of dysentery. Because she had done this without the parents' knowledge, however, and because she had had a reputation for several years for working witchcraft, she was arrested, interrogated under torture, and banished.[45] This was the only case of its kind, however.[46] Others – like the trial of Catharina Leimbach discussed later in this chapter – involving anxieties about harm done to infants or childbearing women were rare; harm to older children crops up only slightly more frequently.[47] It was only the malevolence of Anna Maria Knöspel, who was banished for witchcraft in 1689, that was imagined by her neighbours in particular connection with children and childbearing: she was thought to have bewitched one child and was barred from the lying-in festivities of female neighbours after one had allegedly fallen ill after Knöspel had washed her bed-linen.[48] On the whole, then, in Rothenburg the crimes of witchcraft and infanticide were not conflated and the idea of the witch as the inverse of the good mother whose main aim was to harm infants and parturient women was merely one facet rather than the central core of the way in which the area's inhabitants imagined witches.[49] As the Magdalena Dürr case suggests, in its most extreme form this idea may have had more purchase at the elite rather than the popular level.

A 'poisoning' housewife? Margaretha Rost, 1641

Twelve years after Magdalena Dürr's execution another case of witchcraft came
to the attention of the council which was also rooted in a problematic marriage.
Forty-year-old Michael Rost, a vine-dresser from the village of Finsterlohr,
appeared in the city chancellery on 21 July 1641 to claim that his twenty-seven-
year-old wife Margaretha had bewitched him. She was his third wife; they had
been married for six years and had one child (an eighteen-month-old girl) still
alive in 1641. Rost explained to the authorities that poverty had driven him to
go and work in the vineyards on the River Main in the spring, despite the fact
that Margaretha had objected to his going and had offered to sell some of her
clothes if he would stay at home. Rost returned to Finsterlohr after two weeks
but on the way was 'shot' in the left thigh in such a manner that he continued
his journey in considerable agony. It is unclear what condition Rost suffered
from but the way in which he described the sudden onset of pain showed that
he believed it was caused by bewitchment. Margaretha came to meet her husband before he reached home and relieved him of the belongings he was carrying. Rost spent the day after his return working wretchedly in his own small
vineyard – despite Margaretha's pleas that he desist – but the pain in his leg
worsened and he had been virtually bedridden ever since. Margaretha often put
her hand onto his thigh as they lay in bed together to try to relieve his pain but
this only made it worse; according to Rost her compassion was a sham.[50]

After several weeks of suffering Rost decided to seek relief from the Little
Miller of Buch am Wald, a cunning man so renowned locally that he had been
mentioned by name in an ordinance issued against the use of white magic by the
council in 1639.[51] As Buch was some distance from Finsterlohr, Rost was
bedridden, and Margaretha was pregnant, she asked a friend, Jacob Ardolt of
Rothenburg, to visit the miller on behalf of Rost. Ardolt obliged and returned
with a packet of seeds to be boiled in a draught for Rost to drink and two
charms, one to tie onto his painful leg and another to hang round his neck.
These remedies had no effect, however, so in late May as Margaretha was about
to give birth to their next child Rost asked the village midwife if her husband,
Jörg Bohs of Finsterlohr, would go to the miller on his behalf. Bohs made the
trip without Margaretha's knowledge and brought back the same trio of remedies that Rost had already tried, which proved again to be ineffectual. The baby
which Margartha subsequently bore died rapidly after its birth.[52]

Thereafter Rost's suffering increased. One night in June the pain in his leg
was so bad that he could not sleep and for the first time accused his wife of
having caused it, blamed her for the fact that none of the miller's remedies were
helping, and begged her to lift the bewitchment. Margaretha insisted that she
was innocent and offered to visit the miller herself in order to discover who had

really caused it. The next day, less than four weeks after giving birth, she went to Buch herself with Ardolt to consult the miller, who gave them the same remedies as before, with an additional charm for Rost's leg. The miller refused to identify the person who had bewitched Rost, however.[53] Rost's leg subsequently improved enough to allow him to work in his vineyard for a few days, but on 2 July the familiar cycle of events began again: the pain returned, he accused Margaretha of having caused it, and she went to Rothenburg to ask Ardolt to visit the miller in the hope that the latter would clear her name by identifying someone else as the cause of her husband's suffering. Ardolt returned with different remedies and instructions from the miller: three charms which Margaretha – without Rost's knowledge – was to boil in his food when she prepared his next three meals, another charm that she was to place in their bed-straw, and some seeds that she was to brew in a draught for them both to drink. Despite the fact that the miller had told Margaretha that she must put the remedies into effect, Rost insisted on inspecting them, and Margaretha duly showed him the seeds and bed-straw charm. Rost subsequently felt so strange ('as if the room were full of thick fog') that he got out of bed and threw both items out of the house. He later searched his wife's clothes for the other three charms which he knew the miller had sent but was unable to find them. Margaretha told him that she had hidden them elsewhere so that she could boil them in his food secretly.[54]

Rost's suspicions against his wife increased after this point. Shortly afterwards he awoke at night with his throat feeling blocked. Thinking he was going to choke, he drank some water, only to start expectorating what he described as 'spermatic, evil-smelling matter, frequently and by the handful'.[55] As his wife was suffering from a vaginal discharge at the time he accused her of having put this 'waste stuff' into his throat while he was asleep.[56] He then became suspicious of all the food that Margaretha prepared for him, thinking she was trying to posion him. When Margaretha brought him dumplings to eat Rost made her take a bite out of them before he would eat any. Those that Margaretha had tested first in this way tasted fine but any dumplings which Rost ate whole made him feel 'strange in the head'.[57] He also had suspicions about a baked egg and some wine that Margaretha persuaded him to consume; he had felt so ill as a result that he had had to make himself sick with a purgative. Matters came to a head on 18 July when a pancake which Margaretha had cooked made Rost feel so strange that he had gone to his brother's house to purge himself and had stayed and eaten his meals there until 20 July. He had then decided that the only answer to his predicament was to drive his wife out of their house, which he did with the aid of a stick. His suffering did not abate, however, so he brought the matter before the council in the hope of that it would intervene and rid him of Margaretha.[58]

The council took a statement from Ardolt on 23 July and interrogated Margaretha the day after.[59] She put a different gloss on the events which had been interpreted as evidence of her identity as a witch by Rost. She had only tried to stop Michael from going away to work because he had enough to do in his own vineyard, she explained, and because she had been pregnant at the time and wanted him near at hand.[60] She had met him on his return home before he reached their house, not because of any supernatural prescience about his whereabouts, but because a cavalryman riding through Finsterlohr had told her that he had seen Michael outside the village.[61] She probably also only refused to give Rost the three charms which Ardolt had fetched from the miller on his third visit to Buch because she wanted to follow the miller's instructions – that she brew them secretly in Rost's food – rather than from any sinister motive, as Rost suggested.[62] Indeed, Margaretha did everything possible to ameliorate Rost's sufferings. She went to Rothenburg to persuade Ardolt to consult the miller; she slept on the floor for the fortnight preceding her confinement to leave Rost the comfort of their bed; she made the trip to Buch herself less than four weeks after giving birth; and she prepared all sorts of food for the bedridden Rost thereafter.[63] The problem for Margaretha was that once Rost was convinced that she had bewitched him any of her actions could be construed by him as further evidence of her maleficent abilities: if it made him feel worse it would confirm his suspicions of her and if it made him feel better it would simply prove that she had the ability to unwitch as well as bewitch. Rost's comment that Margaretha's compassion was a sham – a deception with which to conceal her identity as a witch – poignantly encapsulates the impossible situation in which she found herself.

Margaretha explained Rost's allegations against her by telling her interrogators that he was 'odd in the head', 'strange and melancholy'.[64] She also asked her interrogators to exhort Rost to better behaviour if they were to continue living together,[65] although the only complaint she made against him at this stage was that he had forced her to resume having sex with him on only the fourth day after her recent confinement, an action at odds with contemporary cultural expectation that a wife had the right to rest from intercourse for six weeks after giving birth.[66] The miller of Buch also became convinced that marital discord caused by Rost's strange ideas rather than witchcraft was the cause of the couple's problems. Despite repeated requests by Ardolt and Margaretha to identify the person responsible for Rost's suffering he had refused with increasing impatience to name names, explaining that this was too risky a thing for him to do.[67] During Ardolt's final visit to Buch he lost patience with Rost entirely, describing his suspicions against Margaretha as foolish fancies and advising Ardolt to tell Rost to trust his wife.[68] The remedies given to Ardolt by the miller on this occasion also seem to have been aimed at restoring marital harmony rather than just curing Rost's leg: one of the charms was to be placed in the couple's bed while the draught brewed from the seeds was to be drunk by them both rather than Rost alone.

The council also ultimately treated the Rost case as one of marital dishar-mony, despite the fact that Rost's allegations against his wife became even wilder during a confrontation staged between the couple in gaol on 26 July. Rost now suggested that Margaretha had been responsible for the death of the baby she had recently given birth to and that she had killed her stepson (Rost's child by a pre-vious wife) eighteen months earlier by means of poisoned dumplings. Margaretha explained that the baby had died because she had spent the fortnight before its birth sleeping in discomfort on the floor and that her stepson had died after being tortured by marauding soldiers.[69] She countered Rost's accusations with one of her own, claiming that he had offered her an abortifacient to get rid of the baby she had borne in June once he had realised she was pregnant with it.[70] These new allegations were serious but, doubtless because there were no witnesses to them other than the Rosts themselves, the council decided against investigating them further and instead to end the case as quickly as possible. After much exhortation Rost was persuaded to acknowledge his mistake in having accused his wife of witchcraft and to ask her, God, and the council for forgiveness for his actions. Rost and Margaretha were then formally reunited over a handshake and drink of wine.[71] They were released from custody on payment of their costs without further punishment, despite the fact that they had both used the services of a cun-ning man and that Rost had tried to give his wife an abortifacient.[72] The council's aim was to restore marital harmony rather than to punish either spouse in a way which would have made conjugal reconciliation impossible.

Rost believed not only that Margaretha had deliberately incapacitated him by harming his leg, but that she had tried to choke him with her bodily waste-matter and to poison him with bewitched food, and that she might even have been responsible for the deaths of their children. She thus appears in his narra-tive as the archetype of the evil housewife, an imaginary construct by means of which Diane Purkiss has suggested that early modern English women who accused other women of witchcraft were able 'to negotiate the fears and anxi-eties of housekeeping and motherhood'.[73] What is striking about the Rost case, however, was that this fantasy was articulated by a man, suggesting that it could be used by men as well as women to negotiate a wider range of fears and anx-ieties than those specific to married female accusers. Rost seems to have used it in 1641 in order to make sense of what he imagined to be a battle of wills between himself and his wife around the issues of provision, food and sex which Rost was terrified of losing.

As a day-labouring vinedresser with a small vineyard of his own to work in Rost would have been able to maintain his household on only the margins of subsistence at the best of times.[74] That times were hard for Rost in 1641 can be seen by the fact that he felt compelled to go and work on the River Main (because, as he put it, 'the cupboards were bare of foodstuffs'),[75] and by the fact that the council did not fine the Rosts at the end of the case.[76] With Margaretha's impending childbed Rost doubtless felt that the onus was on him to restock the cupboards and may thus have regarded her plea that he stay at home and her offer to sell some of her clothes to generate some income as defiance of his will, as well as a slighting of his ability to provide for the family. Who else but Margaretha would have shot him in the leg, therefore, after he had gone away to work against her wishes? The pain which ensued stopped Rost from working (which was what he seems to think Margaretha wanted all along), but it also – paradoxically – gave him a reason for not working and may thus have constituted the ideal excuse for any of his imagined inadequacies as a provider for his family. Rost's case thus suggests that we need to see anxieties about the ability to provide not just in the gender-specific sense of housewifely preparation of food but in a broader sense that could incorporate men's anxieties about their ability to generate income in order to guarantee the survival of their households.[77]

As Rost's suspicions against Margaretha grew they focused increasingly on the food and drink she offered him, which he imagined tasted strange and made him feel ill. This idea can be understood in the context of contemporary anxieties about witches' poisons, which were believed to be 'the opposite of nourishment . . . a power, which consumed the body from within'.[78] It can also be understood in the context of early modern marital conflicts, which might revolve around food: a wife's failure to prepare adequate meals on time or a husband's dissatisfaction with the fare on offer could spark arguments symptomatic of more intractable conjugal problems.[79] In Rost's case his reaction to the food offered to him by Margaretha symbolised the profound mistrust he had come to feel for his witch-wife and what he saw as her counterfeit concern for him; the miller also realised this when he urged Ardolt on his final visit to tell Rost to eat the meals Margaretha prepared for him as a gesture of reconciliation.[80] Rost did not do so, however, and instead felt so fearfully dependent on his wife for the preparation of food and of the miller's counter-magical remedies that his only answer was to flee their home to his brother's house and the safety of the cooking of a surrogate wife in the person of his sister-in-law.[81]

Rost also imagined and expressed inadequacies in the context of a perceived battle of wills with his wife around the issue of sexual intercourse. Rost admitted in custody that he had had sex with Margaretha shortly after she had given birth to their child in early June but tried to excuse his behaviour by saying that she had bewitched him into doing so and that he had only had sex with her because it had relieved the pain in his leg. There may have been another explanation, however, again involving a perceived act of defiance by

Margaretha. Margaretha told her interrogators that Michael had often complained that he could not get at her properly when she was pregnant; this was probably a reference to the fact that he had been unable to have satisfactory intercourse with her at this time. Rost, however, said that Margaretha had not always submitted to his sexual will and that this defiance had led him to conclude she must be a witch.[82] His early resumption of their sexual relations during Margaretha's lying-in period can therefore be seen as Rost's attempt to reassert his sexual will after the pregnancy. By encroaching on Margaretha's lying-in period, Rost was also denying her the right to refuse him her body as well as seeking to assert his authority as a husband in the only way left to him in his bedridden state.

Rost was not the only man in early modern Rothenburg to imagine his wife as a witch: Benedict Wücherer of Schmerbach, for example, cut his wife's throat shortly after their marriage in 1627 for this reason.[83] Like Rost, Michael Bendig of Detwang believed that his wife had lamed him and was called before the Consistorium in Rothenburg in 1613 for having consulted cunning men about the matter, including the Sorcerer of Aub who had beaten Bendig's wife in the couple's cellar as part of Bendig's 'cure'.[84] However, many other men doubtless suffered illness without accusing anyone, much less their wives, of being witches. What particular facets of Rost's character and experience may have predisposed him to accuse Margaretha of witchcraft in 1641?

One facet may have been the fact that he was, as Margaretha put it, 'odd in the head'. His strangeness was noted in 1660 when he was called before the Consistorium for 'foolish' behaviour: he had refused to take communion, had muttered critically throughout the pastor's sermon, and had gone round Finsterlohr telling other villagers not to attend church. He had then given the members of the Consistorium such a strange explanation for his behaviour and had spoken in such wild tones that they simply told him to home and subsequently asked his brother why he could not control Rost more effectively. This incident and the way in which it was handled suggest that Rost's behaviour was so peculiar that the members of the Consistorium deemed him resistant to reasoned discussion or formal punishment.[85] Glimpses of Rost's strangeness and particularly a paranoia which he expressed through suspicions of witchcraft can be seen in the 1641 case. He had told Margaretha that he suspected both of his former wives of having been witches, a fact which suggests that this paranoia predated his marriage to Margaretha.[86] It certainly increased during June and July of 1641. He came to think not only that his wife was a witch who was attempting to harm him but also that the miller's remedies had turned against him and were making him feel ill. He even came to think that his eighteen-month-old daughter was part of the conspiracy: after Margaretha protested that she and the child never fell ill after eating the same food as Rost, Rost asked pointedly 'how am I to know what you two are up to?'[87] Given that witchcraft was the product of the fears and fantasies of the accusers' imagination in the early modern period it is thus not surprising that a man who seems to have been particularly fearful and fanciful would be more prone than others to see his wife's witchcraft as the cause of his suffering.

We should not, of course, forget that Rost was suffering in 1641 from a pain in his leg which, as he described it, felt like someone was turning a knife in his thigh.[88] In addition to this physical suffering, Rost probably also felt anxiety about whether his condition would improve and about how long his family would be able to survive without him working regularly. The particularly perturbing aspect of his condition may have been the fact that it rendered him bedridden, so that he was forced to become ever more physically dependent on Margaretha. Lyndal Roper has suggested that it may have been the peculiar situation of the lying-in period, with the recently delivered mothers dependent on their lying-in maids for the fulfilment of their physical needs while they themselves were bedridden and experiencing feelings of 'depression, immobility and passivity', which helped explain why they projected their anxieties onto these maids by accusing them of witchcraft in early modern Augsburg.[89] It seems likely, however, that the anxieties engendered by such feelings of immobility and passivity were not exclusive to women during the lying-in period or indeed to women at all but, as the Rost case suggests, could be felt by anyone whose illness or infirmity rendered them bedridden, immobile, and dependent on others. In such a situation it is hardly surprising that certain individuals accused someone else of having caused their condition by means of witchcraft. In so doing they tried to assuage their terror at their own increasing powerlessness by seeking vengeance against the malevolent power of the alleged witch whom they believed had caused their suffering.

Domestic authority usurped?: Catharina Leimbach, 1652

The idea of the witch that Diane Purkiss suggested as a 'usurper of the authority of other women over the domestic realm' has particular resonance for a witchcraft case that occurred in the village of Wettringen in 1652.[90] It began on 26 August, when fifty-two-year-old Hans Schürz brought his eight-year-old daughter Barbara into Rothenburg to report that she claimed to have been seduced into witchcraft by their next-door-neighbour, the blacksmith's wife Catharina Leimbach, who was fifty-three or fifty-four. Two years previously Catharina's daughter Magdalena had allegedly enticed Barbara over to the smithy by saying that Catharina had cooked something good to eat. Once at the smithy, however, Catharina and her maidservant, Barbara Bratsch, had taken

Barbara Schürz into the barn and made her repeat some strange words, at which point the devil had appeared. After this initiation rite Catharina had often come into the Schürz household at night to take Barbara out of her bed, usually in order to make her milk her family's cows into a pail which Catharina had taken back to the smithy with her, but sometimes in order to take Barbara with her on a fire-iron to a witches' dance. This had been held in a house near Leitsweiler and Catharina's husband, daughter and maidservant had also attended: the participants had feasted, danced, kissed each other and forsworn God. Hans Schürz explained that he and his thirty-eight-year-old wife Eva (Barbara's stepmother) had not been able to prevent Barbara from being snatched away by Catharina even if she slept between them in their bed. Barbara had also told him that Catharina was able to milk the Schürz's cows in the smithy by means of a magical ritual involving a stick.[91] As a self-confessed witch Barbara was gaoled, and she duly repeated her tale of witchcraft to her interrogators.[92] Catharina Leimbach, her sixty-three-year-old husband, Mathes, and their former maidservant, twenty-three-year-old Barbara Bratsch, were gaoled and interrogated about the girl's claims on 30 August.[93]

Mathes Leimbach had moved to Wettringen in 1617 and taken over the smithy at the time of his marriage to Catharina in 1619. They had had eight children, although only twelve-year-old Magdalena still lived with them in 1652.[94] Bratsch had been a maidservant at the smithy from February 1650 until February 1652, when she had gone into service in innkeeper Hans Düring's household.[95] Catharina, Mathes and Bratsch denied that there was any truth in the claims made by Barbara Schürz and explained that the whole affair was the result of enmity which had arisen between the two households owing to an event that had occurred in May 1651. Eva Schürz's cows had stopped giving milk and, concerned that witchcraft was the cause of this problem, she had performed a magical ritual to identify the alleged witch responsible. Bratsch had entered Eva's house – in search of a stray lamb belonging to Catharina which Catharina had sent her to find – while Eva was performing this ritual. As a result Eva assumed that Bratsch was the witch who was to blame for her cows' poor milk-yield and accused her accordingly. Bratsch denied the allegation and the two women began to quarrel. Eva contemplated accusing Bratsch of witchcraft before the council but was persuaded against this by other villagers. The dispute was finally settled by village officials at Wettringen's inn during the summer of 1651, to Eva's detriment; she had to pay almost 2 gulden in costs and was told to stop slandering Bratsch.[96] Relations between the Schürz and Leimbach households unsurprisingly deteriorated rather than improved thereafter.[97] As Catharina's daughter Magdalena later told the authorities, since this settlement she had not been allowed to go into the Schürz house or to talk to Barbara Schürz because her parents were at odds with Eva.[98] Under interrogation Catharina admitted that she had been angry with Eva, whom she held responsible for driving Bratsch away from the smithy.[99]

The lamb incident and the reactions it produced on the parts of Eva, Bratsch and Catharina are comprehensible only in light of the fact that by May 1651 Eva already believed Catharina to be a witch. As it was believed that older witches passed on knowledge of witchcraft to those with whom they were closely associated and especially to those over whom they held power, it was logical for Eva to assume that Catharina had taught her witchcraft to Bratsch, for Bratsch to leave the smithy as soon as possible after Eva accused her of witchcraft in order to sever her ties to Catharina, and for Catharina to be angry at Eva for Bratsch's departure. Eva believed that Catharina was a witch because Catharina had had a reputation in Wettringen for around eighteen years for being able to make unusually large amounts of butter and cheese from the milk of her cows.[100] Early modern Germans understood their communal economies in terms of finite resources, in which one household was thought able to produce more than its fair share only at the expense of others,[101] while witchcraft was conceptualised as magical theft, by means of which one household was able secretly to steal what rightfully belonged to another.[102] The combination of these two beliefs meant that any actual or perceived success in terms of production or enrichment on the part of one household ran the risk of being understood as the result of witchcraft by others. When Eva's cows stopped giving milk in 1650, therefore, it made sense for her to assume that Catharina was magically stealing their milk and that it was this theft rather than Catharina's skill which accounted for the latter's apparently more successful dairying. That envy of the apparent economic success of the Leimbach household relative to that of the Schürz household was a crucial motivating factor behind the suspicions of witchcraft can also be seen in the comment made by Hans Schürz that the smith and his wife did little work, but ate and drank well.[103] It is impossible to ascertain whether Catharina really was the best dairywoman in Wettringen, although one clue to the gaining of her reputation lies in the testimony of Appolonia Völzner, who said that Catharina had boasted to her about how much money she had made from the sale of her butter and cheese at the parish fair at Insingen in 1651.[104] Boastfulness was a dangerous habit in early modern communities, as it excited the envy that was often the key motivating factor in the making of witchcraft accusations. Perhaps Catharina's boastfulness earned her a reputation for suspiciously successful dairying that was rooted more in perception than reality.

Eva Schürz had been born and raised in Wettringen, so would long have known of Catharina's reputation.[105] However, three events that occurred in 1649 and 1650 would have increased her fear of the older woman. Eva had married Hans Schürz, a widower from Bronnholzheim, and taken possession of the house next to the smithy after her father died in 1649; her own widowed stepmother, Barbara Weber, continued to live with the couple and Barbara Schürz, Hans's daughter by a previous wife.[106] Eva gave birth to the couple's own first child soon after their marriage. She had an arduous labour which lasted for two days, until Catharina Leimbach came into the birthing-chamber and touched her, whereupon she bore the child with the next contraction. This suggested to Eva that Catharina had a mysterious power over her ability to give birth, a power which became connected in Eva's mind with the rapid deaths of this and her second baby by Schürz. That this was the case can be seen by the fact that in mid-August 1652 Eva consulted a soothsayer about the likely success of her ongoing third pregnancy. The soothsayer repeated the story of the birth of Eva's first child, referring to a woman who had suddenly enabled her to give birth after hours of labouring in vain to do so. As soothsayers usually confirmed whatever pre-existing suspicions against others their clients hinted at to them, we can conclude from this account that Eva was worried about Catharina's power over her in relation to the birth of her third child and that the soothsayer had confirmed her anxieties. It was therefore not surprising that the witchcraft matter reached crisis-point with the formal accusations of the Leimbach household members in August 1652, a month before Eva was due to give birth to her third child.[107]

The second event which helped persuade Eva that Catharina was a witch was the fact that in 1650 the milk-yields of Eva's cows began to decline. Eva linked this misfortune to the Leimbach household by means of an exchange she had had with Catharina through Catharina's daughter, Magdalena. She claimed that Catharina had sent Magdalena to the Schürz household with a gift of meat and herbs, asking in return that Eva send her the first milk from her pregnant cow as soon as it calved. Eva had refused to comply with this request, despite the fact that Magdalena had apparently been sent by her mother to request the milk three times. Shortly after this exchange the Schürz's newborn calf fell ill, allegedly after Magdalena had stroked it, and Eva had managed to keep it alive only with difficulty. Since then the Schürz's cows had never yielded the expected amount of milk and Eva doubtless became convinced that Catharina's witchcraft, mediated through the words and actions of her daughter Magdalena, was to blame.[108]

The third factor which helped crystallise Eva's suspicions against Catharina was the fact that she seems to have suspected that Catharina was trying to usurp her rightful authority as stepmother over Barbara Schürz. Eva claimed that Catharina was in the habit of taking Barbara into her house when Hans Schürz was not at home. One episode from 1650 had taken on particular significance for Eva. She claimed that Catharina had kept Barbara at the smithy for two days in Schürz's absence. When Schürz returned Eva had complained to him about this; he had gone outside and called across to the smithy that Barbara should be sent home immediately. She had not appeared, so Schürz had gone into the smithy and dragged her out himself, while Catharina apparently begged him not to beat the girl.[109] For Eva, the idea that Catharina had the power to draw Barbara into her own house probably burgeoned into the idea that Catharina had the power to initiate Barbara into those arts of witchcraft which she was also apparently teaching to her own daughter and maidservant. Eva's worst fears about Catharina's usurpation of her maternal authority over Barbara were doubtless confirmed when Barbara began claiming that Catharina was able to take her out of her parents' bed at night and to make her steal her stepmother's milk.

Catharina either denied that the incidents which Eva recounted had occurred at all or set them in the context of innocent social intercourse between neighbours. She denied that she had constantly kept Barbara at the smithy away from her parents; Barbara had once hidden in the smithy out of fear of her father but this had been an isolated incident.[110] Catharina had once sent Eva a gift of meat and herbs but this had been in return for a butchering implement lent to her by Eva; she denied that she had sent Magdalena to ask Eva for her cow's first milk or that Magdalena had made Eva's calf fall ill and explained that Eva's cows yielded little because she gave them insufficient fodder.[111] Catharina had an equally matter-of-fact explanation for the birth of Eva's first child. She said that the women who had attended Eva had treated her harshly: when she had arrived later she had settled Eva differently in her bed, at which point she had had the baby. It was thus Catharina's milder treatment of Eva rather than any supernatural power which had helped her give birth. Catharina also had an explanation for the rapid deaths of Eva's first two babies, testifying that Eva's own stepmother had said that Eva had been too lazy to breastfeed them properly.[112]

Despite the fact that Hans Schürz's report of his daughter's seduction into witchcraft triggered off the Wettringen witch-trial, his wife was almost certainly the main driving force behind it: Eva gave three formal statements about Catharina to the council (two of them apparently unsolicited) and it was her anxiety around which the case revolved.[113] Barbara Schürz doubtless constructed her seduction narrative, in which Catharina was the villain of the piece but in which she was also assisted by Magdalena Leimbach and Barbara Bratsch, out of the suspicions which her stepmother had voiced against Catharina and the Leimbach household since 1649. Barbara Schürz also began to talk publicly about witchcraft in the summer of 1651, which coincided with the quarrel between Eva and Bratsch and the deterioration of relations between the Schürz and Leimbach households.[114] Eva's anxiety about Catharina was predicated not only upon Catharina's pre-existent reputation for witchcraft and threatening

proximity but also on Eva's sense of failure as a housewife relative to Cather-
ine's actual or perceived success in this role. Take dairying as an example.
Ensuring that the household had a plentiful supply of dairy produce was one of
the early modern housewife's most important duties; these were essential
foodstuffs for her family and any surplus could be sold for cash at local markets.[115] The failing milk-yields of Eva's cows were thus a symbol of her inade-
quacy as a housewife as well as a threat to the well-being of her household; it is
unsurprising that she tried to assuage her sense of failure by projecting it onto
the apparently better dairywoman, Catharina, whom she blamed for stealing
her cows' milk.[116]

This dynamic of guilt, envy, fear and hatred also prompted Eva to imagine Catharina as a witch in relation to another role central to the status of the
early modern housewife: that of bearing and raising children successfully.
Again, Eva may have compared herself to Catharina and found herself wanting.
Catharina had borne and raised at least one child – Magdalena – to early adulthood successfully, while Eva had yet to see one of her babies survive infancy.
Eva had problems in giving birth, whereas she believed that Catharina had
expertise in easing the birthing process. Eva also imagined that Catharina
had a greater degree of control over Barbara Schürz than she herself had. Her
own relationship with Barbara was strained: Mathes and Magdalena Leimbach
told the authorities that Eva beat Barbara so severely that Barbara had run away
and expressed a desire to hang herself, while Bratsch's stepfather testified that
Eva beat Barbara harshly when Hans Schürz was not at home.[117] These individuals may have had a vested interest in portraying Eva as violent, but the manner
in which Eva and her stepmother, Barbara Weber, sought to play down their
allegations suggested that they were not without foundation. Eva admitted
having beaten Barbara but excused herself by saying that she had never done
her great harm and that Barbara misbehaved terribly when Schürz was away,
while Weber stated that Eva never gave the child more than two blows at once.
She added that there had been so much discord between Eva and Hans on Barbara's account that she wished she did not live with the couple.[118] Eva thus
seems to have been able to control Barbara with difficulty and only by means
of violence, while imagining that Catharina held such sway over the girl that
she could tempt her to the smithy and keep her there for days without any need
for violence and against her stepmother's wishes. Either consciously or uncon-
sciously Eva measured herself as an unsuccessful housewife against her perception of Catharina as successful and coped with the uncomfortable
discrepancies she perceived by imagining Catharina to be a witch. However, as
had been the case with Michael Rost, Eva may also have been especially prone
to fears about witchcraft because she was weak-minded. The Leimbachs
claimed that the Weber family from which she came was 'foolish' and that

she had gone out of her senses when the settlement with Bratsch went against her in 1651.[119]

Eva's suspicions against Catharina may never have reached the attention of the council, however, had her stepdaughter not begun to talk openly of witchcraft: her tale of seduction into witchcraft by Catharina triggered formal proceedings against the Leimbachs without the need for her parents to make specific accusations against them, thereby risking a counter-accusation of slander. It also helped ensure that sympathy on the part of the councillors throughout the trial lay with the Schürz rather than the Leimbach household. As had been the case in earlier trials involving self-confessed child-witches, the councillors found it difficult to believe that a child could fabricate an unfounded narrative of witchcraft, while Catharina's refusal to confess was perceived by them as insolent obstinacy and thus as additional evidence of her likely identity as a witch.[120] Catharina was the most harshly treated of all the suspected Wettringen witches: she was questioned most frequently and severely in custody and was tortured five times with thumbscrews during her final interrogation.[121] After steadfastly refusing to confess to witchcraft she was released unpunished on 5 October, although the surety she had to swear before leaving gaol listed the allegations the Schürz family had made against her in tones which implied that they were more credible than Catharina's denials of guilt.[122] Mathes Leimbach was not tortured but, being old and infirm, suffered severely from the cold during his incarceration.[123] He was released on 9 October but the trial proved to be his financial and physical ruin. His business had collapsed as a result of his long absence from the smithy, while the fact that his wife had been tortured and thus rendered dishonourable meant that no apprentices were willing to continue working for him.[124] Moreover, the council imposed such a punitive level of bail – of 200 Reichstaler – on Mathes as a condition of his release that this was tantamount to an exorbitant fine. He paid 70 Reichstaler in cash but had to surrender his work-tools and the income from two fields and one piece of woodland to the council in lieu of the remaining amount.[125] Mathes died eighteen weeks after his release from gaol, doubtless as a result of his suffering during the trial.[126] This was not the end of the matter for the Leimbachs, however. Catharina and Magdalena were finally banished from Rothenburg's hinterland in 1656, ostensibly for having failed to live in peace with their neighbours, after Hans Schürz had again claimed that Catharina was plaguing his daughter in 1654 and after Wettringen pastor Nicolaus Rosenbach reported that Magdalena Leimbach had offered to teach another young girl in the village witchcraft.[127] Their banishment had probably been engineered by a pro-Schürz faction in Wettringen which Catharina – by then a poor widow – was powerless to resist. The two Barbaras escaped more lightly. Barbara Bratsch, who had also denied all the allegations of witchcraft, was released unpunished on 7

October 1652, although she had to pay the costs of her lengthy stay in gaol.[128] Barbara Schürz, the cause of all the trouble, was released from gaol in late September 1652, kept in the city hospital to gain religious instruction until May 1653, then returned to her parents.[129] They seem to have lost patience with her, however: she was sent away into service by her father after 1654.[130]

The Wettringen witch-trial offers an excellent example of the way in which fear and envy of a threat to her domestic authority could encourage one women to imagine another as a witch. We should, however, beware of understanding this case and others like it simply in terms of the ongoing tension between the women involved. It was rather the outcome of an ongoing tension between the households of Eva and Catharina which also drew in their children, servants and husbands. The popular belief in witchcraft as knowledge transferred within the household meant that Eva assumed that Catharina had passed her skills on to her daughter and her maidservant; accordingly Eva imagined them as culpable for the illness of her calf and the falling milk-yields of her cows. Moreover, although Mathes assumed only a minor role in Barbara Schürz's witchcraft narrative, the fact that he was arrested and interrogated suggests that the council at least entertained the possibility that it was dealing with an entire household of witches, even if it assumed that Catharina was the main culprit.[131] The hostility of the members of the Leimbach household was likewise imagined to affect the entire Schürz family: Barbara most directly, as she was plagued by Catharina, but Eva and Hans as well, as they worried about their cows' failing milk supply, Barbara's suffering and Eva's pregnancy.

This belief that knowledge of witchcraft was passed on within households by the older to the younger generation had deep roots in Rothenburg and its hinterland villages. In the witch-trial involving the Brosam family of Wettringen in 1561 villagers testified that Barbara Brosam had learned witchcraft from her parents-in-law, while in 1563 Appolonia Kellner and her children Appolonia, Anna and Georg of Finsterlohr were involved in a case in which popular opinion suggested that the siblings had gained their reputations as witches from their mother.[132] The idea that knowledge of witchcraft was transferred along the maternal line is suggested in other Rothenburg cases: the mothers of Anna Maria Knöspel and Barbara Schmezer were reputed witches, while both the mothers and grandmothers of Anna Weh and Babelein Kuch enjoyed this dubious honour.[133] In cases like that of the old herdsman of Gebsattel, however, men were imagined as the main carriers of reputations for witchcraft within their families. The old herdsman emerged as a reputed witch in the trial of Margaretha Hörber in 1627, discussed in Chapter 4. He cropped up again in testimony given during the trial of Margaretha Horn of Bettenfeld in 1652, discussed in Chapter 6. Margaretha's first marriage at the age of twenty-four had been to Martin, the old herdsman's son. As a result of the herdsman's reputation it was said of Margaretha upon this marriage that 'she will now also learn witchcraft'.[134] Aware of the risk of gaining a reputation as a witch by association, Margaretha had not allowed her parents-in-law into her house in Gebsattel. Fortunately for her her husband had died soon after their marriage, thereby freeing her of her bad name, as one of her neighbours put it.[135] The old herdsman and his children had all had reputations as witches so strong that even by 1652 people would have nothing to do with one of his surviving sons-in-law.[136] These comments also show that contemporaries imagined a reputation for witchcraft as like a disease: the more contact you had with people already infected, the more likely you were to develop the contagion yourself.[137] The centrality of the idea of witchcraft as knowledge passed on within households also explains why individuals could first gain reputations as witches at very young ages, even if they were not formally accused of witchcraft until much later in their lives, if at all. Reputations could be gained by children simply by virture of being born into reputed witch-families,[138] by adolescents as a result of going into service with reputed witch-mistresses[139] and by young adults as a result of marrying reputed witches.[140]

Viewing the Wettringen case simply in terms of an ongoing tension between the two housewives involved also risks blinding us to the importance of the seduction narrative to its dynamic and outcome. This narrative, in which a child or teenager claimed to have been forced or persuaded into learning witchcraft by an older witch, had first surfaced officially in the witch-trial involving six-year-old Hans Gackstatt in 1587.[141] It was expanded upon in the cases involving Margaretha Hörber in 1627, Margaretha Harter in 1629, and Brigitta Hörner in 1639[142] and would figure even more centrally in later seventeenth-century trials.[143] The elites took such narratives seriously because the idea that witchcraft was a learned art was enshrined both in demonology and in law,[144] and because they found it hard to believe that youngsters were capable of fabricating stories of witchcraft that were entirely without foundation.[145] The seduction narrative also made sense at the popular level because it was an extension of the idea that witchcraft was passed on by older witches to youngsters over whom they had influence: in the Wettringen case, for instance, Catharina's alleged seduction of Barbara Schürz would have been understood by her parents as an attempt by the Leimbachs to gain a new recruit for their 'witch-household'. However, the seduction narrative was imagined in more strongly gendered terms than the idea of witchcraft as knowledge passed on within families, as the latter belief allowed for transference along male lines. Apart from Leonhardt Maas, who was accused of helping his wife Anna to seduce their maidservant, Anna Margaretha Rohn, into witchcraft in 1664,[146] and Hans Böhm, of whom it was implied in 1690 that he had tried to encourage Hans Adam Knöspel to continue his alleged witchcraft, men were absent from the seduction narratives of self-confessed child-witches.[147] The classic figure in these narratives was an adult woman who was or had been married: either the mother of the child in question, or another woman who occupied a quasi-maternal role in relation to the child, such as a godmother, a mistress, an aunt, or an adult woman with whom the child had a close and possibly affectionate relationship.[148]

The gendering of the seduction narrative probably occurred for two reasons: once established within popular discourse it was likely to be heard and repeated by children with the key element of the adult female seductress at its core. The first explanation for its gendering was the early modern household division of labour, which ensured that adult women had the greatest responsibility for the care and education of children of both genders within the household, especially in the early years of their lives, and continued to exercise control over and to teach the arts of housewifery to their daughters and maidservants.[149] As one key way of imagining witchcraft in Rothenburg was as the inverse of these positive nurturing and educative roles it was hardly surprising that women were also most easily imagined in the role of the seducer in seduction narratives, persuading children to dedicate themselves to the devil instead of God and teaching them how to do harm rather than good. This way of categorising women as good or bad teachers is evident in the testimony of eight-year-old self-confessed witch Brigitta Hörner in 1639. She claimed that her mother had taught her to say the Lord's Prayer, the Creed and the Ten Commandments – and had, in other words, been a good mother to her – while her godmother had taught her witchcraft and to swear instead of praying. Her godmother had been a bad mother to her – in other words, a witch.[150]

The second reason which explains the gendering of the seduction narrative and the importance which this narrative gained in the dynamic of the Rothenburg witch-trials was the fact that it was taken so seriously by the Rothenburg elites: the idea of innocent children being corrupted by the influence of evil women seems to have hit a nerve with councillors and their advisers throughout the early modern period. It is impossible to explain exactly why this was the case, although some hypotheses can be offered. At one level, of course, this idea was simply a slightly different version of the traditional demonological idea, found in texts like the *Malleus Maleficarum*, that witches were expected to dedicate their offspring to the devil.[151] It may have caused the councillors such concern, however, because Lutheran thinking had elevated the importance of women's role as housewife and mother at the same time as Lutheran domestic ideology held mothers largely responsible for the early religious education of their children.[152] Perhaps because Lutheranism had, in theory at least, increased women's influence over their children, fears that women may have chosen to exercise this influence to evil rather than good purpose may have grown in the

minds of male Lutheran elites and predisposed them to believe the seduction
narratives of self-confessed child-witches. The Rothenburg councillors and their
advisers may also have found it psychologically satisfying to imagine themselves
as the benevolent and protective fathers who were needed to free these powerless, innocent child-witches from the clutches of their evil female seducers and
to guide them back onto the path of Lutheran piety.[153] As educated, pious men
who wielded the sword of justice over their subjects, they would have believed
themselves best fitted for this task and may have enjoyed the fact that such child-
witches were usually compliant players in trial dramas, not only admitting to
their own witchcraft but also throwing themselves on the councillors' mercy.[154]
The latter seem to have imagined such witch-trials as a struggle for the child's
soul between themselves and God on one side against the devil and evil women
on the other, either because they were in the habit of conceptualising the world
in terms of polar opposites,[155] or because this way of thinking allowed them to
curb the power of the mother and reassert the power of the father over the
family, at least in fantasy.

Male witches: 'masculine' witchcraft?

As the fate of Mathes Leimbach in the 1652 Wettringen witch-trial reminds us,
we must not forget that men could be accused of witchcraft and suffer as a
result: they constituted 24 per cent of the overall total of witches tried in the
Holy Roman Empire.[156] The percentage of males involved in witch-trials in
Rothenburg was, at 29.2 per cent, slightly higher than this overall imperial
average, because the figures include self-confessed child-witches and individuals who were questioned or investigated on suspicion of witchcraft by the city
council without becoming the subject of a full, formal trial.[157] Males became
involved in witch-trials in Rothenburg in five different ways. The first was as
alleged sabbat-attenders: Margaretha Hörber, for example, claimed to have
seen three men (including the old herdsman of Gebsattel) as well as nineteen
women at sabbats in 1627.[158] The second was as self-confessed boy-witches
who, like their female counterparts, claimed that they had been seduced into
witchcraft by adult women.[159] In both types of cases the Rothenburg council
treated the males involved in much the same way as it did females. As far as both
male and female sabbat-attenders were concerned, the council was unwilling
to pursue investigations against them with any severity because it feared that to
do so would cause witch-trials to escalate and because it was uncertain whether
or not to believe stories of sabbats.[160] Self-confessed boy witches – like girls in
the same position – tended to be taken seriously by the council and were
regarded as in need of better religious instruction and of rescuing from the

clutches of their evil seducers rather than punishment. The boys' youth rather than their gender thus shaped the handling of their cases. Hans Gackstatt was treated more harshly in 1587 but the council's severity towards him can be accounted for by its initial uncertainty about how to treat child-witches and by Hans' inconsistency under interrogation.[161]

The third way in which men could become involved in witchcraft trials was, to use Rolf Schulte's terminology, as 'secondary witches' who were related to women who were also suspected of witchcraft.[162] Paulus Brosam (in 1561) and Mathes Leimbach (in 1652), who were arrested with their wives, and Georg Kellner, who was arrested with his mother and sisters in 1563, fall into this category, as do Leonhardt Maas and Georg Adam Knöspel, who were both formally questioned at the same time as their wives were questioned (Maas) and tried (Knöspel) for witchcraft in 1673 and 1689, respectively.[163] In all these cases, however, the related women were the main focus of the council's investigation into the allegations of witchcraft: they were also far more likely to be tortured and punished than the men with whom they were arrested. None of the men listed above were tortured and only Georg Adam Knöspel (who was banished with his wife) was technically punished, although the punitive surety demanded of Mathes Leimbach was tantamount to a severe fine.[164] The milder treatment and punishment of these secondary male witches was due partly to the fact that they figured less significantly in the initial accusations of witchcraft made against their families. In all five of the cases listed above the related women – Barbara Brosam, Appolonia Kellner, Catharina Leimbach, Anna Maas and Anna Maria Knöspel – were at the centre of the witchcraft allegations that led to their trials. Paulus Brosam was accused of having helped his wife in her witchcraft, for example, but it was Barbara Brosam whom Hans Lautenbach claimed had pressed him while he slept, while Barbara Schürz imagined Mathes Leimbach as a member of a household of witches but focused her witchcraft narrative on Leimbach's wife, Catharina.[165] More importantly, however, the Rothenburg councillors and their advisors accepted but then accentuated this gender-bias against women in their handling of these cases, for reasons discussed later. This can be seen in the fact that they consistently failed to act on the hints about men's maleficient powers dropped by witnesses when they could have chosen to do so. Witness testimony from Wettringen in 1561, for example, suggested that Paulus Brosam was also a witch, as his mother, father and uncle were all reputed to be able to work witchcraft, while in the 1652 Wettringen case Hans Schürz and another villager suggested that both Catharina and Mathes Leimbach were reputed witches: the council ignored these and similar insinuations in other cases.[166]

The fourth way in which men could become involved in witchcraft trials – and in their own right rather than as the accomplices of female witches – was as cunning men who were imagined as capable of working maleficent as well as beneficient magic. There were only two cases of this type in early modern Rothenburg, underlining the fact that neither the councillors nor their subjects were in the habit of conflating black and white magic.[167] In early modern Holstein, by contrast, the authorities had by the seventeenth century come to regard and try cunning folk as witches, with the result that erstwhile cunning men formed the majority of men tried in their own right for witchcraft.[168] Fifty-year-old Christoph Vogel from the village of Bettwar was one of the two Rothenburg cunning men accused of witchcraft: in February 1687 he was accused by a peasant couple from Seldeneck of having caused the condition of their son's diseased leg to deteriorate after he had tried to cure it. The council showed little interest in investigating his case in depth and banished him from Rothenburg and its hinterland just two days after his arrest.[169] The other case of this type centred around a Rothenburg joiner, Hans Georg Hofmann, who had a reputation for being able to find misplaced or stolen objects: he had, for example, tried to help a friend, blacksmith Endres Vogt, find a lost hammer with a ritual he took from a book he possessed which dealt with this art.[170] The events which led to his downfall began in the summer of 1604, when a man called Georg Gering complained in a tavern about a sum of money of his which had gone missing. Endres Vogt heard Gering's complaint and told him that Hofmann would be able to find the money. Gering promised Hofmann 50 gulden if he could do so and Hofmann, with Vogt's help, subsequently searched Gering's property for the money using a treasure-seeking ritual.[171] In custody Hofmann claimed that this ritual, which had been taught to him by another joiner while on his travels as a journeyman, had merely involved the use of a special plant.[172] However, other witnesses – including Vogt – who testified in the case claimed that Hofmann had performed a more sinister rite aimed at gaining power over the devil, whom Hofmann claimed had taken Gering's money.[173] Unfortunately for all parties concerned, Hofmann failed to find the money.

Hofmann's treasure-seeking activities may never have reached the attention of the authorities but for events which occurred in March 1605. David Walther, a member of the Rothenburg social elite, asked Hofmann's friend and fellow joiner Michael Pfund, to make him a table and delivered the wood for it to Pfund's workshop. Pfund was unable to complete the work as requested, so Walther complained about him to the council, claiming that he feared Pfund had sold the wood he had been given. In order to ensure that the table was finished quickly and to thereby restore good relations with Walther, Pfund asked Hofmann to finish the table, which he did. The table was delivered to Walther's house in mid-March.[174] Strange noises allegedly began to emanate from the house and rumours soon abounded that it was haunted and that Hofmann, as a reputed cunning man with power over the spirit-world, was to blame.[175] The idea was that Hofmann had conjured up spirits to help him finish the table as quickly as possible but had then been unable to banish them again. This suspicion arose so rapidly against Hofmann because of his association with Pfund, who also had a reputation as a worker of magic. Some years earlier Pfund had been called before the Consistorium in Rothenburg on charges of possessing a book of ritual magic,[176] and in February 1605 he had stengthened his reputation by saying that he would die during the year, a comment which had been understood by listeners as evidence of his ability to foretell the future.[177] Pfund also had a reason — Walther's complaint against him — for wanting to bewitch the table.

A gullible servant or passer-by may have heard unusal noises in Walther's house after the table had been delivered and started the rumours about the poltergeist because of the pre-existing reputations of Hofmann and Pfund, or perhaps Walther started or encouraged the rumours as part of a continuing vendetta against Pfund. Whatever the case, talk about the table became rife and prompted Hofmann's arrest and official enquiry into his reputation and treasure-seeking activities on 4 April.[178] Under interrogation Hofmann admitted that he had searched for Gering's money but only using the plant ritual and that Endres Vogt was now testifying against him on this matter out of malice.[179] Hofmann also said that, while he had made the table for Walther, he bore no responsibility for the fact that it was haunted. He denied that he had made a pact with the devil for the sake of material gain or that he could conjure and ban spirits.[180] Futher information was then gathered from witnesses about both Hofmann and Pfund. Pfund, however, had judiciously developed an illness which rendered him bedridden at this point, so the case continued to focus on Hofmann, who denied on 9 April that he and Pfund had used their books of magic to cause the haunting of Walther's house.[181] The council then asked jurists Friedrich Prenninger and Michael von Berg about how to proceed in the case. Prenninger advised the council to end the matter by banishing Hofmann for his use of magic whereas von Berg felt that Pfund could be questioned because of his suspicious reputation and that Endres Vogt could be asked about his own involvement in the treasure-seeking and the apparent malice which he bore Hofmann and which might prejudice his testimony against the joiner.[182]

The bedridden Pfund was questioned in his house on 12 April; he denied that he was a sorcerer and that any untoward methods had been used to make the table.[183] By 13 April Hofmann had decided that his only hope was to try to shift the blame for the poltergeist onto Pfund. He now claimed that Pfund had said angrily that he would make the table for Walther in the devil's name; the implication was that this was tantamount to a curse. He also claimed that his own stepfather, who had been apprenticed to Pfund as a boy, had told him that he had seen Pfund use a book in order to conjure spirits which he had then set to work for him.[184] Hofmann's strategy backfired, however, as his stepfather refused to confirm this new allegation against Pfund.[185] The council made one last attempt to harmonise the testimony of the three protagonists in the case on 15 April when Hofmann was confronted with Pfund and Endres Vogt in gaol. Unfortunately for the council all three stuck to their stories: Hofmann blamed Pfund for the poltergeist and Vogt for initially getting him involved in the treasure-seeking, Pfund denied that he had raised the poltergeist, while Vogt did all that he could to emphasise Hofmann's sinister abilities as a cunning man.[186]

There the case ended. No further action was taken against Vogt and Pfund, who were never arrested, despite the fact that Pfund was as 'guilty' of involvement in the matter of the poltergeist as Hofmann and the fact that Vogt had also been involved in the treasure-seeking. Hofmann was not questioned again but was banished from Rothenburg and its hinterland for his use of the forbidden arts of treasure-seeking and spirit-conjuring on 17 April.[187] Clues as to why all three men were treated mildly can be found in the legal opinions on the case. Prenninger advised the council against torturing Hofmann, not only because there was insufficient evidence to justify this course of action but also because he feared that Hofmann would complain formally against the council to the Emperor if he were tortured.[188] This was because torture dishonoured an individual and would have made it difficult for Hofmann, as a craftsman to whom honour was particularly important, to earn a living after the trial. The effect that even spending time in gaol could have on a craftsman's reputation was noted by von Berg, who suggested that Hofmann should be released from custody after promising to desist from treasure-seeking as imprisonment alone was sufficiently shameful to damage his ability to earn his living for the rest of his life.[189] This unwillingness to damage honour and earning capability through imprisonment and torture may help explain why the council showed little enthusiasm for arresting Pfund and Vogt, especially if it feared that they might also seek redress from the Emperor. Urban craftsmen may thus have enjoyed better protection than Rothenburg's rural subjects against arrest and torture for allegations of witchcraft because of their status as well as their gender.[190] Case-specific circumstances also influenced the course of Hofmann's case, however. Prenninger noted that the alleged haunting of Walther's house was causing a stir in Rothenburg and encouraging the common people in their ungodly beliefs about witchcraft; a sermon preached to try to quieten talk about the poltergeist had had little effect. Prenninger recommended ending the case rapidly to avoid further public scandal, advice which the council, given its concern with maintaining order in the city, doubtless took to heart.[191]

The final type of male involvement in the Rothenburg witch-trials was when men were accused of maleficient witchcraft in their own right and without any pre-existing reputation as cunning men. Only one case of this sort progressed as far as a formal investigation during the early modern period, although there were undoubtedly other suspected maleficient male witches in the area who were never brought to the attention of the authorities. On 22 December 1662 blacksmith Georg Leupolt, who was in the last throes of an illness which had plagued him since October 1660, sent his wife Appolonia to the chancellery to accuse their neighbour, wheelwright Michael Würth, of having caused his illness by means of a bewitched drink.[192] Georg died six days later and Appolonia pursued the allegation against Würth on his behalf, bringing forward more evidence to prove Würth's identity as a witch. She claimed that in 1662 she had heard Würth threaten to bewitch another man, Burckhard Roth, so that he would dry up like a turnip, and that she had heard him say that he could work magic in order to blind people using their urine. She also told the council that Würth had bewitched a pear-tree belonging to Michel Klein.[193] Klein confirmed that this had happened in early 1660, claiming that Würth had touched the tree with his hand and left a mark as if the tree had been scorched with a red-hot iron; it had borne no fruit since the incident.[194] Further evidence against Würth was provided by potter Michael Albrecht, by Veit Rueg, the pastor of Kirnberg, and by wheelwright Johannes Georg. Albrecht claimed that Würth had talked to him about methods of causing illness by means of poisoned drinks during a conversation they had had about Leupolt's illness, while Rueg claimed to have heard Würth say that he wished that he had caused Leupolt greater suffering after Leupolt had died and Würth had discovered that a formal complaint had been brought against him as responsible for Leupolt's illness. In both instances Würth's words had been construed by his listeners as confirmation of the suspicion that he had bewitched Leupolt to death. Johannes Georg's evidence pertained not to Leupolt's illness but to a book of ritual magic allegedly possessed by Würth. After Würth had performed less successfully than expected at a shooting contest in Waldmannshofen Würth's wife (Barbara) had told Georg that this had been due to magic which had been used against Würth. Würth had been unable to protect himself because he had forgotten to take his book of ritual magic with him. This book had allegedly been given to Würth by a man called Hans Stanninger who Barbara claimed was a powerful sorcerer from Ansbach.[195]

Despite the fact that Würth had been accused of bewitching another man to death the council proceeded with caution in the handling of his case: he was not formally questioned until 28 February, was further questioned on only two subsequent occasions (14 March and 5 May), and was never taken into custody.[196] The fact that he was not arrested gave Würth the freedom of movement to pursue strategies in his own defence. In late March he went to Ansbach to ask Johann Christoph von Eyb, Hans Stanninger's lord, to question Stanninger under oath about whether he had ever given Würth a book of ritual magic.[197]

Würth went again to Ansbach in early July to seek legal advice on his case, having been given permission to travel there by the council under the pretence of needing to go there for work purposes.[198] He did not return to Rothenburg, however, having decided that the risk of arrest at this stage of proceedings was too great. He was later seen in Rothenburg's hinterland but city officials failed to capture him there.[199] The legal investigation against him was therefore never completed; he was banished in absentia with his wife on 1 August 1663.[200] The council's caution in acting against Würth was doubtless based on the principle which had governed its handling of the 1605 case discussed above: its unwillingness to damage the reputations of craftsmen by means of over-hasty arrest and torture. There are also hints that Würth was socially moder-ately well connected in Rothenburg, a fact that would also have discouraged the council from hasty action.[201] Finally, Rothenburg's councillors and their advis-ers may have been slower to act against Würth than they had been to act against accused female witches like Catharina Leimbach and Margaretha Horn in 1652 because he was a man and because they found it easier to believe that women rather than men were workers of maleficient magic.[202] In his analysis of the gender-bias of early modern demonology, Rolf Schulte has suggested that the association between women and witchcraft was more marked among Protes-tant and particularly Lutheran writers than it was among Catholic demonolo-gists.[203] The gender-bias of Protestant demonology may therefore have influenced the council's reaction to the Leupolts' accusations against Würth to the latter's advantage, in the same way that it probably helped shape the coun-cil's milder treatment of male secondary witches in comparison to that of their female relatives.

On the rare occasions when he was questioned Würth denied that he had bewitched either Georg Leupolt or Michel Klein's tree or that he had threat-ened to bewitch Burckhard Roth. He admitted that Hans Stanninger, with whom he had had business dealings in Rothenburg, had once taught him a ritual which allegedly helped the performer to fire a rifle as accurately as possible, but denied that Stanninger had given him a book of magical arts.[204] It was Würth's exchange with Stanninger, which had occurred in 1659, which first suggested to Georg and Appolonia Leupolt that Würth might be a witch. In 1663 Appolonia claimed that Georg, who had been eavesdropping through a wall dividing their respective households at the time, had heard Stanninger teaching Würth various magical arts and had assumed that Stanninger had also given Würth the book in which they were written.[205] Georg may thus have begun to feel anxiety about Würth's magical powers which was accentuated by Würth's threatening proximity to the Leupolts. Georg was thus predisposed to blame the sudden onset of his illness after consuming a drink given to him by Würth in Würth's house in 1660 on Würth's witchcraft. The Leupolts' suspicions against Würth were then confirmed by a cunning man, Dr Hirsch of Dürren-hofen, who assured them that Georg's illness had been caused by witchcraft, and by the fact that Würth had done nothing more than shake his head when Georg had said to him that he believed that Würth had given him poison to drink.[206] Once the Leupolts began to suspect Würth of witchcraft all of his actions could be construed as sinister by them: if he visited the bedridden Georg regularly this was perceived as a threatening invasion of the Leupolts' domestic space, but a failure on Würth's part to visit Georg was interpreted as evidence of the secret malice which he bore the blacksmith.[207] Würth does not seem to have done much to help his own situation, however, as he seems to have had a habit of expressing his opinions with a forthrightness that some of his neighbours may have found threatening. On discovering that the Leupolts had accused him formally of witchcraft, for example, Würth admitted having said that Leupolt would have died less peacefully had he (Würth) first brought a slander-suit against him.[208] Würth was either too convinced of his own right-eousness or too tactless to realise the danger that existed in thus speaking aggressively against a person for whose death he was held responsible.

After Würth had fled Rothenburg the city councillors arrested his wife Barbara and interrogated her three times.[209] Barbara had figured only margin-ally in the allegations raised against her husband. Appolonia Leupolt had once said that she held Würth and Barbara responsible for Georg Leupolt's illness, but otherwise centred her allegations of maleficium entirely on Würth.[210] The only other evidence against Barbara was Johannes Georg's allegation that Bar-bara had told him about her husband's book of magic in the context of her recounting of Würth's misfortune at the shooting contest in Waldmann-shofen.[211] The councillors seem to have decided to arrest Barbara partly out of frustration with the fact that Würth himself had escaped their jurisdiction, and partly as a result of their belief that women were more likely than men to be workers of maleficium. However, when Barbara was banished on 8 August her surety referred only in cautious terms to the possibility that she may have assisted Würth in his witchcraft: in custody she had been told that she was to be banished for her obstinacy under questioning and the false testimony she had given. The latter comment was a reference to the fact that, after consistently denying knowledge of any book of magical arts possessed by her husband, she admitted during her final interrogation that he had possessed at least one such book and that she had tried to persuade him to take it with him to Wald-mannshofen to help ensure success in the shooting-contest. Barbara claimed, however, that Würth had destroyed the book in early May 1663.[212] The impor-tance of books of ritual magic in this trial and the trial of Hans Georg Hofmann in 1605 points to the existence of beliefs about a particularly masculine way of learning magical arts which was linked to, yet distinct from, the idea that magic

was passed on within the household and which may have had particular significance in the urban context. When pressed about whether or not he possessed
any such books during questioning in the chancellery on 28 February Würth
would admit only that he had owned two such books during his life. His father
had given him one but he had destroyed it so that his children would not be
encouraged to use magic; he had obtained the second in Nuremberg while
working there as a journeyman.[213] Hofmann also referred to having learned
magical rituals for treasure-seeking while travelling as a journeyman and both
he and Pfund were suspected of possessing books of ritual magic, a charge not
levelled at any of the women involved in witch-trials in Rothenburg.[214] It
may therefore have been the case that urban craftsmen, who were most likely
to be literate and mobile, were believed most likely to learn magic from books
and ideas exchanged in the context of their work, instead of – or in addition
to – learning magic within the household. Intriguingly Hofmann and Würth
were both believed to have gained their maleficient powers from books of
what appear to have been beneficient magical rituals. Perhaps the attempt by
the authorities in Rothenburg to teach their subjects that all magic was evil
had had some, albeit tangential effect, insofar as it had encouraged certain
citizens to become more anxious about the malevolent potential of such books
of white magic.[215]

Conclusions

Anyone, of any age and either gender, could plausibly be imagined to be a witch
in early modern Rothenburg; the witch-trials that occurred there involved a
wide range of alleged witches, from six-year-old Hans Gackstatt, who claimed
to have gone night-flying with his mother in 1587, to eighty-eight-year-old
Anna Maas, accused of seducing her maidservant into witchcraft in 1673. The
range of suspects was so broad because witchcraft was understood primarily as
an art taught by older experts to people younger than themselves or with
whom they lived in close proximity: technically anyone – men and children
included – could learn and practise it. The range of alleged witches was also
broad because suspicions of witchcraft could arise in many different situations
of social conflict. They also sprang chiefly from the anxieties and fantasies of
those individuals who accused others of witchcraft. Again these anxieties and
fantasies were diverse, but were often played out around the accuser's feelings
of fear and envy of the alleged witch as someone able to exercise power over
onself and one's household. Men and women could both be imagined as capable of working maleficient magic in this manner and the disturbing abilities of
the witch to enrich her- or himself illicitly by means of magic at the expense of

others and to jeopardise the material survival of other households was likewise not gender-specific. For example, Georg Leupolt believed that Michael Würth had bewitched him by means of a poisoned drink in a manner which severely affected his ability to work and led ultimately to his death: Michael Rost held very similar beliefs in relation to his wife Margaretha's malevolent magical powers in 1641.[216] Würth's visits to the bedridden Leupolt were also imagined by the Leupolts as a sinister invasion of their household space in the same way that Eva Schürz gradually came to imagine the visits of Catharina or Magdalena Leimbach or Barbara Bratsch to her house as connected to Catharina's malevolent power as a witch over the Schürz household. Hans Georg Hofmann's alleged conjuring of spirits to enable him to complete his work as a joiner more rapidly can also be understood as similar to Catharina Leimbach's alleged theft of the milk of Eva Schürz's cows: both were imagined as attempts at enrichment by dishonest, magical means. In the same way that Malcolm Gaskill has argued for England, then, men as well as women could be imagined as witches in early modern Rothenburg because 'specific circumstances, relationships and, above all, the fear of maleficium took precedence over an unqualified appreciation of the sex of the suspect in the mind of the accuser'.[217]

Awareness of this point should not, however, blind us to the fact that women were still more likely to be accused of witchcraft than men in early modern Rothenburg and, once accused, were more likely than men to face trial and what was – by Rothenburg standards – severe legal treatment.[218] From the context of beliefs about witchcraft which were potentially gender-neutral, then, emerged accusations of witchcraft which were gender-biased although by no means gender-specific. Several factors meshed together to explain this gender-bias. The first was a broad tendency on the part of the area's inhabitants, probably based on a centuries-old and quintessentially misogynistic way of conceptualising magic, to believe that women were more likely than men to practice maleficient magic and that men were more likely than women to practice beneficient magic. This was a very loose belief system, however, which allowed for much overlap between the genders. The second factor which shaped the gender-bias of witchcraft accusations was the gendered division of household labour which helped ensure that women – as housewives and mothers – were more likely than men to be involved in the daily practice of nurturing skills such as food production and preparation, child-care, and so on. As maleficient magic was often imagined as the inverse of these positive skills – as the desire and abilty to posion and harm rather than to nurture – it was thus more likely that women rather than men would be imagined as possessing them. Thirdly, anxieties about witchcraft were often imagined and articulated around the issue of the breaching of household boundaries in early modern Rothenburg and its hinterland villages, as accusers began to perceive the entrance of suspected witches into their domestic space as threatening rather than welcome. These anxieties were more likely to be played out between women than men because women were more often involved in the domestic exchanges to offer and request assistance or to lend and borrow utensils and foodstuffs which necessitated frequent visits between neighbouring households, either in person or by means of children or servants sent on their behalf. Finally, as housewives and mothers women also played teaching roles within the household, passing on rudimentary religious knowledge to their children and housewifery skills to their daughters and maidservants. Again, this rendered them more vulnerable to being imagined as witches as the latter were believed likely to want to pass on their knowledge of witchcraft to those over whom they held power.

None of the above ways of imagining maleficient magic categorically excluded men, however, while the fact that much witchcraft belief revolved around the idea of the passing on of knowledge within a household encouraged contemporaries to think of witches in terms of suspect families – including both men and women – rather than individuals. Moreover, as the cases involving Michael Rost and Georg Leupolt have shown, men as well as women could use the fantasy of the witch as the personification of the power to negatively affect all aspects of nurture and nourishment in order to articulate their fears about their own inabilities to provide properly for their families and about the terrifying pain and immobility that they suffered as a result of disease. This fantasy was also flexible enough to allow men like Michael Würth to be imagined as witches and was not – as the work of Purkiss, Roper, Jackson and Ahrendt-Schulte discussed at the beginning of this chapter implies – predominantly restricted to a women's sphere of work, belief and conflict within which it was drawn on just by women in order to play out anxieties over their relative status as good housewives and mothers. The most that can be concluded from the Rothenburg material is that the gender-bias in terms of beliefs about magic and in terms of the household division of labour which helped shape this fantasy encouraged men, women and children to imagine women as witches more readily than they would men. There were two reasons why women aged between thirty and sixty formed the majority of people formally involved in witchcraft trials in Rothenburg, with women in their fifties slightly more at risk of such involvement. The first was that, while many of these women had gained their reputations as witches at much younger ages, the general reluctance of the area's inhabitants to accuse their neighours formally of witchcraft meant that they could live for many years within their communities before such a formal accusation was finally made. The second reason was the fact that the age of between forty and sixty was a period of life during which contemporaries believed the exercise of power to be at its peak. It was therefore also likely

that witches were believed to be at the peak of the exercise of their malevolent powers at this time of their lives; they would therefore have excited
greater fear and envy and a greater willingness to make formal accusations in
their neighbours as a result.[219]

The gender-bias which encouraged the citizens of Rothenburg and the
peasants of its rural hinterland to imagine women as witches more readily than
men was more marked at the elite level, where the influence of the city councillors, their legal advisors, and medical and theological experts combined to
ensure that women accused of witchcraft were more likely to be formally prosecuted than their male counterparts and also to suffer more severely as a result
of the rigours of the legal process. For economic, political and legal reasons the
Rothenburg elites were more reluctant to take formal legal action against men
suspected of witchcraft, especially if they were urban craftsmen. However, the
elites' gender-bias against women in their beliefs about and actions against
alleged witches was probably also shaped by a Lutheran view that women were
more likely to become witches than men. This was not because of women's
sexual lust: indeed, significant concern about or focus upon the alleged sexual
congress of accused witches with the devil is absent from the Rothenburg
witch-trials. Women were rather believed more likely to submit to the devil
because they were the weaker of the two genders in terms of character, intellect and piety.[220] This gender-bias was probably shaped by the writings of scep-
tics such as Johann Weyer who strongly emphasised the idea that the devil drew
most of his recruits from among the ranks of pitiful, weak-minded, impious
women as a way of playing down the power of witches and of arguing against
the necessity for witch-trials.[221] Elite treatment of alleged witches was also
shaped by Lutheran teaching about women's ideal roles as pious and dutiful
wives and mothers: the councillors may have found it easier to believe that
women like Magdalena Gackstatt, Magdalena Dürr, Catharina Leimbach and
Margaretha Horn really were witches because their behaviour was apparently
so at odds with elite expectations about Lutheran feminine ideals.[222] Finally, the
growing importance of the seduction narrative to the Rothenburg witch-trials
also helps explain why women rather than men were more likely to be accused
of and tried for witchcraft, especially in cases involving self-confessed child-
witches. It was women's *educative* role as teachers of rudimentary religious
knowledge and the skills of housewifery to their children and servants and their
general power over youngsters within the household which made seduction
narratives so credible to listeners at all social levels in early modern Rothenburg: all were able to recognise and fear the actual or perceived influence for
good or evil of women as housewives and mothers over the young. Among the
city councillors, their advisers and their subjects, then, the seduction narrative
sprang from and helped foster an anxiety about the power of witches to

corrupt the young which helped shape and sustain the gender-bias of the Rothenburg witch-trials because it was a narrative which could be directed most plausibly against adult women who were or had been married.

Notes

1 46 individuals, or 70.8 per cent of the 65 individuals listed in the Appendix.
2 39 individuals, or 84.8 per cent of 46 females.
3 See Rowlands, 'Stereotypes and statistics', Tables 9.3–9.5.
4 Of 39 women aged 21 and above, 28 or 71.8 per cent were married, 9 or 23.1 per cent were widows, and 2 or 5.1 per cent were single.
5 Purkiss, *The Witch in History*, pp. 91–118, especially pp. 94, 100.
6 Roper, *Oedipus and the Devil*, pp. 199–225, especially pp. 208–212. Deborah Willis also uses psychoanalytical models to argue that 'witches were women . . . because women are mothers', in *Malevolent Nurture*, p. 6.
7 Ahrendt-Schulte, *Zauberinnen in der Stadt Horn*, pp. 213–243, especially pp. 225–227. Brauner, in *Fearless Wives and Frightened Shrews*, and Hayes, in 'Negativizing nurture and demonizing domesticity', also use the idea of the witch as the inverse of the good housewife.
8 Jackson, 'Witches, wives and mothers', pp. 73, 74.
9 RStA Interrogation Book A887 fols 548r–549v, 552r–553r, 554v. For full trial-records, see fols 545r–594v.
10 *Ibid.*, fols 553v–554r.
11 *Ibid.*, fols 545v, 546r, 549v–550r.
12 *Ibid.*, fols 552v, 545v, 551v, 547r.
13 *Ibid.*, fol. 562v.
14 *Ibid.*, fol. 551v.
15 *Ibid.*, fols 551v, 550r, 547r: 'keins Mans wert, grob, unsauber.'
16 *Ibid.*, fols 554r, 545v.
17 See pp. 19–20 for discussion of the importance of honour and the damage that could be done to it by slander.
18 On this idea, see Rublack, 'Pregnancy, childbirth and the female body', pp. 90–93.
19 RStA Interrogation Book A887 fols 548r–550r.
20 *Ibid.*, fols 555r–556v.
21 *Ibid.*, fols 557r–560v.
22 *Ibid.*, fols 561r–566r.
23 *Ibid.*, fols 567r–571v.
24 *Ibid.*, fols 574r–575r.
25 *Ibid.*, fols 576r–580r.
26 *Ibid.*, fols 581r, 582r.
27 *Ibid.*, fols 583r–586v.
28 *Ibid.*, fol. 591v.
29 *Ibid.*, fol. 559v: 'sehr . . . wunderbar und seltsam.'
30 *Ibid.*, fol. 587r.
31 *Ibid.*, fol. 584r.
32 Jackson, 'Witches, wives and mothers'.
33 RStA Interrogation Book A887 fol. 564r: 'dz jenige so eins also heisse seye schuldig daran'.
34 This may also have been the case with the self-confessed witches studied by Louise Jackson who were probably victims of physical or sexual abuse, see Jackson, 'Witches, wives and mothers', pp. 73–74.
35 RStA Interrogation Book A887 fol. 585r.
36 *Ibid.*, fols 592r–594v.
37 *Ibid.*, fols 561r–561v.
38 *Ibid.*, fol. 560r.
39 *Ibid.*, fols 572r–572v.

40 *Ibid.*, fol. 573r.

41 See Rowlands, 'Women, gender and power', Chapter 3.

42 See on this point Davis, *Fiction in the Archives*, pp. 77–110.

43 On the Lutheran idealisation of women's domestic role, see Chapter 3, pp. 94–96 and n. 76.

44 See RStA Interrogation Book A909 fols 188r–399v and Appendix for details.

45 RStA Surety Book A849 fols 296r–298r.

46 Perhaps the frequency of this type of trial in Augsburg was, as Robin Briggs suggests, due to the fact that one or two cases generated enough publicity 'to create a local syndrome which led to a modest trickle of cases over several decades', Briggs, *Witches and Neighbours*, p. 281. According to Tom Robisheaux, witchcraft accusations emerged from the lying-in period 'in only a minority of cases' in south-western Germany, 'Witchcraft and forensic medicine', p. 203.

47 See for example StAN Ro. Rep. 2092 fols 53r–54r; RStA Interrogation Book A908, statement by Endres Klenckh (11 July 1671); StAN Ro. Rep. 2087 fols 746r–751r.

48 *Ibid.*, fols 621r–622r, 623r, 636r–638r, 652r, 700r–700v.

49 Most of Rothenburg's infanticide cases involved unmarried maidservants; mention of witchcraft was absent from their interrogations, see Rowlands, '"In great secrecy"'. Elsewhere infanticide and witchcraft became more conflated; see for example Maria Tausiet's work on Aragon, 'Witchcraft as metaphor: infanticide and its translations'.

50 RStA Interrogation Book A896 fols 250r–250v; for full trial-records, see fols 250r–279v. This way of imagining bewitchment is depicted in an illustration in Ulrich Molitor's 1489 work *De Lamiis*, in which a man's leg is bewitched by an arrow shot from a bow by a witch, see Dresen-Coenders, 'Witches as devils' concubines', p. 60.

51 RStA Ordinances A363 fols 279r–282r.

52 RStA Interrogation Book A896 fols 251r–252r.

53 *Ibid.*, fols 252v–253r.

54 *Ibid.*, fols 253v–254v: 'vndt er vermeint, die stube seye voll dicken Nebels'. Margaretha gave the charms to Finsterlohr's pastor soon afterwards after Rost fetched the pastor to his house so he could take communion, see *ibid.*, fol. 255r.

55 *Ibid.*, fols 255r–255v: 'biss er angefangen ein dergleichen spermatische . . . vbel stinckende Materey haufig vndt handtvollweiss ausszuwerfen'. Rost's interrogators noted that this was how Rost described the matter, fol. 255v.

56 'Sie ihme im schlaff solche wüste ding in halss gestecket haben müste', *ibid.*, fol. 255v. It is unclear whether Margaretha was menstruating or suffering from a postpartum vaginal discharge. Given that she had given birth in late May or early June and that menstruation recommences eight weeks after delivery in women who do not breastfeed, the latter explanation seems more likely. Rost described his wife as suffering from her 'womanly illness' ('wegen ihrer Weiblicher Kranckheit vngelegenheit gehabt', fol. 255v).

57 *Ibid.*, fol. 256r: 'gar selzamb im Kopf'.

58 *Ibid.*, fols 256r–257r.

59 See *ibid.*, fols 258r–260r (Ardolt); fols 261r–266v (Margaretha).

60 *Ibid.*, fol. 261v.

61 *Ibid.*, fol. 262r.

62 *Ibid.*, fol. 264v, where this is implied.

63 *Ibid.*, fols 262v–265v, 267r.

64 *Ibid.*, fol. 266r: 'Ihr Mann sey eben ein Recht wunderlicher Kopf . . . selzam vndt melancholisch.'

65 *Ibid.*, fol. 266v.

66 *Ibid.*, fol. 262v.

67 *Ibid.*, fol. 259r. The miller was probably cautious about confirming his customers' suspicions of witchcraft because he had already been arrested and questioned by Rothenburg's council about his activities as a cunning man in 1624, although released without punishment; see RStA Account Book R528 fol. 116v.

68 RStA Interrogation Book A896 fols 259v–260r. We are reliant on Ardolt's account of his visits to the miller for this information. As Margaretha's friend Ardolt may have been tempted to present her favourably in his statement. However, his account of the miller's growing impatience with Rost has a convincing ring and his description of his visits to Buch and the remedies with which he returned accord with those given by the Rosts.

69 *Ibid.*, fols 267r–267v.

70 *Ibid.*, fol. 269v.

71 *Ibid.*, fol. 271r.

72 For their sureties, see *ibid.*, fols 273r–275v (Margaretha); fols 277r–279r (Michael).

73 Purkiss, *The Witch in History*, p. 93.

74 On the poverty of vinedressers in early modern Rothenburg, see Vice, 'Vineyards, vinedressers and the Peasants' War'.

75 RStA Interrogation Book A896 fol. 250r: 'nach dem er keine lebensmitel mehr im Vorrath gewüst.'

76 *Ibid.*, fols 275r–275v, 279r.

77 Being a good provider for his family was lauded in many early modern German conduct-books as one of the main duties of the married man, see Hendrix, 'Masculinity and patriarchy', pp. 185–186, 193.

78 Ahrendt-Schulte, *Zauberinnen in der Stadt Horn*, p. 223: 'Gift wurde allgemein als Gegenteil von Nahrung verstanden, eine Kraft, die den Körper von innen aufzehrt.'

79 For examples, see RStA Interrogation Book A850 fols 262r–270v; Roper, *The Holy Household*, pp. 176–185.

80 RStA Interrogation Book A896 fol. 260r.

81 *Ibid.*, fol. 256v.

82 *Ibid.*, fols 269r–269v.

83 See Chapter 1, n. 111.

84 StAN Ro. Rep. 2090 fols 120r–121r.

85 StAN Ro. Rep. 2096 fols 266r–278r.

86 RStA Interrogation Book A896 fol. 261v.

87 *Ibid.*, fol. 268v: 'weiss ich nicht wass Ihr beede mit einander gemacht'.

88 *Ibid.*, fol. 252v.

89 Roper, *Oedipus and the Devil*, pp. 209–210, 211–213.

90 Purkiss, *The Witch in History*, p. 100.

91 StAN Ro. Rep. 2087 fols 1r–3r; for full trial-records, see *ibid.*, fols 1r–164r. For an image which shows a witch magically milking her neighbour's cows through an axe handle from Johann Geiler von Kaiser's *Die Emeis* (1517), see Hayes, 'Negativizing nurture and demonizing domesticity', p. 182.

92 StAN Ro. Rep. 2087 fols 4r–8v.

93 *Ibid.*, fols 10r–14v (Catharina); fols 15r–17r (Bratsch); fols 17v–20r (Mathes). Catharina's daughter Magdalena was not arrested but questioned formally at the smithy.

94 Mägerlein, *Familienregister der Pfarrgemeinde Wettringen*, p. 331.

95 StAN Ro. Rep. 2087 fol. 15r.

96 For accounts of this incident see *ibid.*, fol. 11r (Catharina); fols 15v–16r (Bratsch); fols 18r–18v (Mathes); fols 32r–32v (Eva).

97 *Ibid.*, fol. 19r.

98 *Ibid.*, fol. 24r.

99 *Ibid.*, fol. 48r.

100 See *ibid.*, fols 33r, 35v, 36r–36v, 38r and 38v for testimony about Catharina's reputation.

101 This idea can also be seen in the witchcraft accusations against Diederich Flade in Trier and Christoph Wendler von Bregenroth in Hohenberg: both were wealthy urban newcomers who were believed to have used their influential positions to enrich themselves unfairly at their communities' expense, see Dillinger, 'Richter als Angeklagte'. For the newest analysis of the Trier witch-trials, see Voltmer, 'Zwischen Herrschaftskrise'.

102 On this idea, see Ahrendt-Schulte, *Zauberinnen in der Stadt Horn*, pp. 229-235.

103 StAN Ro. Rep. 2087 fol. 61v.

104 *Ibid.*, fols 36r–36v.

105 Mägerlein, *Familienregister der Pfarrgemeinde Wettringen*, p. 457.

106 *Ibid.*, pp. 457 and 539; StAN Ro. Rep. 2087 fol. 33r.

107 For Eva's account of the birth of her first child and her consultation of the soothsayer, see *ibid.*, fols 31v–32r. Mägerlein's *Familienregister der Pfarrgemeinde Wettringen*, p.457, lists only one child born to Eva before 1652 (Eva, born 27 September 1650, died 2 October 1650), but Eva refers clearly to two babies born since her marriage in 1649 which both died quickly after birth. Her third pregnancy was successful: she bore Magdalena (one of only two of her children to survive to adulthood) on 25 September 1652, see *ibid.* Barbara Schürz suggested that Eva was worried about Catharina's power over her childbearing ability, StAN Ro. Rep. 2087 fol. 14r.

108 *Ibid.*, fols 55r–55v.

109 *Ibid.*, fols 30v–31r.

110 *Ibid.*, fol. 44v.

111 *Ibid.*, fols 46r–46v, 47v.

112 *Ibid.*, fols 48v–49r.

113 For Eva's statements, see *ibid.*, fols 30v–32v, 55r–56v, 74v–76v.

114 *Ibid.*, fols 1r–3r, 4r, 21v. Barbara seems to have told her story against Catharina in order to win her stepmother's favour and to gain her father's attention. Barbara's witchcraft narrative – which included details of encounters with a black man who had torn off her apron – may also have been a means by which she articulated her trauma at the fact that she had been sexually abused some time before the trial in 1652. She described an act of intercourse with an adult man in great detail to her step-grandmother and was also found to have lost her virginity after being examined by the city midwives on 27 September 1652. It seems most likely that she had been raped, probably by a stranger, while working or wandering by herself in the village fields. For details of this aspect of the case, see *ibid.*, fols 21v–22r, 34v, 53r–53v, 34r, 91r, 87r, 125r–126r, 129r–131r, 133r–133v.

115 See Purkiss, *The Witch in History*, pp. 96–97, on the importance of dairying to early modern housewives.

116 Purkiss suggests that this psychological dynamic was crucial to stories of witchcraft told by female accusers in early modern England (*ibid.*, pp. 91–118), while Nancy Hayes argues that the German witch was constructed as 'a terrifyingly powerful and aggressive depriver of nutrition and . . . life itself . . . a demonic mother who challenges God's natural beneficence', in 'Negativizing nurture and demonizing domesticity', p. 197.

117 StAN Ro. Rep. 2087 fols 19r, 22v, 38v.

118 *Ibid.*, fols 31r, 33v.

119 *Ibid.*, fols 11r, 18r: 'närrisch'.

120 See pp. 187–192 for discussion of the idea that an accused witch's refusal to confess was increasingly perceived as evidence of her identity as a witch by the councillors.

121 StAN Ro. Rep. 2087 fols 79r–86r. For Catharina's other interrogations, see fols 10r–14v, 44v–49r.

122 *Ibid.*, fols 92r–93r.

123 *Ibid.*, fols 43v–44r.

124 *Ibid.*, fols 119r–120v, 135r–135v.

125 *Ibid.*, fols 117r–118r. Mathes also had to pay the costs of his and Catharina's stay in gaol.

126 *Ibid.*, fol. 147r.

127 *Ibid.*, fols 151r–152v, 148r–149r, 154r–154v.

128 *Ibid.*, fols 115r–115v.

129 *Ibid.*, fols 144r–145v. The councillors did not lose sympathy with Barbara and deem her worthy of punishment even after the fact that she had lost her virginity had been established; see above, n. 114.

130 This was according to pastor Nicolaus Rosenbach, *ibid.*, fol. 163r.
131 For the interrogations of Mathes, see *ibid.*, fols 17v–20r, 41r–44r, 64r–65v.
132 For case details, see pp. 18, 22, 25 and Appendix.
133 See StAN Ro. Rep. 2087 fols 704r–705v (Knöspel); RStA Interrogation Book A925 fols 104v–105r (Schmezer); the 1582 Oberstetten case is discussed pp. 24, 26–27, 30–31, and in Rowlands, 'Eine Stadt ohne Hexenwahn' (Weh); the Hilgartshausen case involving Hans Gackstatt is discussed in Chapter 3 (Kuch).
134 'Sie werde nunmehro Trutenwerk auch lernen', RStA Interrogation Book A898 fol. 518v; see also fol. 514v.
135 *Ibid.*, fol. 518v.
136 *Ibid.*, fols 519r–519v. Michael Würth, the wheelwright accused of witchcraft in 1663 whose case is discussed pp. 164–168, passed on a reputation for witchcraft to his stepson Georg Adam Knöspel, who was banished with his wife Anna Maria after her trial for witchcraft in 1689, see StAN Ro. Rep. 2087 fols 679r, 628r–628v.
137 This idea of witchcraft as like a contagious disease is also suggested by David Sabean in *Power in the Blood*, p. 105, and helps explain why people in Rothenburg's hinterland who lived in close proximity to alleged witches would threaten to move out of their villages: see for example RStA Bettenfeld Village Acts A491 fol. 49v.
138 This was the case with Babelein Kuch, see n. 133, and p. 85. Johannes Dillinger has one example from Electoral Trier of a twenty-five-year-old man who had had a reputation as a witch for forty years, so powerful was the stigma of being born into a witch-family, see Dillinger, '*Böse Leute*', pp. 204–205.
139 This was the case with Barbara Bratsch; for another example of a maidservant in this position, see RStA Interrogation Book A908, trial of Appolonia Glaitter of Windisch-Bockenfeld, statement by Margaretha Lang (29 July 1671).
140 This was the case with Margaretha Horn, discussed earlier in this paragraph. For further discussion of the young ages at which people could first gain reputations as witches, see Rowlands 'Witchcraft and old women'.
141 See Chapter 3.
142 The Hörber and Harter cases are discussed in Chapter 4; the Brigitta Hörner case on p. 62.
143 See the trials involving Margaretha Fischer (1668), Anna Margaretha Rohn (1673), Hans Christoph Emmert (1676), Hans Adam Knöspel (1689), and Hans Caspar Kürrlein (1709) listed in the Appendix.
144 See for example Radbruch, *Die Peinliche Gerichtsordnung*, p. 52; Kramer, *Der Hexenhammer*, Part II.
145 This was particularly the case if it suited the council's legal and political priorities to take their confessions seriously; compare for example its treatment of the cases of Margaretha Hörber and Margaretha Harter discussed in Chapter 4. On the difficulty contemporaries experienced in doubting children's confessions, see Walz, 'Kinder in Hexenprozessen', p. 220.
146 RStA Interrogation Book A909 fols 275r–276v, 277r–280v.
147 StAN Ro. Rep. 2087 fols 754r–756r, 765r, 766v, 767v, 761r–764r. Brigitta Hörner claimed in 1639 that she had been baptised in the devil's name by the pastor of Spielbach but that she had been taught witchcraft by his wife (her godmother), see RStA Interrogation Book A895 fols 165r–165v, 166r–170v.
148 The following youngsters accused the following women of having seduced them into witchcraft: Hans Gackstatt accused his mother in 1587 (see Chapter 3), as did Hans Adam Knöspel in 1689 (see StAN Ro. Rep. 2087 fols 620r–739r); Margaretha Hörber accused the village midwife, with whom she had had an affectionate relationship, in 1627 (see pp. 106–107); Brigitta Hörner accused her godmother in 1639 (see n. 147); Anna Margaretha Rohn accused her mistress in 1673 (see n. 146); Margaretha Fischer accused her foster-mother in in 1668 (RStA Interrogation Book A906, documents involving Margaretha Fischer and Susanna Lamer, 20–29 August 1668); Margaretha Harter accused the old herdswoman with whom she went begging in 1629 (see p. 125); Hans Caspar Kürrlein accused his aunt in 1709

(RStA Interrogation Book A938 fols 297r–373v), as did Hans Christoph Emmert in 1676 (see Schraut, 'Niederstetten 1676').

149 On the gendered division of household labour, see Ahrendt-Schulte, *Zauberinnen in der Stadt Horn*, pp. 35–42, 225–227; Briggs, *Witches and Neighbours*, pp. 267–269; Purkiss, *The Witch in History*, pp. 91–118; Sharpe, 'Witchcraft and women in seventeenth-century England', pp. 188–192; Wunder, *'Er ist die Sonn', sie ist der Mond'*, pp. 89–117. We can see it clearly around the issue of dairying and childbirth in the Wettringen witchcraft case of 1652, see pp. 150–156. The important educative influence of women over their children is discussed pp. 94–96.

150 RStA Interrogation Book A895 fols 166r–170v.

151 See Chapter 2, n. 39.

152 See Chapter 3 n. 76.

153 That Lutheran urban men could imagine and want themselves protrayed in this role is seen in a stained-glass window painted for Nuremberg's city council by Christoph Murer in 1598. Here the just government of the councillors is symbolised by the Christian virtues about to rescue a chained, naked child from the clutches of an evil old man (symbolising a Jew) and an evil old woman (symbolising a witch); see Zika, 'Kannibalismus und Hexerei', p. 103. As near neighbours with similar political and religious views, it seems reasonable to assume that Rothenburg's councillors would have shared this way of imagining their own good government with the Nuremberg councillors.

154 This stood in marked contrast to what the councillors perceived as the deliberate defiance of adult women who refused to confess their witchcraft, a theme discussed pp. 187–192.

155 On the idea that early modern demonology was organised in terms of polar opposites in which women were classified on the negative side of the equation, see Clark, 'The "gendering" of witchcraft in French demonology'.

156 Schulte, *Hexenmeister*, p. 81. In other regions of Europe the percentage of men tried as witches ranged from 5 per cent in the Bishopric of Basel to 92 per cent in Iceland, *ibid.*, p. 86. No explanation exists for these wide variations.

157 Nineteen males out of a total of sixty-five people.

158 RStA Interrogation Book A886 fols 269(a)r, 287r; this case is discussed pp. 105–124.

159 See the cases of Hans Gackstatt (1587), RStA Interrogation Book A877 fols 532r–579v; Hans Christoph Emmert (1676), Council Meeting Minutes B45 fols 630v–631r, Account Book R531 fol. 234v, Schraut, 'Niederstetten 1676'; Hans Adam Knöspel and Hans Georg Nunn (1689-94), StAN Ro. Rep. 2087 fols 620r–863v; Hans Caspar Kürrlein (1709), RStA Interrogation Book A938 fols 297r–373v.

160 The reasons for this reluctance are discussed in Chapters 1 and 2.

161 See Chapter 3.

162 Schulte, *Hexenmeister*, pp. 234–242: 'primary' male witches were those accused in their own right, *ibid.*, pp. 215–234.

163 See RStA Interrogation Book A858 fols 14r–36r, Surety Book A846 fols 433v–435v, 438v–441v (Brosam); Interrogation Book A861 fols 497r–513v, Surety Book A847 fols 353v–355v (Kellner); StAN Ro. Rep. 2087 fols 1r–164r (Leimbach); RStA Interrogation Book A909 fols 188r–399v (Maas); StAN Ro. Rep. 2087 fols 621r–739r (Knöspel).

164 None of the men were tortured: Leimbach's wife and Kellner's mother and one of his sisters were tortured. Kellner was also the only member of his family to escape banishment in 1563. Knöspel was technically banished on account of his debts, his poor household discipline and his wife's bad reputation, but it made religious and economic sense for the council to banish him with his wife rather than to divide the couple.

165 See pp. 14–23 for discussion of the Brosam case; pp. 150–160 for the Leimbach case.

166 RStA Interrogation Book A858 fols 28r–31v (Brosam); StAN Ro. Rep. 2087 fols 36r–36v, 61v (Leimbach).

167 See Chapter 2 for discussion of this point.

168 Schulte, *Hexenmeister*, pp. 228–234.

169 RStA Interrogation Book A921 fols143r–150v.
170 RStA Interrogation Book A884 fols 539r–539v, 549r, 553v; for full trial-records, see fols 510r–612v.
171 *Ibid.*, fols 511r–518v.
172 *Ibid.*, fols 528r–528v.
173 *Ibid.*, fols 513r–514v, 515v–516v.
174 *Ibid.*, fols 523r, 531r–532r, 571v–572v, 591r–591v.
175 *Ibid.*, fols 526v–527r, 610v–611r.
176 *Ibid.*, fols 536v, 569v–570v.
177 *Ibid.*, fols 510r–510v, 524v–525r.
178 *Ibid.*, fols 610v, 559v.
179 Vogt probably testified against Hofmann to try to deflect attention away from his own role in the treasure-seeking.
180 *Ibid.*, fols 526r–533r.
181 *Ibid.*, fols 534r–550r.
182 *Ibid.*, fols 556r–560r (Prenninger); fols 563r–567r (von Berg).
183 *Ibid.*, fols 569r–573v.
184 *Ibid.*, fols 574r–577r.
185 *Ibid.*, fols 580r–583v.
186 *Ibid.*, fols 584r–588v.
187 *Ibid.*, fols 610r–612v.
188 *Ibid.*, fol. 559r.
189 *Ibid.*, fol. 567r.
190 Compare for example the treatment of Hofmann, Pfund and Vogt with that of Mathes Leimbach in 1652, p. 156.
191 *Ibid.*, fols 556r–560r. Prenninger was very scathing about the credulity of the lower orders in his report.
192 RStA Interrogation Book A902 (unpaginated), Appolonia Leupolt's statement (22 December 1662). Case-documents continue until 15 June 1664, when Barbara Würth asked to be allowed to return to Rothenburg, a request refused by the council on 22 June 1664.
193 *Ibid.*, Appolonia Leupolt's statement (17 January 1663).
194 *Ibid.*, Michel Klein's statement (17 January 1663).
195 *Ibid.*, statements by Johannes Georg (17 January1663) and Michael Albrecht (22 January 1663); letter from Veit Rueg (5 February 1663).
196 *Ibid.*, Michael Würth's testimon (28 February, 14 March, and 5 May 1663).
197 *Ibid.*, letter from Würth to Rothenburg's council, 30 March 1663. Von Eyb refused to question Stanninger unless Rothenburg's council asked him to do so. The council complied, but von Eyb failed to question Stanninger until 9 April and did not send his testimony to Rothenburg until 27 July 1663; see *ibid.*, letters exchanged between Rothenburg's council and von Eyb dated 30 and 31 March 1663, 27 June 1663, 27 July 1663.
198 *Ibid.*, letters from Würth to Rothenburg's council, 1 and 3 July 1663.
199 *Ibid.*, report of sightings of Würth in Rothenburg's hinterland and order to rural officials to capture him, 31 July 1663.
200 *Ibid.*, Barbara Würth's surety, 1 August 1662.
201 For these hints, see See RStA B27 (Chronicle by Johann Georg Albrecht), 1663; RStA Interrogation Book A902, letter by Würth written between 3 and 15 April 1663.
202 See pp. 150–160 for discussion of Leimbach's case; pp. 180–192 for discussion of Horn's.
203 Schulte, *Hexenmeister*, pp. 107–177, especially pp. 116–120, 165–170.
204 RStA Interrogation Book A902, Würth's testimony, 28 February 1663.
205 *Ibid.*, Appolonia Leupolt's statement, 6 March 1663.
206 *Ibid.*, Appolonia Leupolt's statement, 22 December 1662.
207 *Ibid.*, Appolonia Leupolt's statement, 22 December 1662; Würth's testimony, 28 February 1663.

208 *Ibid.*, Würth's testimony, 28 February 1663.

209 *Ibid.*, Barbara Würth's interrogations, 21, 23 and 27 July 1663.

210 *Ibid.*, Appolonia Leupolt's statement, 29 December 1662.

211 *Ibid.*, Johannes Georg's statement, 17 January 1663.

212 *Ibid.*, Barbara Würth's interrogation, 27 July 1663, and surety sworn on 1 August 1663.

213 *Ibid.*, Würth's testimony, 28 February 1663.

214 For Hofmann and Pfund, see RStA Interrogation Book A884 fols 528r, 539r–539v, 549r, 553v, 536v, 569v–570v. None of Rothenburg's accused female witches admitted to or were questioned about possessing books of ritual magic, although some referred to magical rituals passed on between women within the household verbally. For an example, see the Shrove Tuesday cleaning ritual referred to by Margaretha Horn, p. 181.

215 For discussion of the Rothenburg authorities' attempt to police the use of white magic, see pp. 68–75.

216 I thus disagree with Ingrid Ahrendt-Schulte, who implies that the idea of the witch as poisoner was gender-specific to women (as one aspect of the construct of the witch as the inverse of the good housewife), see Ahrendt-Schulte, *Zauberinnen in der Stadt Horn*, pp. 213–243, 225–227.

217 Gaskill, 'The Devil in the shape of a man', p. 161. The idea that witchcraft accusations emerged from various social conflicts and for many different reasons is also emphasised by Gaskill in 'Witchcraft in early modern Kent'; by Briggs in *Witches and Neighbours*; by Behringer in 'Witchcraft studies in Austria, Germany and Switzerland'; by Rummel in 'Vom Umgang mit Hexen und Hexerei'; and by Dillinger in '*Böse Leute*'. This work challenges older approaches to the study of witchcraft which suggested that the background to witchcraft accusations could be explained by just one dominant model of social conflict. The main proponents of the latter theory are Thomas in *Religion and the Decline of Magic* and Macfarlane in *Witchcraft in Tudor and Stuart England*. Radical feminist explanations of witch-hunts (such as Barstow's *Witchcraze*, or Hester's *Lewd Women and Wicked Witches*) can also be criticised for trying to reduce the complexity of witch-trials to one broad model of alleged social conflict: that of men's hatred or fear of women.

218 See Appendix for overview summary of cases.

219 For discussion of the connections between age and women's vulnerability to accusations of witchcraft; see Rowlands, 'Stereotypes and statistics', and 'Witchcraft and old women'.

220 See Schulte, *Hexenmeister*, pp. 116–120.

221 See Rowlands, 'Stereotypes and statistics', for discussion of this sceptical position and its gender-bias. There were copies of Weyer's *De Praestigiis Daemonum* and another well-known sceptical work, Johann Georg Gödelmann's *Tractatus de magis, veneficis et lamiis* in Rothenburg's Consistorial library; it seems probable that this strain of sceptical demonology influenced the ideas of some of the councillors and their advisers. We know that it influenced the opinion written by Superintendent Georg Zyrlein in the case of Margaretha Hörber (see pp. 53–54), which in turn influenced the council's handling of subsequent cases of self-confessed child-witches.

222 Their cases are discussed in Chapter 3 (Gackstatt), pp. 136–143 (Dürr), pp. 150–160 (Leimbach) and pp. 180–192 (Horn).

6

'God will punish both poor and rich': the idioms and risks of defiance in the trial of Margaretha Horn, 1652

While it is possible to attribute the restrained pattern of witch-hunting in early modern Rothenburg to the interaction of the beliefs and the legal and social priorities of both the councillors and their subjects, we must not forget another factor that was vital in ensuring that most of the Rothenburg witch-trials were unlikely either to end in verdicts of guilt or to spiral out of control into chain-reaction type 'witch-panics'. This was the courage of the men and most especially the women, who formed the majority of those accused of witchcraft, in bearing the psychological and physical suffering caused by the experience of incarceration, interrogation and perhaps even torture without breaking down and admitting that they were witches. The reluctance of the council to resort to torture rapidly and without restraint, in addition to the knowledge that verdicts of guilt in witch-trials were the exception rather than the rule in Rothenburg, were doubtless crucial in giving many prisoners in the city gaol the strength of mind to resist the pressure to confess. However, they also drew on and displayed their own resources of piety, anger, desperation and stoicism to help bolster this resistance. One accused witch called Margaretha Horn not only refused to confess to witchcraft in 1652 but also developed a sophisticated rhetoric of defiance against the city council and its handling of her case in the course of her interrogation. Her trial is of such interest because it underscores particularly effectively the point that women on trial for witchcraft were not 'mere mouthpieces of a patriachal elite', whose statements and confessions were simply forced re-hashings of that elite's demonology.[1] On the contrary – and despite the fact that power over the trial process lay ultimately with the council – alleged witches were capable of contributing to and of shaping the course of interrogations in idiosyncratic ways. At the same time, however, the trial of Margaretha shows that it was becoming increasingly problematic for women accused of witchcraft in early modern Rothenburg to articulate defiance against their accusers and the council without this defiance being interpreted as additional evidence of their alleged identity as witches.

A swarm of fleas

On 6 August 1652 sixty-year-old Margaretha Horn, who lived in the village of Bettenfeld with her husband Hans and two unmarried daughters, Eva and Cordula, was arrested on suspicion of having caused a swarm of fleas to plague her nearest neighbour, Leonhard Gackstatt. According to Gackstatt the fleas were everywhere: in his house and garden and in the clothes and bedding of all the family members, who had been bitten bloody by the insects. Nor could they be got rid of; after strenuous cleaning and airing efforts the fleas would return to the house within the hour.[2] Gackstatt claimed that Margaretha had caused the fleas to infest his house by means of a ritual she had carried out on Shrove Tuesday of 1652. Margaretha was supposed to have swept out her own house, to have deposited the waste onto Gackstatt's dung-heap and to have stuck the broom with which she had done the sweeping on top of the waste, thereby magically transferring the dirt and vermin from her own house to his. In custody Margaretha admitted having carried out the ritual cleaning and depositing of waste but explained that she had done so with no evil intentions, that she had not put the waste onto Gackstatt's dung-heap, and that many other women of the area also practised this custom of sweeping out on Shrove Tuesday: one of her married daughters had learned of it while in service in Rothenburg several years earlier.[3] Any fleas that existed in Gackstatt's house were not the result of her witchcraft but of his bad housekeeping; all seven members of his household apparently slept in the same room as his chickens, pigs, calves and goat. Margaretha also alluded at this point to the great enmity which Gackstatt possessed against her: he had sought to take her life before, she claimed, and was now trying to make a witch out of her by falsely accusing her of having created the fleas.[4]

The allegation made by Gackstatt against Margaretha was, in fact, the final stage in a feud between them which may have begun as early as 1639, when Margaretha had moved from Gebsattel to Bettenfeld, but which by 1652 involved all members of the Horn and Gackstatt households and was common knowledge in Bettenfeld. Gackstatt may have believed that Margaretha was a witch from 1639 because her first marriage had been into the family of the old herdsman of Gebsattel, whose members were all reputed witches; by 1652 – and in addition to the flea-swarm – he also blamed her for the low milk-yields of his cows. For her part, Margaretha held Gackstatt responsible for the death of her son Michael, claiming that Gackstatt's violence towards Michael had caused the internal injuries of which he had later died.[5] The events of Shrove Tuesday in 1652 brought the tension between the two households to an open breach: Hans Horn and Gackstatt almost came to blows over the alleged flea-making ritual, armed with a hoe and axe, respectively, while it prompted their wives and children to taunt and throw stones at each other.[6] Hans Horn tried in vain to restore accord between the households through the mediation of neighbours in May, then – presumably in desperation, as it was a high-risk strategy – reported to the council in Rothenburg in late June that Gackstatt had accused one of his own sons of adultery six years earlier.[7] This pre-emptive strike, which constituted an attempt to shift official attention onto the alleged wrongdoings of the Gackstatt family and away from the fleas, backfired badly, however. Gackstatt countered Horn's accusation with the allegations of witch-craft against Margaretha and it was Margaretha who was taken into custody to suffer the rigours of a formal trial.[8]

From the beginning the councillors approached the case as if Gackstatt's story was the most credible version of events and viewed Margaretha's protes-tations of innocence as an unhelpful stumbling block to the smooth progression of the trial. This was surprising, as Margaretha's reference to the enmity which Gackstatt bore her should have encouraged them to investigate his allegations against her as stringently as possible. The councillors could, for example, have attempted to establish the relative credibility of Gackstatt and Margaretha by asking their neighbours for evidence about their reputations. However, this was not done until late August and after Margaretha had already been interrogated three times, and even then these other witnesses were only asked about Mar-garetha's reputation and not Gackstatt's.[9] The councillors could also have decided to treat Gackstatt's allegations as slander and placed the onus on him to prove them. They did not take this course of action, despite the fact that Mar-garetha repeatedly asked them to do so and despite the fact that they had adopted this approach in several other previous witch-trials.[10] Three case-speci-fic factors probably encouraged the councillors to handle the case in a manner which worked to Margaretha's disadvantage. The first was the fact that Gack-statt was a subject of the Margrave of Brandenburg-Ansbach, a powerful, Lutheran, neighbouring territorial lord with whom the councillors probably thought it best not to lock judicial horns by taking Gackstatt into custody in Rothenburg. Gackstatt was thus not arrested in the course of the case: he merely gave two statements to the council on 28 August and 20 September and never had his testimony tested under the pressure of formal questioning.[11] The second factor which worked against Margaretha was the advice given to the council by its theological and medical advisors about Gackstatt's allegations. On 8 August the council asked Superintendent Georg Zyrlein and another leading urban cleric, Michael Renger, and the city physicians, Josaphat Weinlin and Johann Georg Sauber, the question which was central to the case, that of whether the infamous flea-swarm had a natural or supernatural cause.[12] On 11 August the clerics penned a short, terse response to the council in which they were unwill-ing or unable to comment on the origins of the fleas and which stood in marked contrast to the exceptionally detailed and explicitly moderating opinon Zyrlein had written on the case of Margaretha Hörber in 1627.[13] The physicians were less cautious. In a much lengthier report to the council on 13 August they deduced – without going to Bettenfeld to see it for themselves – that the flea-swarm had been produced unnaturally from demonic causes rather than naturally from corrupt matter. This was because it was unusually large, because it plagued only Gackstatt's house rather than any others, and because it could not be got rid of by the usual means. The physicians' report, which constituted the first of its kind in the history of the Rothenburg witch-trials, was thus extremely harmful to Margaretha because it gave the councillors expert confirmation of what they seem to have thought about the fleas all along. The physicians also condemned the act of ritual Shrove Tuesday magic to which Margaretha Horn had already confessed, thereby implying that it might have been the cause of the flea-swarm.[14] Both theologians and physicians recommended that the council seek further advice on how to proceed against Margaretha from legal experts, although the council chose not to do this until 9 September when it asked jurist Georg Christoph Walther for his opinion on the case.[15]

The third factor which unwittingly prejudiced the councillors against Margaretha was her behaviour in custody: the final summary of her crimes listed her insolent and insulting speech as evidence which had added weight to the suspicion that she was a witch.[16] The first signs of her impatience with the way in which the council was handling her case emerged towards the end of her first interrogation on 6 August. After a series of questions about the flea-swarm which were worded in a manner which implied an assumption of her guilt in having caused it she was asked by Michael Schwarz and Johann Ludwig Völcker, the two councillors deputised to question her, about how she thought her case was to proceed and how she thought she would gain her release from gaol. She said simply that 'my lords will know what to do' and maintained that the onus lay on Gackstatt to substantiate his allegations.[17] She was then asked whether she wanted to make the customary plea to the council for her release. She replied that 'the authorities did not carry the sword of justice for nothing' and that 'they will know how it ought to be used'.[18] She requested justice rather than clemency because she believed herself innocent, but to the councillors her refusal to beg for mercy was doubtless perceived as defiance of their paternal benevolence. Moreover, her comment that the councillors would know how the sword of justice ought to be used implied that they were using it improperly in assuming that she was guilty of witchcraft.

Margaretha's responses to questions grew increasingly impatient during her second interrogation on 12 August. For example, Schwarz and Völcker pointed out that Gackstatt swore she had caused the flea-swarm, to which she responded that 'if he said much he must also prove much'.[19] Her interrogators

also claimed that it was known that she made and used salves, the implication
being that these were her means of bewitchment. She replied that she made
salves for her family's medicinal use and that apothecaries also made salves, the
implication being that apothecaries were not accused of witchcraft as a result.[20]
She expressed her hatred of Gackstatt with increasing vehemence, calling him
a liar, a whoremonger, and someone who cursed and caused evil.[21] On this
occasion she did ask the council for mercy in the name of the Last Judgement
but refused to be cowed into making a confession of witchcraft.[22] On being
threatened with torture she proclaimed her innocence and said that God would
punish her accusers; on being offered help if she confessed she said that 'my
lords could help by judging the case according to imperial law', with the implication that they were failing to do so.[23] It was at the end of this second interrogation that the case took a surprising turn. Schwarz and Völcker asked her to
tell them about an angel she claimed had come to her in gaol a night or two earlier and she obliged, telling them that the angel, which had been small and
which had spent the night sitting on her lap, had comforted her by telling her
that her soul belonged to God.[24] Her interrogation stopped at this point, doubtless because her interrogators needed advice from the rest of the council on
what to make of the angel's alleged appearance.

Details of the angel's next nocturnal visit to Margaretha dominated her
third interrogation on 16 August when she began to use the angel's voice not
only as a far more powerful means of articulating her impatience with the way
in which the council was handling her case but also as a way of criticising the
council's administration of justice more generally and of threatening it with
dire retribution if it did not set its house in order. In so doing Margaretha
shifted the dynamic of the questioning process in her favour, so that her interrogators were hanging on her every word and at one point even allowed her to
leave the room so that she could have more time to recall what the angel had
said to her. She also devised a way of refusing to respond to her interrogators
when it did not suit her: she claimed that the angel had told her to remain silent
if they asked any 'evil' questions.[25]

Margaretha began by remembering that the angel had said the following
rhymes to her, the second a more succinct version of the first:

> You have been given up to the executioner,
> God give the councillors the Holy Ghost, so that they consider the matter
> properly,
> You have cried out for the Emperor's law,
> God give the councillors the Holy Ghost, so that they reach their verdict justly.[26]

> If my lords do not reach their verdict justly,
> They will lose their imperial law.

> If my lords do not want to run a good council,
> He [the Emperor] will set a new council in their place.[27]

Further exhortation to recall what the angel had said brought further criticism from Margaretha. She implied that the council's implementation of the law was motivated by the desire for profit rather than for justice and criticised the preachers of Rothenburg for not speaking out against this.[28] The world was evil, she said, and God would punish it if the council did not:

> If the authorities do not punish their city and rural subjects, then God will punish both poor and rich with the flux [dysentery], ten times more severely than they have been punished with the war [the Thirty Years' War], so that no-one will be able to remain free of the stench.[29]

Margaretha added that if Gackstatt caused her death with his accusations she would call him to account at the Last Judgement.[30]

In making these pronouncements Margaretha was building on the idea she had alluded to at the end of her first interrogation: that the council would exercise its legal power justly only by confirming her innocence. Through the angel's voice in the two rhymes, however, she added a threatening nuance: that the council would lose its power if it found her guilty. By referring to the imperial law she wished to be judged by and which she suggested the council risked losing if it acted against her illegally, Margaretha reminded her interrogators that there was a power beyond Rothenburg in the person of the Emperor to which the council historically owed its political and judicial autonomy. She also reminded the council that it was ultimately accountable to the Emperor for its exercise of judicial power and that it was possible for the council's subjects to seek redress from the Emperor if they felt that the council had exercised this power arbitrarily. These reminders may have struck a particularly raw nerve among Rothenburg's councillors in 1652. Since the late 1630s the ever-increasing taxes imposed by the council on its citizens and subjects to pay the war-debts incurred by the city, coupled with the secrecy with which all council business was shrouded, had created a popular suspicion that the council was made up of close relatives who dealt dishonestly and in their own interests with the citizenry's money. In 1645 a citizen had been arrested for accusing the mayor of stealing the townspeople's money after an edict had been issued ordering all citizens who could no longer pay their taxes to suffer the quartering of two or three soldiers in their houses. The tension reached crisis-point in April 1652 when a deputation of angry citizens demanded that the council submit its annual accounts to public scrutiny. The council refused to comply with this request so the citizens took their complaints to the Emperor; the dispute was finally resolved (largely in the council's favour) in 1653.[31]

This dispute formed the backdrop against which the case against Margaretha was tried, and her comments were calculated to remind the councillors of the threat of imperial displeasure which was hanging over them. Her reference to a possible loss of power for the councillors at this time may also have reminded them of another threatening force – that of popular discontent – to which they could hardly afford to remain impervious: the events of the Peasants' War of 1525, when the patrician oligarchy had been ousted from government of the city on a tide of social and religious unrest, was hardly such a distant memory.[32] God was the third and most powerful force with which Margaretha threatened the council. Through the threat of the dysentery epidemic if the council failed to wield the sword of justice properly Margaretha again touched a raw elite nerve. The Thirty Years' War had just visited devastation – including epidemics which respected neither wealth nor status – on Rothenburg and its hinterland unprecedented in the area's history.[33] Moreover, for many years and in an attempt to steer their subjects away from sin the Rothenburg authorities had stressed the idea that the sins of the individual invited the wrath of God upon the whole community.[34] Margaretha had learned this lesson well but turned it against the councillors by suggesting that it was possible for them to behave in a manner which threatened divine retribution for rich and poor alike. Her reference to the fact that she would call Gackstatt to account for his false accusations at the Last Judgement can also be interpreted within this egalitarian theological framework. She was reminding the councillors that earthly injustice would not go unseen and unpunished by God and that everyone – themselves included – would be called to account for their actions on that day when earthly distinctions of wealth and status would finally be rendered meaningless.

The angel which Margaretha claimed to have encountered was doubtless not an entirely strategic creation on her part. She seems to have been a woman of very steadfast faith who might well have believed that God would send a divine emissary to her in her hour of need, particularly as Lutheran pastoral teaching had, for over a century, aimed to convince people that they were permanently surrounded by angels which 'stirred feelings of fear and anxiety, as well as bringing comfort and solace'.[35] The way in which she described her first encounter with the angel certainly suggests that his appearance may have sprung from her desire for comfort and companionship in her cell. When pressed for more details about the angel's appearance she said that he was like a person but as small as a two-year-old child, with a head like an apple, no hair, and bare, white feet.[36] This description, coupled with the fact that Margaretha later said that the angel was called Michael and that she had held him on her lap, suggests that she may also have imagined the angel as her deceased son Michael for whose death she held Gackstatt responsible.[37] It was when she realised how avidly her interrogators were interested in the angel's words, however, and when she realised what she could say to them through the angel's voice, that Margaretha began more deliberately to express her defiance through this new channel and to shift the emphasis of her rhetoric from her personal impatience with the council to articulate broader contemporary public discontents.

What she said about the angel and the way in which she said it was also very similar to the pronouncements made by the *c*. 150 popular prophets whose stories we know about from other Lutheran areas of early modern Germany. These prophets commonly claimed to have had had encounters with angels who asked them to tell their contemporaries to repent, although they sometimes also used their prophecies in order to make political points.[38] For example, in 1648 a vintner called Hans Keil from the Württemberg village of Gerlingen claimed to have met an angel in his vineyard who allegedly threatened the people of Württemberg with collective punishment if they did not repent, and criticised the authorities for their extortionate taxes. David Sabean has shown that Keil fashioned his description of the encounter and the angel's words from sermons he had heard and from devotional literature, songs and broadsides – particularly about visions experienced by other people – he had read.[39] Margaretha probably drew on similar cultural resources for her prophecy in 1652. Even if unable to read, she would have heard the theme of divine retribution for sin dealt with in sermons and council ordinances and would doubtless have heard songs, rumours and recitations of broadsides dealing with visions and wonders during the tempestuous years of the Thirty Years' War. She may even have known of Keil's prophecy, as verbal and written accounts of it had circulated in southern Germany before the Württemberg authorities managed to quash them in 1648.[40]

Of course, the problem with the strategy of defiance employed by Margaretha was that the power to categorise the being she claimed had appeared to her in custody as either good or evil lay entirely in the hands of the councillors and their advisers. Sure enough, when jurist Georg Christoph Walther was finally asked for his opinion on the case on 9 September he noted caustically that one would have to be a 'simple sheep' indeed to believe that Margaretha's visitor had been a good angel: it was far more likely to have been the devil in disguise, who made a habit of visiting his imprisoned confederates, the witches.[41] Conversing with the devil was subsequently cited against Margaretha as one of the strongest proofs of her identity as a witch and of which she had to purge herself by suffering torture.[42] Another problem for Margaretha was that she was defiant at all: her increasingly impatient protestations of innocence, which to a modern-day reader of her trial-documents show immense strength of will on her part, were almost certainly perceived as obduracy and insolence by the men questioning her and the councillors and their advisers who deliberated on her case. This was because they were members of a patrician, urban,

Lutheran elite who expected subservience from their peasant subjects and who, as Sigrid Brauner has suggested, measured the women they encountered by the standard of the demure, obedient housewife they had been educated to understand as the feminine ideal and who were therefore particularly disconcerted when they encountered verbally assertive women in the context of witch-trials.[43] As a peasant and a woman, Margaretha Horn should have shown herself doubly submissive to the authority and mercy of the councillors in the questioning process. That she did not do so must at one level have piqued their egos. At another, it would have encouraged them to believe that she was wilful and unnaturally hard-hearted and therefore more likely to be a witch.

Margaretha's verbal defiance was mirrored for the councillors by what they perceived to be her physical defiance, which they regarded as additional evidence of her true yet still concealed identity as a witch. For example, her apparent inability to shed tears during her time in custody counted as a presumption of guilt against her from first to last, the first time that this had happened in a witch-trial in Rothenburg.[44] As physicians Weinlin and Sauber explained, tears came from the fluid in which the human heart swims. When the heart was moved by emotion this water flowed to the eyes to produce tears.[45] Margaretha's failure to cry in custody signified an absence of the emotions of fright and sorrow proper to her situation if she were innocent of the alleged witchcraft and suggested to the men watching her that the devil rather than God held sway over her heart. It also signified that she was unnatural corporeally as well as emotionally, and therefore more likely to be a witch, because one way in which witches' bodies were imagined at this time was as harder and drier than the open, leakier body of the normal woman, dominated as it was by cold and wet humours.[46] Margaretha told her interrogators that Gackstatt's accusations had caused her such grief that she had already cried herself out but this prosaic explanation for her inability to shed tears in custody was ignored by the councillors, despite the fact that physicians Weinlin and Sauber conceded that it was at least medically plausible.[47]

The council made a last attempt to break Margaretha's resistance during her final interrogation on 22 September. After again refusing to confess to any acts of witchcraft she gave vent to her rage against Gackstatt, expressing the hope that he would burn in hell and be torn by as many demons as she had shed tears. She was then subjected to two further ordeals intended to help establish her 'true' identity as either a witch or a godly woman. First she was asked to recite a prayer. She did so perfectly until she came to a line which called on God to protect her from the devil, at which point she muddled the words. She was probably simply too tired or confused at this point to remember the prayer correctly, but her failure in reciting it counted as another presumption of guilt against her, despite the fact that her frequent protestations of piety throughout her time in custody might have been expected to suggest to her interrogators that she was a woman of stalwart faith. She was then examined for the insensible mark on her body which demonological lore held that the devil left on witches as a sign of their allegiance to him. The executioner stuck a needle into likely spots on her back so that she bled profusely and in the process discovered a suspicious mark between her shoulder-blades which allegedly did not bleed and was insensible. Again, Margaretha's prosaic explanation for the mark – that it was the scar of an abcess she had suffered some years earlier – was ignored. With these additional presumptions of guilt against her and in the face of her continuing obduracy she was finally tortured with thumbscrews five times, as hard as the executioner could turn them, as her interrogators noted. Even this level of physical suffering failed to force Margaretha into producing the desired confession of witchcraft, however, and the interrogation ended with her calling again to God to comfort her in her suffering.[48] A day later jurist Georg Christoph Walther wrote an opinion on her case in which he pointed out that she had purged herself of the presumptions of guilt which had existed against her by suffering torture and that any further judicial action against her would be unlawful. The council should therefore err on the side of caution, leave the ultimate judgement of innocence or guilt in so uncertain a matter as witchcraft to the all-seeing power of God, and release her from custody.[49] In writing this opinion Walther appears to have been blissfully unaware of the fact that he was, ironically, advising the councillors to do what Margaretha had wanted all along: namely to try her case according to the precepts of imperial law and in a manner for which they would be able to answer with a clear conscience to God at the Last Judgement.

The council decided to follow Walther's advice and freed Margaretha on 1 October, although on the basis of a surety which, far from exonerating her, implied that she might well have been guilty of witchcraft.[50] But why were the councillors even at this late stage of the case unwilling to relinquish their suspicion that Margaretha might indeed have been a witch, despite her consistent insistence on her own innocence? Her defiant behaviour had been crucial in prejudicing the council against her throughout the case but may have been of particular significance during her final interrogation when it seems to have reached an apogee of insolence and obstinacy in the councillors' eyes. It was noted that Margaretha laughed on being threatened with torture, a reaction which may have stemmed from desperation or hysteria on her part but which would have strengthened her interrogators' perception of her as non-submissive, hard-hearted and witch-like.[51] After understandably but unwisely wishing the torments of hell upon Gackstatt she also as good as cursed her interrogators with the observation that 'he who does me an injustice, must fry and suffer there [in Hell] eternally'. She also told them to look to their salvation, with the implication that they were setting this at risk by their unfair treatment of her.[52] That her interrogators continued to think that Margaretha was a witch who was concealing her true identity beneath a sham of godliness can be seen in the fact that they continued to regard her as supernaturally hard of emotion and body. They noted that she barely cried out while suffering torture and that her hands seemed hardly bruised or bloody at all at the end of her ordeal; her supposed physical insensibility was listed in the final summary of her case as another of the presumptions of guilt of witchcraft which had existed against her.[53]

The careful noting by her interrogators of all manner of evidence of per-ceived defiance on the part of Margaretha Horn was a new development in the witch-trials that occurred in Rothenburg: it also happened, although to a less detailed degree, in the case of Catharina Leimbach, the blacksmith's wife from Wettringen, whose trial for the alleged bewitchment of eight-year-old Barbara Schürz began on 30 August and ended with her release from custody on 5 October 1652.[54] It is, of course, impossible to claim with certainty that Mar-garetha and Catharina were qualitatively more 'defiant' than any of the women who had been tried for witchcraft in Rothenburg in the past, although the use by Margaretha of the angel's prophecy to criticise the council's application of the law suggests that her resistance of authority was unusually marked and sophisticated. Margaretha and Catharina both seem to have possessed excep-tional strength of will, an unshakeable faith in their own righteousness, and a vivid sense of God's commitment to them.[55] Such traits may have been parti-cularly strong in women of middle years, for whom age had strengthened their sense of identity. The self-reliance and piety of Margaretha and Catharina may also have been strengthened because they and their families had managed to survive the ravages of the Thirty Years' War, which was no mean achievement, given that Bettenfeld and Wettringen had suffered population losses of 58 per cent and 76 per cent, respectively during the war years.[56] That both women were more concerned about answering to God rather than to the council for their actions is conveyed clearly in their interrogations and, while this was the-ologically an entirely correct position for them to adopt, it probably discom-fited the councillors to be so clearly reminded of the limits of their earthly jurisdiction by two peasant women.

It is equally difficult to say with certainty why the councillors evinced such concern with the issue of defiance in the witch-trials of 1652. They may have been particularly sensitive to the issue of popular defiance of their author-ity because of the on-going dispute with their subjects over the issue of their taxation policies, especially as Margaretha Horn had said during her third inter-rogation that she would make public the angel's criticisms of the council on her release from gaol.[57] The councillors were probably also more generally con-cerned about the issue of witchcraft in the summer of 1652 because they were faced with what for Rothenburg constituted an unprecedented 'outbreak' of witch-trials: Mathes Leimbach, Barbara Bratsch and Barbara Schürz as well as Catharina Leimbach and Margaretha Horn were all in gaol at the same time between late August and early October as claims of witchcraft against them were investigated. However, another reason for the relatively severe treatment of both Catharina and Margaretha by the councillors and for their increased concern with the women's apparent defiance may have been a shift in their perception of what constituted a valid proof of possible guilt in cases of witchcraft.

Generations of councillors and their advisers had long recognised that witchcraft, as a secret crime, was exceptionally difficult to prove at law.[58] Throughout the early modern period they remained largely reliant on verbal testimonies and an evaluation of their relative credibility in order to arrive at verdicts in witchcraft trials, with the essential question remaining: who should be believed, the alleged witch who maintained her innocence or her accuser who claimed she was guilty of witchcraft? However, in the course of the seventeenth century – and particularly in 1652 – the councillors began to display greater enthusiasm for certain physical indicators of an alleged witch's innocence or guilt which could be both observed and tested, at least according to the logic of demonological lore. Thus in the trial-records of Catharina Leimbach and Margaretha Horn great emphasis was placed by the authorities on the fact that neither woman was able to shed tears while in custody, on the fact that Margaretha had a mark on her body which did not bleed when pricked and that she was barely bruised by the thumbscrews, and on the fact that both women displayed unnatural emotions in custody by, for example, laughing when about to be tortured.[59] Various reasons may explain why the councillors suddenly chose to place such emphasis on these pieces of evidence when most of them appear to us to have had perfectly plausible, non-supernatural explanations. One councillor may have recently read a demonological treatise which discussed these physical 'proofs' of guilt or had heard of them having figured in witch-trials elsewhere. He may then have used his influence to help raise their evidential status in 1652 as a way of keeping Rothenburg abreast of the latest methods of witch-identification. Another possibility is that the trial-records are showing us the effects of a vicious circle, in which Margaretha's initial defiance in custody encouraged the councillors to suspect that she was a witch and thus to interpret any evidence that they saw subsequently in a way which would confirm this suspicion. However, in the case of Margaretha we may also be seeing the first glimpses of a long and complex legal development by means of which physically tangible and observable evidence, ideally seen and evaluated by male experts, was gradually being elevated in status in comparison to verbal testimony as a more valid form of legal proof. That this process was shaped by a class and gender dynamic is also suggested by in her case: throughout, the councillors valued the consistent verbal testimony of this redoubtable middle-aged peasant woman less highly than they did the external clues to her identity which they could observe and evaluate for themselves. Thus they ignored her prosaic explanations for her failure to shed tears and for the mark on her back, for example, and chose instead to 'see' these phenomena as deeply sinister. Of course, the more Margaretha protested her innocence, the more defiant she appeared to the councillors. Her trial therefore also shows that it was becoming increasingly difficult for women accused of witchcraft in Rothenburg to deny their guilt without behaving in ways which risked being interpreted by the authorities as witch-like.

Late seventeenth-century changes

None of the individuals involved in the 1652 witch-trials were found guilty of or punished for the crime of witchcraft. However, various features of these trials suggest that the councillors in Rothenburg and their advisers were beginning to adopt a more severe attitude towards alleged witches. In both cases the councillors chose consistently to regard the testimony of the accusers rather than the accused as more credible, in both cases the main suspects (Catharina Leimbach and Margaretha Horn) were tortured fairly severely, and in both cases the wording of the sureties on which the women were released were so grudging as to barely exonerate them of suspicion. In the trial of the Leimbachs, moreover, such punitive bail conditions were imposed on Mathes Leimbach that they almost certainly ruined his family financially.[60] These changes in council attitude discernible in 1652 were the precursors of a more general shift in attitude towards and handling of witch-trials which was to become more marked in Rothenburg in the second half of the seventeenth century. This shift was not significant enough to shatter the general pattern of restraint in terms of the number and outcome of witch-trials in the city: the years c. 1650–c. 1700 saw no mass episodes of trials and executions and verdicts of guilt in witch-trials were still the exception rather than the rule.[61] However, from about 1650 the Rothenburg authorities seem to have become more convinced of the reality and threat of witchcraft than they had been before, more inclined to give accusers rather than accused witches the benefit of judicial doubt during trials, and less confident in their ability to handle cases quickly and in the interests of social harmony.

These changes can be seen in various aspects of later seventeenth-century trials. Accused witches had to work harder to convince the council of their innocence in the context of an interrogation process which became lengthier and more intimidating. Appolonia Glaitter of Windisch-Bockenfeld, who was accused of witchcraft in 1671, was incarcerated for fifty-two days, interrogated six times and tortured with thumbscrews three times before finally being released from gaol, despite the fact that the case against her consisted of a flimsy tissue of dubious circumstantial and hearsay evidence woven together by neighbours who admitted from the outset that they bore her malice.[62] The trial of Glaitter was also significant for two other features which likewise support the idea that the council had lost confidence in its ability to resolve witch-trials satisfactorily. The first was the fact that, for the first time in the history of witch-trials in Rothenburg, the council asked the legal faculty of a university (Tübingen) for advice on the case; it then looked to the university of Altdorf for advice on a witch-trial which occurred in 1673.[63] The *Carolina* had advised judges to seek advice in this manner in 1532 but the council had never hitherto felt the need to do so, having relied almost exclusively on its own municipal jurists for expert legal opinion.[64] The council also, unusually, looked to an external jurist, Johann Höfel of Schweinfurt, for advice on the trials for witchcraft of Michael Würth in 1663 and Anna Margaretha Rohn in 1673.[65] Secondly, the paperwork on the trial of Glaitter was extremely voluminous, running to around 300 pages of statements, interrogations and legal opinions. Other late seventeenth-century trials generated similar or even greater amounts of documentation, suggesting that the councillors were finding it increasingly difficult to arrive at clear conclusions about guilt or innocence in instances of alleged witchcraft.[66]

The above observations are not intended to suggest that expert opinion in witch-trials necessarily worked to the detriment of the alleged witch. In the case of Glaitter it was primarily the careful and scornful demolition of the circumstantial evidence against her by the Tübingen jurists – plus the ultimate willingness of the council to follow their advice – which helped ensure Glaitter's release from custody.[67] In other cases, however, expert opinion had more detrimental effects on accused or self-confessed witches. While the Rothenburg jurists consistently adhered to the idea that legal caution was better than legal excess in witch-trials throughout the early modern period, by the later seventeenth century the Rothenburg clerics and physicians called on to offer their opinions on such trials were most likely to do so in ways which supported the idea that witchcraft was real and thus in need of more severe handling. For example, in the trials of Margaretha Horn in 1652 and Anna Margaretha Rohn in 1673 the testimony of city physicians served to encourage the council to believe that supernatural rather than natural phenomena were at hand: the flea-swarm plaguing Leonhardt Gackstatt in the trial of Margaretha and the bizarre emergence of needles from a wound in her arm in the trial of Rohn.[68] The clerics also played roles in certain late seventeenth-century witch-trials which probably helped heighten anxieties about witchcraft felt by the councillors and their subjects. Intensive pastoral care doubtless only helped convince self-confessed witch Anna Margaretha Rohn, who claimed that she was being plagued by witches and the devil from 1664, of the reality of her disturbing fantasies and to persuade her to repeat them with increasing vehemence until the council had little choice but to begin formal judicial proceedings against her in 1673. In 1692 the foremost ecclesiastical official in Rothenburg, Superintendent Sebastian Kirchmeier, became even more deeply embroiled in a witch-trial. He tried to start a mass-hunt in the city by means of the intimidating and leading questioning of two individuals already gaoled on charges of witchcraft, although his endeavours stemmed as much from a desire to settle personal scores as they did from a genuine theological conviction about the need to eradicate witches.[69]

Expert opinion, then, could have positive or negative effects on witch-trials from the point of view of alleged witches and potential suspects. In the same way it is possible to regard the voluminous documentation produced by the later seventeenth-century trials as not necessarily and unequivocally detrimental to the cause of the accused. Tom Robisheaux has suggested that the very volume of expert opinion and written documentation in such trials could actually slow down the whole judicial process, which might make guilty verdicts less likely, or even cause it to collapse altogether. This was because medical and legal experts interpreted the signs of bewitchment at length and within specialised forms of learned discourse which non-expert magistrates found increasingly difficult and time-consuming to consider. As Robisheaux writes in conclusion regarding a long and complex witch-trial from the Lutheran county of Hohenlohe in 1672: 'what slowed a witch trial like this one, what made conviction difficult for the authorities, was the legal process of reconciling so many different and complex ways of reading the signs of bewitchment'.[70] However, while allowing for these provisos and acknowledging the need to evaluate the severity or otherwise of trial-processes on a case-by-case basis, I would still argue that we can – overall – read the greater reliance by the Rothenburg councillors on expert and particularly external opinion and the increasingly voluminous nature of trial-documentation in the later seventeenth century as evidence of an increase in their own uncertainty about how best to handle witch-trials. By looking at the Rothenburg witch-trials over the whole early modern period it is possible to see that this uncertainty constituted a change from an earlier conciliar attitude which had been defined by four main factors: a scepticism about certain aspects of witchcraft based on the *Canon episcopi* and Lutheran theology; a legal caution in witch-trials based on judicial precepts regarding slander and moderate interpretation of the *Carolina*; a humility which encouraged the council to leave the ultimate verdict in witch-trials up to God rather than to reach definitive conclusions about guilt or innocence themselves; and a concern for social harmony which the council believed witch-trials were more likely to destroy than affirm.[71] These factors had tended to influence trial-procedure to the advantage of accused witches up until about 1640, whereas the greater uncertainty evinced by the council in the later seventeenth century tended to have the opposite effect.

Why might the council have become more uncertain in its handling of witch-trials and perhaps even more anxious about the threat that witches and the devil posed to the souls of its subjects in the second half of the seventeenth century? One reason may have been the fact that Rothenburg itself, rather than the city's hinterland, provided the context for an increasing number of witch-craft cases in the course of the seventeenth century. The years 1605 and 1629 saw the trials of Hans Georg Hofmann and Barbara Rost, while in 1639 self-confessed child-witch Brigitta Hörner disturbed the city with her tales of witchcraft. Another self-confessed witch, Anna Margaretha Rohn, unsettled both the councillors and her fellow citizens for even longer, suffering spectacular fits from 1664 until 1673 which she claimed were the result of her enthralment to witches and the devil.[72] Then in the 1690s a large-scale witch-trial threatened to erupt in the city hospital as a result of the allegations of self-confessed child-witch Hans Adam Knöspel, who had been quartered there and who infected other inmates with his stories of witchcraft.[73] It may ironically have been the case that the council unwittingly helped accelerate the spread of ideas and anxiety about witchcraft from the rural to the urban populace by its policy of housing self-confessed child-witches in the city hospital, a fate first experienced by Margaretha Hörber in 1627.[74] The fact that several seventeenth-century witch-trials and some of the most spectacular episodes of self-confession occurred against an urban backdrop thus probably made the problem of witchcraft and how to resolve it particularly pressing and even personal to the councillors, given the myriad personal connections that linked them to the city's inhabitants.

Another reason for the councillors' increased uncertainty about how best to handle cases of witchcraft in the second half of the seventeenth may have been the fact that they had lost confidence more generally in their own political power and significance. The Thirty Years' War inflicted more damage on Rothenburg and its rural hinterland than any other episode of conflict in the area's history. As a result of the council's equivocal policies in the early war years, the fact that Rothenburg had the misfortune to be situated at an important crossroads of troop movements, and the fact that its medieval defences were woefully inadequate to resist the might of seventeenth-century armies, the area suffered terribly at the hands of both sides in the conflict. Between 1622 and 1631 imperial and Catholic League troops were quartered in and marched through the city's hinterland, then in 1631 Rothenburg was taken by the Swedes and then by imperial forces in what became known as Rothenburg's year of misery and lamentation. Between 1631 and 1635 and again between 1640 and 1648 Rothenburg was at the centre of the Franconian war-zone, with Bavarian, Swedish, French and imperial troops marching through and living off its land. By 1648 about 70 per cent of the hinterland's population was dead or had fled the area, many farms and fields had been destroyed or fallen into disrepair and disuse, many village churches had been damaged, formal religious life in the hinterland had all but collapsed, and all citizens and subjects had been squeezed to the point of financial exhaustion for the contributions demanded by the frequently changing resident armies. The scale of damage was reflected in the length of time it took to rectify: in some rural areas sixty years passed before pre-war levels of productivity were again attained.[75] Overall this terrible experience may have made the councillors realise that, for all their claims to authority within the city, they were of little or no significance politically and essentially powerless militarily within Germany as a whole, at the same time as it had highlighted particularly starkly their inability to fulfil adequately their traditional role as the *Schutz und Schirmherr* or 'protector' of their subjects. At a psychological level, then, the impact of the memory and aftermath of the war on the councillors' collective self-confidence from the 1650s may have manifested itself in a greater degree of uncertainty and inconsistency in their handling of witch-trials.[76]

The council may also have felt that it had to treat accused witches more severely from the mid-seventeenth century onwards because of increased popular pressure to do so. That a certain proportion of the council's subjects was becoming impatient with its relatively lenient treatment of suspected witches is suggested by the final opinion written on the 1652 witch-trials by jurist Georg Christoph Walther. Walther advocated freeing Margaretha Horn and Catharina Leimbach from custody because they had purged the presumptions of guilt which had existed against them by suffering torture but pointed out to the councillors that to end their trials in this manner would cause critical talk among the populace. Walther stated that people were already saying that the council had no heart for punishing witches and proceeded against them too timidly, and the defensive tone in which he offered justifications for the release of the two women hints at the level of popular criticism he either knew about or expected to be voiced. It was all very well, he noted, for people with no responsibility for criminal justice to express their opinions on trials, but verdicts had to be left to those who bore responsibility for them. To execute someone was a weighty matter and one could never deliberate for too long in cases involving capital sentences. Moreover, secular authorities could act no further in criminal cases than was allowed to them by the constraints of legal procedure and by God; if God kept a matter hidden from them they had to leave any punishment of it to God's final judgement. It was presumptuous for people to think that they could intervene in the meting out of divine justice.[77]

How might we account for the popular impatience with the handling of witch-trials by the council which Walther's comments suggest was apparent in 1652? Had the council's subjects become more concerned about witches and their activities by the mid-seventeenth century or were they expressing long-standing levels of concern more openly? The former was probably the case but the relationship of distrust which had developed between the council and its subjects over the former's financial policies by the 1650s may have encouraged more open expression of popular dissatisfaction with council rule.[78] It is, of course, impossible to prove that the inhabitants of Rothenburg and its rural hinterland were more fearful of witches in 1652 than they had been a century earlier: an emotion cannot be plotted on a graph. However, the events of the Thirty Years' War described above may well have created the context within which concern about witchcraft could more easily be fostered, particularly after 1631 when the impact of the war on Rothenburg and its hinterland was most severe. Against the backdrop of material damage to life, limb and property provided by the war Rothenburg's subjects may have become generally more desperately and selfishly fearful for the survival of themselves and their families. It seems reasonable to suggest that their fears of the threat of witches to the things which helped guarantee that survival – their health, food supply and livestock – might have grown as well. Moreover, the experience of living in this area during the war, when the threat of death due to epidemic disease or at the whim of marauding soldiers was ever-present, must also have had a psychological impact, perhaps causing the anxieties of those individuals who were already prone to fear of death, disease, misfortune and witchcraft to become even more heightened.[79]

The Thirty Years' War may also have provided a context within which the inhabitants of Rothenburg and its hinterland were able more rapidly to gain knowledge of a more diverse set of beliefs about witchcraft and of different ways of handling witch-trials from other parts of Germany as a result of the frequent troop and population movements in and out of the area. As we saw in Chapter 4, in 1629 Catholic cavalrymen quartered in Rothenburg's hinterland tried to start a witch-hunt in order to terrorise the locals and to show them and the city council how witches should best be treated. It is possible that the soldiers involved in this episode had been in or near the Franconian Catholic prince-bishoprics of Würzburg and Bamberg, within which exceptionally severe witch-trials were raging at this time and wanted to pass on this example of Catholic severity to the 'lenient' Rothenburg Lutherans.[80] An idea expressed by Brigitta Hörner, the eight-year-old orphan who told stories of witchcraft in 1639, also appears to have had a Catholic source and may have spread more rapidly to Rothenburg via Catholic troops. Brigitta claimed that she was a witch because she had been baptised as such by the pastor of her home village of Spielbach. This was the first time that the idea of a witches' priest who could baptise children in the devil's name emerged in a Rothenburg witch-trial; in the opinion that he wrote on the trial of Brigitta jurist Georg Christoph Walther noted that this was a Catholic notion rooted in an erroneous belief in the sacral power of priests and one of which he had learned while conversing with a Catholic jurist from Würzburg.[81] In addition to hearing of this idea from the nearby city Würzburg, Rothenburg's subjects may also have learned – again via soldiers – of the case of the alleged witches' priest Michael Campensis, a Jesuit who was executed for witchcraft in Trier in 1627 in a case which subsequently gained significant notoriety.[82] These learning processes may have raised popular concern about witchcraft and, more importantly, given Rothenburg's inhabitants harsher yardsticks against which to measure the handling of witchcraft accusations by the council.

There is also evidence to suggest that there was an increased emphasis on and concern with matters supernatural during the Thirty Years' War among at least some sections of Rothenburg's population. The chronicle of Rothenburg during the war years written by Sebastian Dehner abounds in examples of strange signs allegedly seen by the city's inhabitants: fiery skies in 1630, 1640, 1642 and 1646, three suns in the heavens in 1630, 1636 and 1645, a pond in which the water changed into blood in 1646, and so on. In 1640, 1645 and 1654 mysterious banging, rumbling and wailing noises apparently emanated from the town-hall to suggest that it was haunted, although Dehner may have emphasised these in his chronicle as part of his criticism of the council's financial policies in order to imply that the councillors were in league with the devil. Most disturbing of all were the cries of a strange bird which became known onomatopoeically as the Uhu in 1640, 1645 and 1654. While steadfast Lutherans would have understood these signs as exhortations from God to repentance – and this was how Superintendent Zyrlein interpreted the cries of the Uhu in sermons preached in the 1640s and 1650s – those of weaker faith may have regarded them as elements within an imagined set of darker portents of disorder and evil into which witches and their activities could also easily be incorporated.[83] The attempts by the council to strengthen Lutheran piety among its subjects suffered severely during the war years. Organised religious life in the hinterland collapsed: twenty-one of the thirty-two rural parishes suffered vacancies for anything up to thirty-three years and ecclesiastical visitations of the rural hinterland were suspended between 1621 and 1642.[84] Once resumed, they would record with lamentations the lack of basic religious knowledge possessed by peasants who had grown up during the war.[85] The city parishes were not as badly affected but formal urban religious life would also have been significantly disrupted by the war. Whatever small success the council and Consistorium may have had in persuading its subjects away from belief in both black and white magic before the 1620s would thus have been adversely affected by the traumatic events of the next two decades.

By the 1640s and 1650s, then, the impact of the Thirty Years' War may have created a context within which fears about witchcraft were more likely to arise among the city's subjects and be taken more seriously by the city councillors. This was because the war radically accentuated the likelihood of and thus the fears about material hardship and death for the area's inhabitants, because it raised their general sensitivity to the presence of the supernatural in everyday life, and because it produced the financial problems which caused particularly strong feelings of dissatisfaction with council policy to emerge among the populace. Moreover, it is likely that the psychological impact of the war continued to be of significance for the inhabitants of Rothenburg and its rural hinterland in the second half of the seventeenth century as stories of war experiences were told and memories about its horrors perpetuated. This was because the efforts to rebuild and repopulate the hinterland villages, to reinvigorate the agrarian economy and to replenish the city's finances dominated the policy-making of the council and the lives of its subjects throughout this period, and because the area's material well-being and very existence as an independent political entity continued to be threatened by military aggression from the 1670s onwards, this time on the part of the French armies of Louis XIV.[86]

In postulating this scenario I do not want to suggest that the inhabitants of Rothenburg and its rural hinterland became *en masse* more credulous about witchcraft, more fearful of witches, and thus keener to see them punished as a result of their experiences and memories of war during the seventeenth century. For certain people such experiences may have led to a strengthened trust in God rather than a greater fear of witchcraft; this – ironically – seems to have been the case for Catharina Leimbach and Margaretha Horn, the two main suspects of the witch-trials of 1652. Moreover, there are hints to suggest that the spectrum of popular opinion about witchcraft described in Chapter 1, within which some people were terrified of witches while for others they were the subject of humour, was still present in Rothenburg in the seventeenth century. In the opinion that he wrote on the 1605 trial of Hans Georg Hofmann, for example, jurist Friedrich Prenninger conceded that the alleged presence of a poltergeist in David Walther's house was causing much concern in Rothenburg, especially among those who were weak of faith. However, Prenninger also noted that some people thought the matter a joke, with one unnamed individual claiming that if the noise in Walther's house stopped he would make noises in his own house in order to fool people into thinking that it too was haunted.[87] A similar sense that the level of popular fear about witchcraft was still far from uniform and that popular opinion was still divided on the question of how severely to treat accused witches was also conveyed in the opinion written by jurist Georg Christoph Walther on the 1652 witch-trials. Walther pointed out to the council that, in addition to expecting criticism from those who thought it had treated Catharina Leimbach and Margaretha Horn too leniently, it should also expect criticism from those who felt that it had treated them too harshly in having tortured them.[88] Here we can see that the concern for personal honour and the awareness of the adverse effects which torture could have on the honour of an individual and his or her family, rather than fear of witchcraft, could still define popular responses to particular trial-episodes.

What is suggested by the overall tone, length and handling of the post-1650 witch-trials in Rothenburg, then, is a more complex and by no means wholesale shift in attitude towards witchcraft on the part of successive generations of city councillors, their advisers and their subjects. The councillors seem to have become less confident in their own sense of authority and in their traditional religious, legal and political precepts for the resolution of witch-trials. At the same time they appear to have become more aware of the divisions of popular opinion regarding their handling of witch-trials and to have found it harder to know which faction of popular opinion to please: that which wanted more severe council action or that which thought the council was already acting too severely. In calling more frequently on external and expert opinion in order to help it reach trial-verdicts the council was reflecting as well as perhaps exacerbating its own uncertainty and confusion over what to think about witches, particularly as the city's own clerical and medical experts tended to influence later seventeenth-century witch-trials in ways which were more likely to heighten rather than lessen the concern that witchcraft posed a genuine threat to the city and its subjects which needed combating. Moreover, while a spectrum of attitudes towards witchcraft ranging from derision to terror existed at all social levels throughout the whole early modern period, it may have been the case that the experience and memory of war caused the delicate balance within this spectrum to swing perceptibly in favour of greater fear of and credulity about witches from the mid-seventeenth century onwards. It was thus only the dogged insistence of the Rothenburg jurists that due legal restraint should not be abandoned in witch-trials, the ultimate unwillingness of the councillors to ignore this legal advice, even in cases when they appear to have believed in the guilt of an alleged witch, and the resolute refusal by individuals like Margaretha Horn to confess to being witches which ensured that late seventeenth-century Rothenburg did not see more trials, verdicts of guilt and executions for witchcraft.

Notes

1 Purkiss, *The Witch in History*, p. 91. Purkiss criticises feminist historians for assuming that women witnesses in witch-trials were such 'mouthpieces', and for their preoccupation with torture and execution which reduces the accused witch to 'a tortured, voiceless body' which was 'nothing but an instructive spectacle of violation and dismemberment', *ibid.*, p. 14.

2 RStA Interrogation Book A898 fols 480r, 487r, 493r, 512r. For full case-documents, see *ibid.*, fols 485r–535v; A491 Bettenfeld Village Acts fols 45r–57r.

3 This custom of Shrove Tuesday sweeping to rid the house of vermin is recorded in the *Hand-wörterbuch des deutschen Aberglaubens*, ed. Bächtold-Stäubli, vol. 2, pp. 1249–1250.

4 RStA Interrogation Book A898 fols 486r–490r (Margaretha's first interrogation, dated 6 August 1652). It is possible to reconstruct Gackstatt's accusations from the questions put to Margaretha; no formal statement from Gackstatt was recorded until 28 August 1652. Margaretha's daughters Eva and Cordula had helped their mother with the Shrove Tuesday sweeping and Gackstatt tried to shift the focus of the investigation onto Cordula in a later statement dated 20 September 1652 (fols 532r–524v) but Rothenburg's council never questioned or arrested her or Eva.

5 For references to their feud, see *ibid.*, fols 487r–488r, 510r, 512v, 517v–518r. For references to Margaretha's previous marriage in Gebsattel, see *ibid.*, fols 514r–514v, 517r–519v.

6 *Ibid.*, fols 489v, 523v.

7 *Ibid.*, fols 485r, 517v.

8 The wife of Bettenfeld's herdsman made the first official report to the council about Gackstatt's flea-swarm, *ibid.*, fol. 480r. Margaretha later claimed that she had done this at Gackstatt's bidding, fol. 487r. If so this was clever of Gackstatt as it enabled him to bring his accusation against Margaretha to the council's attention without taking personal responsibility for it. The council had briefly investigated Horn's allegations against Gackstatt's family (fols 481r–483r) but apparently took no further action.

9 *Ibid.*, fols 513r–514v.

10 For Margaretha's pleas, see *ibid.*, fols 489v–490r, 497r. For discussion of other trials where witchcraft accusations were treated as slander, see pp. 23–24.

11 For Gackstatt's statements, see *ibid.*, fols 512r–512v, 523r–524v. Rothenburg's council may have thought it best to avoid further conflict with the Margrave because in the summer of 1652 it was involved in a dispute with him over the issue of ecclesiastical visitations in the seven parishes of Rothenburg's hinterland for which he still held patronage rights, see StAN Ro. Rep. 2089 fols 187r–203v.

12 RStA Interrogation Book A898 fol. 493r.

13 *Ibid.*, fol. 495r. For Zyrlein's opinion in the Margaretha Hörber case (discussed pp. 53–54. 114–115), see RStA Interrogation Book A886 fols 283r–286v.

14 RStA Interrogation Book A898 fols 503r–505r.

15 StAN Ro. Rep. 2087 fols 57r–60r. Walther's opinion covered both Margaretha's case and that involving the members of the Leimbach household and Barbara Schürz which was under investigation at the same time and which is discussed pp. 150–160. For this reason it is bound with the Leimbach case documents in a volume of the Consistorium's records in the Nuremberg State Archive. The council may have delayed asking Walther his opinion on Margaretha's case because of her introduction of the angel into the proceedings and because of the opening of the case involving the Leimbach household on 26 August.

16 RStA Interrogation Book A898 fol. 533v.

17 *Ibid.*, fols 486r–490r, especially fol. 489v: 'solches werden meine Herrn ausszuüben wissen'.

18 *Ibid.*, fol. 490r: 'die Obrigkeit trage dass Schwert nicht vmb sonsten, werde wissen wie Sies brauchen solle'.

19 *Ibid.*, fol. 497r: 'Möge sagen was Er wolle, ob Er viel sage, müste Er auch viel beweisen.'

20 *Ibid.*, fol. 499r. For an account of how witches were believed able to make fleas out of salves from the case involving Hans Christoph Emmert in 1676 (listed in the Appendix, see

Schraut, 'Niederstetten 1676', p. 159.
21 *Ibid.*, fols 497v, 498v.
22 *Ibid.*, fol. 498v.
23 *Ibid.*, fols 499r–499v: 'die Hern können helffen, die können ja solches richten wann sie das Recht vnd ritterlich Keyserlich Recht brauchen wollen.'
24 *Ibid.*, fols 500r–500v.
25 *bid.*, fol. 510r.
26 *Ibid.*, fol. 507v:
> Mann hat dir anbotten, den Hencker vnd darnach dir ringen,
> Gott gebe den Herren den heyligen Geist, dass sie sich wol besinnen,
> Du hast geschreyen nach Keysers Recht,
> Gott gebe den herrn den heyligen Geist, dass sie führen ihren Urtl recht.
27 *Ibid.*, fol. 509r:
> Wann meine Herren nit führen Ihr Urtheil Recht,
> So vierlieren Sie Ihr Keyserlich recht.
> Wann meine Herrn nit führen wollen ein gueten Rath
> Woll er setzen einen neuen Rat.
28 *Ibid.*, fol. 509v.
29 *Ibid.*, fol. 510r: 'Daferne die Obrigkeit Ihre Statt vnd Vnterthoenen Vfm Landt, nicht straffen theten, dass Gott mit der Ruhr . . . vnd sonsten dermassen arme vnd reiche, Zehenmal mehr alss vorhin mit dem Krieg Straffen wollen, dass Niemand vor gestanck bleiben könne.'
30 *Ibid.*, fol. 506v.
31 For details of this dispute, see Winterbach, *Geschichte der Stadt Rothenburg*, vol. II, pp. 131–132; Heller (ed.), *Rothenburg ob der Tauber im Jahrhundert des grossen Krieges*, pp. 148–149; Rank, *Die Finanzwirtschaft der Reichsstadt Rothenburg*, pp. 125–129; Weigel, *Rothenburger Chronik*, p. 222; RStA B25 (Chronicle by Nikolaus Göttlingk), fols 315v–316r (which dates the first submission of complaints by the citizenry to the Emperor to 27 April 1651 and which names Michael Würth – who was accused of witchcraft in 1663, see Appendix – as one of the ringleaders in the dispute). Weigel argues that the dispute led to the introduction of minute-keeping for council-meetings in 1653 (*Rothenburger Chronik*, p. 222) but this practice was not in fact started until 1664.
32 For details of the Peasants' War in Rothenburg, see Quester, *Das Rad der Fortuna und das Kreuz*; Baumann (ed.), *Quellen zur Geschichte des Bauernkriegs aus Rotenburg an der Tauber*.
33 See Heller (ed.), *Rothenburg ob der Tauber im Jahrhundert des grossen Krieges*, pp. 36–146; Moritz, *Die Folgen des Dreissigjährigen Krieges*, pp. 54–90.
34 See for example the council's reference to the need to publish ordinances against the use of magic in order to deflect God's wrath from the inhabitants of Rothenburg and its hinterland, RStA Ordinances A363 fols 279r–282r (1639).
35 Gordon, 'Malevolent ghosts and ministering angels', pp. 101–102.
36 RStA Interrogation Book A898 fols 507r–507v.
37 *Ibid.*, fol. 509r.
38 Beyer, 'A Lübeck prophet in local and Lutheran context', especially pp. 168–169, where Beyer notes that in a Lutheran context 'saints were exchanged for angels, who were usually dressed in white'. A case of witchcraft from seventeenth-century Rye in England also uncovered claims of the appearance of prophetic angels by one Anne Taylor, see Gregory, 'Witchcraft, politics and "good neighbourhood"', p. 45.
39 Sabean, *Power in the Blood*, pp. 61–93.
40 *Ibid.*, pp. 79–82.
41 StAN Ro. Rep. 2087 fols 59v–60r. Walther referred to Margaretha as the Flea Woman (die Flohfrau) in this opinion as if her guilt were proven rather than still a matter of supposition.
42 RStA Interrogation Book A898 fol. 533v.
43 Brauner, *Fearless Wives and Frightened Shrews*, especially pp. 113–119.
44 RStA Interrogation Book A898 fols 489r, 493r, 533v.

45 *Ibid.*, fols 504v–505r.
46 This idea is explored by Diane Purkiss in *The Witch in History*, pp. 119–144, especially pp. 121, 125–127.
47 RStA Interrogation Book A898 fols 489r, 504v. As the physicians also pointed out, however, the problem was that no-one but Margaretha knew whether she really had cried so much.
48 *Ibid.*, fols 526r–532v. The mark had already been found on Margaretha's back during her fourth interrogation, see *ibid.*, fol. 521v. The only other alleged Rothenburg witch who had hitherto been examined for a witches' mark – although not pricked in this manner – was Magdalena Dürr, whose case is discussed pp. 136–143; see RStA Interrogation Book A887 fols 569v–570v.
49 StAN Ro. Rep. 2087 fols 95r–97v.
50 RStA Interrogation Book A898 fols 533r–534r. The shame of the witchcraft trial dogged the Horn family for years afterwards. In order to try to restore his family's reputation Hans Horn was forced to beg Rothenburg's council for a formal attestation to his wife's good character in 1659. This was grudgingly given in 1660. See *ibid.*, fols 535r–535v and Bettenfeld Village Acts A491 fols 45r–49v for details of the aftermath of the trial.
51 RStA Interrogation Book A898 fol. 530v.
52 *Ibid.*, fol. 531r: 'wer mir vnrecht thut, muss immer vnd ewig dorten braten vnd leyden'.
53 *Ibid.*, fols 532r–532v, 533v.
54 See pp. 150–160 for a full discussion of this case.
55 For their interrogations, see RStA Interrogation Book A898 fols 486r–490r, 497r–500r, 506r–510v, 520r–521v, 526r–532v (Margaretha); StAN Ro. Rep. 2087 fols 10r–14v, 44v–49r, 79r–86r (Catharina).
56 Moritz, *Die Folgen des Dreissigjährigen Krieges*, pp. 89–90.
57 RStA Interrogation Book A898 fol. 509v.
58 This point is discussed on pp. 32–33, where I argue that it tended to encourage Rothenburg's councillors to treat witchcraft cases with caution.
59 For the evidence pertaining to Margaretha, see RStA Interrogation Book A898 fols 493r, 530r–530v, 532r–532v, 533v. For that pertaining to Catharina, see StAN Ro. Rep. 2087 fols 46v–47r, 48r, 49r, 83v, 85v.
60 The Wettringen case is discussed on pp. 150–160.
61 See Appendix for an overview of the later cases. As this period forms a distinct episode in the history of Rothenburg's witch-trials, I intend dealing with it in a separate monograph. Anna Margaretha Rohn in 1673 and Barbara Ehness in 1692 were executed for witchcraft during this period, although in both cases there were specific circumstances which helped explain why the authorities deemed the death-penalty deserved: Rohn was a self-confessed witch who had claimed that she was in the devil's clutches for nine years before her trial and who also confessed to infanticide, while Ehness had attempted murder by means of poison.
62 RStA Interrogation Book A908 (unpaginated), case-documents dated from 11 July to 11 October 1671. Glaitter's case is discussed in Rowlands, 'Witchcraft and old women'.
63 For the Tübingen jurists' opinion in the Glaitter case, see RStA Interrogation Book A908, document dated 19 August 1671. For the Altdorf jurists' opinion on the Anna Margaretha Rohn case, see RStA Interrogation Book A909 fols 311r–313v, 357r–361v. The councillors had also asked the Altdorf legal faculty for an opinion in the case of Ulrich Helfer, a man tried for treasure-seeking in 1659, see StAN Ro. Rep. 2087 fols 254r–255r, 296r–307r. In 1692 Rothenburg jurist Johann Georg Krauss drafted a request for advice to the Tübingen legal faculty during the trial for witchcraft of Barbara Ehness but did not send it, see RStA Interrogation Book A925, letter from Krauss dated 23 May.
64 Radbruch, *Die Peinliche Gerichtsordnung*, pp. 130–131. The council had called on the two Nuremberg jurists (Gugel and Hardessheim) to whom it paid an annual retainer for advice on the allegations of witchcraft which arose in the village of Oberstetten in 1582, see RStA Interrogation Book A875 fols 221r–223v.

65	RStA Interrogation Book A902 (unpaginated), opinion dated 2 February 1663 (Würth); Interrogation Book A909 fols 352r–355r, 368r–371r (Rohn).

66	For other long cases see for example the trials of Barbara Ehness in 1692 (RStA Interrogation Book A925 fols 1r–129v); of Anna Maria Knöspel, her son Hans Adam Knöspel and Hans Georg Nunn between 1689 and 1694 (StAN Ro. Rep. 2087 fols 620r–863v); and of Anna Margaretha Rohn in 1673 (RStA Interrogation Book A909 fols 188r–399v).

67	See n. 63 for details of the Tübingen opinion.

68	RStA Interrogation Book A898 fols 503r–505r (physicians' report in Horn's case); Interrogation Book A909 fols 206r–208r, 227r–229r, 266r–267r, 274r, 337r–338r, 372r–375v (physicians' reports in Rohn's case). Rohn's admission that she herself had faked the appearance of the needles from her wound was ignored by the council – another example of their late seventeenth-century tendency to 'see' as sinister phenomena which had prosaic explanations.

69	See n. 66 for details of the trials of Anna Margaretha Rohn, Hans Adam Knöspel and Barbara Ehness. In 1692 Kirchmeier tried to persuade Ehness and self-confessed child-witch Hans Adam Knöspel, who was still being held in the city hospital after his trial in 1689, to accuse other individuals whose names he fed to them of witchcraft.

70	Robisheaux, 'Witchcraft and forensic medicine', pp. 212–213.

71	These themes are discussed in Chapters 1 and 2.

72	See RStA Interrogation Book A884 fols 510r–611v (Hofmann); Interrogation Book A888 fols 1r–32v (Rost); Interrogation Book A895 fols 165r–174v, 408r–420v (Hörner); Interrogation Book A909 fols 188r–399v (Rohn).

73	See nn. 66 and 69 for details of Knöspel's case.

74	Hörber's case is discussed pp. 105–124.

75	For details of the course of the Thirty Years' War in Rothenburg and the devastating impact it had on all aspects of life in the city and its rural hinterland, see Heller (ed.), *Rothenburg ob der Tauber im Jahrhundert des grossen Krieges*, pp. 36–190; Schmidt, 'Auswirkungen des Krieges auf Stadt und Land'; Rank, *Die Finanzwirtschaft der Reichsstadt Rothenburg*; Moritz, *Die Folgen des Dreissigjährigen Krieges*, especially pp. 54–90, 132–176; StAN Ro. Rep. 2096 fols 33r–65r.

76	Diane Purkiss also points to the psychological effects of the English Civil War, although she argues that they caused a more specific 'crisis in masculinity' which some men coped with by directing violence at 'the figure of the witch as a condensed, displaced image of all there was to fear', 'Desire and its deformities', pp. 105–106.

77	StAN Ro. Rep. 2087 fols 95r–97v.

78	This popular dissatisfaction with the council's financial policies is discussed earlier in this chapter in the context of the Margetha Horn trial; see n. 31.

79	Kunstmann also alludes to the possibility that the impact of the Thirty Years War may have encouraged greater anxiety about witchcraft in Nuremberg, which also experienced unusually severe witch-trials after the war in 1659 and 1660, see *Zauberwahn*, pp. 196, 200–201.

80	For details of the severe trials in the Franconian prince-bishoprics see Behringer, *Hexenverfolgung in Bayern*, pp. 236–241.

81	RStA Interrogation Book A895 fols 171r–173r; for full case-documents, see *ibid.*, fols 165r–174v, 408r–420v. See also Rowlands, 'The "Little witch girl"'.

82	For discussion of this case, see Schad, 'Ein Priester auf dem Scheiterhaufen', and 'Kriminalfall Michael Campensis'.

83	For the many signs and portents recorded by Dehner for the war years, see Heller's edition of Dehner's chronicle, *Rothenburg ob der Tauber im Jahrhundert des grossen Krieges*, pp. 36–37, 49, 54, 109, 121, 122, 123, 124, 125, 127, 128, 129, 130, 132, 133, 139, 140, 144, 146, 148, 175, 181, 182, 185, 189–190, 232–233. See *ibid.*, p. xvi for the idea that Dehner was critical of the council's taxation policies.

84	On the rural parish vacancies, see Moritz, *Die Folgen des Dreissigjährigen Krieges*, pp. 17–32, 151–159. On the lack of ecclesiastical visitations, see StAN Ro. Rep. 2096 fol. 33r.

85 See for example *ibid.*, fols 69r–71r (visitation of 1652), fols 250r, 258r (visitation of 1660).

86 The attack by French armies in 1688, for example, destroyed much of the work which had been done in Rothenburg's hinterland to restore the damage done by the Thirty Years' War, see Moritz, *Die Folgen des Dreissigjährigen Krieges*, pp. 158–159. For details of the lengthy rebuilding programme undertaken by Rothenburg's council after the Thirty Years' War, see *ibid.*, pp. 132–176.

87 RStA Interrogation Book A884 fols 556r–560r.

88 StAN Ro. Rep. 2087 fols 95r–97v.

Conclusion

In Rothenburg and its hinterland four factors interacted to ensure that the area experienced a restrained pattern of witch-trials and only three executions for witchcraft throughout the early modern period. The first was a willingness on the part of the councillors and their judicial advisers to treat and punish a significant proportion of the witchcraft allegations with which they were confronted as slanders.[1] This happened most often during the second half of the sixteenth and early part of the seventeenth century, but was still possible in later years: allegations of witchcraft were handled in this way by the council in 1668 and 1709, for example.[2] The councillors' policy in this regard had the effect of discouraging their subjects from making formal accusations of witchcraft for fear of failing to prove them at law and thereby incurring punishments for slander. However, the councillors and their subjects also shared a concern about the value of personal honour which they believed that thoughtless talk about witchcraft could diminish. These concerns made most people cautious about speaking openly about witchcraft, both during trials and in the course of everyday social interaction. The narratives told by the child-witches of Rothenburg were thus so shocking to contemporaries and posed such a severe test of the authorities' restrained handling of witchcraft allegations because they broke and threatened to permanently loosen the conventions that traditionally governed and constrained how people in the area spoke about witchcraft.

The second factor which limited the severity and scale of witch-trials in Rothenburg was the refusal on the part of the elites to abandon normal legal procedure in the handling of witch-trials, a factor which was also of paramount importance in explaining the relative paucity of witch-trials in other parts of Germany.[3] Torture was used with restraint and often not at all in the Rothenburg trials, thus ensuring that all accused (as opposed to self-confessed) witches were able to maintain their denials of guilt. Serious legal action was never taken against those individuals accused by self-confessed witches of having been seen at witches' dances. This was due partly to an elite scepticism about the reality of the witches' dance that was influenced by the medieval *Canon Episcopi*, partly to a judicial scepticism about the validity of the testimony of self-confessed witches, and mainly to an elite desire not to see individual witch-trials escalate into large-scale witch-panics. The councillors did begin to take physical signs of witchcraft – such as the alleged inability to cry or supposed witches' marks on suspects' bodies – more seriously as forms of proof in trials from the mid-seventeenth century. However, as this change was not accompanied by a major policy shift in terms of the application of torture in witch-trials, it did not increase the risk of chain-reaction-type witch-panics occurring.

The caution with which the councillors and their legal advisers treated witches at law during the early modern period was not – as Kunstmann suggests for Nuremberg – the result of 'a progressive striving for justice', but stemmed rather from a conviction on their part that witchcraft was so problematic a crime to prove unequivocally that the ultimate punishment of suspected witches was best left to the all-seeing wisdom of God.[4] This idea was partly rooted in a judicial appreciation of the difficulty of reaching definitive conclusions about guilt or innocence in the case of the secret crime of witchcraft. However, it also had important roots in elite religious belief. Successive generations of Rothenburg councillors reached decisions in witch-trials on the basis of a sense of humility which encouraged them to think that some problems were so testing that they were best left to God to solve. They also had a sense of anxiety that if they mistakenly executed the innocent along with the guilty during witch-trials then they would have to answer to God for this at the Day of Judgement. Bad secular government also risked bringing the wrath of God down upon the whole community. As the seventeenth century progressed the councillors and their advisers became less sure about how best to serve God through their handling of witch-trials – by prosecuting witches severely or leniently? – although they usually solved their dilemma by erring on the side of caution. They were consistently reluctant to execute anyone for witchcraft (interpreted either as maleficium or apostasy) and instead continued to impose the late-medieval punishment of banishment on alleged witches, although only in the most serious of cases.[5] Of the three women executed as witches in Rothenburg between 1500 and 1800, two had committed other crimes (infanticide and attempted murder by means of poison) which were anyway deemed worthy of the death penalty. The third, Anna Margaretha Rohn, was a mentally unstable self-confessed witch who was largely the architect of her own downfall in 1673.[6]

Political priorities perceived to be of fundamental importance by the city councillors also helped ensure that witchcraft was never zealously prosecuted in Rothenburg. One of these priorities was the councillors' belief that the judicial autonomy of Rothenburg and its right to freedom from external interference in the exercise of its judicial power were best expressed and maintained by quashing rather than fostering witch-trials. This idea was articulated most clearly during the trial of Hans Georg Hofmann in 1605, when jurist Friedrich Prenninger warned the council of the risk that Hofmann would complain to the Emperor if he were tortured without sufficient legal justification, although Margaretha Horn also articulated an awareness of the possible intervention by the Emperor in Rothenburg's affairs if the council mishandled her trial for witchcraft in 1652.[7] In both cases the council took the warnings about the risk of imperial intervention to heart in their handling of the trials. The trials involving Margaretha Hörber in 1627 and Margaretha Harter in 1629 suggested that a religious edge had been added to the council's assertion of its judicial autonomy: council handling of both cases affirmed its right not only to try alleged witches but to try them in a certain – cautious – manner in the face of perceived Catholic challenges to its authority.[8] The council's willingness to seek advice from legal experts external to Rothenburg in problematic late seventeenth-century witch-trials can thus be seen as a small but significant shift away from this earlier self-confident assertion of judicial autonomy.

Of even greater influence on its cautious handling of witchcraft allegations than its concern with judicial autonomy was the council's concern with maintaining social stability in Rothenburg and its hinterland villages. From the 1560s, successive generations of city councillors realised that the economic and military strength of the hinterland was likely to be damaged by the social tensions caused by large-scale trials and executions for witchcraft. The idea that the social and economic well-being of a community was likely to be damaged rather than strengthened by witch-trials also shaped the council's reaction to narratives of witchcraft told later in an urban context. The council tendency to treat people who told stories of witchcraft publicly – whether individuals who accused others of witchcraft, self-confessed witches, or those who spread rumours about witchcraft – as more of a threat to good social order than the alleged witches themselves can be most clearly seen in its handling of the witchcraft cases involving the Brosams from Wettringen in 1561, the Kellner family from Finsterlohr in 1563, Margaretha Seitz from Oberstetten in 1587, Leonhardt Brandt from Steinach in 1602, and Hans Georg Hofmann, Barbara Rost and Brigitta Hörner from Rothenburg in 1605, 1628 and 1639, respectively.[9] It was probably also at work in other cases, however. Moreover, although all of the factors which helped ensure the restrained pattern of witch-trials in Rothenburg were vitally important, this concern about the social damage that severe witch-trials could do to communities was arguably the most important, as it remained constant throughout the early modern period whatever other changes of belief about witchcraft were expressed by the councillors and their advisers.[10] The emphasis on social order suggests that older concerns, rooted in the medieval idea of maintaining the social peace for the sake of the urban commune as a whole, continued to help shape the councillors' mild legal treatment of witchcraft throughout the early modern period and ensured that the city and its hinterland were protected against even the large waves of fierce witch-hunting which broke out elsewhere in Franconia in the 1590s and 1620s.

The inhabitants of Rothenburg and its rural hinterland also played their part in helping ensure that the area never experienced large-scale, severe witch-trials by means of their lack of enthusiasm for making formal accusations against neighbours whom they suspected of witchcraft. This unwillingness stemmed from a bundle of inter-related factors. In legal terms individuals who may have wished to make witchcraft accusations doubtless realised that they had a slim chance of proving them at law, while both they and witnesses in witch-trials were aware of the punishments for slander they risked incurring by speaking incautiously about witchcraft. These concerns, plus a sense of the value of social harmony and personal honour which they shared with the councillors and their advisers, encouraged the inhabitants of the area to feel that non-legal methods were the most effective for combating the threat of witchcraft. Moreover, most of the Rothenburg witch-trials show that a wide spectrum of popular attitudes towards alleged witches existed: in each case some people expressed deep feelings of hostility and envy towards alleged witches, others simply laughed about them, while the middle-ground of popular feeling about alleged witches and how best to cope with them was characterised by pragmatism rather than a deep-seated desire to see them executed. Popular dissatisfaction with the council's cautious handling of witch-trials may have grown during the seventeenth century and popular and elite anxiety about the threat posed by witchcraft may have increased as a result of the material and psychological impact of the Thirty Years' War on the area and its inhabitants. However, as the legal opinion written by jurist Georg Christoph Walther in 1652 demonstrated, popular opinion about witchcraft and how it ought best to be handled was never uniform in Rothenburg and its hinterland.[11] Crucially, popular opinion in favour of more severe action against witches was never so widespread nor so vehemently articulated – even during years of hardship – that the council felt obliged to accede to it.[12]

The Rothenburg evidence thus suggests that those areas most likely to be characterised by a restrained pattern of witch-trials in early modern Germany were those in which a significant majority of the ruling elites came to realise that the social, economic and political stability of their territories was likely to be damaged rather than strengthened by severe and large-scale witch-hunts. This way of thinking was effective, however, only if it could be put into practice: it was thus crucial for the ruling elites who were of this opinion to be able to maintain or assert control over the judicial processes by means of which alleged witches were tried. They also had to help ensure – perhaps chiefly by punitive measures such as the punishment of slander – that their subjects did not bring irresistible pressure in favour of more severe action against witches to bear upon them. Protestant demonology which emphasised the idea that many aspects of witchcraft were delusions caused by the devil might help support such a moderate elite viewpoint, as might a confessionally neutral awareness of the difficulty of proving witchcraft accusations unequivocally at law. It was not the size, cohesion or location of a territory which made it more or less likely to fall prey to the horrors of large-scale witch-trials in early modern Germany, then, but rather the question of whether and for how long this set of restraining factors pertained in its particular case. In Rothenburg and its hinterland they were kept essentially intact throughout the whole early modern period, sparing the lives of many individuals who might otherwise have been executed for witchcraft.

NOTES

1 Authorities elsewhere also tried to dampen enthusiasm for the making of witchcraft accusations by punishing or threatening with punishment those who had named or who sought to name others as witches: see the examples from Munich and Nuremberg cited in Chapter 1, n. 104. As I pointed out on pp. 23–24, however, the deterrent effect of suits and punishments for slander on the making of witchcraft accusations remains under-researched for early modern Germany.

2 See the cases involving Margaretha Fischer (1668) and Hans Caspar Kürrlein (1709) in the Appendix.

3 This point is made by Kunstmann for Nuremberg (*Zauberwahn*, p. 191); by Behringer for Munich ('Schieternde Hexenprozesse', p. 75); and by Schmidt for the Palatinate (*Glaube und Skepsis*, p. 480).

4 Kunstmann, *Zauberwahn*, p. 199: 'ein fortschrittliches Streben nach Gerechtigkeit'.

5 An unwillingness to impose the death penalty for witchcraft was also characteristic of Nuremberg and the Palatinate, see Kunstmann, *Zauberwahn*, p. 197; Schmidt, *Glaube und Skepsis*, pp. 131–137, 479.

6 One perhaps surprising aspect of the Rothenburg council's handling of witch-trials was that it did not categorise self-confessed witches like Rohn as suffering from melancholy, or mental instability. This medical idea was only occasionally relevant and only in relation to people who claimed to have been bewitched (like Michael Rost in 1641: see pp. 146, 149–150).

7 See pp. 162–164 for the Hofmann case; pp. 180–192 for the Horn case.

8 Both Schmidt for the Calvinist Palatinate and Kunstmann for Lutheran Nuremberg suggest that a mild approach to witch-trials there may have been maintained in conscious opposition to what was perceived to be excessive Catholic persecution of witches, see Schmidt, *Glaube und Skepsis*, p. 480, Kunstmann, *Zauberwahn*, pp. 176, 199–200.

9 These cases are discussed in Chapters 1, 2 and 5.

10 Kunstmann suggests that a similar concern on the part of the Nuremberg council to protect the city's social and economic well-being helped explain its unwillingness to hunt witches, see *Zauberwahn*, pp. 199–200. Schmidt downplays the importance of the Palatinate authorities' political priorities in explaining the restrained pattern of witch-trials in his conclusion to *Glaube und Skepsis* (pp. 475–482); on this point see also Walter Rummel's review of *Glaube und Skepsis*. However, as Rummel points out, Schmidt's book clearly demonstrates that the Palatinate authorities asserted control over – and moderate handling of – witch-trials in order to protect their own subjects against being dragged into trials in other territories and to curb the enthusiasm of neighbouring nobles who fostered witch-hunts as a way of encroaching

upon the judicial competence of the Palatinate courts. This suggests that political priorities were as important in shaping the handling of witch-trials in the Palatinate as they were in Rothenburg and Nuremberg.

11 For Walther's opinion, see pp. 196–7, 199–200.

12 Neither Kunstmann nor Schmidt deal in much depth with the issue of the role that the lower orders played in shaping the pattern of witch-trials in Nuremberg and the Palatinate. For Nuremberg Kunstmann merely says that there is no evidence that the lower orders contributed to the mild handling of witch-trials, although he concedes that they did not put pressure on the council for more severe action against witches, *Zauberwahn*, p. 175. Schmidt suggests for the Palatinate that the lower orders tended to want more severe witch-hunts and were only restrained in this desire by the moderate elites, *Glaube und Skepsis*, pp. 477, 137, although a more detailed account of the role of the lower orders in the Palatinate witch-trials may be impossible because of the poor survival of the trial-records (*ibid.*, p. 20). In 'Witch-craft and judgement', Scribner also points to the idea that, where witchcraft was not treated as an exceptional crime by the authorities, it was more likely to be viewed pragmatically by the lower orders, who might then also see excessive and severe witch-trials as doing more harm than good.

Appendix: trials for witchcraft in Rothenburg ob der Tauber, 1549–1709

Date of trial	Name of alleged witch(es); status (if known); fate (1 denotes execution) (I)	Age of alleged witch(es) at trial (? denotes age has been estimated) (II)	Trial evidence of pre-existing reputation as a witch (III)	Accusers; fate of accuser(s) (if applicable) (IV)
1549	(1) *Dorothea, widow (of at least four years) of Rothenburg citizen Caspar Klennckh.* Possibly of middling to high status? Gaoled; interrogated under torture; banished for sorcery and fornication.	? May have had children of marriageable age, suggesting she was in her forties or fifties.	None.	Probably *Jorg Bubenleben of Rothenburg* (married), her children's guardian, upon whom she had allegedly tried to inflict the pox through witchcraft. It was also alleged that she had had sex during her widowhood.
1561	(2) *Barbara, wife of Paulus Brosam of Wettringen;* (3) *Paulus* was accused of having helped Barbara in her witchcraft. Gaoled; interrogated; released after paying their costs and promising to reappear before the council if the matter went any further.	? Had six young children, the last one less than a year old; probably married twelve years. Assuming this was their first marriage and they had married at c. twenty-five and c. twenty-seven, they were probably in their late thirties in 1561.	Wettringen's pastor claimed that Barbara had been reputed a witch for ten years and had been taught witchcraft by her parents-in-law, Elisabetha and Veit Brosam. Elisabetha, Veit and Veit's brother, Hans, had also had reputations as workers of witchcraft since the Peasants' War (1525), suggesting that they were in their sixties or seventies by 1561.	*Hans Lautenbach and his brother-in-law, baker Leonhart Immell, of Wettringen,* as the result of a feud with the Brosams. Lautenbach was married and probably in his fifties or sixties by 1561. Immell was probably married and older than the Brosams. Gaoled; interrogated; banished (Immell) and put in the pillory and banished (Lautenbach) for slander.

| 1563 | (4) *Appolonia, wife of Georg Schneider, and her children by her first husband, Cuntz Kellner;* (5) *Appolonia, wife of carpenter Leonhard Bretner;* (6) *Anna, wife of donkey-drover Michel Arnns; and* (7) *Georg Kellner, all of Finsterlohr.*

All four were gaoled and interrogated: Appolonia senior (thumbscrews once, strappado once) and Anna (thumbscrews once) were tortured; the three women were banished for slander and quarrelsomeness; Georg was released unpunished. | ? With two married daughters, Appolonia senior was probably at least in her fifties by 1563. (She was known as 'old Appolonia', although this was probably to distinguish her from Appolonia junior.) Her daughters were probably in their mid-to-late twenties or early thirties in 1563; Georg was probably younger. | Appolonia senior had been reputed a witch in Finsterlohr for at least twenty-nine years by 1563. With a reputed witch for a mother, Appolonia, Anna (also rumoured to be a witch by 1563) and Georg had probably been at risk of acquiring similar reputations from a young age. | *Appolonia's son-in-law, Leonhardt Bretner, and his wife Appolonia junior, of Finsterlohr,* called Appolonia senior and Anna witches and Georg 'king of the witches' as part of a family feud. Bretner and his wife had hit hard times and felt that Appolonia senior and Anna were refusing to help them.

Bretner: gaoled; interrogated; banished with his wife for slander. |
| 1571 | (8) *Magdalena, widow (of at least five years) of citizen/rope-maker Caspar Weinmayr of Rothenburg.* Poor; working as a lying-in maid by 1571.

Gaoled; interrogated under torture; banished for attempted poisoning and fornication. | ? The fact that she had not remarried after the death of second husband Weinmayr suggests she was possibly in her late forties–early fifties. | She had been rumoured a witch in Rothenburg for many years. | *Albrecht Bernpeck, of Rothenburg (married),* whose new-born baby she had allegedly tried to poison with mercury.

It was also alleged that she had had sex during her widowhood and that she might have been responsible for her husbands' deaths. |

1572	(9) Anna, wife of Hans Eck of Tauberscheckenbach. Gaoled; interrogated; released on payment of costs and told to keep the peace with her sister.	? She could have been any age from her late twenties to her fifties. Given that she and her sister were both married, it is perhaps most likely that they were in their thirties or forties.	None, other than her sister's accusation.	Anna's sister Kunigundt, wife of Georg Richter, citizen/nail-maker of Rothenburg, accused Anna of laming her husband through witchcraft. Kunigundt: gaoled; interrogated; released on the same conditions as her sister.
1582	(10) Gertraud, widow (of seven years) of herdsman Leonhardt Durmann; (11) Anna, wife (since 1570) of Melchior Schneider; (12) Anna, wife of butcher Georg Weh, all of Oberstetten. None of them were gaoled, questioned or punished.	? Neighbours described Anna W. as young and Gertraud and Anna S. as 'advanced in years'. Gertraud seems to have had a daughter who was probably at most a teenager in 1582, while Anna S. had had at least one husband prior to Melchior S., by whom she had had three surviving children, so both were probably in their fifties in 1582.	None against Anna S.. Gertraud had been reputed a witch for at least eight years and had a brother who was a cunning man. Anna W's mother and grandmother were reputed witches, so she would have risked acquiring the same reputation from a relatively young age.	Margaretha, wife of Burckhardt Seitz, of Oberstetten, claimed she had seen the trio at a witches' feast. She was married with children still living at home and was probably older than Anna W. but younger than Anna S. and Gertraud. Margaretha: gaoled; interrogated; released on payment of costs after promising to reappear before the council if the matter went any further.

1587	(13) *Magdalena, wife of Martin Gackstatt; her son, (14) Hans; (15) Anna, wife of Jörg Brodt; (16) Babelein, daughter of Hans Kuch junior, all of Hilgartshausen.* All four were gaoled and interrogated; Magdalena (strappado once) and Hans (two floggings, thumbscrews once) were tortured; Anna and Babelein were definitely released unpunished; Magdalena and Hans almost certainly were as well.	? Magdalena was probably not older than her mid-forties in 1587 (as Hans was aged six), and may have been younger. Anna was about thirty, Babelein about thirteen.	Suspicions of witchcraft had first arisen against Magdalena ten or twelve years earlier. No evidence against Anna, although there are hints that Babelein's mother (probably aged early thirties) and grandmother (probably in her fifties or sixties) were also reputed witches.	*Hans Gackstatt, Magdalena's six-year-old son,* claimed to have been taken to a witches' dance by his mother, and that he had seen Anna, Babelein and other village women there: see column (I) for his fate.
1602	(17) *Katharina, wife of Franz Kupfer; (18) Anna, wife of Jörg Stahl; (19) Elisabeth, wife of Daniel Kraft; (20) Katharina, wife of mason Michael Lientschner; and (21) Appolonia, wife of carpenter Leonhardt Holenbuch, all of Steinach.*	? Daniel Kraft was thirty-seven in 1602, so his wife Elisabetha was probably two–three years younger than him, at around thirty-four–thirty-five. The other couples may have been of the same generation as the Krafts (mid-to-late thirties).	Only Appolonia H. had a pre-existing reputation of at least six years' – and probably longer – standing.	*Blacksmith's apprentice Leonhardt Brandt,* of Steinach, claimed to have seen the five women at a witches' gathering. Brandt was unmarried but betrothed, so was probably in his mid-twenties in 1602. Gaoled; interrogated; released under the same conditions as had pertained to Margaretha Seitz in 1582.

1605	(22) *Hans Georg Hofmann and* (23) *Michael Pfund, citizen/ joiners of Rothenburg.* Both had fallen on hard times by 1605. Gaoled; interrogated; banished (Hofmann); formally questioned with no further action taken (Pfund).	? Pfund was in his fifties or – more probably – sixties, as Hofmann's stepfather had been his apprentice twenty years earlier, and was probably married. Hofmann was married and probably in his late twenties or early thirties.	Hofmann had offered his services as a treasure-seeker for at least a year. Pfund had been called before the authorities before 1605 for allegedly possessing a book of magical arts.	Hofmann was arrested on the basis of rumours circulating in Rothenburg to the effect that he and Pfund had bewitched a table they had made for Herr David Walther.
1627	(24) *Margaretha Hörber of Gebsattel,* claimed she had been seduced into witchcraft by Ursula, the old midwife of Gebsattel and her own mother, and taken by Ursula and (25) *Ursula's daughter Eva to* witches' dances where she had seen nineteen women and three men, including (26) *the old herdsman of Gebsattel.* Gaoled for seven months; interrogated; kept in the city hospital for two more months; released on payment of costs after promising to live a Christian life. Eva was formally questioned; enquiries were made about the herdsman but no action was taken against him.	Margaretha was thirteen when her trial began in 1627 and fourteen when finally released from custody in 1628. Her mother and Ursula were dead by 1627. Eva had married in 1627 after eighteen years in service, aged probably around thirty. The old herdsman was possibly at least in his fifties if not sixties to warrant this epithet: he had one son who had been aged probably in his mid-to-late twenties in 1616 (see the Margaretha Horn trial, 1652, for more details).	None for Margaretha's mother, Ursula or Eva; the old herdsman was reputed a witch in Gebsattel.	*Margaretha* claimed she was a witch herself: see column (I) for her fate.

Date	Name and action	Age		Notes
1628–29	! (27) *Magdalena, wife of Hans Dürr of Standorf.* Gaoled; interrogated; tortured (thumbscrews twice); executed (beheaded then burned).	Twenty-eight or twenty-nine.	None.	*Magdalena was arrested on suspicion of having killed her eleven-week-old baby. She confessed to this crime and also claimed that she was a witch, having been seduced into witchcraft by her own mother (who had died three months earlier): see column (1) for her fate.*
1629	(28) *Anna Maria, wife of Georg Bezold, one of the five Rothenburg mayors.* No action taken against her.	? Georg Bezold was sixty-two in 1629 and had been married to third wife Anna Maria since 1609. She had had her last child by him in 1618, which suggests that she was at least in her late forties–early fifties by 1629.	None.	*Barbara Rost, a maid in the Bezolds'* service spread rumours that her mistress was a witch. Rost was probably in her late twenties–early thirties by 1629; she had made one abortive attempt at marriage eight years earlier. Gaoled; interrogated; banished for slander.
	(29) *Johann Georg Schnepf, Rothenburg city councillor.* No action taken against him.	Twenty-eight.	None.	*Rost and schoolboy Bernhard Wunsch of Rothenburg spread rumours that Schnepf had attended a witches' dance.* Wunsch had to formally revoke this allegation.

1629	(30) *Anna Dieterich, herdswoman and widow (since 1627) of Untereichenroth, and* (31) *Margaretha Harter of Bovenzenweiler*, who claimed to have been seduced into witchcraft by Dieterich. Both were poverty-stricken and begged in order to survive. Gaoled; interrogated; Harter was flogged in gaol and banished for slander; Dieterich was released unpunished.	Dieterich was sixty-one; Harter fifteen. Dieterich was rumoured to be a witch; these rumours emanated mainly from her son and especially her daughter-in-law, with whom she had lived and been at odds since the death of her husband.	*Margaretha* was forced into accusing Dieterich by Catholic troops quartered in the area who hoped to start a witch-hunt: see column (I) for her fate.
1639	(32) *Brigitta, daughter of day-labourer Endres Hörner and his wife Ursula of Spielbach*. Endres was long dead by 1639; Ursula had turned to begging after his death and died in 1638. Brigitta claimed to have been seduced into witchcraft by her godmother, Brigitta, the wife of pastor Johann Mauck of Spielbach, who was also dead by 1639.	Brigitta was nearly eight; Johann Mauck had been forty-two in 1631; his wife Brigitta had probably been the same age or two–three years younger. Only Brigitta suspected her godmother of witchcraft.	*Brigitta* claimed she was a witch herself: see column (I) for her fate.

1639	Gaoled; interrogated; sent to the Rothenburg hospital for three months; released. She was discovered, dead, in Steinbach in October 1640, after her relatives had refused to take her in.			
1641	(33) *Margaretha, wife of Michael Rost of Finsterlohr.* Both were gaoled; interrogated; released after promising to live peacefully with one another.	Margaretha was twenty-seven and Rost's third wife; Rost was forty. They had been married for six years and had had three children: one was still alive.	Only Rost thought his wife was a witch.	*Michael Rost* accused his wife of witchcraft and asked the council for a divorce. Evidence suggests that he was mentally unstable: see column (I) for his fate.
1652	(34) *Margaretha, wife of Hans Horn of Bettenfeld.* Gaoled; interrogated; tortured (thumbscrews, five times); released after paying her costs and promising to reappear before the council if the matter went any further. The Horns still lived in Bettenfeld in 1659.	Margaretha was sixty in 1652, as was Hans, her third husband. She had first married at the age of twenty-four in 1616.	Margaretha risked acquiring a reputation for witchcraft in 1616 after marrying Martin, the son of the old herdsman of Gebsattel (a reputed witch: see the Margaretha Hörber case, 1627, for details). However, Martin died quickly after their marriage, sparing her the worst effects of a long association with the family. She told the council she had been a godmother twenty-six times as proof of her good reputation.	*Margaretha's nearest neighbour Leonhard Gackstatt of Bettenfeld* accused her as part of an ongoing feud with her and her family. Gackstatt was neither gaoled nor formally questioned, probably because he was a subject of the Margrave of Brandenburg-Ansbach.

1652

(35) *Catharina, wife of blacksmith (36) Mathes Leimbach of Wettringen, their daughter (37) Magdalena, their maidservant (38) Barbara Bratsch, and (39) Barbara, the daughter of Hans Schürz and stepdaughter of his second wife Eva, the Leimbachs' nearest neighbours.*

Catharina, Mathes, Barbara B. and Barbara S. were gaoled and interrogated; Catharina was tortured (thumbscrews, five times). Catharina, Mathes and Barbara B. were released, but the Leimbachs had to pay a punitive amount of money as surety. Magdalena was formally questioned. Mathes died shortly after the trial as a result of the privations he had suffered; Catharina and Magdalena were finally banished from Wettringen in 1656. Barbara S. was sent from gaol to the Rothenburg poor-house, then released in 1653.

Catharina was fifty-three or fifty-four in 1652; Mathes was sixty-three. Mathes had moved to Wettringen in 1617 and married Catharina in 1618; their youngest child (of eight), Magdalena (aged twelve), still lived with them. Bratsch was twenty-three. Hans Schürz was fifty-two, his wife Eva thirty-eight or younger; they had married in 1649. Hans' daughter Barbara from his previous marriage was eight.

Catharina had had a reputation for working magic for at least eighteen years.

Barbara Schürz claimed to have been seduced into witchcraft by Catharina and taken by her to witches' dances which Mathes and Bratsch also attended: see column (I) for her fate. Hans Schürz brought his daughter's accusations before the council in 1652 but his wife had been increasingly suspicious of Catharina since 1649–50; relations between the two households broke down in 1651. Evidence suggests that Eva Schürz was mentally unstable.

1663	(40) *Michael Würth, citizen/wheelwright of Rothenburg and his wife (41) Barbara,* who was accused of having helped him in his witchcraft. Würth was formally questioned but fled Rothenburg before he could be gaoled. Barbara was gaoled and interrogated: both were then banished.	? Probably at least in his early to mid-forties - possibly older; his wife was probably of around the same age.	Suspected for at least two–three years before he was formally accused.	*Würth's neighbour Appolonia, wife of Georg Leupolt, a farrier of Rothenburg,* accused Würth of having caused the illness from which Leupolt had suffered for over two years before his death in December 1662, and of other acts of maleficium.
1668	(42) *Susanna, wife of Anthoni Lamer of Adelshofen and her foster-daughter (43) Margaretha Fischer,* a maidservant from Habelsee. Susanna was formally questioned; Margaretha was gaoled; interrogated; banished for slander.	? Susanna was called an old woman by neighbours; Margaretha was seventeen.	None, although Susanna's husband Anthoni called her an old witch publicly.	*Margaretha* claimed that Susanna had seduced her into witchcraft; later she admitted that she had fabricated the charge to revenge herself on her foster-mother for ill-treatment she had suffered at her hands as a child: see column (I) for Margaretha's fate.
1671	(44) *Appolonia, wife of Georg Glaitter of Windisch-Bockenfeld.* Almost certainly fairly wealthy.	Fifty-six. She was born and lived all her life in W.-Bockenfeld. Glaitter was her fourth husband. Her first	Appolonia had long had a reputation as a witch, perhaps from the age of eleven: the possibility that her mother	*Appolonia's nearest neighbour Endres Klenckh, and his wife, Appolonia,* accused Appolonia of having bewitched their

1671

Gaoled; interrogated; tortured (thumbscrews, three times); released after paying costs and swearing a surety.

marriage – at eighteen – had lasted from c. 1633–c. 1637; the second from c. 1637/8–c. 1662/3; the third from c. 1662/3–1664/5.

had also been reputed a witch might account for Appolonia's early reputation. She stated that she had only married her second husband (at age twenty-two–twenty-three) on condition that he defend her against witchcraft accusations. Trial evidence reached back to an act of alleged bewitchment by Appolonia in c. 1641, when she would have been c. twenty-six; see Rowlands, 'Witchcraft and old women', for details.

daughter. Klenckh was aged c. forty-two in 1671 and had been in Appolonia's service as a twelve-year-old around 1641. Klenckh was supported in his accusations by his eighty-two-year-old father, Michael. None of the Klenckhs were gaoled during the trial.

1673

! (45) *Anna Margaretha, daughter of Philip Rohn, citizen/plasterer,* (46) *Anna and her husband* (47) *Leonhardt Maas, cutler, and* (48) *Andreas Spahn, all of Rothenburg.*
    Anna Margaretha was gaoled; interrogated; tortured (thumbscrews twice); executed (beheaded and burned). The others were all questioned formally.

Anna Margaretha was twenty-two; Anna Maas was eighty-eight: Leonhardt Maas was probably the same age as his wife; Spahn was twenty-two. Anna Margaretha had begun having fits in 1664, claiming that she was being plagued by the devil and her mistress Anna Maas, that the latter had seduced her into witchcraft, and that Leonhardt Maas and Andreas Spahn had assisted in the seduction process.

No-one other than Anna Margaretha thought that she or Anna Maas were witches.

Anna Margaretha confessed to being a witch herself and also accused Anna and Leonhardt Maas and Andreas Spahn. During her trial Anna Margaretha also claimed to have committed multiple acts of infanticide: see column (I) for her fate.

1676

(49) *Hans Christoph, the son of Georg Emmert of Habelsee,* claimed that he had been seduced into witchcraft by his aunt, Barbara Emmert of Dunzendorf, who had taught him how to conjure fleas and taken him to witches' dances with her mother Dorothea.

He was gaoled, interrogated in Rothenburg, then sent to Uffenheim, as the Rothenburg council mistakenly thought that Barbara E. came from Custenlohr and was thus subject to the jurisdiction of the Brandenburg-Ansbach authorities in Uffenheim. Hans Christoph was interrogated and beaten in gaol in Uffenheim, then released on payment of costs. His aunt and her mother were interrogated and released unpunished by the Hatzfeld authorities in Niederstetten, to whose jurisdiction they belonged and who had refused to send them to Uffenheim for trial; see Schraut, 'Niederstetten 1676', for details.

Hans Christoph was fourteen; Barbara, the wife of Hans Emmert was thirty, her widowed mother Dorothea was sixty (see Schraut, 'Niederstetten 1676', pp. 158, 160).

None.

Hans Christoph confessed to being a witch himself and accused his aunt and her mother: see column (I) for their fates.

1687	(50) *Christoph Vogel, a poor lodger from Bettwar.* Gaoled; interrogated; banished.	Aged around fifty, he was almost certainly married and had six children.	He was known as a speaker of blessings to cure disease.	The *Vögeleins Bauer of Seldeneck and his wife* accused Vogel of having made their eight-year-old son's diseased leg worse instead of better after attempting to cure it.
1689	(51) *Anna Maria, wife of (52) Georg Adam Knöspel, citizen/weelwright of Rothenburg, and their son (53) Hans Adam Knöspel.* Anna Maria was gaoled; interrogated; banished. Hans Adam was gaoled; interrogated; sent to the city's hospital. He died in 1698. Georg Adam was questioned formally; deprived of his citizenship and banished.	Anna Maria and her husband were fifty; Hans, who suffered from epilepsy, was eleven.	Anna Maria had been reputed a witch ever since moving to Rothenburg, probably in her twenties. She had probably had a reputation from an early age because her mother, a blind eighty-year-old, still living in Haltenbergstetten, had long been reputed a witch there. Georg Adam Knöspel also had a reputation as a witch and was called 'Witch-Knöspelein' in 1689. This was due to the fact that he had been the stepson of reputed witch Michael Würth and son of Barbara Würth (see 1663 for case details).	*Hans Adam* claimed that his mother had seduced him into witchcraft and taken him to witches' dances. Other charges of maleficium were brought against her by neighbours after her arrest. Georg Adam was questioned by the council on account of his wife's reputation and his son's confessions: see column (I) for their fates.

1690	(54) *Appolonia Schwärz, a poor widow of Rothenburg and* (55) *Hans Böhm, formerly the blacksmith of Gailnau, living in Rothenburg's hospital by 1690.* Both were formally questioned, but no further action was taken.	? To have given up work and gone into the hospital, Hans B. may have been of advanced age, as there is no reference to him suffering from any physical infirmities. ? As a poor widow who sold fruit in the market to support herself and who lodged with Barbara Ehness (see next case), Appolonia S. may have been at least past childbearing age (i.e. in her late forties—early fifties).	Probably reputed witches before 1690, although no evidence on length of reputations.	*Hans Adam Knöpel,* who had been sent to live in Rothenburg's hospital after his parents' banishment in 1689, accused Appolonia S. and Hans B. of being witches in 1690. *Barbara Röder of Rothenburg* also claimed that Appolonia S. had bewitched her young daughter.
1692	! (56) *Barbara, widow of Hans Ehness of Rothenburg.* Poor: her father Matthes Ebert had been a vinedresser and beggar, her husband a day-labourer. Gaoled; interrogated; tortured (thumbscrews once); executed (beheaded then burned).	Forty-one. She had been married to Ehness (c. thirty years her senior) for thirteen years without having any children; witnesses described her as an old woman.	None. She was arrested on suspicion of having poisoned her lodgers and confessed to this, the poisoning of her husband, her seduction into witchcraft by her godmother at the age of eight or nine, and her attendance at various witches' dances since then. She later retracted this confession of witchcraft but was executed anyway for attempted poisoning.	*Hans Ruopp, who lodged with Barbara Ehness,* accused her of having poisoned himself, his wife, and their 4 children (not fatally) after she put arsenic into their milk-broth.

(57) Johann Craft, pastor of Taubersscheckenbach; (58) Appolonia, wife of citizen/butcher Johann Crämer of Rothenburg; (59) Adelheit Jäger of Rothenburg; (60) Barbara Schmezer of Rothenburg, wife of a minor city official; (61) Anna Schöppler of Rothenburg, formerly in service in the city's hospital; (62) Barbara Weiser, who was probably a widow, as she paid to live in the city's poorhouse. 　　All the women were formally questioned; enquiries were made about Craft, but no further action was taken.	Craft was fifty;? Appolonia C. was probably at least of middle age, as Crämer was her fourth husband. No evidence for Adelheit J. or Anna S. ?Barbara S. was probably at least in her fifties, if not older, as she testified that she had raised six children; ? Barbara W. was probably also at least in her fifties.	Adelheit J. and Barbara S. were both alleged to have had bad reputations for a long time. Barbara S.'s mother had been accused of witchcraft in Dinkelsbühl, so Barbara S. may have acquired her reputation from her.	*Hans Adam Knöspel, Hans Georg Nunn (see below) and Barbara Ehness* claimed to have seen them at witches' dances. Ehness later retracted her accusations, however, explaining that she had been fed the names by one of the pastors who had visited her in gaol.
1692–94 (63) *Hans Georg Nunn*, inmate of Rothenburg's hospital. 　　Questioned formally; no further action.	? A boy, probably of similar age to Hans Adam Knöspel (ten–twelve).	None.	Copying the example of *Hans Adam Knöspel*, with whom he shared a room in the city's hospital, *Hans Georg* claimed that he had been seduced into witchcraft and taken to witches' dances, where he had seen other alleged witches (see above).

| 1709 | (64) *Anna, widow of cobbler Johann Eberhard Schumacher of Rothenburg, and her nephew,* (65) *Hans Caspar Kürrlein.* Both were gaoled; interrogated; released; Kürrlein was first flogged in gaol for slander. | Fifty-three; married to Schumacher from the age of twenty-one to thirty-three, then widowed for twenty years. Hans Caspar was twelve. | Anna's daughter-in-law suspected her of being a witch; moreover, Anna's nickname was Flea-Anna, suggesting she may have had a reputation for being able to conjure fleas. | *Hans Caspar* was encouraged to claim that he had been seduced into witchcraft by Anna by *Anna's daughter-in-law, Maria Appolonia.* Maria Appolonia was married to Anna's son, Johann Eberhard Schumacher junior, and had an extremely bad relationship with Anna. There is also evidence to suggest that she was mentally unstable. *Maria Appolonia:* gaoled; interrogated; banished with her husband for slander. |

Note: The names of alleged witches and, where appropriate, their accuser(s), are highlighted in italic.

Bibliography

Primary sources

Rothenburg City Archive (Stadtarchiv Rothenburg; abbreviation RStA)

Blood Books (*Blutbücher*) 1501–1782: B329, B330, B331, B332, B333, B665.
Surety Books (*Urfehdenbücher*) 1501–1601: A842, A843, A844, A846, A847, A849, A851, A853, A855, A857.
Interrogation Books (*Urgichtenbücher*) 1552–1765: A852, A854, A858, A861, A870, A873, A874, A875, A877, A884, A886, A887, A888, A895, A896, A898, A902, A906, A908, A909, A911, A920, A921, A925, A938, A981.
Municipal Account Books (*Rechnungsbücher*) 1530–1777: R524–R540 inclusive.
Civil Court Books (*Stadtgerichtsbücher*): B304.
Peasants' Court Books (*Bauerngerichtsbücher*): B316, B317.
Detwang Village Court Books (*Detwang Gerichtsbücher*): B327, B328, B659.
Village Acts (*Dorfakten*): A105–A166, A491, A719, A739, A753, A754, A769, A515, A539, A597, A599.
Minutes of Council Meetings (*Ratsprotokolle*): B45.
Records of Council Elections (*Ratswahlbücher*): B186, B186a.
Marriage Acts (*Matrimonialakten*): A1477.
Council Ordinances (*Ordnungen und Rechtssatzungen*): A362, A363, A365, A366a, A1269, AA122a.
Lists of Council Appointees: B511.
Notebooks of Mayor Johann Georg Styrzel, 1637–1707: B198.
Books of Legal Opinions and Jurists' Correspondence: B230, B231, A372–A382, A390, A394.
Chronicles of Rothenburg: B25 (by Nikolaus Göttlingk); B27 (by Johann Georg Albrecht).
Council Library: Nos 463, 284–286 (Theology Section), No. 68 (Miscellaneous Section).
Die Rechtssatzungen der Reichsstadt Rothenburg ob der Tauber, complete list of all the ordinances drawn up by Rothenburg's council, compiled by Ludwig Schnurrer, 1988.

Familienregister der Pfarrgemeinde Wettringen, edited by Fritz Mägerlein, 1977.
Gebsattel im 17. Jahrhundert. Register Kirchenbuch Gebsattel, 2 vols, edited by Hanns Bauer, undated.

Archive of the Parish Church of St Jakob, Rothenburg

Auszug aus den Consistorialacten des ehemal. Rothenburg. Consistorium, compiled by Johann Ludwig Schäfer, undated, eighteenth century.

Nuremberg State Archive (Staatsarchiv Nürnberg; abbreviation StAN)

Minutes of the Nuremberg City Council (*Ratsverlässe*): Rep. 60a.
Nuremberg Council Correspondence (*Briefbücher*): Rep. 61a.
Books of Legal Opinions, Nuremberg (*Ratschlagbücher*): Rep. 51 and Rep. 51a.
Rothenburg Repertorium, Records of Rothenburg's Consistorium (*Konsistorialakten*): 2086, 2087, 2089, 2090, 2091, 2092, 2096.

Printed primary sources

Baumann, F. L. (ed.), *Quellen zur Geschichte des Bauernkriegs aus Rotenburg an der Tauber*, Tübingen, Bibliothek des litterarischen Vereins in Stuttgart, 1878.
Hartmann, J. L., *Neue Teuffels-Stücklein*, Frankfurt am Main, 1678.
Hartmann, J. L., *Greuel des Segensprechens*, Nuremberg, 1680.
Heller, K. (ed.), *Rothenburg ob der Tauber im Jahrhundert des grossen Krieges; Aus der Chronik des Sebastian Dehner*, Ansbach, Verlag Fr. Seybold, *c.* 1913.
Kramer, H. (Institoris), *Der Hexenhammer. Malleus Maleficarum*, translated by W. Behringer, G. Jerouschek and W. Tschacher; G. Jerouschek and W. Behringer (eds), Munich, Deutscher Taschenbuch Verlag, 2nd edn, 2001.
Radbruch, G. (ed.), *Die Peinliche Gerichtsordnung Kaiser Karls V. von 1532 (Carolina)*, Stuttgart, Philipp Reclam Jun., 6th edn, ed. A. Kaufmann, 1996.
Rücker, D., *Mundus personatus, Dass ist Die vermumbte verkehrte Welt Oder die grosse Welt-Mascarada*, Windsheim, 1688.
Sehling, E. (ed.), *Die evangelischen Kirchenordnungen des XVI. Jahrhunderts*; Vol. XI: Bavaria, Part I: Franconia, Tübingen, Verlag J. C. B. Mohr (Paul Siebeck), 1961.

Secondary sources

Ahme, E., 'Wertung und Bedeutung der Frau bei Martin Luther', *Luther*, 35:1 (1964), 61–68.
Ahrendt-Schulte, I., *Zauberinnen in der Stadt Horn (1554–1603): Magische Kultur und Hexenverfolgung in der Frühen Neuzeit*, Frankfurt am Main and New York, Campus Verlag, 1997.

Bächtold-Stäubli, H. (ed.), *Handwörterbuch des deutschen Aberglaubens*, 10 vols, Berlin and New York, Walter de Gruyter, 1987.

Barstow, A. L., *Witchcraze: A New History of the European Witch Hunts*, San Francisco and London, Pandora, 1994.

Bedal, K., *Mühlen und Müller in Franken*, Munich and Bad Windsheim, Verlag Delp, 2nd edn, 1992.

Behringer, W., 'Scheiternde Hexenprozesse: Volksglaube und Hexenverfolgung um 1600 in München', in R. van Dülmen (ed.), *Kultur der einfachen Leute: Bayerisches Volksleben vom 16. bis zum 19. Jahrhundert*, Munich, C. H. Beck, 1983, 42–78.

Behringer, W., *Hexenverfolgung in Bayern: Volksmagie, Glaubenseifer und Staatsräson in der Frühen Neuzeit*, Munich, Oldenbourg, 1987.

Behringer, W., 'Kinderhexenprozesse: zur Rolle von Kindern in der Geschichte der Hexenverfolgung', *Zeitschrift für Historische Forschung*, 16 (1989), 31–47.

Behringer, W., 'Weather, hunger, fear: the origins of the European witch hunts in climate, society and mentality', *German History*, 13 (1995), 1–27.

Behringer, W., 'Witchcraft studies in Austria, Germany and Switzerland', in J. Barry *et al.* (eds), *Witchcraft in Early Modern Europe*, Cambridge, Cambridge University Press, 1996, 64–95.

Bensen, H. W., *Historische Untersuchungen über die ehemalige Reichsstadt Rotenburg*, Nuremberg, Riegel and Wiessner, 1837.

Beyer, J, 'A Lübeck prophet in local and Lutheran context', in B. Scribner and T. Johnson (eds), *Popular Religion in Germany and Central Europe, 1400–1800*, London, Macmillan, 1996, 166–182.

Bezold, R. W. von, *Die Verfassung und Verwaltung der Reichsstadt Rothenburg ob der Tauber (1172–1803)*, Nuremberg, Verlag J. L. Stich, 1915.

Biesel, E., '"Die Pfeifer seint alle uff den baumen gesessen". Der Hexensabbat in der Vorstellungswelt einer ländlichen Bevölkerung', in G. Franz and F. Irsigler (eds), *Methoden und Konzepte der historischen Hexenforschung*, Trier, Spee Verlag, 1998, 289–302.

Bostridge, I., 'Witchcraft repealed', in J. Barry *et al.* (eds), *Witchcraft in Early Modern Europe*, Cambridge, Cambridge University Press, 1996, 309–385.

Brauner, S., *Fearless Wives and Frightened Shrews: The Construction of the Witch in Early Modern Germany*, Amherst, University of Massachusetts Press, 1995.

Briggs, R., *Witches and Neighbours: The Social and Cultural Context of European Witchcraft*, London, HarperCollins, 1996.

Briggs, R., 'Verteidigungsstrategien gegen Hexereibeschuldigungen: der Fall Lothringen', in G. Franz and F. Irsigler (eds), *Methoden und Konzepte der historischen Hexenforschung*, Trier, Spee Verlag, 1998, 109–128.

Burghartz, S., *Leib, Ehre und Gut: Delinquenz in Zürich Ende des 14. Jahrhunderts*, Zurich, Chronos Verlag, 1990.

Clark, S., 'Protestant demonology: sin, superstition and society (*c.* 1520–*c.* 1630)', in B. Ankarloo and G. Henningsen (eds), *Early Modern European Witchcraft: Centres and Peripheries*, Oxford, Clarendon Press, 1990.

Clark, S., *Thinking With Demons: The Idea of Witchcraft in Early Modern Europe*, Oxford, Oxford University Press, 1999 paperback edn; first published 1997.

Clark, S., 'The "gendering" of witchcraft in French demonology: misogyny or polarity?', *French History*, 5 (1991), 426–437.

Cunningham, H., *Children and Childhood in Western Society Since 1500*, London, Longman, 1995.

Dannheimer, W., *Verzeichnis der im Gebiete der freien Reichsstadt Rothenburg o. T. von 1544 bis 1803 wirkenden ev.-luth. Geistlichen*, Nuremberg, Egge Verlag, 1952.

Davis, N. Z., *Fiction in the Archives: Pardon Tales and their Tellers in Sixteenth-Century France*, Stanford, Stanford University Press, 1987.

Dillinger, J., 'Hexenverfolgungen in Städten', in G. Franz and F. Irsigler (eds), *Methoden und Konzepte der historischen Hexenforschung*, Trier, Spee Verlag, 1998, 129–165.

Dillinger, J., 'Richter als Angeklagte: Hexenprozesse gegen herrschaftliche Amtsträger in Kurtrier und Schwäbisch-Österreich', in H. Schnabel-Schüle (ed.), *Vergleichende Perspektiven, Perspektiven des Vergleichs: Studien zur europäischen Geschichte von der Spätantike bis ins 20. Jahrhundert*, Mainz, Verlag Philipp von Zabern, 1998.

Dillinger, J. *Böse Leute*: Hexenverfolgungen in Schwäbisch-Österreich und Kurtrier im Vergleich, Trier, Spee Verlag, 1999.

Dixon, C. S., *The Reformation and Rural Society. The Parishes of Brandenburg-Ansbach-Kulmbach, 1528–1603*, Cambridge, Cambridge University Press, 1996.

Dresen-Coenders, L., 'Witches as devils' concubines: on the origin of fear of witches and protection against witchcraft', in L. Dresen-Coenders (ed.), *Saints and She-Devils: Images of Women in the 15th and 16th Centuries*, London, Rubicon Press, 1987, 59–82.

Endres, R., 'Zur wirtschaftlichen und sozialen Lage in Franken vor dem Dreissigjährigen Krieg', *Jahrbuch für fränkische Landesforschung*, 28 (1968), 5–52.

Endres, R., 'Der Dreissigjährige Krieg', in A. Kraus (ed.), *Handbuch der bayerischen Geschichte. Vol. 3, part I: Geschichte Frankens bis zum Ausgang des 18. Jahrhunderts*, Munich, C.H. Beck, 3rd edn, 1997, 486–495.

Erler, A. and Kaufmann, E. (eds), *Handwörterbuch zur deutschen Rechtsgeschichte*, 3 vols, Berlin, Erich Schmidt Verlag, 1971 (I), 1978 (II), 1984 (III).

Fletcher, A., *Gender, Sex and Subordination in England 1500-1800*, New Haven, Yale University Press, 1995.

Gagliardo, J. G., *Germany Under the Old Regime, 1600-1790*, London, Longman, 1991.

Gaskill, M., 'The Devil in the shape of a man: witchcraft , conflict and belief in Jacobean England', *Historical Research*, 71 (1998), 42–171.

Gaskill, M., 'Witchcraft in early modern Kent: stereotypes and the background to accusations', in J. Barry *et al.* (eds), *Witchcraft in Early Modern Europe*, Cambridge, Cambridge University Press, 1996, 257–287.

Gawthrop, R. and Strauss, G., 'Protestantism and literacy in early modern Germany', *Past & Present*, 104 (1984), 31–55.

Gersmann, G., '"Gehe hin und verthedige dich!" Injurienklagen als Mittel der Abwehr von Hexereiverdächtigungen – ein Fallbeispiel aus dem Fürstbistum Münster', in S. Backmann *et al.* (eds), *Ehrkonzepte in der Frühen Neuzeit. Identitäten und Abgrenzungen*, Berlin, Akademie Verlag, 1998, 237–269.

Ginzburg, C., *The Cheese and the Worms. The Cosmos of a Sixteenth-Century Miller*, London, Penguin, 1992.

Gordon, B., 'Malevolent ghosts and ministering angels: apparitions and pastoral care in the Swiss Reformation', in B. Gordon and P. Marshall (eds), *The Place of the Dead: Death and Remembrance in Late Medieval and Early Modern Europe*, Cambridge, Cambridge University Press, 2000, 87–109.

Gray, M. W., *Productive Men, Reproductive Women. The Agrarian Household and the Emergence of Separate Spheres during the German Enlightenment*, New York and London, Berghahn Books, 2000.

Gregory, A., 'Witchcraft, politics and "good neighbourhood" in early seventeenth-century Rye', *Past & Present*, 133 (1991); 31–66.

Haustein, J., 'Martin Luther als Gegner des Hexenwahns', in H. Lehmann and O. Ulbricht (eds), '*Vom Unfug des Hexenprocesses'. Gegner der Hexenverfolgung von Johann Weyer bis Friedrich Spee*, Wiesbaden, Verlag Otto Harrassowitz, 1992.

Hayes, N., 'Negativizing nurture and demonizing domesticity: the witch construct in early modern Germany', in N. J. Miller and N. Yavneh (eds), *Maternal Measures: Figuring Caregiving in the Early Modern Period*, Aldershot and Burlington, Ashgate, 2000, 179–200.

Heller, K., *Rothenburg ob der Tauber in Wehr und Waffen*, Rothenburg ob der Tauber, Verlag J. P. Peter, 1920.

Hendrix, S., 'Masculinity and patriarchy in Reformation Germany', *Journal of the History of Ideas*, 56:2 (1995), 177–193.

Henningsen, G., 'The greatest witch-trial of them all: Navarre, 1609–1614', *History Today*, 30 (November 1980), 36–39.

Hermelink, H. (ed.), *Die Matrikeln der Universität Tübingen, 1477-1600*, 2 vols, Stuttgart, Verlag W. Kohlhammer, 1906 (I), 1931 (II).

Hester, M., *Lewd Women and Wicked Witches: A Study of the Dynamics of Male Domination*, London, Routledge, 1992.

Jackson, L., 'Witches, wives and mothers: witchcraft persecution and women's confessions in seventeenth-century England', *Women's History Review*, 4 (1995), 63–83.

Karant-Nunn, S. '*Kinder, Küche, Kirche*: social ideology in the sermons of Johannes Mathesius', in A. C. Fix and S. C. Karant-Nunn (eds), *Germania Illustrata. Essays on Early Modern Germany Presented to Gerald Strauss*, Kirksville, Sixteenth Century Journal Publishers, Inc., 1992, 121–140.

Kunstmann, H. H., *Zauberwahn und Hexenprozess in der Reichsstadt Nürnberg*, Nuremberg, Schriftenreihe des Stadtarchivs Nürnberg, 1970.

Labouvie, E., *Zauberei und Hexenwerk: Ländlicher Hexenglaube in der frühen Neuzeit*, Frankfurt am Main, Fischer Taschenbuch, 1991.

Labouvie, E., 'Hexenspuk und Hexenabwehr: Volsmagie und volkstümlicher Hexenglaube', in R. van Dülmen (ed.), *Hexenwelten: Magie und Imagination*, Frankfurt am Main, Fischer Taschenbuch, 1987, 49–93.

Labouvie, E., *Verbotene Künste: Volksmagie und ländlicher Aberglaube in den Dorfgemeinden des Saarraumes (16.–19. Jahrhundert)*, St Ingbert, Röhrig Verlag, 1992.

Langbein, J. H., *Prosecuting Crime in the Renaissance: England, Germany, France*, Cambridge, Massachusetts, Harvard University Press, 1974.

Leder, K., *Kirche und Jugend in Nürnberg und seinem Landgebiet 1400 bis 1800*, Neustadt an der Aisch, Verlag Degener & Co., 1973.

Lorenz, D., 'Vom Kloster zur Küche: die Frau vor und nach der Reformation Dr. Martin Luthers', in B. Becker-Cantarino (ed.), *Die Frau von der Reformation zur Romantik. Die Situation der Frau vor dem Hintergrund der Literatur- und Sozialgeschichte*, Bonn, Bouvier Verlag, 1980, 7–35.

Lorenz, S., 'Brenz' Predigt vom Hagel und die Hexenfrage', *Blätter für württembergische Kirchengeschichte*, 100 (2000), 327–344.

Macfarlane, A., *Witchcraft in Tudor and Stuart England. A Regional and Comparative Study*, London, Routledge, 2nd edn, 1999; 1st edn, Routledge & Kegan Paul, 1970.

Maclean, I., 'The law of defamation and the theory of meaning in Europe 1500–1630', *Journal of the Institute of Romance Studies*, 1 (1992), 147–164.

Merzbacher, F., *Die Hexenprozesse in Franken*, Munich, C. H. Beck, 1957.

Merzbacher, F., 'Geschichte des Hexenprozesses im Hochstifte Würzburg', *Mainfränkisches Jahrbuch für Geschichte und Kunst*, 2 (1950), 162–185.

Midelfort, H. C. E., *Witch Hunting in Southwestern Germany, 1562–1684: The Social and Intellectual Foundations*, Stanford, Stanford University Press, 1972.

Midelfort, H. C. E., *A History of Madness in Sixteenth-Century Germany*, Stanford, Stanford University Press, 1999.

Müller, A., *Gebsattel. Chronik eines fränkischen Dorfes*, Rothenburg ob der Tauber, Schneider Druck GmbH., 1989.

Müller-Wirthmann, B., 'Raufhändel: Gewalt und Ehre im Dorf', in R. van Dülmen (ed.), *Kultur der einfachen Leute: Bayerisches Volksleben vom 16. bis zum 19. Jahrhundert*, Munich, C. H. Beck, 1983, 79–111.

Purkiss, D., *The Witch in History: Early Modern and Twentieth-century Representations*, London and New York, Routledge, 1996.

Purkiss, D., 'Desire and its deformities: fantasies of witchcraft in the English Civil War', *Journal of Medieval and Modern Studies*, 27:1 (1997), 103–132.

Quester, E., *Das Rad der Fortuna und das Kreuz. Studien zur Aufstandsperiode von 1525 in und um Rothenburg ob der Tauber und ihrer Vorgeschichte*, Rothenburg ob der Tauber, Verlag des Vereins Alt-Rothenburg, 1994.

Rank, K., *Die Finanzwirtschaft der Reichsstadt Rothenburg ob der Tauber während des Dreissigjährigen Krieges*, Erlangen, Palm & Enke Verlag, 1940.

Robisheaux, T., 'Witchcraft and forensic medicine in seventeenth-century Germany', in S. Clark (ed.), *Languages of Witchcraft: Narrative, Ideology and Meaning in Early Modern Culture*, London, Macmillan, 2001, 197–215.

Robisheaux, T., 'Zur Rezeption Benedict Carpzovs im 17. Jahrhundert', in H. Eiden and R. Voltmer (eds), *Hexenprozesse und Gerichtspraxis*, Trier, Paulinus Verlag, 2002, 527–543.

Roper, L., *Oedipus and the Devil: Witchcraft, Sexuality and Religion in Early Modern Europe*,

Routledge, London and New York, 1994.

Roper, L., 'Will and honour: sex, words and power in Reformation Augsburg', *Radical History Review*, 43 (1989), 45–71.

Roper, L., 'Mothers of debauchery: procuresses in Reformation Augsburg', *German History*, 6 (1988), 1–19.

Roper, L., *The Holy Household: Women and Morals in Reformation Augsburg*, Oxford, Clarendon Press, 1989.

Rowlands, A., 'Witchcraft and popular magic in early modern Rothenburg ob der Tauber', in B. Scribner and T. Johnson (eds), *Popular Religion in Germany and Central Europe, 1400–1800*, London, Macmillan, 1996, 101–118.

Rowlands, A., 'Monstrous deception: midwifery, fraud and gender in early modern Rothenburg ob der Tauber', in U. Rublack (ed.), *Gender in Early Modern German History*, Cambridge, Cambridge University Press, 2002, 71–101.

Rowlands, A., 'Stereotypes and statistics: old women and accusations of witchcraft in early modern Europe', in S. Ottaway *et al.* (eds), *Power and Poverty: Old Age in the Pre-Industrial Past*, Connecticut, Greenwood, 2002, 167–186.

Rowlands, A., '"In great secrecy": the crime of infanticide in Rothenburg ob der Tauber, 1501–1618', *German History*, 15 (1997), 179–199.

Rowlands, A., 'Witchcraft and old women in early modern Germany', *Past & Present*, 173 (2001), 50–89.

Rowlands, A., 'The "Little witch girl" of Rothenburg', *History Review*, 42 (March, 2002), 27–32.

Rowlands, A., 'Eine Stadt ohne Hexenwahn. Hexenprozesse, Gerichtspraxis und Herrschaft im frühneuzeitlichen Rothenburg ob der Tauber', in H. Eiden and R. Voltmer (eds), *Hexenprozesse und Gerichtspraxis*, Trier, Paulinus Verlag, 2002, 331–347.

Rublack, H.-C., 'Success and failure of the Reformation: popular "apologies" from the seventeenth and eighteenth centuries', in A. C. Fix and S. C. Karant-Nunn (eds), *Germania Illustrata. Essays on Early Modern Germany Presented to Gerald Strauss*, Kirksville, Sixteenth Century Journal Publishers, Inc., 1992, 141–165.

Rublack, U., 'Pregnancy, childbirth and the female body in early modern Germany', *Past & Present*, 150 (1996), 84–110.

Rummel, W., 'Vom Umgang mit Hexen und Hexerei. Das Wirken des Alltags in Hexenprozessen und die alltägliche Bedeutung des Hexenthemas', in G. Franz and F. Irsigler (eds), *Methoden und Konzepte der historischen Hexenforschung*, Trier, Spee Verlag, 1998, 79–108.

Rummel, W., *Bauern, Herren und Hexen: Studien zur Sozialgeschichte sponheimischer und kurtrierischer Hexenprozeße, 1574-1664*, Göttingen, Vandenhoeck & Ruprecht, 1991.

Rummel, W., 'Rezension von Jürgen Michael Schmidt, *Glaube und Skepsis. Die Kurpfalz und die abendländische Hexenverfolgung 1446–1685*, Bielefeld 2000', in *PERFORM*, 2 (2001), Nr. 5 (1 September 2001), URL: www.sfn.uni-muenchen.de/rezensionen/rezp20010515.htm.

Sabean, D. W., *Power in the Blood: Popular Culture and Village Discourse in Early Modern*

Germany, Cambridge, Cambridge University Press, paperback edn 1987; 1st edn, 1984.

Schad, H.-J., 'Ein Priester auf dem Scheiterhaufen: Auf der Spur einer menschlichen Tragödie des Auwer Hexenpastors Michael Campensis', *Jahrbuch Prüm*, 12 (1971), 66–70.

Schad, H.-J., 'Kriminalfall Michael Campensis – Spurensicherung nach 350 Jahren', *Heimatkalender für den Kreis Bitburg Prüm*, 1976, 84–7.

Schattenmann, P., *Die Einführung der Reformation in der ehemaligen Reichsstadt Rothenburg ob der Tauber (1520–1580)*, Gunzenhausen, Verlag für bayerische Kirchengeschichte, 1928.

Schattenmann, P., 'Rothenburger Studenten in vorreformatorischer Zeit (1350–1580)', *Jahresbericht des Vereins Alt-Rothenburg*, 1928, 29–46.

Schmidt, H., 'Das Kriegsjahr 1628', *Fränkischer Feierabend*, 2 (1954), 57–64.

Schmidt, H., 'Vordringender Hexenwahn, 1627–1629', *Fränkischer Feierabend*, 2 (1954), 77–94.

Schmidt, H., 'Aberglaube, Hexenwahn', *Fränkischer Feierabend*, 7 (1959), 60–72.

Schmidt, H., 'Auswirkungen des Krieges auf Stadt und Land: Vom Aufbau des Volksbestandes', *Fränkischer Feierabend*, 6 (1958), 49–53.

Schmidt, J. M., *Glaube und Skepsis. Die Kurpfalz und die abendländische Hexenverfolgung 1446–1685*, Bielefeld, Verlag für Regionalgeschichte, 2000.

Schnurrer, L., *Rothenburg im Mittelalter. Studien zur Geschichte einer fränkischen Reichsstadt*, Rothenburg ob der Tauber, Verlag des Vereins Alt-Rothenburg, 1997.

Scholz Williams, G., *Defining Dominion; The Discourses of Magic and Witchcraft in Early Modern France and Germany*, Ann Arbor, University of Michigan Press, 1996.

Schormann, G., *Der Krieg gegen die Hexen: Das Ausrottungsprogramm des Kurfürsten von Köln*, Göttingen, Vandenhoeck & Ruprecht, 1991.

Schraut, E., 'Niederstetten 1676. Barbara Emmert aus Dunzendorf und ihre Mutter Dorothea, genannt Schopfendöra, werden der Hexerei verdächtigt', in W. Krüger (ed.), *650 Jahre Stadt Niederstetten*, Niederstetten, 1991, 158–165.

Schubert, E., 'Gegenreformation in Franken', *Jahrbuch für fränkische Landesforschung*, 28 (1968), 275–307.

Schulte, R., *Hexenmeister: Die Verfolgung von Männern im Rahmen der Hexenverfolgung von 1530–1730 im Alten Reich*, Frankfurt am Main, Peter Lang Verlag, 2000.

Schwerhoff, G., *Köln im Kreuzverhör: Kriminalität, Herrschaft und Gesellschaft in einer frühneuzeitlichen Stadt*, Bonn, Bouvier Verlag, 1991.

Schwillus, H., '"Der bischoff lässt nit nach, bis er die gantze statt verbrennt hat": Bemerkungen zu der 1745 veröffentlichten Liste der unter Fürstbischof Philipp Adolf von Ehrenberg wegen angeblicher Hexerei hingerichteten Menschen', *Würzburger Diözesan-Geschichtsblätter*, 49 (1987), 145–154.

Scribner, R. W., 'Witchcraft and judgement in Reformation Germany', *History Today*, 40 (April 1990), 12–19.

Sebald, H., *Der Hexenjunge. Fallstudie eines Inquisitionsprozess*, Marburg, Diagonal-Verlag, 1992.

Sharpe, J. A., 'Witchcraft and women in seventeenth-century England: some northern evidence', *Continuity and Change*, 6 (1991), 179–199.

Steinmeyer, E. von (ed.), *Die Matrikel der Universität Altdorf, 1575–1809*, 2 vols, Würzburg, Universitätsdruckerei H. Stürtz A.G., 1912.

Strauss, G., *Luther's House of Learning: Indoctrination of the Young in the German Reformation*, Baltimore and London, Johns Hopkins University Press, 1978.

Strauss, G., 'Success and failure in the German Reformation', *Past & Present*, 67 (1975), 30–63.

Stuart, K., 'Des Scharfrichters heilende Hand – Medizin und Ehre in der Frühen Neuzeit', in S. Backmann *et al.* (eds), *Ehrkonzepte in der Frühen Neuzeit. Identitäten und Abgrenzungen*, Berlin, Akademie Verlag, 1998, 316–347.

Tausiet, M., 'Witchcraft as metaphor: infanticide and its translations in Aragon in the sixteenth and seventeenth centuries', in S. Clark (ed.), *Languages of Witchcraft: Narrative, Ideology and Meaning in Early Modern Culture*, London, Macmillan, 2001, 179–195.

Thomas, K., *Religion and the Decline of Magic*, London, Weidenfeld & Nicolson, 1971.

Ulbricht, O., 'Der Einstellungswandel zur Kindheit in Deutschland am Ende des Spätmittelalters (ca. 1470 bis ca. 1520)', *Zeitschrift für historische Forschung*, 19 (1992), 159–187.

Vice, R. L., 'The village clergy near Rothenburg ob der Tauber and the Peasants' War', *Archiv für Reformationsgeschichte*, 82 (1991), 123–145.

Vice, R. L., 'Vineyards, vinedressers and the Peasants' War in Franconia', *Sonderdruck aus dem Archiv für Reformationsgeschichte*, 79 (1988), 138–157.

Voltmer, R., 'Zwischen Herrschaftskrise, Wirtschaftsdepression und Jesuitenpropaganda. Hexenverfolgungen in der Stadt Trier (15.–17. Jahrhundert), *Jahrbuch für westdeutsche Landesgeschichte*, 27 (2002), 137–207.

Wagner, E., 'Hexenglaube in Franken heute', *Jahrbuch für fränkische Landesforschung*, 30 (1970), 343–356.

Walinski-Kiehl, R., 'Godly states: confessional conflict and witch-hunting in early modern Germany', *Mentalities*, 5 (1988), 13–24.

Walz, R., 'Kinder in Hexenprozessen: Die Grafschaft Lippe 1654–1663', in G. Wilbertz *et al.* (eds), *Hexenverfolgung und Regionalgeschichte: Die Grafschaft Lippe im Vergleich*, Bielefeld, Verlag für Regionalgeschichte, 1994, 211–231.

Walz, R., 'Schimpfende Weiber. Frauen in lippischen Beleidigungsprozessen des 17. Jahrhunderts', in H. Wunder and C. Vanja (eds), *Weiber, Menscher, Frauenzimmer: Frauen in der ländlichen Gesellschaft 1500–1800*, Göttingen, Vandenhoeck & Ruprecht, 1996, 175–198.

Weigel, M. *Rothenburger Chronik*, Rothenburg ob der Tauber, Buchdruckerei Gebr. Schneider, 1904.

Wiesner, M., 'Luther and women: the death of two Marys', in J. Obelkevich *et al.* (eds), *Disciplines of Faith: Studies in Religion, Politics and Patriarchy*, London and New York, Routledge & Kegan Paul, 1987, 295–308.

Willis, D., *Malevolent Nurture: Witch-Hunting and Maternal Power in Early Modern England*, Ithaca and London, Cornell University Press, 1995.

Winterbach, J. D. W. von, *Geschichte der Stadt Rothenburg an der Tauber und ihres Gebietes*, 2 vols, Rothenburg an der Tauber, 1826 (I), 1827 (II).

Woltering, H., *Die Reichsstadt Rothenburg ob der Tauber und ihre Herrschaft über die Landwehr*, 2 vols, Rothenburg ob der Tauber, Verlag des Vereins Alt-Rothenburg, 1965 (I), 1971 (II).

Wulz, G., *Die Prenninger von Erding: eine bayerische Gelehrtenfamilie*, Munich, Verlagsanstalt Gebr. Giehrl, undated, *c.* 1929.

Wunder, H., *'Er ist die Sonn', sie ist der Mond: Frauen in der frühen Neuzeit*, Munich, C. H. Beck, 1992.

Ziegler, H.-P., *Die Dorfordnungen im Gebiet der Reichsstadt Rothenburg*, Rothenburg ob der Tauber, Verlag des Vereins Alt-Rothenburg, 1977.

Zika, C., 'Fears of flying: representations of witchcraft and sexuality in early sixteenth-century Germany', *Australian Journal of Art*, 8 (1989), 19–47.

Zika, C., 'Kannibalismus und Hexerei: die Rolle der Bilder im frühneuzeitlichen Europas', in H. Röckelein (ed.), *Kannibalismus und europäische Kultur*, Tübingen, Edition Diskord Verlag, 1996, 75–114.

Unpublished theses

Herzog, K.-P., 'Das Strafensystem der Stadt Rothenburg ob der Tauber im Spätmittelalter' (Inaugural Dissertation for the Legal Faculty of the Julius-Maximilians-University of Würzburg, 1971).

Moritz, G., 'Die Folgen des Dreissigjährigen Krieges und der Wiederaufbau in der Rothenburger Landwehr' (Zulassungsarbeit zur Wissenschaftlichen Prüfung für das Lehramt am Gymnasien, Erlangen, 1980).

Plummer, M. E., 'Reforming the Family: Marriage, Gender and the Lutheran Household in Early Modern Germany, 1500–1620' (DPhil thesis, University of Virginia, 1996).

Rowlands, A., 'Women, Gender and Power in Rothenburg ob der Tauber and its Rural Environs, 1500–c.1618' (DPhil thesis, University of Cambridge, 1995).

Vice, R. L., 'The German Peasants' War of 1525 and its aftermath in Rothenburg ob der Tauber and Würzburg' (DPhil thesis, University of Chicago, 1984).

Index

Notes: All subject entries listed relate to Rothenburg and its hinterland, unless other-wise specified as relating to Germany generally or to other parts of Germany. All individuals listed as reputed, accused, self-confessed, or executed witches, as child-witches, and as individuals slandered as witches; as accusers and slanderers; and as cunning men or women, are from Rothenburg or its hinterland villages. After page references, 'n.' indicates the number of a note on that page.